The APRIL FOOL'S DAY LAWYER

COLIN O'NEILL

The April Fool's Day Lawyer © 2025 Colin O'Neill

All Rights Reserved. No part of this book may be reproduced in any form or by any electronic or mechanical means including information storage and retrieval systems, without permission in writing from the author. The only exception is by a reviewer, who may quote short excerpts in a review.

This book is a work of non-fiction. This publication is designed to provide accurate and authoritative information in regards to the subject matter covered. It is sold with the understanding that neither the author nor the publisher is engaged in rendering legal, investment, accounting, or other professional services. For privacy reasons, some names, locations, and dates may have been changed.

These are the memories of the author, from their perspective, and they have tried to represent events as faithfully as possible.

Printed in Australia

Cover by Melinda Childs @studioorchard

Internal design by Book Burrow

www.bookburrow.com.au

First printing: August 2025

Paperback ISBN 978-1-7638-6910-3

eBook ISBN 978-1-7638-6911-0

Distributed by Lightning Source Global

A catalogue record for this work is available from the National Library of Australia

BOOKS BY COLIN O'NEILL

From Vietnam Nasho to Catching School Crooks

A Question of Arson

The April Fool's Day Lawyer

CONTENTS

Prologue	1
Legal Eagle	8
Guilty or Not Guilty?	13
Another String to One's Bow	45
Aspects of the Law of Employment	50
Once a Bankrupt, Always a Bankrupt?	77
Perils of Liquidation-Directors Beware	93
Industrial Accidents	114
Don't Drink, Take Drugs, Then Drive	126
Family Violence and Intervention Orders	142
Coward's Punch	182
Issues with the NDIS	197
Firearms and Other Weapons	213
Bail or No Bail	238
Victims of Crime	256
Court Diversion Program	289
Virtual Court	299
Fool for a Client	313
A Blight on the Legal Profession	320

The Lawyer is a Snitch	335
The Jury is Still Out	369
Time to Call Stumps	382
Acknowledgements	389
Glossary	392
Bibliography	423
Magazines/Journals/Reports/Articles	424
Principal Reference Websites	431
List of Cases	432
List of Legislation	441
International Covenants and Declarations	450
Newspaper and Other Media References	451
About the Author	471

PROLOGUE

On Wednesday, 9 July, 1969, I ceased to be a soldier in the Australian Army and my Certificate of Discharge reminded me of my total effective service in Australia of 365 days and outside Australia as a Vietnam Nasho of 365 days. Despite some reservations, I was about to return to civilian life as a public servant with Victoria Police.

The use of public servants in police line ups had not changed since 1967, with the only difference being that such lines ups were mostly conducted on the vacant sixth floor of the new building at the rear of Russell Street. For whatever reason, I was still being chosen to be part of line-ups and, on Tuesday, 26 March, 1974, I stood alongside two persons in custody for murder and armed robbery. The men were Barry Robert Quinn and his then alleged accomplice, Robin West. Quinn was shorter than me, but he was placed right beside me due to our similar build and hair style.

Homicide detectives then brought in a witness who was asked to look along the line of men, see if he could recognise the person, or persons, who robbed him at gunpoint, then walk up to him and tap him on the shoulder. The witness was wearing a sling as, apparently, he had been wounded during the robbery allegedly committed by Quinn and West. The well-built male witness walked along the line, stopped in front of me, then took one step to my left and let go with a round-arm right hook, knocking Quinn to the floor. I just stood there in sheer bloody amazement before police quickly escorted the witness away. My adrenaline was pumping.

Quinn was subsequently sentenced for two murders but, unfortunately, he happened to share a Jika Jika maximum security cell with another murderer, who was just as dangerous and violent, by the name of Alex Tsakmakis. To put it bluntly, Tsakmakis was a psychopath.

It was never going to end well with Tsakmakis in 1984, dousing Quinn with industrial glue and then flicking lighted matches at him, sending him to an early grave. Tsakmakis, or I should use his jail nickname "the Barbeque King", also copped his right whack some four years later when Russell Street bomber, Craig Minogue, belted him over the head with a pillowcase full of dumbbells and then claimed self-defence to murder, all to no avail. Minogue has now been in prison for 37 years and will never be released, unless the Victorian Parole Board is satisfied that he is in imminent danger of dying or is so seriously incapacitated, he does not pose any risk to the community.

There would be two defining chapters in my life in 1974 which would result in a total change in direction, although a number of years apart. The first chapter began with the advertisement in the Victoria Public Service Gazette for the C1 classified position of Security Control Officer with the Victorian Education Department and my subsequent successful application for the prevention and detection of school crime, notably catching school crooks.

My exposure to criminals with Victoria Police, albeit in police line ups, had obviously whet my appetite to go down this path, but it became apparent that my job as head of school security would not be without its moments of peril. I was to find out on many occasions over the next 19 years that school crime was not just "kiddie crime".

This was blatantly obvious when I responded to a silent alarm at a school in the northern suburbs one evening and was the first unit to arrive. After positioning myself 20 metres from an open school window, a bag was suddenly thrown out, followed by a short male offender. When he landed on the ground, I told him he was under arrest and to lay down with his arms where I could see them. After telling me to 'get fucked,' he took off. Within seconds, my trained German shepherd, Edo, had the screaming offender down on the ground with a nasty bite on his leg. I handcuffed him, told him he was under arrest and asked his name.

'Normie Faure, you prick,' was his reply.

I knew the background of the Faures. In particular, I knew his cousin, Keith Faure, and that they had both carried out a bank robbery in Clifton Hill in 1976 and shot police officer, Michael Pratt, who happened to be driving past.

I very quickly placed Faure into the rear of my vehicle with Edo and, hoping there were no other Faures watching, I made a quick dash for Heidelberg Police station. I could always return to the school later to secure it, so I told our control room to inform responding police who I had in custody. I did have a fleeting brain wave to see if I could find his motor vehicle but quickly changed my mind. On the way to placing him in a police cell, my now not-so-good mate, Normie, left me in no doubt that he would get me back and it wouldn't be pleasant. I must admit, I didn't sleep well that night after the adrenaline once again wore off.

Our friend was actually on parole for the Clifton Hill bank job and was now back in prison to see out his eight years that he first received in 1977. Knowing his history and his not-so-veiled threat, I always thought he would come after me on his release and the outcome would not be to my liking. In June 1984, Normie asked his prison mate, Vincenzo Delouise, who was about to be released from custody, to look after his de facto, a very attractive heroin addict by the name of Darlene. Normie was to be released some weeks after Vince and thought nothing of asking his cell mate to make sure he took care of her until then.

The old adage, "never introduce your donah (girlfriend) to a pal", particularly another crook, was overlooked by Normie. Vince, being the lad he was, certainly looked after the highly sexed Darlene and Normie, on his release, was to subsequently find out she was sleeping, not only with him, but also Vince on alternative nights.

It was always going to finish badly and better Vince and Normie, than me. When Normie discovered what was going on, he and Vince had a knife fight and stabbed each other to death. The following morning, I was greeted with the news on the radio about two well-known Melbourne rogues who had met their maker. No loss to mankind and good riddance to Norman Leslie "Normie" Faure. I think Constable Michael Pratt may have received some satisfaction from that outcome as well. I certainly did and it demonstrated that school crime and catching crooks was not without its dangers.

Following many other arrests in our schools over the next

19-odd years, one further arrest by me, which was brought before the court, would finally persuade me to another direction in life. In regards to this offender, I was once again the first responding unit to arrive, so I quietly proceeded to the outside of the school building in alarm where I observed a male, around the age of 25–30 years, methodically searching several areas. I waited for him, knowing the Police Dog Squad would not be far off. He then opened a set of double doors, threw some items out and was about to depart with his goodies, or so he thought. I really had no choice but to place him under arrest before the police dog arrived. To say he was a smart arse is an understatement, but I handcuffed him and waited for police.

A few months after I made a statement to Eltham Police, our miscreant was pleading not guilty as, according to his version of events, he had simply been walking through the school grounds around midnight minding his own business when, without cause, I placed him under arrest. The matter was listed at the Eltham Magistrates Court where, after giving compelling evidence of what I observed on responding to a silent alarm and why I arrested the offender, I was subjected to vigorous cross examination by his barrister.

He said words to the effect, 'Mr O'Neill, I put it to you the defendant was simply walking through the school grounds and you placed him under arrest without reason, that's correct, isn't it?'

Luckily, I recalled learning from an experienced member of the Police Arson Squad to keep your answers short and, where possible, limit them to one word. After looking around the court room, I replied, 'No.'

He then responded, 'So you say, Mr O'Neill, you had good reason to arrest him?'

My reply was, 'Yes.'

The barrister then put the same question again about walking through the school grounds and his client being detained without cause. By this stage, I was getting rather annoyed and said words to the effect of, 'You have already asked me that question.'

Learned counsel tried it again and I just looked at him and then said, 'I have already responded to that question.'

He kept at me, causing me to say, 'Sorry but I don't understand your line of questioning.'

His blunt reply was, 'Don't you understand the Queen's English?'

Now, I was more than aware of conducting myself in a professional and appropriate manner, but my reply was exactly the opposite because of my annoyance and frustration to his repeated line of questioning.

'Yes, she lives in England!'

The Magistrate, understandably, was very unimpressed, as was the police prosecutor, who both gave me a dressing down and I left the court with my tail between my legs. The defendant also left, but at least I got to go home that night whereas he didn't, due to his guilty verdict. He had priors for burglary and was sentenced to a term of imprisonment.

In my position as Manager, Security Services Group, Victorian Directorate of School Education, this defining moment, amongst others, including my "run in" with Normie Faure, was when I thought I could do a better job than some of these lawyers, so could I consider a career in law? I had already decided my days of catching school crooks were fast coming to an end, so studying for a law degree now beckoned.

My final arrest was to take place in the early hours of

the morning at a school in Mount Martha when the portable buildings were entered, activating the silent alarm. I was only living a few minutes away and, on arrival at the school, I observed a rather large "gentleman" in the corridor between the two connected portables. Aware that police back up was only a few minutes away, I decided to keep him under observation.

The offender quickly changed my decision when he gathered his ill-gotten goodies and began to leave the portables. Leaving me with no choice, I had to introduce myself, but he took off down the road adjoining the school, with me giving chase. Unfortunately for him, he only made it to a roundabout near the school when he saw a police divvy van fast approaching so, realising the game was up, he lay down on the road where I handcuffed him.

Although he was my last arrest after 19 years of working in school security, I had no doubt that there would be many more who would suffer the same fate as our total school arrests were now in the order of almost 10,000 since the inception of silent school alarms.

The game was also up for me as in September 1993, my final chapter in catching school crooks was over when I left the Victorian Public Service to complete my final year of a law degree and start another interesting chapter in my life. I was admitted as a barrister and solicitor on April Fool's Day, 1996. Such annual custom on 1 April involves playing practical jokes on the recipient and then yelling out, 'April Fool!' Time would tell though whether only a fool would want to practice law.

1
LEGAL EAGLE

After completing 1994 as a full-time student, and without the constant day to day commitment of reducing school crime, I finally graduated from La Trobe University with a Bachelor of Arts and Bachelor of Laws with Honours. In order to graduate with Honours, you had to obtain a minimum of a distinction in all subjects and then complete a thesis of not less than 10,000 words. For some unknown reason, my thesis was on War Crimes Prosecutions, not that I witnessed any such crimes during my service in Vietnam.

The graduation was alongside fellow students of the calibre of Don McKenzie, who would later be appointed as senior lecturer at Monash University before practicing as a solicitor. Conor O'Brien, who would become a partner in the successful legal practice of Doogue and O'Brien, Solly Gerber, now a much sought after taxation barrister, and Stella Stuthridge who, after working as a solicitor in the area of criminal law in Bendigo, was subsequently appointed as magistrate presiding in Shepparton and more recently, as the supervising Magistrate for Family Violence.

I fondly recall Solly sitting the open book Corporations Law exam in our final year and, after about two hours of a three-hour exam, he got up and left while we all continued, needing the three allocated hours. Solly would later say he had done enough to pass so why finish the exam? Needless to say, he achieved a pass with a high distinction. No wonder he excels in taxation law. His other claim to fame he brags about is that he is the first Australian to have visited every country in the world and can prove it with no less than 14 filled passports.

The story of Her Honour Stuthridge was an upbringing of living in a violent home where, unfortunately, she witnessed family violence committed against her mother and younger siblings. Her Honour graduated from high school in Altona with a commitment and passion for social justice, including studying criminology and sociology, before being amongst the first-year law students at La Trobe. I never had the pleasure of appearing in her court but have no doubt she is certainly a well credentialed appointment in the new role, supervising the specialist Court for Family Violence and I wish her well.

Our excellent lecturers included John Willis, who was admitted as a barrister and solicitor in April 1974 and then signed the Bar Roll in May 1987. John specialised in criminal law and I always found his lectures of interest as he would include many practical examples, no doubt taken from his extensive client experience. Dr Chris Corns also practised as a criminal barrister and specialised in such areas as criminal appeals, procedure and, of course, advocacy. Dr Corns is also a co-author of a number of books, including "Criminal Appeals and Reviews". Along with John, now known as Professor

Willis, in 2010, he was awarded the Dean's Teaching Award for outstanding contribution regarding lecturing in advocacy skills.

One subject I and many others struggled with, was Administrative Law, taught by Professor Roger Douglas. That was certainly no reflection on this learned gentleman. Our final exam in this subject saw a number of students leaving the exam centre, upset and unable to finish. I must admit the questions being asked just didn't seem to make any sense, or perhaps were termed that way to get the best out of the student. Somehow, I scraped through and probably owe the good professor a thank you.

Part of our training included a short in-house period at the Preston Legal Aid Office under the supervision of Rob Thyssen and Caitlin English. Rob would subsequently sign the Bar Roll in 1999 and I would, in due course, brief him as counsel regarding a number of criminal matters. Ms English, or I should say, "Her Honour", would later be appointed as a magistrate sitting for 13 years, followed by an appointment as deputy state coroner and then, more recently, as a County Court judge.

As further part of my training and hopefully closer to a successful career as a barrister and solicitor, I observed over a number of days, the trial of police detectives, Cliff Lockwood and Dermott Avon, in the Supreme Court for the alleged 1989 murder of Walsh Street suspect, Gary Abdallah. They were represented by Robert Richter, who was appointed as a QC in November 1985, and Phillip Dunn QC. Their defence was, to say the least, brilliant, in particular Richter's final address, with both being found not guilty by a jury.

Mind you, on graduation I did have a choice to practice in law, or alternatively, undertake a role as a lecturer, perhaps in the area of employment law. Thanks to Don McKenzie, I also had an interest and leaning towards industrial and employment law, not just criminal law.

After deciding that my new career would be as a "legal eagle" or solicitor, I commenced my articles of clerkship in February 1995 with Hall Solicitors in Mornington. In due course, I would be welcomed in a baptism of fire, to say the least, and struggle to find my wings. As an articled clerk, I had no standing in a court of law and would need to seek leave to appear. My principal was John Hall, a now well-respected barrister and mediator, who determined that as he was unavailable, I would need to appear in the Dromana Magistrates Court and seek an adjournment of a criminal matter.

This was to be my first appearance in court as a lawyer. Well, not really, as I was only an articled clerk. So, with some trepidation I presented myself at court to await my fate. On seeking leave from the presiding magistrate to appear, I was told by a smiling Hal Hallenstein, 'Mr O'Neill, it is with much pleasure I give you leave to appear.'

I had never seen His Worship smile before and certainly not when I liaised with him at school fires when he was state coroner, but his welcome was very much appreciated on this occasion.

Unfortunately, I was not to be so lucky a few weeks later when the same scenario arose and I needed to seek leave to appear and request an adjournment. I went through the same procedure, politely introducing myself as an articled clerk and asked for leave to appear. His Worship, Robert Tuppen, was not so accommodating and said, 'No, Mr O'Neill, I won't give you leave but I will stand the matter down and suggest you get your principal down to court quick smart.'

With some reservation on my part, I was admitted as a barrister and solicitor of the Supreme Court on 1 April, 1996. I was presented before the court in my wig and gown by John as my principal and he thought it was very appropriate that I should be admitted on such a day. I would remind John though it was yours truly who came up with the new name for his practice, "The Law Firm". Maybe he was right though as only a fool would want to practice law as, certainly over many years, I would get to represent my own rogues gallery. Then again, I was admitted to practice on April Fool's Day in 1996.

2
GUILTY OR NOT GUILTY?

One of the many legal principles that was first drummed into us as budding lawyers, albeit struggling students, was the presumption of innocence. In other words, if charged with a criminal offence, a person is considered innocent until proven guilty beyond reasonable doubt[1], as the legal burden to prove such guilt remains with the prosecution[2].

If there is any doubt, the person charged must be acquitted. This presumption of innocence is in line with article 14(2) of the *International Covenant on Civil and Political Rights 1966* as is the right to a fair trial and legislated in Victoria pursuant to section 25(1) of the *Charter of Human Rights and Responsibilities Act 2006*(Vic).[3]

---

1   Refer section 141 *Evidence Act 2008*(Vic).

2   Also refer section 141 of the *Evidence Act 1995*(Cth).

3   Also see Part 2.6 of the *Criminal Code Act 1995*(Cth).

However, there are some offences in Victoria known as strict liability offences which means, 'You do the crime; you do the time.'

This, in effect, determines that the prosecution does not have to demonstrate the guilty act (actus reus) was committed with a guilty mind (mens rea), unless such crimes occurred by way of a defence under reasonable mistake of fact[4], for example, driving whilst suspended or failing to stop for police. This mistake-type defence is not available in strict liability offences, such as drink and drug driving, as there is no requirement to demonstrate intent.

One of the dilemmas faced was whether my clients should plead guilty or not guilty or try the reasonable mistake defence. What I was to find in many of my matters, the brief of evidence was so overwhelming with, not only statements by the police informant but corroborating witness statements, of what had taken place on the commission of the criminal act, it would leave my client with not much leeway, other than to plead guilty. I would certainly give the client both scenarios to either enter a guilty or not guilty plea and, on most occasions, they would follow my advice. Well almost.

The advantage of an early guilty plea was they would receive a sentence discount, and I was to find, particularly in the Magistrates Court, the presiding magistrate would say on sentencing, 'If it was not for the early guilty plea, I would have sentenced you to a term of imprisonment.'[5]

---

4   see *Proudman v Dayman* [1941] HCA 28-67 CLR 536.

5   see section 6AAA - sentence discount for guilty plea- *Sentencing Act 1991*(Vic) and section 362A of the *Children, Youth and Families Act 2005*(Vic) also see *R v Lanteri* [2006] VSC 225 for an explanation of the sentencing process by Gillard J.

Guilty pleas and sentencing also provided for a broad indication from the courts any likely custodial sentence if the defendant was to plead guilty. In the County and Supreme Courts, the accused could make application for an early sentence indication, but only if the prosecution first consented and there was also agreement from the judge.[6]

The Magistrates Court sentence indication scheme is more flexible and can be provided at any time during the hearing of the matter, including whether an immediate term of imprisonment would be imposed, or what type of sentence would be likely such as a community corrections order.[7] It should be also noted that the Magistrates' Court could hear certain indictable offences in its jurisdiction stream which were triable summarily[8].

It was against this learning of theory and, at times, complex legislation that I was now about to enter the jungle and nuances of criminal law. My first appearance, now as a bona fide solicitor, was in the Frankston Children's Court representing a juvenile charged with burglary. My nerves were shot being my first real appearance, but I settled down slightly after having a dry retch in the toilet earlier before appearing in court. My client pleaded guilty, on my advice, given that he was arrested, would you believe, inside a school, following detection by a silent alarm system. I certainly did not tell him and his parents about my previous occupation catching school crooks. I suggested a guilty plea, under the circumstances, would be the preferred option and I was correct with the sentence being an adjourned undertaking of good behaviour.

---

6   see Part 5.6 of the *Criminal Procedure Act 2009* (Vic).

7   see Part 3.3 of the *Criminal Procedure Act*.

8   Ibid.

My foray into criminal law certainly got off to a rocky start after that, when I suddenly found myself as Duty Lawyer at the Dromana Magistrates Court, despite my very limited experience. In those days, Victoria Legal Aid (VLA) would appoint law practices to provide a duty lawyer, and it was not uncommon to appear on behalf of many defendants over a full day, for a measly fee of $300.

I appeared before Her Worship, Heather Spooner, and the first case related to two Vietnamese poachers caught by Fisheries and Wildlife officers. They had breached the Fisheries Regulations for abalone poaching, having around 60 abalone in their possession with the limit being only 10. My new clients could not speak any English and trying to get instructions was a nightmare. Ms Spooner was not impressed and suggested the matter be stood down in order to arrange for an interpreter before I could proceed with any plea.

In the interim, I appeared for a local resident charged with lighting a fire on a total fire ban day, in addition to an assault charge. Both charges carried significant penalties, including imprisonment with the charge of lighting the fire under *the Country Fire Authority Act 1958* (Vic) and the common assault charge pursuant to section 23 of the *Summary Offences Act 1966* (Vic). My client determined that rubbish in her back yard needed to be taken care of, so she lit a fire, despite knowing it was prohibited. On arrival of the Country Fire Authority (CFA), she was not impressed and, instead of putting out the flames, she squirted the CFA members with water, hence a charge of assault. It must have been my lucky day as the abalone poachers got off with a reasonably minor fine, while my fire lady received a good behaviour bond (GBB) with a donation to the CFA.

A GBB is an adjourned undertaking to comply with certain conditions and can be imposed either with or without conviction. The period for such is normally around 12 months but can be imposed for up to five years. In the event of any breach, the defendant can be resentenced for the initial offending, but I didn't think my fire lady would be seen in court again.

It wasn't long before I would appear before Mr Tuppen again, but this time at the Melbourne Magistrates Court. I was representing a brothel owner, who I shall name "Madam Lash". She specialised in sexual masochism and, would you believe, I honestly had no idea what that type of service was all about.

In Victoria, following a working party set up by the Kennett Government, legislation was put in place to control prostitution and the like. The *Prostitution Control Act 1994* (Vic), which is now legislated as the *Sex Work Act 1994* (Vic), regulates the conduct of brothels and escort agencies. To operate a brothel, you need a permit which is subject to council planning controls, including obtaining the relevant licences for both owner–operated brothels and escort workers, the latter to be at least registered.

As part of my understanding and, perhaps to help with my submissions before the court of the charges, I visited the "place of pain". I was to witness firsthand a number of their clients being sexually aroused by the infliction of, what can only be described as torture, mostly by being whipped while their hands and neck were secured, sometimes to a cross. I quickly left the building before attending at the Police Licensing, Gaming and Vice Squad in St Kilda Road to view the footage they had taken at the place of pain, courtesy of an undercover police operative. On watching the vision taken outside the building in the back yard, I quickly determined that Madam Lash had a problem and hopefully a fine would be the best outcome.

Noting I was only in my second year of law as a practising solicitor, I thought with some glee, that perhaps I could still plead entrapment as an excuse. In other words, police acted improperly in order to induce Madam Lash's girls to carry out sexual acts, albeit in the back yard of the premises that resulted in the charges before the court. The fact they didn't have the correct permit or, at the very least, no permit to run what was effectively a brothel, was of course going to be an issue.

My submission before His Worship did not go well. Not only was my matter called up first, but a number of my former colleagues from La Trobe University were sitting in court waiting to appear for their matter to be called. Mr Tuppen welcomed me to his court as now I didn't need to seek leave. First, he jokingly questioned what I was doing in Melbourne as I would normally appear at either the Frankston or Dromana Magistrates Courts. I entered a plea of guilty, then this was followed by the police informant summary. My former so-called colleagues started to giggle as the summary was quite explicit.

The plea would take at least 10 minutes but as soon as I started with the excuse of entrapment by way of mitigation, Mr Tuppen was not impressed. He said words to the effect, 'Mr O'Neill, surely you are not trying to use that as an excuse as part of your plea submission?'

'No, your Worship, I am not but I am just trying to explain what actually happened as a mitigating factor.'

'Really, Mr O'Neill? I has seen the footage so I strongly suggest you move on and tell me why your client should not be heavily fined.'

Move on I did and very quickly as I just wanted to get the hell out of court and away from my now former, so called, university friends, still chuckling away behind me. Madam Lash was fined $1500 with conviction and I left the court, once again with my tail between my legs.

Interestingly, on 2 December 1999, His Worship, Robert Tuppen, had another prostitution matter before him which he again deemed as 'unacceptable, dirty, exploitative and distasteful'.

On this occasion, one defendant was committed to trial for importing Thai women to work in both legal and illegal brothels, while the other received a six-month suspended sentence. Perhaps my representation was not as bad as I thought, seeing my client was only fined.

His Honour certainly didn't take any rubbish from those appearing before him or, in this case, not appearing. He even described, on one occasion, the editor of the Herald Sun as 'extremely rude for refusing to appear before me', regarding what appeared to be a potentially prejudicial article. This article related to attempted murder charges over the disappearance of Maria Korp. Her husband, Joe Korp, and his mistress, Tania Herman, were charged with attempted murder but Joe committed suicide on the day of Maria's funeral and Herman was sentenced to 12 years imprisonment with a nine-year non-parole period[9]. Mr Tuppen's issue was, and quite rightly so, that the article had the potential to sway any jury trial, and His Honour reminded the editor of the principle of fair reporting. At least it wasn't me on this occasion getting the rap over the knuckles.

In practising law, I was to find I would often take on

---

9   *R v Tania Lee-Anne Herman* [2005] VSC 234.

a number of similar matters, one after the other. In another similar case, my client was in breach of our prostitution laws, operating and advertising her services from her home on the Mornington Peninsula. I obtained the relevant instructions from this very attractive lady and then, as we are required to do, discussed legal costs stating I would need at least $1,000 up front to appear on the court return date.

My client quickly responded that perhaps we could come to "another arrangement", in other words, her "femme fatale" services would be provided to me in lieu of legal costs. It's fair to say that from that moment on, when I needed to obtain further instructions, I arranged for one of our other staff to always be present during our conference.

It wasn't long before I was back appearing at Frankston Magistrates Court. This time for a client named John who was charged with a number of burglary and theft of property offences to feed his drug habit. The thorough police brief left him with no choice but to plead guilty. He had about five to six pages of convictions but none for assault or similar behaviour, such as resisting arrest. As I did with all clients, I advised John, when appearing in court, he needed to dress appropriately, preferably in a suit or at least smart casual. On the day of the guilty plea, he turned up in a very bright coloured tank top with all his tattoos on display.

I certainly have nothing against tattoos, but his form of attire in the circumstances was really not appropriate to appear in court. I strongly suggested he needed a smart, casual shirt and, as a Myers department store was located across from the court precinct, he could go there and buy a shirt. Unfortunately, he didn't have any cash on him, so I gave him $50 which he was to pay back in due course. After disappearing for about 20 minutes, he returned in a very smart, long-sleeved casual shirt.

Well done, John! At least, he now looked presentable to go before the presiding magistrate. As we were walking into court, he handed me back my $50 note.

I exclaimed, 'I thought you didn't have any cash?'

John's reply was, 'I didn't. I just helped meself.'

Perhaps shoplifting was another one of John's favourite pastimes.

It must have been his lucky day as he escaped being sentenced to a term of imprisonment and ended up with community service and a fine.

Unfortunately, John's luck was to runout as on Good Friday in 1998 when he was shot dead by police. Apparently, John was breaking into an ATM in Bentleigh in the early hours of the morning when he was confronted by police. He was armed with a claw hammer, no doubt to use as a breaking implement. After being warned by police to put the weapon down, he approached them allegedly in a threatening manner and he was shot at least three times. A coronial investigation followed, and the finding was justifiable homicide, although Coroner Graeme Johnston did call for the use of stun guns or tasers by police.

I was rather saddened at the outcome for John as I found him to be very pleasant and, in my view, he didn't have a bad bone in his body, other than breaking into various establishments to feed his drug habit.

I had another client in my early days who put on a brave face when I told him the likely outcome would be a short term of imprisonment. He was charged with assault offences and, as he had a few priors for similar behaviour and only fines with conviction, in all likelihood he would go to jail on this occasion. On the day of the guilty plea at Frankston Magistrates Court, I sought his instructions as to whether he wanted me to lodge an appeal and also apply for bail if he was sentenced to a term of imprisonment.

The client with a brave face said, 'Nah, I'll be right. I can handle myself inside so don't bother applying for bail.' He further told me he was 'pretty tough' and could 'look after himself in any event'.

The presiding magistrate, on listening to the police summary and after seeing his priors, told me in no uncertain terms, by way of a sentence indication, that my client would be going to jail, regardless of what I submitted as part of my plea. Halfway through making my submission, I noticed His Worship reach under the bench facing the court, a sure sign that my client was definitely going inside, as he buzzed for court security who would shortly be accompanying my client to the cells.

Three months was the sentence and, a short time later, I visited my client in the cells in case he had changed his mind and wanted to appeal the sentence and apply for bail. What a gibbering mess he was, and I wondered, *What happened to Mr Toughness?* He was literally bawling his eyes out and whimpering, 'Get me out of here, please apply for bail, I can't handle this.'

The lesson he learnt was that jail is a scary and lonely place. He was granted bail and, on appeal in the County Court, his luck changed, and he was given a community corrections order (CCO), with conviction.

In typical fashion and, no doubt due to my early inexperienced years as a lawyer, I tried to run a plea of self-defence regarding another client who had been charged with a number of counts of assault involving one victim. The way I saw it, he was only protecting himself from being assaulted. Surely self-defence was a good argument? While our laws recognise the right of any person to protect themselves from an attack or even a threatened attack, it has to be necessary and certainly proportional, given the set of circumstances.

The problem I had and, as rightly pointed out to me by His Honour who I had also incorrectly called "Your Worship", 'Mr O'Neill, please don't try and run that argument before me, your client belted the victim on at least four occasions, broke his jaw and put him in hospital.'

So much for my learned plea with the new title for magistrates from 2004 being "Your Honour", not "Your Worship". He was lucky not to be sentenced to a term of imprisonment but received a CCO of 18 months with conviction and to complete 250 hours of unpaid community work.[10]

A CCO is now the only community-based sentencing order that can be imposed by magistrates. They replaced other orders known as an intensive corrections and management order and an order for combined custody and treatment. A CCO, which can be with or without conviction, has a maximum of two years if ordered in the Magistrates Court and five years in the County or Supreme Courts and can include up to 600 hours of unpaid community work, which will require a pre-sentence report before making the order.

The order can be subject to conditions, such as notifying police of any change of address and a drug and alcohol assessment in the event the court is satisfied the criminal offending was

---

10   see section 7 (1) of the *Sentencing Act*.

contributed to by drug or alcohol dependence. The court can also impose restrictions and conditions on the use of drugs or alcohol including rehabilitation, together with, as applicable, restrictions on movement and residence, associations with certain individuals, curfews and court monitoring. Recent data released by the Sentencing Advisory Council determined that in the County and Supreme Courts, CCOs were imposed in 12 per cent of matters heard with 6 per cent in the Magistrates Court, with the latter imposing fines as its most common penalty.

I was to find that alcohol certainly played a large part in respect of some clients being brought before the court in all types of matters. One, in particular, was regarding Jack (not his real name), who was a young man of only 19 years of age and for some reason decided breaking into a clothing store at 3am in the morning to steal clothes would be a good idea. Jack was from a very well-respected family, well educated, had no priors and the combination of binge drinking and consumption of anti-depressant medication was not a good idea. When he woke up on the morning after his brazen burglary and on realising what he had done, he discarded most of the clothing off a local pier.

It was fortunate in Jack's matter that I tendered to the court a very persuasive psychological report, which set out his debilitating mental health disorder. In addition, Jack had already made restitution to the owner of the burgled premises, which was another factor in the court placing him on a GBB without conviction.

Alcohol and possibly drugs also played a part in a client who was charged with assaulting a St John ambulance volunteer after a heavy day at the local races. The problem for my

23-year-old client, Ron (not his real name), was he was facing a mandatory six-month imprisonment courtesy of sections 18 and 31 of the *Crimes Act* 1958 (Vic)(Crimes Act) and section 10AA of the Sentencing Act, noting under section 31 there is a maximum penalty of five years imprisonment for such an assault on an emergency worker. Such custodial sentence was brought about by the Andrews Government in 2018 by the *Justice Legislation Miscellaneous Amendment Act 2018*(Vic), following the assault of a paramedic by two women who had escaped a term of imprisonment.

The definition of emergency worker under section 10AA of the Sentencing Act defines such workers as either police officers or protective service officers as defined in the *Victoria Police Act 2013* (Vic), paramedics and operational members within the meaning of the *Ambulance Services Act 1986*(Vic), operational members on duty under the CFA Act and the *Fire Rescue Victoria Act 1958*(Vic), with volunteer emergency workers as defined in the *Emergency Management Act 1986*(Vic). An emergency worker also includes custodial officers such as prison officers, police escort officers and youth justice officers[11].

It should be noted the mandatory penalty of six months specifies such circumstances of why a mandatory jail term is not appropriate. Special circumstances include impaired mental functioning but not brought about solely as a consequence of self-induced drugs or alcohol intoxication. This type of plea submission to the court as a mitigating factor certainly assisted a young woman charged with assaulting a police officer, including kicking him to the ground. Her lawyers, in early July 2023, persuaded Magistrate Rosemary Falla in the Melbourne Magistrates Court that special circumstances applied due to

---

[11] see *Corrections Act 1986*(Vic).

the past traumatic family history of the defendant and that she achieved good grades whilst at school.

Four offenders in the Melbourne County Court were not so fortunate when they assaulted police officers and were not only charged under section 31 of the Crimes Act, but also affray.[12] Whilst His Honour Judge Johns accepted the offenders had excellent rehabilitation prospects, were in stable relationships and employment, and two of the offenders suffered from a traumatic childhood, sentencing included 15 months imprisonment with an eight month non-parole period.[13]

In the case of Ron, in his drunken and perhaps drug induced stupor he passed out and was being attended to by the volunteer. He lashed out, striking a minor blow to the volunteer which didn't cause any significant injury, other than a slight chest bruise. He was subsequently charged with assault of an emergency worker.

In my view, I failed to see how the volunteer fell under the emergency worker definition as none of the relevant acts determined that it applied to St John ambulance workers. This argument initially fell on deaf ears with police prosecutors at a summary case conference and it was not until a second mention before the presiding magistrate, that we finally reached agreement with Ron pleading to the alternative section 23 assault charge under the Summary Offences Act. My plea included the mitigating circumstances surrounding the assault, together with three glowing character references. Given he had no prior convictions, Ron was placed on a good behaviour bond with an order to make a donation to the St John's Ambulance.

---

12   see section 195H of the Crimes Act.

13   see further *DPP v Trent Potts, Phillip O'Donnell, Jake Houldcroft and Jake Mitchell* [2022] VCC 1825.

I continued to represent young offenders in the Children's Court which has two main divisions, namely one for family and the other for criminal matters. A child in respect of criminal responsibility is defined as under the age of 18 and of, or over, the age of 10 at the time of the alleged offending but does not include a person who was of or above the age of 19 years at the time a proceeding was commenced in court.

For all matters outside criminal charges, a child is defined as under 18 years of age. This means the age of criminal responsibility for a child to be arrested, charged or jailed must be at least 10 years of age. Victoria does have a caution program in place for first time juvenile offenders, but it will depend on the seriousness of the crime and the impact on the victim. The Victoria Police Manual sets out all the factors that must be taken into consideration and when or if any charges should be laid.

Case in point, when a caution was given to a client's young son of 15 years of age after being detected inside his local high school equipped with CCTV. On the day in question, in company with two friends, they saw an open window into a classroom so decided to climb inside and walk around for something to do. Not a good choice as the school reported the entry to police and the culprits were quickly identified. The client's son was interviewed by police and consideration could have been given to a charge of unlawfully being on the premises. However, as a first-time offender and given no damage was caused and he admitted guilt, not that he had any choice given the CCTV footage, he was cautioned, which was consented to by his parents and who were present when the caution was given. Such caution will remain in a police brief register for future reference if needed. Further cautions may be given but again depending on the seriousness of the offending.

There is also a plea option available by way of diversion under section 356 of the CYF Act which commenced on 1 January 2017 under the Children's Court Diversion Service (CCYD). The CCYD provides for eligible juveniles who appear before the Court's Criminal Division to be placed on a diversion, but not for serious offences which are subject to a fixed penalty or sentence. There must be acceptance of the conduct that resulted in bringing the young offender before the court and a typical diversion plan may include a letter of apology to the victim and consenting to the activity requirements, as further outlined in the plan. If, of course, the offending is committed when drunk or alcohol affected, the court may order appropriate counselling and if associated with violence, an anger management program

New South Wales has a similar caution and diversion program in place for specific offences under the *Young Offenders Act 1997*(NSW), which applies to juveniles between the age of 10-17 at the time of the offending, with the aim of diverting the young offender out of the court system. Victoria's Sentencing Act defines a young offender as under the age of 21 and case law determines a youthful offender as aged between 21-25 years, which the court may take into account when sentencing. The young age of the offender is one factor to be considered by the court and as determined by the Court of Appeal,[14] rehabilitation is one of the three primary sentencing considerations, the other is not being sentenced to an adult prison unless there is no option.[15]

In Australia, in all jurisdictions a juvenile under the age

---

14   *R v Mills* [1998] VSC 241.

15   the three general principles were affirmed in *Azzopardi v The Queen* [2011] VSCA 372.

of 10 years cannot be determined guilty of a criminal offence.[16] Between the age of 10 to 14 years, the common law doctrine known as the presumption of *doli incapax*, (Latin phrase meaning 'incapable of evil'), which assumes that a child under 14 years of age is not sufficiently intellectually and morally developed to appreciate any wrongdoing and cannot form any criminal intent. This means the police prosecutor must be able to demonstrate the child knew such criminal conduct was seriously wrong before they can be found guilty.

For example, in *RP v The Queen* [2016] HCA 53, the High Court of Australia determined that the prosecution's evidence did not rebut the *doli incapax* presumption and stated:

> *What suffices to rebut the presumption that a child defendant is doli incapax will vary according to the nature of the allegation and the child. A child will more readily understand the seriousness of an act if it concerns values of which he or she has direct personal experience. Rebutting [the doli incapax] presumption directs attention to the intellectual and moral development of the particular child. Some 10-year-old children will possess the capacity to understand the serious wrongness of their acts while other children will not.*[17]

The same rationale was applied in the March 2022 pack murder of 16-year-old Declan Bates in which an accomplice, who was 13 years old at the time, was successful in arguing such legal principle being found not guilty of murder or manslaughter in concert with other gang members. Supreme

---

16   see section 344 of the CYF ACT and section 4M of the *Crimes Act 1914*(Cth).

17   [para 12].

Court Justice Incerti accepted evidence that the defendant was suffering from complex ADHD and psychiatric issues[18]. Declan's family gained little comfort from this decision despite his accomplices previously being sentenced on their guilty plea, one for murder with a 15-year term of imprisonment and two others for manslaughter and intentionally cause serious injury, both receiving less jail time. At the time of writing, it remains to be seen whether Her Honour's ruling will be appealed with other perpetrators still to be tried.

The Children's Court Criminal Division has jurisdiction to determine all matters summarily, except any offences resulting in death. Committal proceedings are conducted in the Children's Court, but the more serious matters, such as murder and manslaughter, arson causing death and culpable driving resulting in death, will then proceed either in the County or Supreme Court. The hearing of matters in the Children's Court also allows members of the public to attend such proceedings, unless the sitting magistrate determines they should be excluded.

This was readily apparent in one matter I acted in for a young 13-year-old client charged with offences of indecent assault against a young female. Her parents were very vocal, bordering on being abusive to my client and his mother outside the court and then sat in the open court glaring at both me and my client. I addressed the magistrate of what had transpired outside and asked they be excused from sitting in court. All to no avail, but Her Honour did suggest that they needed to conduct themselves appropriately, or she would have no hesitation to having the matter heard in a closed court. I did try to submit the *doli incapax* defence as part of my submissions,

---

18   *DPP v PM* [2023] VSC 560.

even with a report from a psychologist. The magistrate was having none of that as it was clear from the evidence presented by the police prosecutor that my client understood what he did was wrong, given the nature of the offending, which clearly was of a serious nature.

The prosecutor referred to case law involving offending of a sexual nature and quoted from the Victorian Court of Appeal in *R v ALH* (2003) 6 VR 276[2003] VSCA 129:

> *In case of person under the age of 14 but not under the age 10, the Crown has to prove that they knew their conduct was seriously wrong. It is a rebuttable presumption that can be rebutted sufficiently by the act or acts constituting the offence in conjunction with the age of the defendant... Some acts may be so serious, harmful or wrong as properly to establish requisite knowledge of the child; others may be less obviously serious, harmful or wrong or may be equivocal or may be insufficient.*

The upshot was, however, my young client was placed on an undertaking to be on good behaviour without conviction and, given the exceptional circumstances of the offending, the bond was for a period of 12 months.

Unfortunately, in statistics released by the Crime Statistics Agency (CSA), juvenile crime continues to rise for the age bracket of 10 to 17 years with an increase compared to 2021 of 18.2 per cent in 2022 in particular committing assaults, robberies and even murder. More troubling was those offending between the age of 10-14 with a total of 5882 crimes being committed, an increase of 37 per cent and noting such an increase was the highest number for the previous five years. Aggravated burglaries by juveniles were also particularly noted with entries into unlocked homes to steal motor vehicles, showing an increase in 2022 by 15.4 per cent.

In the past year alone, Victoria Police had a total of 600 juvenile offenders on their watch list, in other words, they were keeping a watchful eye over them, as 280 of those were recidivist offenders in respect of aggravated burglaries, with many being repeatedly released on bail only to continue committing crime. Since 2022, according to the CSA, there has been a further surge in juvenile crime with a total of 20,041 offences being committed by those in the 10-17 age bracket during the previous 12 months, while in 2023 crimes committed by juveniles between 14-17 years of age rose a staggering 30 per cent.

The minimum age of 10 years in respect to criminal culpability has however been a sore point now for many years. The Australian Government, to date, has totally rejected pressure to amend its legalisation. This has led, in frustration of the failure to implement a national law amendment, to a recent decision by the Victorian Government to amend the CYF Act in which a juvenile can be arrested, charged or jailed, except for such serious crimes as murder, raising the age of criminal responsibility to 12 years in 2024 with further consideration to 14 years of age in 2027.

The concern was due to the previous year from September 2023 saw an increase in home burglaries, by offenders in the age bracket between 10-14, of a staggering 44.6 per cent, compared to the previous year. Obviously, in a few years, we won't have to be overly concerned about this sort of increase as the offences won't be considered crimes in any event.

This proposed 2027 amendment has, however, been supported by the Law Institute of Victoria President, Tania Wolff, when she said:

This is the minimum standard (increase the age to 14 years) set by the United Nations and is backed by medical research which shows children go through significant cognitive development at this age.

These amendments have also received further support, including from various justice advocates and in particular from the Victorian Aboriginal Legal Service, as there are clear concerns in placing children as young as 10 in juvenile detention. On the other hand, former Victorian Chief Commissioner of Police, Kel Glare, stated in response that, in his opinion, such a move would be the 'height of stupidity... there are all kinds of adult criminals who'd use 13-year-old kids as a tool to commit their offences. I think it's almost inevitable this will increase crime.'

This view was also supported by Victorian Chief Commissioner of Police, Shane Patton, when he said, 'There'll will(still) be a victim of crime but the child won't be able to be held accountable at law.'

The Victorian Government may, however, be minded to also consider the age of criminal responsibility in other countries such as Canada and Israel setting it at 12 years of age, while Japan is lower at 11 years of age. Unsurprisingly, at least 28 USA states do not impose a set minimum for criminal responsibility, while prosecutions under USA Federal law sets it at 11 years of age. The Australian Council of Attorneys-General in their 2021 "Age of Criminal Responsibility Working Group" review and their subsequent report proposed an increase in line with Canada and Israel to 12 years of age.[19]

The Northern Territory Labor Government passed a bill

---

19   See Council of Attorneys-General, Age of Criminal Responsibility Working Group Terms of Reference, Communique 23 November, 2018.

in November 2022 to amend its criminal code to raise the minimum age of criminal responsibility from 10 to 12 years.[20] This amendment was as a consequence of a recommendation set out in the report of the Royal Commission into the Protection and Detection of Children in the Northern Territory. The amendment to the *Criminal Code Act 1983*(NT) then came into law on 1 August, 2023 and was to also simplify the *doli incapax* statutory test, but victims of such crimes would still have access to financial support under the *Victims of Crime Assistance Act 2006* (NT). The amendments also removed any record of prior offending by children under this new minimum age of criminal responsibility. However, two years later, in October 2024, its now Country Liberal Party Government brought it back to 10 years of age.[21]

The ACT became the first government, however, to pass a bill in November 2023, raising the age of criminal responsibility, with some exceptions in respect to serious offending, to 14 from 1 July 2025.[22] In addition, the ACT has codified the statutory test of *doli incapax* into legalisation, as will Victoria.

It is a foregone conclusion that the Victorian Government will increase the age of criminal responsibility, even as juvenile crime is at an all-time high, particularly in respect to home invasions. Regardless, they may also need to have a closer look at the "Embedded Youth Outreach Program" (EYO program), which emanated from a series of initiatives involving police and justice youth workers. A similar type of initiative first gained prominence as far back as 1947 with the establishment of the

---

20   *Criminal Code Amendment (age of criminal responsibility) Bill* 2022.

21   *Criminal Code Amendment Act 2024*(NT).

22   *Justice (Age of Criminal Responsibility) Legislation Amendments Bill 2023.*

St Kilda Boys Club now known as the St Kilda Police and Citizens Club, as a consequence of a few local youths stealing apricots from the front garden of its founder, Olive Johnston. Their overall mission is to prevent crimes being committed by young people and provide them with other options as part of their character building and offering them support and services, including participation in a range of sporting activities.

The EYO program involves a police officer in partnership with a youth worker, offering after hours liaison and support to youths under arrest, trying to uncover what the reasons were for committing crimes. It was aptly put by Sergeant Hawkes of Werribee Police who said, 'The whole arrest, charge, bail, remand, court system, justice system, youth detention can't be just the answer.'

This ingrained notion of "arrest, punish and release" was also closely examined in 2018 in a multi-agency working partnership overseen by the Department of Justice and Community Safety with the aim of determining ways to deter youths from our criminal justice system.

Another initiative, which has gained some prominence, is what is known as the P.A.R.T.Y Program. Certainly not a party in a normal sense. It involves a prevention program where those participating listen to firsthand experiences from front line police and paramedics, for example, which, no doubt, would have an impact on young people and their offending which may have resulted in traumatic consequences. Such a program also includes visiting hospital emergency and intensive care units, which in itself drives the message home and hopefully changes lives for the better.

While legal representation must be treated seriously and appropriately, at one point I even tried to introduce some humour into my submissions in a guilty plea. This time it was before His Honour, Julian Ayres, at Dromana Magistrates Court. My client, being the owner of a dog called Diesel, was charged under the *Domestic Animals Act 1994* (Vic) with three counts of "found at large outside their premises". Whilst these charges are not criminal in nature, it is still contingent on the prosecution to prove the case beyond reasonable doubt. The maximum penalty pursuant to section 23(1) of this act is not more than six penalty units, but between sunset and sunrise, the penalty increases to not more than 10 penalty units. Yet, if you own a cat and are charged with such an offence, the fine is only one penalty unit for a first offence and three penalty units for any subsequent offence.

In my opening submission, with supporting photos of the installed preventative measures, including metal stakes, I referred to Diesel as Houdini, as no matter what my client put in place, the dog kept digging his way out. Houdini, of course, was a well-known escape artist and illusionist and it seemed to me the dog was in the same league. My client even tried medicating the animal, to no avail. It's fair to say, the gallery in court all had a good laugh but His Honour was not impressed, particularly when the shire prosecutor also referred to the dog as Houdini. Mr Ayres, very gruffly, warned both of us that the dog's name was not Houdini, so stop calling him that. At least I tried to humour the court and, in any event, Houdini, sorry Diesel's owner, was let off with a fine without conviction of $300 with shire costs of $125.

Two not guilty pleas before a jury, both in the County Court of Victoria, were to follow the committal proceedings with me as instructing solicitor. The committal process in the Magistrates Court applies to cases listed for trial by judge and jury and such procedures are set out in sections 95-157 of the Criminal Procedure Act. Such a proceeding allows the defence, following disclosure of evidence by the prosecution, to "test the evidence" and cross examine their witnesses with leave of the court. Ultimately, it is for the presiding magistrate to determine whether there is sufficient evidence to support a conviction for the defendant to be committed to stand trial.

The committal process often referred to as a "mini trial" by a number of legal commentators, has a number of critics with calls for such proceedings to be discontinued. Victims of Crime Commissioner, Fiona Mc Cormack, is of the view such a process only results in further victim harm and trauma. In addition, it allows defence lawyers to not only intimidate prosecution witnesses but also use such a process as a delaying tactic. This opinion was also shared by Victorian Law Reform chair, Tony North KC, who was also of the view committal proceedings were not an effective procedure, in any event, in recognising weak prosecution cases with presiding magistrates not committing for trial only around one to two per cent of matters.

In March 2020 and largely brought about the significant case delays caused by the COVID-19 pandemic, the Supreme Court of Victoria introduced a fast-tracking committal procedure with an up-front election by the accused to stand trial in respect of murder and/or manslaughter and related charges.[23] Already, around 35 per cent of those accused of murder have accepted such a process without the need for a committal in the Magistrates Court.

The *Juries Act 2000*(Vic) applies to both criminal and civil trials, with the latter consisting of usually six people, but

---

23   see sections 143 and 144 of the Criminal Procedure Act.

sometimes up to eight, in order to determine the amount of compensation by way of damages a person should be paid, if any. In respect to a criminal trial in either the Victorian Supreme Court or County Court, the jury consists of 12 members but in trials expected to be lengthy, up to 15 people are on the jury for either a trial in the Supreme or County Courts. The County Court is the principal criminal division trial court, except in respect to treason or murder and related offences, which falls under the jurisdiction of the Supreme Court.[24]

Jurors have an important role to play in our criminal justice system, to not only protect the rights of the accused, but to ensure and participate in the proper administration of justice. Jurors must, however, be mindful that they can be held in contempt, particularly for conducting their own research and making enquiries about matters before them at trial, to ensure they only deliberate on the evidence before them. The conduct of jurors is regulated by Part 10 of the Juries Act in addition to the *Jury Directions Act 2015*(Vic).

The misconduct of a juror was highlighted in the Victorian Supreme Court trial of Ricardo Barbaro, who was charged with the murder, in May 2020, of Ellie Price. Despite the explicit instructions of Justice Lasry to the jury panel not to make their own enquires about the case before them, one juror ignored this instruction by undertaking personal research on the internet, resulting in the trial being abandoned, much to the frustration of, not only His Honour, but all participants. This particular juror under section 78A of the Juries Act now faces a penalty of 120 penalty units, which could be in the order of $22,000. There is also a common law offence of attempting to corrupt,

---

[24] also see sections 46 and 47 of the Juries Act-failure to reach unanimous verdict-also see Victorian Law Foundation-Jurors Handbook 2012.

influence, instruct or induce a jury or jurors to reach a verdict in favour of one side, despite the evidence before them.[25]

In my first County Court trial I acted for a former school principal charged with sexual assaults against one of his students and, as the police brief was rather lacking in some areas on the client's instructions, we proceeded as a plea of "not guilty" following a Magistrates Court committal. I briefed John Williams of Counsel who, at the time, was practising in criminal law and his wife, Jillian, would later be appointed as Judge in the Federal Court of Australia. It was my first foray into a jury trial and, even as an instructing solicitor, I found it very demanding but John in his usual fashion excelled with the client being found not guilty.

This trial was quickly followed by another one in the County Court with a client charged with sexually abusing his younger sister. The plethora of charges under the Crimes Act included a number of sexual assaults and the remainder also included incest. It was certainly a learning experience for me. In consultation with the barrister I briefed, what I found unusual was that it was determined our client would plead guilty to one charge of sexual assault at the start of the trial but not guilty to all other charges.

In my opinion, at the time and with all of three years of practice to date, this course of action seemed very risky. The dilemma was whether this guilty plea would have an adverse impact on the defendant in respect to the remaining charges. The answer was no, it didn't, and the judge properly instructed the jury on the admissions made in respect of the guilty plea.[26] After a four-day trial and a short deliberation by the jury,

---

25   see section 320 of the Crimes Act.

26   see section 222 of the Criminal Procedure Act.

our client was found not guilty of the remaining charges and received a nominal sentence for the charge of sexual assault.

This was followed by a very short interaction with an outlaw motorcycle gang (OMCG) that I won't name for obvious reasons. In my view, their conduct was clearly in breach of the Crimes Act and two of their members should have been charged with fraud and at least obtain a "financial advantage by deception". Section 82 of the Crimes Act defines such an offence as, 'A person who by any deception dishonestly obtains for himself or another any financial advantage', giving rise to imprisonment of a maximum of 10 years. In order to prove the offence, it must be undertaken by the prosecution as detailed in section 81 of the Crimes Act, that not only did the defendant engage in deception but amongst other elements as a result of that conduct, obtained ownership, possession or control of property.

In this particular matter, I was acting for Malcom Howell as the trustee in bankruptcy. Before he could take possession of the bankrupt's property, to wit a rather large house in the southeast suburbs, the OMCG moved in as soon as the house was vacated on the alleged basis, they had an equitable interest and, as a consequence, they lodged a caveat claiming an interest in the property. Not that they had any such interest. On discussing the matter with the Victoria Police OMCG Task Force set up at the time, it seemed this type of brazen conduct was happening on a regular basis.

As the removal of the caveat was urgent, we applied to the Supreme Court to achieve this. We believed we had a sound prima facie argument that the OMCG had no right whatsoever to the property, either on legal or equitable grounds. The difficulty was, our application could be tied up in the court proceedings for some time as a Notice of Appearance was filed by lawyers acting for the OMCG. We had no doubt our application would be successful with a significant costs order against the OMCG caveator, but time was of the essence.

Given the police really had no choice but to view the matter as a civil dispute, charges under the Crimes Act were not on their agenda and, even if charges were laid, I doubt the OMCG would have simply entered a guilty plea. On that basis, I was left with the trustee's firm instructions to see if the matter could be resolved by way of a financial settlement, which it was but only after a lengthy discussion on site at the property in dispute. My dealings with the OMCG certainly left me in no doubt they were not angels and they rode off with a substantial trust account cheque.

I also learnt very quickly never to tell my client the likely outcome of the sentencing by a court. I wouldn't now say to a client, for example, 'Don't worry, I will get you out of this mess with a small fine or good behaviour bond.'

What I was to learn later on, the best answer to give is the best- and worst-case scenario. For worst case, it would be what the Crimes Act stipulated as a penalty, noting it could be a term of imprisonment and, best case, given the client's antecedents on what a court might determine. This would, of course, depend on the plea material and if the client had any priors for similar offending.

Case in point was a client who I will call Dick (not his real name). It was in regard to his forced entry into a home and the stealing of a television set. Now Dick had no priors and, for all intents and purposes, was a clean-living man in his early 30s and usually gainfully employed. On this particular day, after becoming very stressed when driving to a job interview, he stopped his car before walking into a house, after knocking on the door, and then proceeded to steal a television set in full view of the elderly victims. He drove off with his vehicle registration number taken down by the householders, who were now very confused and minus a television.

On returning home from the successful interview, police were waiting and arrested him. Given he had no priors and had never been in any sort of trouble before and, despite how brazen the aggravated burglary was, he was granted bail by police on his own undertaking to appear in court at a later date. I told him in no uncertain terms that he had no choice but to plead guilty, but I would get him off on a good behaviour bond, so rest easy and don't worry because 'you're in good hands' with my worldly legal experience to date. Of course, as I was a new kid on the block, so to speak, I omitted to tell Dick this type of criminal offending carried a maximum penalty of 25 years imprisonment.

Judgment day arrived at the Lilydale Magistrates Court and, once again, I reassured him he would be going home with a slap over the wrist. Being the last case called for the day at about 3.45pm, it started to ring some warning bells for me. I entered the plea of guilty and, after the police brief summary was read to the magistrate, I did my plea. What a great plea it was, but not according to His Worship. He indicated to me, incredulously, my client would be going to jail and sentenced him to six months imprisonment.

My client, who was taken away into custody, was then locked up in the police cells next door while I made an application for an appeal against sentence, on the basis of it being "manifestly excessive", and bail, which was listed the next morning at Ringwood Magistrates Court.

Naturally, my client needed comforting so I visited him in the lock up to find him curled up in a ball, crying and reminding me of my words, 'You said I would get a bond.'

Well, I stuffed up on that one, but I was successful in getting him out on bail the next morning. Despite my advising him of best-case scenario only, he still had faith in me to do the appeal on sentence in the County Court. Mind you, the fact I offered to do it pro bono (at no charge), may have had something to do with it but I did feel I owed him that much. Appeal day arrived and I invited Don McKenzie, my former colleague from university, to watch me in action in my wig and gown.

The appeal against sentence was going really well, or so I thought, until the judge asked me a question I had absolutely no idea about. It went something along the lines of whether I had considered a certain piece of legislation and from the way he put the question, His Honour surmised I obviously should have known about it. For a fleeting moment, I had a "Dennis Denuto" moment. Dennis was a likeable and certainly well-intentioned, but incompetent bumbling suburban lawyer in the 1997 Australian film, "The Castle".

Having no idea, as well as being embarrassed, I politely excused myself before His Honour, reached across to the prosecutor and asked him very quietly, 'What in hell is the judge talking about?'

He told me the answer with a smile on his face. Trying to put on a good act of being unfazed, I went back to my spot, told the Judge, 'Yes, I had considered that,' then finished the now quickly amended submission and sat down. I certainly didn't submit a Dennis Denuto plea with his famous line, 'It's the Constitution, its Mabo, it's justice, it's law, it's the vibe... I rest my case.'

There were two outcomes from this: one being the client received a good behaviour bond, but with some stringent conditions and the second was Don's recommendation that possibly I needed to not just practice predominantly in criminal law. Don was lecturing at Monash University and was about to take up a position with Frankston Technical and Further Education (TAFE). Don's employment experience and background was certainly interesting as he had previously worked as a tradesman, teacher, union official and then as a university lecturer. He would subsequently enter the legal profession and, not only specialise in employment law, but branch out into family law, in particular, intervention orders and also criminal law.

I had already thought about doing some lecturing in the area of industrial and employee relations but, at the same time I would continue to "dabble", sorry, practice in a number of areas of law. However, in my early foray into the legal profession, it became readily apparent that I needed to 'broaden my horizons and add another string to one's bow.'

3
ANOTHER STRING TO ONE'S BOW

Whilst I had a reasonable knowledge of industrial and employee relations, my new path in adding another string to my bow was initially as a lecturer at Monash University National Key Centre in Industrial Relations. As Don Mc Kenzie was now the recently appointed Chief Executive Officer of Frankston TAFE, I effectively took over his role in 1999 lecturing to post graduate students for a master's degree qualification in Industrial and Employee Relations.

In its early days during the 1960s-1970s, Monash was very well-known for student demonstrations, particularly against Australia's participation in the Vietnam War and, of course, conscription. One of the better efforts by student radicals involved forcing our then Prime Minister, Malcolm Fraser, to hide in a basement in a university theatre over the dismissal of the Whitlam Government.

However, this was followed by Monash's much publicised pioneering and research into in-vitro fertilisation (IVF), by Alan Trounson and Carl Woods, leading to the delivery of the first IVF baby in 1980. The university initially only had one campus at Clayton, with approximately 15,000 students, but by 1998 it had a total of eight campuses, including two overseas and in excess of 50,000 students.

My lecturing role would mainly be at the Key Centre under the watchful eye of Professor Gerry Griffin. For the next three years, I would have the pleasure of teaching students in the master's program for Labour and Employment Law. One of my students would be Brian Wright, who would later act as the tutor to my classes at the Victoria University of Technology (VUT) as I was also lecturing there in the Graduate Diploma, Industrial Relations and Human Resource Management. VUT was originally established with the enactment of the *Victorian University of Technology Act 1990* (Vic) and commenced operations in 1992. It is now known as Victorian University under the *Victorian University Act 2010* (Vic).

The expertise of Brian first came to my attention when, on one occasion, I was lecturing students in workers compensation, an area of law that he practiced in as a barrister. On this occasion, he politely interrupted me in a class of 30 students to state that what I was saying about the *Accident Compensation Act 1985* (Vic) was well, shall we say, not quite right.

On his appointment as a Magistrate to the Industrial Division of the Magistrates Court at Melbourne in 2004, he was described as, 'A walking Halsbury when it comes to the law of Workers Compensation.'

Despite appearing in this court a number of times as I progressed through my law career, I never had the opportunity to appear before His Honour to be reminded of our days at Monash and VUT. As I was the only lecturer in the master's program without a master's degree, Gerry advised me it might be a good idea if I gained that qualification. So, it was back to head down and bum up for the next six months, sitting exams and attending to a thesis on "A Right to Costs in the Australian Industrial Relations Commission (AIRC)". Don would subsequently assess my thesis and, despite a number of comments on incorrect references and typographical errors, I graduated with a Masters in Industrial and Employee Relations in May 2001 and continued lecturing at both the Key Centre and Monash Clayton Campus.

Sadly, the Campus Menzies Building was subjected to a shooting rampage on 21 October, 2002 in which a commerce student by the name of Huan Yun "Allen" Xiang shot two students dead and wounded five others, including a lecturer, using a pistol he had obtained as a member of a shooting club. As a mark of respect, the Clayton campus flags were flown at half-mast the day after, followed by a day of reflection on the first anniversary. Xiang was subsequently acquitted due to mental impairment and currently remains under psychiatric care at Thomas Embling Hospital, where he also attacked a consultant psychiatrist with a knife in 2015 but again found not guilty on the grounds of mental impairment[27].

I subsequently lost my tenure when Don returned to Monash University to again take up his lecturing role after completing his three years at Frankston TAFE. I continued in my role at VUT and, for the next few years, I also lectured in the graduate certificate courses at Chisholm Institute (Institute),

---

[27] section 20 of the *Crimes (Mental Impairment and Unfitness to be Tried) Act 1997*(Vic).

which was formerly Frankston TAFE. The Institute was established in 1998 and took its name from Carolyn Chisholm and also the Chisholm Institute of Technology, which initially conducted tertiary courses from 1982 to 1990 before coming under Monash University. The constitution for the Institute is made under the powers conferred by section 3.1.1. of the *Education and Training Reform Act 2006*(Vic).

Carolyn Chisholm was lauded as a civil rights pioneer in the 1850s and her efforts in social justice, firstly working on improving the rights of vulnerable women migrants and helping them find employment with vastly improved working conditions. She then focused her efforts on Victoria by successfully lobbying for adequate accommodation shelter along the roads leading to the Ballarat and Bendigo goldfields. I certainly enjoyed my lecturing role at the Institute over a period of some four years, but it was now time to focus on my legal career.

My role as a practicing lawyer, after two years with John Hall and the Law Firm, saw me branch out into my own practice with Louise Luke as O'Neill Luke and Associates, then with experienced accountant and recently admitted lawyer, Geraldine Behan in November 1990, under the name of O'Neill Behan and Associates. The practice was then further expanded to the area of industrial law, including the drafting of employment contracts.

I would appear in the Industrial Relations Court, during its short-lived tenure up until 1997, and then for the next 20 years, the AIRC. Then with the passing of the *Fair Work Act 2009* (Cth), initially I appeared for Fair Work Australia, which is now known as the Fair Work Commission (FWC). I would also continue to represent clients in the Equal Opportunity

Commission, the Federal Court of Australia, the Industrial Division of the Magistrates Court, Accident Compensation Conciliation Service (ACCS) and the Victorian Civil and Administrative Tribunal (VCAT).

At the same time, for the next 20 plus years, I would also continue to practice in the area of crime, for victims of crime, children's court matters, drink driving and family violence related matters, in particular intervention orders. I also became reasonably proficient in debt recovery for clients, leading, as applicable, to bankruptcy and liquidation. Being a legal practitioner though certainly had its moments of drama and despair, intermingled, of course, with some mirth. However, now with my Master's Degree in Industrial and Employee Relations, it was time to test the theory.

4
ASPECTS OF THE LAW OF EMPLOYMENT

The guiding principles underpinning our industrial relations framework can largely be attributed to a number of international labour organisation standards and conventions drafted by member governments, employers and employees (ILO Conventions), which established the basic fundamental principles of rights for our work force. Such areas covered also included the elimination of all types of forced or compulsory labour, the removal of child labour and discrimination in employment.

These conventions, or protocols, can either be legally binding international agreements, agreed to by member countries or, in some cases, recommendations which provide non- binding guidelines. There are a total of 11 fundamental ILO Conventions applicable to workplace rights, including the Right *to Organise and Collective Bargaining Convention*

1949(No 98), the *Equal Remuneration Convention, 1951(No 100)* and the *Discrimination (Employment and Occupation) Convention 1958(No 11)*.[28]

Initially, the Victorian Employee Relations Commission (ERC) was established by the Kennett Government, following the proclamation of the *Employee Relations Act 1992*(Vic) and ceased functioning on 31 December, 1996. Under section 4 of the *Commonwealth Powers Act 1996* (Cth), its functions were transferred by the Victorian Government under its *Commonwealth Powers (Industrial Relations) Act 1996*(Vic) and such referral of powers would encompass employment matters for all Victorian private and public sector employees, which would then be administered by the Australian Industrial Relations Commission.

Prior to the AIRC, such jurisdiction was at the behest of the Commonwealth Court of Conciliation and Arbitration, which was abolished in 1956, following a decision by the High Court dealing with the separation of powers in Australian law in the Boilermakers' Case.[29] The High Court determined the judicial power of the Commonwealth could not be vested in any tribunal that also had a non-judicial role, giving rise to the establishment of the Commonwealth Conciliation and Arbitration Commission. In 1973, the Australian Conciliation and Arbitration Commission was formed which was subsequently replaced by the AIRC in 1988.

The AIRC would become very relevant regarding matters concerning equal work and equal pay, together with acting

---

28 also refer to *Declaration on Fundamental Principles and Rights at Work* (1998).

29 *R v Kirby: Ex parte Boilermakers Society of Australia* (1956) 94 CLR 254.

as conciliator and arbitrator of unfair dismissal cases, federal awards and enterprise bargaining agreements. The applicable legislation was the *Industrial Relations Act 1988* (Cth) subsequently amended by the *Industrial Relations Reform Act 1993* (Cth). When the Howard Government came into power in 1996, it replaced those two acts when it passed the *Workplace Relations Act 1996* (Cth), legislating workplace rights and conditions.

This was then followed by the enactment of the *Fair Work Act 2009* (Cth) (Fair Work Act), which would cover the overall employment relationship in the majority of workplaces in Australia. In effect, the Fair Work Act sets the boundaries for the minimum standards and regulations of the common law employer and employee relationship, including the terms and conditions of employment now under the administration and oversight of the Fair Work Commission (FWC), which is the governing workplace tribunal.[30].

There is a threshold question that first must be addressed as to what constitutes the difference between an employee and an independent contractor in order for the Fair Work Act to apply. In simple terms, an employee is under a contract of service, normally covered by a modern award and other legislation that is applied to employees and workers for wages, whilst an independent contractor is under a "contract for services" and not subject to any such statutory minimum standards.

The important overriding factor is the "control test" in order to differentiate between the two types of paid services, including but not limited to, who controls the work carried out, who provides the necessary tools and equipment and who is responsible for the income tax deductions. This question

---

30   see its functions as set out in section 576 of the Fair Work Act.

of difference even went to the High Court in *Hollis v Vabu Pty Ltd* [2001] HCA 44 regarding couriers with the decision determining they were employees as the employer, Vabu Pty Ltd, effectively controlled all aspects of their work, including providing uniforms and pay slips.

Further monitor compliance safeguards in the Fair Work Act with the employer–employee relationship saw the establishment of the Fair Work Ombudsman (FWO), with its functions as set out in section 682 of the Fair Work Act. Minimum National Employment Standards (NES) for all employees under the national system were also established under section 61 of the Fair Work Act and came into effect 1 January, 2010. Such standards as working a maximum 38 hour weekly and leave entitlements, including paid family and domestic violence leave, to name a few, cannot be replaced, for example, by awards, enterprise bargaining agreements (EBAs) and common law employment contracts of service, unless specifically allowed under the Fair Work Act.[31]

A number of anti–discrimination laws are also in place in respect of working conditions and possible breaches federally, including, *Racial Discrimination Act 1975*(Cth*)*, the *Sex Discrimination Act 1985* (Cth), the *Disability Discrimination Act 2004*(Cth) and the *Age Discrimination Act 2004*(Cth). In Victoria, working conditions are also covered by the *Long Service Leave Act 1992*(Vic) (LSL Act), *Racial and Religious Tolerance Act 2001* (Vic), *Occupational Health and Safety Act 2004*(Vic) (OHS Act), *Equal Opportunity Act 2010* (Vic) and the *Gender Equality Act 2020* (Vic).

Discrimination and victimisation in the workplace can also be referred to the Australian Human Rights Commission

---

31 see section 62–122 of the Fair Work Act which details the NES.

(AHRC), courtesy of the *Australian Human Rights Commission Act 1986* (Cth). This act stipulates a procedure for the AHRC to investigate and hopefully reach a resolution for workplace complaints of unlawful discrimination based on age, race, sex, sexuality and gender identity and disability. The Victorian Equal Opportunity and Human Rights Commission (VEOHRC) has a similar jurisdiction and human rights complaints, including the majority of those complaints emanating in the workforce, can also be listed with the Human Rights Division of the Victorian Civil and Administrative Tribunal (VCAT).

There is also a further accelerated option available to Victorian employees in respect to employment related claims under the Fair Work Act in the Industrial Division of the Melbourne Magistrates Court.[32] Such workplace issues that can be the subject of a hearing in the Industrial Division include breaches of employment contracts, allegations of unpaid salary, including non-payment of commission, leave entitlements, such as annual and long service leave, and disputes in respect of awards and EBAs under the *LSL Act, Public Holidays Act 1993*(Vic), *Outworkers (Improved Protection) Act 2003*(Vic) *OHS Act* and the *Safe Patient Care (Nurse to Patient and Midwife to Patient Ratios)Act 2015* (Vic).

The Industrial Division does not have jurisdiction in respect to complaints involving allegations of unfair termination, breaches of employee superannuation contributions and workplace issues regarding harassment, bullying or injury. The Industrial Division has a Small Claims Division which deals with claims under $20,000 and a separate procedure for those claims in excess of $20,000. The plaintiff uses the applicable

---

32   see section 4 (2A) of the *Magistrates Court Act 1989* (Vic).

forms under the *Magistrates' Court General Civil Procedure Rules 2010*(Vic).

One of my appearances in the Industrial Division was for a client who was employed by a local law firm. The client had worked as a legal assistant for some eight years and given the length of tenure, termination by notice required the client to provide four weeks' notice of resignation. However, for some reason, when the notice was given, she was terminated summarily the same day and her now ex-employer declined to pay out the period of notice, only paying accrued annual leave. In addition, it was their view that she was not entitled to pro rata long service leave as her length of employment had only been eight years and not 10 years.

Despite my letter of demand for payment of four weeks' notice and referring them to section 6 of the LSL Act, they still determined that their interpretation of employment law and relevant legislation was correct. In addition, they argued my client was in fact a casual employee and not entitled to four weeks' pay in lieu of notice and being a casual, certainly was not entitled to long service leave. I politely referred them to section 3 of the LSL Act which determines that even if she was a casual employee, which we took issue with, the definition of employee incudes a casual. I also referred them to section 28 of the LSL Act where, not only can a court order be made in respect of what is owed, but also a criminal conviction and penalty.

Further, it was again pointed out, that section 6 of the LSL Act in any event specifically provided for payment of such leave after the completion of seven years continuous employment on "ordinary pay equal to $1/60^{th}$ of the employee's total period of continuous employment…". The other difficulty they had was, if she was casual, according to them, why did they pay out accrued annual leave?

We were left with no choice but to file and serve a small claims application in the Industrial Division and, lo and behold, the law firm, as defendant to the proceedings, filed and served a response by way of a defence. Put bluntly, such response did not make any sense whatsoever as they still claimed the client was a casual employee. The matter was quickly listed by the court for a directions hearing and the magistrate, after perusing the defence to the claim, invited them to explain to the court the merits of such a defence.

However, as it was now fast approaching the lunch break, the magistrate said to the principal of the defendant law firm that, in any event, he would stand the matter down and resume at 2pm. In the interim, His Honour suggested to the defendant that perhaps a visit to the Supreme Court library during the lunch interval might prove to be useful. The visit to such library did prove useful as on resumption at 2pm, their response was an admission their defence simply had no merit and would agree to pay the four weeks' pay in lieu of notice and pro rata long service leave.

My application for indemnity costs, being all reasonable legal costs and disbursements as incurred by my client as against court scale costs was, however, rejected by the magistrate. In my view, my client was entitled to be indemnified and reimbursed for her solicitor–client costs as she was left with no alternative than to take out legal proceedings. The magistrate simply took the view, I think, that we had done quite well on the day, with the outcome in my client's favour in any event.

A common law remedy for damages is also available to dismissed employees, in the event they are precluded from commencing proceedings under the Fair Work Act. Whilst statutory unfair dismissal laws have significantly increased the availability of a legal remedy, contractual damages at common law are also available. Wrongful termination of employment usually occurs when an employee is terminated by an employer who is in breach of a contract of service and in the absence of any lawful reason for the termination.

In acting for clients regarding wrongful termination at common law can involve termination of a fixed term employment contract before the completion of the fixed term. A number of these types of matters were generally settled, either without the need to commence legal proceedings for payment of the balance of the fixed term, or by way of court ordered mediation, after the filing and serving of the complaint in the Magistrates Court and if the damages claim was over $100,000, by way of Writ in the County Court.

In situations where there was no fixed term and, in the event there was no justifiable reason to terminate, such as on the grounds of poor performance or misconduct, proper notice must be given to the employee. I was to find in some matters and, in the absence of any written period of notice, the question then would be in the circumstances, what could be considered as reasonable notice? What then needed to be taken into account was the length of service of the dismissed employee, the remuneration paid and more importantly, the seniority and status of the position previously held.

This was particularly relevant in one matter for my client Jim (not his real name), who was on a salary in excess of $200,000, had been in a senior position as a manager overseeing around 30 employees, had been with the employer for nearly seven years and was 60 years old. There was no employment contract in place, just a letter of offer of employment when he first commenced. On termination, the reason was allegedly the employer wanted to take a "new direction". Jim was simply terminated without cause with four weeks' pay in lieu of notice as he was surplus to their needs. Our writ included, amongst other things, a claim for implied reasonable notice based on nine months and, given his employment status with the company, this was deemed to be more than reasonable.

It should be noted that notice periods, based on common law principles, have ranged as high as 18 months as in *Ogilvy & Mather (NZ) Ltd v. Turner* [1996] 1 NZLR 641 and 12 months in *Quinn v Jack Chia (Australia) Ltd* [1992] 1 VR 567. The latter case law was interesting in that, despite a 30-day termination clause in the plaintiff's contract of employment when he first began working with the defendant company, the court held that the overall circumstances at termination, not commencement of employment, applied, noting Quinn had now been promoted to a senior position and on that basis 30 days' notice was not applicable, nor reasonable.

In the case of Jim, the matter was settled and after taking into account that he had mitigated his loss, to a degree, by finding alternate employment, pending the outcome of his legal proceedings, he walked away, under the circumstances, with a reasonable settlement. The lesson to be learnt though regarding the question of implied reasonable notice, or lack thereof, will on most occasions result in an expensive outcome that an employer will not be happy with. I would always advise my employer clients to always ensure and not just limited to senior employees, that you have a properly drafted employment contract in place, including a clear and precise termination clause.

It would be fair to say I lost count of the number of

clients I represented initially in the AIRC and then the FWC for applications concerning allegations of a dismissal being harsh, unjust and unreasonable. Section 382 of the Fair Work Act determines that an employee covered by either a modern award or an enterprise agreement cannot be unfairly dismissed if they have completed a minimum period of employment of six months, or in the case of a small business employer of less than 15 staff, for a period of 12 months.[33]

Further, section 333 of the Fair Work Act refers to an exclusion under a high-income threshold and Regulation 2.13 of the *Fair Work Regulations 2009*(Cth) provides a formula for determining such threshold, which currently sits at $162,000, meaning if an employee earns in excess of that amount, they are precluded from making an unfair dismissal claim.

It should be noted that unfair dismissal exclusions include: employees who resign unless they were forced to, meaning they were constructively dismissed; were not under a training contract which terminated at the end of a specified period; those demoted but did not involve a significant remuneration or duties reduction; employment contracts for a specified time and task and, of course, independent contractors, also known as subcontractors, engaged under a contract for services.[34]

With a constructive dismissal, it wasn't unusual to receive instructions, particularly from an employer client now served with an unfair dismissal claim, where they claimed in defence that the employee had resigned. The only problem was, on discussing the matter further, my client's information would be

---

[33] see section 383 of the Fair Work Act for minimum period and section 23 of the Fair Work Act for definition of small business employer. Also see the Small Business Fair Dismissal Code.

[34] see section 386 of the Fair Work Act for meaning of dismissed.

that the employee was told, 'You either resign or I will sack you,' which is a typical case of constructive dismissal.[35]

Of course, the dismissed employee must be able to demonstrate they were left with no alternative to resign due to the employers' conduct. Such conduct, giving rise to a constructive dismissal, may also include a reduction in remuneration, demotion and even a significant relocation in employment. In respect of the latter, I acted for one ex-employee who was left with no choice but to resign, following his relocation from his normal suburban workplace to Mildura, which was some 500 kilometres away.

Casual employees are generally excluded from making such applications unless they worked on a regular and systematic basis and had a reasonable expectation of on-going employment.[36] In a genuine redundancy exclusion, section 389 of the Fair Work Act sets out what is deemed to be a proper dismissal based on redundancy, but employers need to be careful in situations if the person considered to be redundant to the business needs could have been redeployed, either within their company or an associated entity. If redeployment was an option but the employee was made redundant, this could give rise to a claim for unfair dismissal based on the fact it was not a genuine redundancy.[37]

The main criterion for what constitutes an unfair dismissal under section 385 of the Fair Work Act is based on the concept of whether the termination was harsh, unjust or

---

35   also see *Mohazab v Dick Smith Electronics* [1995] IRCA 625 for leading case on constructive dismissal- no choice but to resign.

36   see section 384(2)(a)(i) & (ii) also see section 15A of the Fair Work Act for meaning of casual employee.

37   see section 389(2) of the Fair Work Act.

unreasonable. This requires a valid reason for the termination and is largely based on substantive and procedural fairness. In other words, the main reason for termination must be a valid one and procedurally, the employee was notified of the reason for termination and was given a chance to respond to such valid reason, if based on conduct or performance.

With performance related terminations, the FWC will consider whether the employee was appropriately warned about such performance related issues and whether a support person for the employee was present during the termination process. Further procedural requirements also include the size of the employer's entity and if they had the benefit of human resource specialists. The FWC can also take into account any other matters it considers relevant.[38]

The other procedural requirement for applicants alleging unfair dismissal is their Form F2 application must be lodged with 21 days after the day the termination took place.[39] In the event the application is out of time, then the applicant must be able to demonstrate there were exceptional circumstances that gave rise to lodging past the due date.[40]

Employers certainly have a right to lodge a jurisdictional objection if they consider the applicant is precluded, due to not meeting the designated criteria to make such unfair dismissal application. Such objection can also include the application was filed out of time, but you cannot object simply on the basis that the termination was in any event fair. Any objection does not automatically bring a halt to the application and it is not

---

38   see section 387 of the Fair Work Act – criteria for considering harshness.

39   see section 394 of the Fair Work Act.

40   section 394 (3) of the Fair Work Act – exceptional circumstances.

unusual for a member of the FWC to consider the jurisdictional objection at the same time when considering the unfairness of the termination.[41]

I would do many appearances for both employees and employers without briefing Counsel regarding termination of employment matters, but I would also brief eminent barristers such as Chris O'Grady, rightly now King's Counsel (KC), being appointed on 24 November 2015 and Brian Lacy, who would go on to be appointed as a Senior Deputy President of the AIRC, and then as Administrator for Christmas Island and the Cocos (Keeling) Islands before returning to the bar. Brian also served with the Australian Regular Army in South Vietnam and played a very important role coordinating the response and victim recovery of the asylum seeker boat catastrophe in December 2010.

Former special counsel, Rebecca Davern, for Allens Arthur Robinson, then signing the Bar Roll in November 2008, was also a pleasure to brief and amongst many of her matters, she successfully defended a discrimination claim against Monash University and others in the matter of *Chen v Monash University* [2015] FCA 130. The result for Chen, a former senior lecturer and professor at Monash University, was not a good outcome, when she was ordered to pay $900k in indemnity costs, after unreasonably rejecting a settlement offer in respect to unproven allegations of sex discrimination and harassment. Rebecca was also ranked by peer review publication, Best Lawyers, as Melbourne "Lawyer of the Year Labour and Employment Law".

I don't think these learned counsel would have been

---

41   see FWC Unfair dismissals benchbook in respect of the applicable criteria for an unfair dismissal application.

impressed with my first appearance, without counsel, in early 1996 regarding an unfair dismissal claim. I appeared as lead counsel, so to speak, noting I had not yet even considered at this point undertaking any further education in employment law, with Don McKenzie as instructing solicitor in the ERC. We alleged our client, an aged care employee, had been unfairly dismissed, all to no avail. It's fair to say my first exposure as lead lawyer was rather embarrassing as my opponent was a very experienced barrister.

I was subsequently "flogged" with the matter, heard over two days, being ultimately dismissed. Whilst my client had a good argument regarding her unfair termination, it largely fell on deaf ears. Even from day one of the hearing, it was obvious the Commissioner had no sympathy for her and most certainly none for her lawyer, ie. me. I appealed the matter to a Full Bench and again was suitably admonished, losing the appeal with a costs order against my client.

After obtaining my master's degree, it would initially be a further learning curve for me, hopefully with some good outcomes for my clients. In one matter, my client alleged he had been terminated without valid reason, in other words, denied substantive fairness and certainly no procedural fairness, as he was terminated by way of email. As I did with all clients, I would make sure they knew to turn their mobile phone off before entering any court or tribunal room.

My client was in the witness box after being sworn in and I started to take him through his evidence. After asking him to repeat his name for the record as the applicant, his mobile phone started to ring with a very distinctive ring tone. I apologised to the AIRC Commissioner and suggested very politely to my client to turn it off, which he did, or so I thought. I started again and this time, actually got past his name when it rang again. Again, I apologised and I very firmly told my client to turn it off, which he apparently did, or once again, so I thought.

No such luck, as about two minutes into his evidence, that annoying distinctive tone rang again. I left the bar table, walked up to my client, grabbed his phone, stormed out of the hearing room and literally chucked it down the corridor and watched as it bounced a few times. On resuming without any sign of being annoyed, I took him through his evidence. One of my VUT students reminded me in class the following week when she said, 'Gee, you were really pissed off with that phone.'

Apparently, she had been sitting in the corridor waiting to appear in another matter and saw my act of destruction. Not a good look, but the lesson was to always make sure your client's phone is switched off.

I wasn't on my own as a lawyer who sometimes lost it and, on this particular occasion, it would be the client who had been terminated by a law practice for alleged unethical conduct as a legal practitioner. My role was to represent him in a conciliation as, quite clearly, he had been terminated unfairly. On the day of the AIRC conciliation, it was obvious he was quite agitated. After hearing my submission as to why the termination was harsh, unjust and unreasonable, the conciliator then asked the respondent law firm for their side of the story of why my client was terminated. They didn't hold back, saying he was 'useless, didn't know the law and should not be practising.'

These remarks greatly annoyed my client and before I knew it, he reached across the table, grabbed the partner from his previous law firm in a head lock and started to throttle him. It certainly brought the conciliation to a very quick unresolved conclusion.

The majority of unfair dismissal applications are usually resolved in the first instance at the conciliation phase, following the lodging of the FWC Form F2 application and after the employer has filed and served a response. My advice was always, whether the client was an employer or a terminated employee, to try and resolve the matter as quickly as possible and without the need for time consuming and costly litigation. The FWC is effectively a no-costs jurisdiction, which means each party to the application must bear their own costs, unless there is an argument that the application was made in circumstances that were vexatious and without reasonable cause.[42]

Lawyers and paid agents have no automatic right to appear in the FWC and must seek leave to appear.[43] Permission to appear is generally sought in accordance with section 596(2)(a) of the Fair Work Act, on the basis that legal representation would enable the matter to be dealt with more efficiently and, if applicable, taking into account the complexity of the matter. In addition, in accordance with section 596(2)(b) of the Fair Work Act, it is usually submitted that it would be unfair not to allow the applicant or respondent to be represented. Costs can also be awarded against such representatives in situations where it should have been readily apparent to them, for example, that such an unfair dismissal application had no reasonable prospect of success.[44]

The primary remedy available to a dismissed employee is reinstatement in circumstances that were deemed to be harsh, unjust and unreasonable. In lieu of reinstatement, if considered

---

42 see section 611 of the Fair Work Act.

43 section 596(1) of the Fair Work Act.

44 see section 401 of the Fair Work Act – Costs orders against lawyers and paid agents.

by the FWC to be inappropriate, payment of up to six months for loss of earnings, less any earnings by the applicant in other employment following termination.[45] The applicant has a duty to mitigate against any loss and make bona fide attempts to find alternative employment, pending the outcome of the unfair dismissal application.

There are number of lessons to be learnt from all of this. With terminated employees, there is usually not a "pot of gold at the end of the rainbow" in respect to compensation for loss of employment by an unfair dismissal. Further, unless you can convince the FWC that reinstatement is appropriate and the employment relationship has not irrevocably broken down, you won't be reinstated. The only matter I acted in where a dismissed employee was reinstated was in circumstances where he had been with the employer for some 18 years and the termination was definitely unfair. However, even in situations like that, there is nothing to prevent the employer, aggrieved by the decision, seeking permission from the FWC to lodge an appeal to the Full Bench of the FWC on the grounds of question of law or significant fact. If granted by way of appeal, it will thereby increase legal costs and delay such reinstatement even further.[46]

A number of Commonwealth workplace laws also protect the majority of employees, including casuals, from discrimination and unfair treatment in the work environment, particularly under the General Protections provisions of the Fair Work Act. Pursuant to Part 3-1 of the Fair Work Act, it includes provision for workplace rights (section 341), protection

---

45   see sections 390-392 of the Fair Work Act.

46   see sections 375A and 604 of the Fair Work Act.

from adverse action in the workplace (see sections 340 and 342) and including industrial activity (section 346).

Other protections under section 351 of the Fair Work Act prohibit employees being discriminated against, including termination on the basis of their race, colour, sex, sexual preference, age, physical or mental disability, marital status, family or carer's responsibilities, pregnancy, religion, political opinion, national extraction or social origin. Section 351 prohibitions are not applicable for any action which is deemed not in breach of anti- discrimination legislation or is based on action taken under the inherent requirements of a business and also some limited good faith action taken in respect of religion.[47] Termination due to an employee's temporary absence due to injury or illness also provides protection to employees, but only in respect of termination and not any matters involving adverse action.[48]

In regard to unlawful termination under the general protections provisions of the Fair Work Act, section 365 provides that a Form F8 application can be made to the FWC in respect to a termination in contravention of such provisions, such application being lodged within 21 days of the termination. All other general protections disputes, not involving termination, are dealt with under section 372 of the Fair Work Act. In the event a termination dispute is not resolved at mediation or conciliation by the FWC in the first instance (section 368), a certificate will be issued showing it is satisfied that all reasonable attempts were made to try and resolve the dispute (section 369). Unless the parties consent

---

[47] also see Fair Work Ombudsman Fact Sheet for General Protections and General Protections benchbook-Exceptions.

[48] section 352 of the Fair Work Act.

to the FWC conducting an arbitration, such certificate then provides for a further 14 days for a Federal Circuit and Family Court application to be made by the terminated employee alleging a general protections dismissal.

If the matter cannot be settled at a court-ordered mediation prior to a contested hearing, the Federal Court can make orders it considers appropriate in the circumstances, pursuant to sections 545, 546 and 570 of the Fair Work Act. Types of orders that can be made in respect to a contravention can include an injunction to prevent, stop or remedy the effects of such contravention, an order awarding compensation for any loss suffered by the person, the subject of a contravention and can also include reinstatement. Employer respondents, for example, need to be aware that if the contravention is proved, the Federal Court can make, under section 546 of the Fair Work Act, a pecuniary penalty order it considers appropriate in the circumstances, to be paid to the aggrieved party. In addition, the Federal Court can, under section 570 of the Fair Work Act, also order that legal costs be paid as incurred by the successful party in the proceedings.[49]

In respect to one particular general protections contravention, I acted for a client by the name of Joseph (not his real name), who had been employed in the position as a salesperson for a period of nearly 18 months. He was married with four children, one of which was, unfortunately, severely disabled, requiring daily medication and care. Joseph was a carer for his disabled child. His employer was aware of the family responsibilities and, despite this, they terminated Joseph due to his absences from the workplace for a week whilst his

---

49   also see FWC General Protections benchbook – Types of order made by the Court.

child was severely ill and in the Royal Children's Hospital in intensive care. This was despite Joseph keeping his employer aware on a daily basis of the reason for his absence, whilst the child remained in hospital.

On advising his employer by telephone that the child was about to be discharged and that he could return to work the following day, the employer terminated his employment over the phone. It should have been evident to the employer they were in breach of the Fair Work Act and, in particular, the general protections provisions, as the absence of Joseph was due to his family and carer responsibilities. He also had sufficient leave credits in any event to cover such absence from the workplace.

A Form F8 general protections application involving dismissal was made to the FWC, alleging Joseph had been unlawfully terminated in breach of section 351 of the Fair Work Act. The remedy sought was compensation for economic and non- economic loss, together with an order that a penalty be paid pursuant to section 546, with legal costs in accordance with section 570 of the Fair Work Act. The respondent employer filed and served a Form F8A response to the general protections application, disputing the chronology of events and that Joseph was validly terminated due to other spurious reasons.

The matter proceeded before a FWC Commissioner who then issued a certificate under section 369 of the Fair Work Act to the effect that all reasonable attempts to resolve the dispute had been or would be likely to be unsuccessful. It was clear to all and sundry that there was a genuine dispute as to actually what had transpired and the facts giving rise to the termination. However, we were very confident of the strength of our case and, lo and behold, at the court-ordered mediation before a registrar, the respondent employer left us in no doubt they wanted to settle the matter.

It was obvious their legal representative had pointed out the risks they ran if the matter proceeded to a contest, including the likely outcome, not to mention an order for costs and a pecuniary penalty. The matter settled with the equivalent of eight months' salary being paid in full, taking into account my client's loss of earnings, which was only around eight weeks, as he had found other employment following the termination. Indeed, the respondent employer may well have not suffered such a financial hit if they had first obtained competent legal advice prior to going down the path of termination and in breach of the general protections.

Failure to obtain legal advice before terminating an employee again became particularly relevant in a general protections claim against one of my employer clients, Joe Bloggs Pty Ltd (not real entity name). This resulted in a protracted and, eventually, time-consuming and costly negotiated settlement at mediation in the Federal Court. The managing director of the client was initially the subject of an application and summons for a personal safety order taken out by one of his female employees, who was alleging she had been sexually harassed by him on a number of occasions. Without obtaining any legal advice other than a short consultation with a duty lawyer, the director consented to such order but, of course, without any admission to liability.

Following the court hearing, the employee was then absent from work for a stress-related illness as a consequence of what had transpired. The absence was supported by medical certificates and a report from a psychologist. A Workcover claim was then submitted alleging a work-related illness based on anxiety and stress due to the sexual harassment. Unfortunately, at this point, my client, without seeking any legal advice, terminated the employee by way of email, without providing any valid reason. Not that there was one.

The now terminated employee immediately sought competent legal advice and filed and served a FWC Form F8 general protections application involving her dismissal. You would think at this point in time the respondent employer would have obtained legal advice, but no, that did not occur. A Form F8A was filed in response which, I was to later ascertain, was rather vague and indeed embarrassing in its denial of any breach of the general protections. To make matters worse, when the parties appeared before a FWC Commissioner in conference, my director client at this point engaged the services of his accountant.

As I was to later explain to the client, that would be the equivalent of me giving him financial advice, which I was certainly not trained to do. The matter was not resolved, apparently because his accountant said they did not have a case to answer. The usual Fair Work Act section 369 certificate was issued followed by a statement of claim as filed in the Fair Work Division of the Federal Court, naming both the employer as respondent and its director on the basis of accessorial liability.

It's fair to say the statement of claim was rather lengthy with over 60 separate paragraphs, complete with particulars alleging contravention of part 3-1 of the Fair Work Act. In particular, there were allegations of various breaches pursuant to adverse action as defined in section 342(1) with the breaches under section 340, breach of workplace rights (section 341), a further workplace rights breach consistent with section 21 of the *Occupational Health and Safety Act* 2004 (Vic)), and a breach of section 351 for reasons including the gender of the applicant.

The statement of claim also alleged there had been a number of breaches based on the unwelcome sexual conduct. The statement also sought as a remedy, or as we say, a "hamburger with the lot", the applicant's loss and damage not only for loss of income as a consequence of the termination of employment, but also for pain and suffering and diminished employment prospects. In addition, the applicant was seeking compensation for an alleged under payment of wages, including applicable shift allowances, leave entitlements and superannuation contributions, together with damages.[50]

On receipt of the statement of claim by way of service, the employer now sought advice and attended my office with their accountant. To say we had a rather vigorous conversation is an understatement, as I made Joe and, of course, his "adviser" aware, in no uncertain terms, that they had a problem and unless it could be resolved as quickly as possible, there was going to be a lot of financial pain. However, at this point in the proceedings, there was no point in making any offers to settle as, in our jargon, all you are doing is effectively "betting against yourself".

We subsequently filed a defence based on the client's instructions denying a substantive number of the allegations, including that the Federal Court did not have jurisdiction to determine the matters raised concerning the alleged breaches

---

50   compensation pursuant to section 545 of the Fair Work Act, pecuniary penalties pursuant to section 546(1) of the Fair Work Act and that such penalty be paid to the applicant (section 546(3)(c), and of course together with legal costs (section 570(2).

of the OHS Act and the Equal Opportunity Act. Under the cover of that objection, we denied the allegations in any event. In addition, the defence, in denying the allegations, also referred to a number of paragraphs in the statement of claim in the usual vernacular as being 'vague, embarrassing, an impermissibly rolled up plea and, in the absence of proper particulars, ought to be struck out.'

Regardless of our client's defence which, on instructions certainly to a degree, had a proper basis, the specific advice I again gave was that this was a matter that needed to be settled at the first available opportunity. In the absence of any settlement at the court ordered mediation and if the matter proceeded to a lengthy contested trial of at last a week some months later, the outcome in my view, would prove very costly for the client, and not just regarding their own legal costs. I would need to engage counsel in any event and, if the Federal Court found in favour of the applicant, the client also ran a very substantive risk of not only compensation being awarded to the applicant, but a pecuniary penalty and most likely an order for payment of the applicant's legal costs.

Common sense prevailed at mediation and, after the usual back and forth in arguments by both sides over nearly a full day, the matter was settled with a significant payment of compensation to the applicant. The settlement and release agreement were in the usual form and executed by the parties, and, of course, including a 'without admission and complete denial of any liability in relation to the proceedings and the allegations.'

A mutual release was agreed to for any further liability, strict confidentiality and, of course, a mutual non–disparagement clause. Suffice to say, the whole exercise for the client was very stressful, time consuming and definitely very costly, given the amount of compensation paid, in addition to their legal fees.

Employers in particular also need to note the FWC has jurisdiction regarding workers seeking redress by way of a remedy against bullying in the workplace.[51] Such a scheme came into effect from 1 January, 2014 and importantly, a worker also includes contractors, subcontractors, outworkers, apprentices, trainees, volunteers and even students undertaking work experience.[52] Any employee who considers they have been bullied in the workplace may apply to the FWC for an appropriate order under section 789FF of the Fair Work Act.

Bullying in the workplace must be treated seriously as in the decision of the Victorian Supreme Court in *Swan v Monash Law Book Cooperative* [2013] VSC 326. An employee was awarded in the order of $600,000 as compensation after her employer failed to adequately deal with allegations of bullying over some five years. In applying with the relevant criteria for workplace bullying, the FWC, in the case of *Ms SB* [2014] FWC 2014, set out the credible and reliable evidence parameters on what constitutes such "unreasonable behaviour" and the "risk to safety and health".

The jurisdiction of the FWC was further amended in September 2021 to include applications for orders regarding workplace sexual harassment. For the 2021-22 financial year, the FWC received a total of 631 applications seeking orders to stop bullying and/or sexual harassment in the workplace.[53]

---

51   see section 789FD (3) of the Fair Work Act for relevant business's covered.

52   see section 789FC of the Fair Work Act.

53   see FWC Annual Report–Access to Justice 2021-22-also see FWC-Sexual Harassment Benchbook.

Employers are also required to eliminate sexual harassment in the workplace by taking reasonable action[54] and the VEOHRC can issue sexual harassment guidelines under section 148 of the Equal Opportunity Act.

It follows, my salutary advice to employer clients, in any event, is always seek legal advice, particularly prior to terminating any employee and, of course, in respect to any employment law matter. Even when they consider they have a substantive valid reason to terminate an employee, my advice is always, take into account and put in place a proper procedure before such termination. In other words, procedural fairness. Many employers would terminate an employee without following any set guidelines and then seek legal advice after the termination.

Even in cases of summary dismissal for serious misconduct, such as fraud, theft and violence, still proceed with caution and always obtain advice from your lawyer prior to termination.[55] Both the courts and the FWC, in respect to summary dismissal, have formed a view that even fighting in the workplace may not justify summary termination, depending on each set of facts. In *Rankin v Marine International Pty Ltd* [2001] VSC 150, the court determined there was no one set parameter for misconduct that justified summary termination without notice.

My advice in those situations and, despite any substantive reason for the termination, was to again put in place a process of procedural fairness regardless, to further mitigate against any allegation of unfair or unlawful dismissal as compared to not only defending a claim but incurring significant on-going legal

---

54 see Part 3 of the Equal Opportunity Act.

55 see rule 1.07 under the Fair Work Regulations for definition of serious misconduct.

costs. Not to mention the time involved in defending such a cause of action, which, of course, could be better spent running their business.

It is apparent our laws relating to employment following a termination are very complex, which can result in many employees being unfairly and unlawfully treated by their employer. The problem that follows is, whilst obtaining legal advice is highly recommended, such employees refrain from taking any action, not only due to the complexity of the legislation and what path to go down, but in some ways, they consider the power balance still tends to remain with the employer.

5
ONCE A BANKRUPT, ALWAYS A BANKRUPT?

Going into bankruptcy has a number of advantages, also many disadvantages, but let's talk about the positive aspects first. The main plus is it allows the bankrupt to basically start again after the standard bankruptcy period of three years and one day has expired. When I say, "start again", it means the now discharged bankrupt has been released from the majority of the debts that led to the bankruptcy. It also has the advantage of preventing unsecured creditors from relentlessly pursuing the bankrupt and, once a trustee is appointed, hopefully there will be a fair distribution to creditors of whatever assets the bankrupt may have had.

The law governing bankruptcy is set out in the *Bankruptcy Act 1966*(Cth), which provides for three main avenues for a person to proceed down that path. First, voluntarily by compiling and filing a debtor's petition with the Australian

Financial Security Authority (AFSA), which sets out the personal details of the applicant proceeding to bankruptcy, including the names of any family members and dependants as applicable and a summary of any income received for the previous 12 months, including any government benefits and pensions.

The Summary of Financial Affairs (SFA) also requires full and proper details of your employment status, superannuation benefits, details of any vehicle(s) in your possession, followed by a requirement to declare the reason for wanting to enter into bankruptcy, either non–business related or, if you operated a business incurring numerous debts.

You must also provide a complete and detailed list of all your assets, including any cash on hand, savings, shares, tools of trade and, of course, any property, such as a family home and if it is jointly owned. The SFA also requires exhaustive details of your liabilities to both secured creditors (e.g. home mortgage) and to unsecured debtors inclusive of all debts, loans and leases as applicable. The person then completing the debtor's petition and SFA must sign a declaration, pursuant to section 267(2) of the Bankruptcy Act for which there is a penalty of 12 months imprisonment for submitting any false information.

The other process in bankruptcy is by application from a creditor who is owed money, by filing and serving a creditor's petition after the service of a bankruptcy notice (BN). The third and final option is to declare a deceased person bankrupt, which can also be by way of a creditor's petition for an order which is obtainable on application from the legal personal representative of the deceased estate.

I acted for a number of medium-sized companies, in particular those supplying steel to various company customers trading under an Australian Company Number (ACN), and those trading under a registered business name with an Australian Business Number (ABN). This meant the person trading under an ABN was the legal entity and therefore legally responsible for the debts incurred by their business.

Initially, if the debtor owed $5,000 or more to my client, such non-payment could be enforced by way of bankruptcy proceedings by establishing the debtor committed an act of bankruptcy.[56] Due to the COVID pandemic, temporary legislative debt relief measures were put in place, so the debt owed had to be $20k or more and the time allowed to respond to the creditor's BN was increased from 21 days to 6 months. From 1 January, 2021, these temporary relief measures ended and the amount set by regulation 10A of the Bankruptcy Regulations 2021 is now a minimum debt(s) of $10k and not more than six years old and the debtor only has 21 days to respond on service of the BN.[57]

It's fair to say that my steel supplier clients "took no prisoners" as they instructed me to pursue any debt aggressively and relentlessly and they would not hesitate to place any customer into bankruptcy, including any company director who had given a personal guarantee to my client. This was regardless of whether there was any likelihood of recovering the debt as owed, even if it was the bare minimum amount and would even be exceeded by their legal costs and disbursements. The latter included filing fees payable to AFSA and the Federal Circuit and Family Court of Australia, such fees now in the order of $4,605.00. My client simply took the view that by putting the

---

[56] see section 40 of the Bankruptcy Act which lists over 20 actions that are deemed to be an act of bankruptcy.

[57] see statutory period–section 5 of the Bankruptcy Act.

company director into bankruptcy, it would be a salutary lesson to other traders putting them on notice to pay the monies outstanding, or 'we will bankrupt you.'

The first step towards bankruptcy would be a letter of demand served, giving the debtor(s) usually 10 days to pay the debt and setting out the repercussions that would follow if said debt was not paid. It is important to note that such letters of demand should not include legal costs, unless it is particularly stated in any terms of a contract that such legal costs will apply. However, even that is questionable and, in my view, you should not add legal costs in any initial letter of demand. The Federal Court in the matter of *ACCC v Sampson* [2011] FCA 165 found a lawyer, in fact, engaged in misleading and deceptive conduct for including costs in the letter of demand.

If there is no response to the letter of demand, which was often the case, legal proceedings would then be commenced by my plaintiff client by way of a complaint in the Magistrates Court for debts under $100,000 and, if exceeding that amount, by way of Writ in the County Court. The following sets out a typical Writ Statement of Claim (by way of example only) for a debt against both the company and its directors, who had gone guarantors:

1. At all material times the Plaintiff is and was (a) a company duly incorporated pursuant to Statute and is capable of suing; and (b) a company in the business of supplying structural steel, plate, merchant bar and tubular products and cutting and drilling services ("the steel products and services").
2. At all material times the First Defendant is and was a company duly incorporated pursuant to the laws of the State of Victoria and is capable of being sued.

3. The Plaintiff, at the request of the First Defendant, sold and delivered steel products and services to the First Defendant during the months of May – June 2019.

Particulars
The request for the supply of steel products and services from the Plaintiff by the First Defendant occurred during the months of May-June 2019 and consisted of either numerous telephone calls from officers, employees and agents of the First Defendant for the supply and delivery of various steel products and services or by attendance at the Plaintiff's premises by officers, employees and agents of the First Defendant to collect the various steel products and services.

4. Tax Invoices were rendered for the supply of the steel products and services in the sum of $1,121,000.67 and the First Defendant is indebted to the Plaintiff in the sum of $1,121,000.67.

Particulars
Numerous Tax Invoices were rendered to the First Defendant by the Plaintiff for various steel products and services during the months of May- June 2019. The Tax Invoices are in writing, copies of which are available for inspection during normal business hours at the office of the Plaintiff's solicitors by appointment.

5. Despite demand, the First Defendant has failed and/or refused to make payment to the Plaintiff which to this date remains due and payable.

Particulars

Full particulars have previously been provided to the First Defendant by the Plaintiff. The Plaintiff has sent monthly statements to the First Defendant and has had its representatives call representatives of the First Defendant. The Plaintiff's solicitors forwarded a letter of demand to the First Defendant on 16 September, 2019, a copy of which is available for inspection during normal business hours at the office of the Plaintiff's solicitors by appointment.

6. Further and/or in the alternative the Plaintiff claims the sum of $1,121,000.67 from the First Defendant on account stated.

7. Further and /or in the alternative at all material times the Second and Third Defendants were Directors of the First Defendant and as Directors, the Second and Third Defendants agreed to act as Guarantors for the First Defendant and entered into and are the Guarantors referred to in a Guarantee ("the Guarantee") made between the Plaintiff and the Second and Third Defendants whereby the Second and Third Defendants unconditionally guaranteed to the Plaintiff the due and punctual payment by the First Defendant of any sum payable of all or any steel products and services whatsoever for which the Plaintiff supplied to the First Defendant and the Second and Third Defendants further agreed to be jointly and severally liable for all monies recoverable from the First Defendant.

Particulars

The Guarantee is in writing and contained in a document signed by the Second and Third Defendant and is available for *inspection at the offices of the solicitors of the Plaintiff between the hours of 9.00am and 5.00pm, Monday to Friday.*

8. Further and /or in the alternative the Plaintiff claims the sum of $1,127,000.67 from the Second and the Third Defendants on account stated.

9. The Plaintiff further claims interest against the Defendants in the sum of $9,703.99 pursuant to a tax invoice issued on 19 August 2019 being tax invoice number 2019-14 being interest due and payable on the sum of $747,057.14 and pursuant to the Plaintiff's general terms and conditions.

Particulars
The tax invoice and the Plaintiff's general terms and conditions are in writing and are available for inspection at the offices of the solicitors of the Plaintiff between the hours of 9.00am and 5.00pm, Monday to Friday.
And the Plaintiff claims:

i. Debt in the sum of $1,127,000.67.
ii. Interest in the sum of $9,703.99.
iii. Interest pursuant to the County Court Act 1958(Vic).
iv. Any amount payable pursuant to A New Tax System (Goods and Services) Tax Act 1999(Cth).
v. Such further or other orders as the Court deems fit.

In the absence of settling the debt by way of a deed of settlement for part payments, or payment in full, in many situations the debtor(s) simply ignored the legal proceedings as served, a summary judgment would then be obtained by way of a court order(s). If, however, the debtor(s) agreed to settling the debt, including legal costs and disbursements, the deed, together with a number of other applicable clauses, would also include the following:

> *In the event (debtor(s)) defaults in making any payment due (whether any instalment or part thereof, or interest or any other sum due) the full amount of the balance of monies then outstanding, including interest and costs which shall become immediately due and payable, and the judgment debtor(s) consent to using this Deed as the basis of (client) making application to a court of competent jurisdiction to place (debtor(s)) into bankruptcy by consent in default of these terms, together with any sums lost as a result of the default, including all interest and costs.*

If the debt as owed is not settled, a further letter of demand, with a copy of the court notice of order (judgment debt), which listed the debt sum outstanding, together with my client's court scale legal costs plus disbursements and interest, would then be sent to the judgment debtor(s) and, in the absence of any agreement for payment, a BN would be filed with AFSA for issuing if the court order was in excess of the minimum statutory amount. In respect of an order against a company, consideration would be given to commencing wind up proceedings.[58]

The BN, with a copy of the court order, would then be personally served on the judgment debtor(s) with a demand for payment within 21 days of service of the BN. Again, in the absence of payment or an agreed payment plan and provided the judgment debtor has made no application for a

---
58   see chapter 6–Perils of Liquidation- Directors be Aware.

compliance extension of time, a creditor's petition can then be filed in the Federal Court and served on the debtor. The petition includes an affidavit executed by the client of the default judgment stating the respondent debtor(s) committed an act of bankruptcy within six months before the presentation of the petition.

On the return date of the petition in the Federal Court, in the absence of settlement or grounds of opposition to the petition, with an accompanying affidavit in support, a sequestration order declaring the judgment debtor bankrupt is entered, appointing a nominated Trustee for control over the now bankrupt's estate. Such order deems said person unable to pay his or her debts and is therefore sequestrated.

The process in obtaining a sequestration order is quite protracted and to ensure compliance and that there are no grounds for rejection of the petition by the court, or to give reason for the judgment debtor to oppose such petition on procedural grounds, the following check list as compiled by legal practice manager, Nadine Smith, is recommended:

1. *Issue BN online with AFSA together with a certified extract of the court order.*
2. *Serve BN on judgment debtor.*
3. *Diarise for 21 days from date of service of BN, noting you only have up to six months to file petition.*
4. *Send letter to trustee requesting trustee's consent to act.*
5. *Draft petition for client to sign affidavit verifying petition, noting date of such petition must be same date as affidavit.*
6. *Conduct bankruptcy search and then prepare and swear affidavit of search of para four of petition, noting this cannot*

be dated before/ on the same date as the petition so do day after client has signed affidavit verifying petition.

7. File affidavit of service of BN, trustee consent to act, affidavit of search of para four and issue petition by way of court online via e-lodgement.

8. Serve on judgment debtor the petition, trustee consent to act, affidavit of service of BN and affidavit verifying para four of petition.

9. File copy of court-issued petition and trustee consent to act with AFSA which must be done within two business days of court issuing of petition.

10. File affidavit of service on judgment debtor of petition by way of court online via e-lodgement.

11. Brief counsel or instructing solicitor to appear on hearing date of petition.

Now, if that is exhausting, there are still more procedural steps as follows:

12. Prepare affidavit of relevant facts (Affidavit of debt that the debt is still owing and arrange for client to sign which must be done the day before the petition hearing).

13. Conduct bankruptcy search and the draft and swear affidavit of search which must be done the day before the petition hearing.

14. Email affidavit of relevant facts and affidavit of search to counsel or instructing solicitor.

15. File original affidavit of relevant facts and affidavit of search by way of court online via e-lodgement.

Now providing the court makes a sequestration order, you are nearly there and finally:

16. *Send sequestration order to trustee and file copy with AFSA which must be done as soon as you receive same, in order to not be fined for late filing.*

Hopefully, all of the above has been completed satisfactorily, noting that whilst there is an option for the court to appoint an Official Receiver in Bankruptcy with delegation to AFSA, this usually only occurs in situations when you have not nominated any registered trustee who consents to act as trustee in bankruptcy.

My preferred option was to always nominate a trustee, but generally many registered trustees will only act providing there is sufficient money or assets in the bankrupt estate to ensure payment of their incurred fees. However, I was able to find one trustee effectively on a speculative basis who was more than prepared to act as trustee in bankruptcy and generally in most matters there would be sufficient funds left over from the bankrupt estate, following proofs of debt being lodged with the trustee.[59] If there were not sufficient funds to pay his fees, his attitude was, 'Well, you win some and you lose some.' In other words, if he missed out on his fees, then so be it and he would simply wait until he was appointed on my instructions as trustee in the next bankruptcy matter.

Although I normally acted for medium-sized business clients in debt collection leading to bankruptcy for sole traders and company directors, there were always clients, particularly sole traders, who would seek my advice when contemplating going into bankruptcy. I would first ensure they had obtained

---

59   see section 84 of the Bankruptcy Act.

relevant financial advice, then determine if there were any avenues open to them, including reaching an agreement by way of negotiation with their creditors to try and avoid the perils of bankruptcy. Following that and if there were no other alternatives, my usual opening line would be, 'Once a bankrupt always a bankrupt.'

I say this on the basis there are a number of distinct disadvantages on entering into bankruptcy as follows, noting this is not an exhaustive list:

1. Whilst bankruptcy encompasses most unsecured debts, it doesn't cover all debts such as fines, including those ordered by a court, child support and maintenance and any government student loans.
2. The standard period for bankruptcy is three years and one day, unless a shorter period can be agreed to with the trustee in bankruptcy by way of sufficient funds to pay all creditors' claims and trustee costs, or the creditors agree to accept the bankrupt's offer for payment of a lesser amount in full and satisfaction of the debt. The period of bankruptcy can be extended, however, for up to eight years and over in situations deemed to be "bad behaviour" by the bankrupt.[60]
3. All divisible property, as defined in section 116 of the Bankruptcy Act, can be placed under the control of the trustee in bankruptcy, which includes houses and land.[61] This results in the trustee effectively becoming the

---

[60] see section 148 of the Bankruptcy Act-misleading conduct by bankrupt and 149D- grounds of objection (also see Part XIV of the Bankruptcy Act.

[61] see section 58 of the Bankruptcy Act–Vesting of property upon bankruptcy-general rule.

legal owner of the property, including jointly owned and property the subject of a mortgage, with the right to sell such asset for the benefit of creditors. It must be noted that equity in a property which is the subject of a Defence Services Home mortgage requires permission from the Department of Veterans' Affairs.[62] Trustee control of any divisible property is, of course, on the basis the sale of such property is commercially viable. In other words, there is sufficient equity in the property.[63]

4. Depending on the number of dependants, the bankrupt's yearly income will be assessed by the trustee in bankruptcy and if the bankrupt earns over a threshold amount, known as the Basic Income Threshold Amount (BITA), one half of the bankrupt's net after tax income will fall to the trustee. The BITA with no dependents is currently (2023) $66,639.30 and, for example, more than four dependants it only increases to $89,296.60. The BITA is updated twice yearly by AFSA, as are other monetary limits. A written application can be made to the trustee by the bankrupt to increase the BITA on hardship grounds and if not successful an appeal can ultimately be made to the Commonwealth Administrative Appeals Tribunal.[64]

5. A bankrupt may also be limited in undertaking certain types of employment; however, the Bankruptcy

---

[62]   see section 45A- *Defence Services Homes Act 1918*(Cth).

[63]   also see section 116 of the Bankruptcy Act and its regulations that lists non-divisible property which is excluded from the trustee noting a bankrupt can retain for their personal use motor vehicles currently at an auction value of $8,550.

[64]   see *Milson & Official Receiver in Bankruptcy* [2004] AATA 275 for a successful appeal on hardship grounds.

Act does not legislate for any restrictions in specific types. A person in bankruptcy will find though that there are a number of eligibility requirements for particular professions and if they are a bankrupt, they may well be precluded from working in a chosen field. For example, accountants, lawyers, tax agents, police and armed forces personnel (not an exhaustive list), may be precluded from employment by the applicable professional association and/or statutory board.

6. In addition to employment restrictions, an undischarged bankrupt will require leave from the Federal Court to be involved in a management capacity with a corporation either as a director, alternate director or secretary.[65]

7. If the bankrupt's reason for filing for bankruptcy is due to gambling debts, such bankrupt can be prosecuted for a criminal offence, provided the gambling debts were incurred within two years of the commencement of the bankruptcy as in section 271 of the Bankruptcy Act.

8. During the period of the bankruptcy, a bankrupt may well be required to surrender their passport and, in order to leave Australia, must first obtain written consent from the trustee in bankruptcy.[66]

9. A bankrupt for the duration of the bankruptcy is restricted to a threshold amount which is currently (2023) $6,771 when obtaining credit, including buying goods or services on credit, hire purchase or by way of cheque and in excess of that amount must declare to the financial lender

---

65   see section 206B of the *Corporations Act 2001*(Cth).

66   see section 272 of the Bankruptcy Act.

they are a bankrupt and failure to do so is a criminal offence under the Bankruptcy Act.[67]

My cautious advice to clients contemplating bankruptcy and those being threatened with bankruptcy by a creditor, is to look at all viable alternatives before going down that path. A bankruptcy, notwithstanding the disadvantages listed above, also has a social stigma attached to it, particularly with family and friends and, of course, close business associates.

There is also a potential issue for the bankrupt in that the trustee can look at past so-called preferential treatment, for example, payments or an asset transfer in favour of an unsecured creditor as against other creditors. In some situations, the trustee can go back for a period of five years prior to the commencement of bankruptcy. If it is deemed as a voidable preference, it can then be clawed back by the trustee.[68]

The other issue for a bankrupt, once discharged from bankruptcy, is endeavouring to obtain a personal loan, mortgage or credit. It will be a problem. Generally, when coming out of bankruptcy, it will still remain on the now discharged bankrupt's credit history which can be anything up to seven years. This means it will affect the person's credit rating and I know of a number of clients following discharge from bankruptcy, who have found it very difficult to be considered anything other than a risk and even in situations when trying to rent a property. Landlords, banks and even employers can conduct a search on the National Personal Insolvency Index (NPII) as it lists the details of the bankruptcy even after discharge.

---

67   see for example sections 269(1)(a) and 304A(1)(j)) of the Bankruptcy Act.

68   see section 122 of the Bankruptcy Act–Avoidance of preferences.

Insurers are able to cancel certain insurance contracts if there is a bankrupt clause that allows them to do so and many insurers will even refuse to renew an insurance policy for a bankrupt. They may even refuse an insurance policy for a person who was previously bankrupt. Minors can also be made bankrupt in certain situations and even debtors who are not Australian citizens can be exposed to bankruptcy if they reside here.[69]

The 2020-21 statistics, as released by AFSA saw only 10,621 new personal bankruptcies, which was nearly a 50 per cent decline compared to the previous financial year. Such decline was certainly influenced by the legislative changes during the pandemic, which also included banks deferring mortgage repayments. It was also obvious the Australian Taxation Office (ATO) and banks, in particular, were not chasing debts due to the impact of the COVID lockdowns. However, as our country has gotten back to some form of normality, it is anticipated personal bankruptcy numbers will start to look like those once again as seen in 2017-2018, which totalled just shy of 35,000. As the saying goes though, you need to consider that perhaps 'Once a bankrupt always a bankrupt.'

---

69   see section 7 and 43 of the Bankruptcy Act.

6
PERILS OF LIQUIDATION – DIRECTORS BEWARE

Liquidation has a number of perils that company directors need to be aware of. Liquidation is the process of winding up a company's structure and its affairs, courtesy of the *Corporations Act 2001*(Cth). It is usually brought about even when a company is solvent, but in most cases, it will be due to insolvency. Such insolvency can be induced by a number of factors such as creditors pressuring the company for payment, debts owed to the company which cannot be recovered and certainly in situations where a struggling company is unable to meet all their tax obligations, in particular pay as you go withholding (PAYG), company tax and employee superannuation entitlements.

If the ATO were to issue a director penalty notice (DPN), the company may be faced with no alternative but to enter into liquidation to avoid their directors being personally liable for the debt of the company. One of the other perils for directors is allowing their company to continue to trade whilst insolvent which, if proven, can have serious outcomes for a director.

However, each situation can be different and whilst there are different types of liquidation in insolvency, such as by creditors and shareholders, there is also a process available of appointing a provisional liquidator, creditors and members voluntary liquidation or a liquidator appointed by the court. It is quite common for an insolvent company to enter into voluntary liquidation, following a special resolution by its members. A members' voluntary liquidation can also take place in respect of a solvent company, but a decision has to be made by its directors to cease trading.

The concept of provisional liquidation occurs when a court appoints a liquidator as a stop gap measure and for the company to resolve its current trading issue. This doesn't necessarily mean, however, that the company will at some stage be placed into liquidation. In some situations, when a company's directors are in dispute over the administration of their business. Such issues, for example, can hopefully be resolved by provisional liquidation and avoid, or at least reduce further consequences for the company. It is not uncommon, following a voluntary administration, for a Deed of Company Arrangement (DOCA) to be agreed to between the parties and its creditors in order for the company to be administered under certain conditions, with the ultimate outcome to be in the better interest of its creditors as opposed to liquidation.

Court appointed liquidation will normally follow an application by a company stakeholder, such as a creditor, to place the company into liquidation for failure to pay a debt or debts.[70] My involvement in advising client creditors in pursuing

---

70   see sections 459A and 459P of the Corporations Act.

a company for a debt and prior to issuing a creditor's' statutory demand for payment of the debt as owed(the demand-Form 509H-section 459E of the Corporations Act), was always to first obtain a Notice of Order (judgment debt) made by the court before issuing and serving the demand. This ensures there is essentially no argument from the debtor company that the debt was due and payable.

This effectively provides the creditor with sufficient grounds to demonstrate the debtor company was insolvent and to commence the winding up process after 21 days, following the service of the demand. In the absence of a judgment debt, the demand pursuant to section 459E must have an accompanying affidavit that verifies the debt is due and payable. Such affidavit is usually sworn or affirmed, if the creditor is a company, by a director or officer of the company.

In any event, even if a demand is accompanied by a judgment order and the company under section 459C (2) of the Corporations Act has failed to comply, the presumption of insolvency can be rebutted provided the debtor company can demonstrate they are solvent. In addition, if the demand was only accompanied, for example, by a director's affidavit, there are significant technical pitfalls where the debtor company can argue the debt was disputed and was not due and payable.

In other words, if there was a genuine dispute afoot and even in situations where it can be demonstrated the debtor company was insolvent, the court could still refuse to issue a winding up order. Hence, it is not an easy path to go down so, right from the outset, I would always advise clients they need to be aware of the compliance requirements and strict procedures of the court, before pursuing the wind-up path.

However, let's assume my client is aware of the pitfalls

so I would always proceed in first obtaining a Court Notice of Order (judgment debt), after following the usual process of a Letter of Demand and, in the absence of settlement, issue court proceedings for the debt as owed. The following is a typical precedent Letter of Demand:

Dear Sir/Madam
Re: Debt – Notice of Intention to Sue

We advise we act for Joe Bloggs Pty Ltd. You are indebted to our client for the balance of $20,600.94 for goods sold and delivered for which full particulars have previously been provided. We are instructed that our client has also sent statements to you and has had its representatives call you concerning the debt.

We are now instructed to commence legal proceedings against you without further notice and enclose herewith by way of service Notice of Intention to Sue. To avoid further costs being incurred against you, we require your cheque no later than 4.00pm on Wednesday, 28 September 2022 in the sum of $20,600.94, such cheque being made payable to Joe Bloggs Pty Ltd.

In the event you choose not to oblige with payment or, alternatively, enter into a payment plan agreeable to our client, our client will instruct us to immediately file a complaint in the Magistrates Court of Victoria without further notice. This may result in further costs against you in the sum of $1,786.40 and the amount owed will have increased on the issuing of the complaint to $22,387.34 plus interest. In the absence of any defence, our client may obtain a judgment against you and by the time the whole process is completed the debt will be in excess *of $23,000.00. Our client may then seek to enforce the debt which could involve the winding up of your company.*

We would strongly recommend that you immediately arrange to make payment in the sum of $20,600.94 or, alternatively, enter into a payment plan agreeable to our client, failing which, proceedings will be commenced without further notice. In the event you wish to discuss any aspect of this matter please contact the undersigned and not our client, or you should seek legal advice and request your lawyers to contact us by the due date.

In many situations, for whatever reason, the debtor company would simply ignore the letter of demand and also ignore the service of the legal proceedings seeking payment. Provided the total amount sought in the demand was at least $4,000,[71] then the demand can be served and, of course, always with a judgment debt attached.

I acted for a number of client companies who once again adopted a "take no prisoners" approach and would not hesitate to wind up a debtor company. In the event no agreement could be reached to pay the debt in full, or even by way of compromise following the letter of demand, court proceedings would be issued. What followed in the absence of terms of settlement or, in most situations, the absence of service of a notice of defence, would then be followed by the demand with copy of the judgment debt attached.

Again, in the absence of a response, noting the judgment company debtor has only 21 days to respond to the demand, an Originating Process (the Writ), together with an affidavit

---

71 see *Corporations Amendment (Statutory Minimum) Regulations 2021*(Cth) as applicable from 1 July 2021.

in support with the demand exhibited, would be filed in the Supreme Court of Victoria. The Writ determines that the application to wind up is made under sections 459(A) and 459(P) of the Corporations Act on the grounds of insolvency; such grounds being the failure of the debtor company to comply with the demand. In addition, a Form 519 must also be filed with Australian Securities and Investments Commission (ASIC) notifying of the court action taken.[72]

In the event the wind-up application is successful at the court return date, a nominated liquidator will be appointed with immediate effect. This then prevents any person from taking any further action against the company in liquidation without leave of the court, including situations following the appointment of a provisional liquidator.[73] It should be noted, however, that section 471C of the Corporations Act allows a secured creditor to realise or otherwise deal with a security interest.

The main role of the court-appointed liquidator, on the grounds of insolvency, is to bring to an end the business affairs of the company now in liquidation and hopefully, pay out any monies to its creditors. Such creditors will be required to lodge with the liquidator a formal proof of debt (POD), setting out in detail with supporting information, what is being claimed by the creditor from the liquidated assets of the company, noting there is a specific time period when such a POD must

---

[72] see sections 465A, 470(1) (a), (b) & (c) of the Corporations Act.

[73] see section 471B of the Corporations Act. Also see *Swaby v Lift Capital Partners Pty Ltd* [2009] FCA 749 at [29], which sets out what factors a court will consider granting leave.

be lodged.[74] The liquidation can then be finalised once the liquidator has completed all investigations, followed by the company being struck off and a final return lodged with ASIC.

There is also a legislative safety net scheme in place for employees whose employer either becomes insolvent or is placed into bankruptcy pursuant to the *Fair Entitlements Guarantee Act 2021*(Cth), which replaced the previous employee entitlements scheme known as the General Employee Entitlements and Redundancy Scheme (GEERS). This allows, on application within 12 months, for compensation to be paid to said employee who meets the eligibility requirements for unpaid salary up to 13 weeks, unpaid annual and long service and redundancy pay up to four weeks per completed year of service, but not unpaid superannuation contributions. The entitlement scheme is not available to those directors appointed within 12 months of the company now in liquidation, including any employee relatives of such director.

Whilst there is no designated time limit in finalising the liquidation, the liquidator is required to complete the task as quickly and efficiently as possible. This will include arranging a meeting of all creditors and, if required, a resolution to be put to a vote of what should be offered to secured and unsecured creditors, employees and, if there is anything left over, to shareholders in a full and final settlement,[75] and, of course, approval of the liquidator's fees. Whilst such fees are unable to be paid until approved by creditors and, in some cases, the court, there may be situations when there are no recoverable assets and the liquidator does not get paid.

---

74   see Forms 535-general claim and 536- claim on behalf of employees – *Corporations Regulations 2001*- 5.6.49.

75   see section 477 of the Corporations Act.

Winding up a company is a rather complex procedure and in all the liquidations I acted in, the nominated liquidator does not generally leave anything to chance and is very diligent in carrying out the liquidation process. There are clearly defined steps a liquidator must follow in the process, including ensuring appropriate updates to all creditors and employees and to investigate the affairs and the available assets of the company. Ultimately, liquidators, as part of their duties, must ensure there is a fair and equal distribution to all creditors of the company from the available assets in liquidation. (i.e. pari passu).

What I was to find and advise my clients accordingly, were in situations where a liquidator discovered and determined the company now in liquidation made payments that were considered to be unfair preferences, they could be "clawed back" from my client as a voidable transaction.[76] What this means is that the liquidated company, prior to being wound up, made a designated payment to the client as an unsecured creditor in respect of goods and services received. Such preference payment was, therefore, in excess of what that particular creditor would have been paid in the event the transaction was to be set aside. This would be on the basis that the creditor was able to prove the debt subsequently in the liquidation process, in other words, on the principle of pari passu.

In more simple terms, a voidable transaction is an unfair preference and once identified by the liquidator, can be claimed, or as we say, clawed back from the creditor as it was paid when the company in liquidation was insolvent. That even includes in situations where such payment was to trigger the insolvency. In order to claw back a deemed voidable transaction, it must have

---

[76] see section 588 FE of the Corporations Act–definition of voidable transaction.

occurred during a relevant period pursuant to sections 588FE and 588 FF of the Corporations Act and generally seen as the six months ending on the relation-back day.[77]

It would be quite common for my clients to receive a letter of demand from a liquidator demanding payment, which had been determined as an unfair preference and therefore considered a voidable transaction. In these types of situations, my response to the demand, providing there was a proper basis, would be on what is known as the "good faith" defence.[78]

The following is a typical precedent letter in response to such a preference payment demand from a liquidator:

Dear Sir,
Re: Fred Nerk P/L (in liquidation) (not entity's real name)

We act for Joe Bloggs Pty Ltd. We refer to your letter dated 20 July, 2022 wherein you make demand for payment for the sum of $128,164.11. For the reasons set out in this letter, we are not prepared to pay that sum. We have instructions to accept service of any proceedings that you wish to issue. Whilst we are not prepared to respond in detail to each of the matters raised in your lengthy correspondence, we suggest you consider the following matters before taking the step of issuing proceedings.

1. The matters raised in paragraph 6(a) of your letter regarding the inadequacy of books and records held by the company are matters which were not known by our client in the relevant period.

---

[77] also refer section 91 of the *Insolvency Law Reform Act 2016* (Cth), which identifies such relation back day in each and every situation.

[78] see section 588 FG of the Corporations Act.

2. None of the detail of the matters set out in paragraph 6(b) and (c) regarding the trading results of the company and the working capital of the company were known to our client at that time. The same applies to demands made by other creditors and the Australian Taxation Office.

3. Our client will rely upon the defence that they had no reasonable grounds to suspect that the company was insolvent when the relevant payments were made by the company. Central to the basis of your claim, to be entitled to repayment of the demanded sum is the assertion made that the purpose of payments made by the company between November 2020 and April 2021 was merely to pay existing indebtedness and not to induce our client to continue to provide services. On our instructions, this assertion is incorrect as it is apparent from the transaction history maintained by our client that it continued to supply the goods and services to the company upon payments being made to it.

If you wish to discuss any aspect of this matter, you should not hesitate to telephone Mr O'Neill of this office.

As can been seen from the above sample letter, the main defence espoused by my clients is that they provided valuable consideration to the transaction and such payment for the goods and services was received in good faith. Importantly, at the time of receiving the payment transaction, the client allegedly had absolutely no idea the company was trading insolvent.

The problem, however, for many of my clients after receiving such a letter of demand from the company liquidator regarding an alleged unfair preference payment, was that to rely on the good faith defence was going to be very problematic. It was obvious at the time of receiving the payment, there were clear indications my clients should have immediately realised the company, now in liquidation, was in trouble, in other words insolvent, at the time of making the payment.

In many cases such obvious indicators were for example: (i) payment for the goods and services by either undated or post-dated cheques and, in one situation, my client explained to me that one payment by cheque had been dishonoured; (ii) On other occasions the client had agreed to enter into a payment arrangement which would be repeatedly breached, yet the client would still continue to provide the goods and services; (iii) Despite numerous defaults in payment by a company indebted to my client, I would still be instructed to issue letters of demand for payment. In the interim, for whatever perplexing reason and despite my learned counsel, my client would still supply the goods and services; (iv) Payments were often made by the debtor company sometimes far in excess of the usual 30-45 days trading terms and (v) the client would also have knowledge of other suppliers having the same sort of payment issues.

While the good faith defence was the usual norm in defending an unfair preference claim by the company liquidator, the examples of the common indicators of company insolvency at the time of the transaction made it very difficult to argue. What usually transpired following my good faith defence letter was the liquidator would still issue legal proceedings to recover the alleged preference transaction and the main crux of our defence, as filed and saved in any event would be, inter alia (amongst other things):

Further, the Defendant says that at the time that each payment was made, the Defendant had reasonable grounds to expect, and did expect, that the company was solvent at the time and would remain solvent even if it made the payment. Further, at the time that each transaction was entered into, the Defendant had no reasonable grounds for suspecting that the company was insolvent at the time or would become insolvent as a result of the transactions and that each transaction was entered into in the ordinary course of trade.

Despite our further bona fide attempts to defend the claim, the liquidator, on most occasions, would know they had a very arguable case and, on that basis, the dispute would normally be settled at the court ordered mediation or prior. Such settlement would be around 60% of what was being claimed and bearing in mind, if it proceeded to trial, notwithstanding the client still had an arguable defence. Common sense would prevail in order to avoid, not only paying the amount claimed, but the liquidator's legal costs and disbursements on the court scale, known as party/ party costs, and were usually around 60-70 per cent of indemnity costs.

With respect to the court scale legal costs and disbursements, what my client also had to be aware of was the repercussions of not accepting what is known as a *Calderbank* offer to settle.[79] Such an offer on a "Without Prejudice Basis Save as to Costs", is a genuine and reasonable offer of compromise to settle the dispute and can include legal costs and disbursements as incurred to date. However, most *Calderbank* offers were for an all-in sum for settlement and usually attractive enough, in

---

79 see *Calderbank v Calderbank* [1975] ALL ER 333.

other words, for the other party to settle the matter without the need for costly and time-consuming litigation.[80]

The bottom line is, if a party rejects the offer and the subsequent outcome, for example, where my client, as defendant at trial, fails to achieve a better result than what was offered by way of compromise, such defendant will have to pay indemnity costs from the date of the offer of compromise. The reverse onus also applies, so in some situations my client as the defendant would also make an offer of compromise in a genuine attempt to settle the dispute at a lesser amount.

If indemnity costs apply, they will be subject to a court order for indemnity costs and will be all reasonable costs incurred by a successful party to the litigation and certainly much higher than party/party costs. In other words, usually the total reasonable costs charged by the lawyers in the legal proceedings.[81]

Liquidators, being the pragmatic people they are, would often make an offer by way of compromise and usually we would settle the matter at some earlier point in the proceeding and get on with the next litigation. Which brings me to the next peril for directors in liquidation. They have a duty to prevent insolvent trading by their company and certainly not continue in business, suspecting they are insolvent and incurring more debts.[82]

Pursuant to section 588S of the Corporations Act, a

---

[80] also see for example offer of compromise under Order 26 of the *Magistrates Court General Civil Procedures Rules 2010* (Vic).

[81] see *Hazeldene's Chicken Farm Pty Ltd v Victorian Workcover Authority* (No 2) [2005] VSCA 298; 13 VR 435 in respect of the principles applied for a court order for indemnity costs.

[82] see section 588G of the Corporations Act.

creditor, with the consent of the liquidator, can commence legal proceedings under section 588M of the Corporations Act against the director(s) of the company in liquidation for a nominated debt that is owed to them. These proceedings would be in the absence of such directors previously providing a written guarantee to the creditor, to be personally liable for the debts of their company and failure to pay subjects them, in any event, to legal proceedings for breach.

The following sets out a typical statement of claim (by way of example only), after giving notice by the creditor to the liquidator to recover a debt against two directors on the basis they had a duty to prevent insolvent trading by their company:

1.   *At all material times the Plaintiff is and was:*

a.   *a company duly incorporated pursuant to Statute and is capable of suing; and*
b.   *a company in the business of supplying structural steel, plate merchant bar and tubular products and cutting and drilling services ("goods and services").*

2.   *The Defendants were at all times material directors of John Smith Pty Ltd (ACN 000 000 000) ("the Company") (not entity's real name).*
3.   *The Plaintiff, at the request of the Company, sold and delivered to the Company or by way of collection by the Company, various goods and services during the months of February 2020 to June 2020 in the sum of $95,000.*

Particulars
The request for the supply of goods and services from the Plaintiff

by the Company occurred during the months of February 2020 to May 2020 on a total of 20 separate occasions.

4. Tax Invoices were rendered by the Plaintiff to the Company for the supply of the steel products and services in the sum of $95,000 ("the debts").

Particulars

A total of 20 Tax Invoices were rendered to the Company by the Plaintiff for various goods and services during the months of February 2020 to May 2020. The Tax Invoices are in writing, copies of which are available for inspection during normal business hours at the office of the Plaintiff's solicitors by appointment.

5. On 18 May 2020 Liquidators of the Company were appointed by virtue of sections 439C(c) and 446A of the Corporations Act, 2001 ("the Act").

6. The Liquidators formed the view that from July 2019 onwards the Company was unable to pay its debts as and when they became due and payable.

Particulars

The Plaintiff refers to a report from the Liquidator dated 20 July 2020, in particular point 4 on page 5 of that report. (the Liquidator's report)

7. On 15 May 2022, the Liquidator gave consent to the Plaintiff to begin proceedings against the Company's Directors for insolvent trading pursuant to section 588S of the Act.

Particulars

The consent is in writing and may be inspected at the offices of the solicitors for the Plaintiff by appointment.

8. *By failing to prevent the Company from incurring debts the Defendants did so in circumstances where they were aware at the time of incurring the debts that:*

a. *there were grounds for suspecting.*
b. *or a reasonable person in a like position of the Defendants in a Company in the Company's circumstances would be aware that at that time the Company was insolvent or become insolvent as a result of incurring the debt or would become insolvent at that time by incurring debts including the debts with the Plaintiff.*

9. *By not preventing the Company from incurring the debts, the Defendants have contravened subsection 588G (2) of the Act.*

10. *By reason of the conduct of the Defendants referred to in paragraph 10 herein, the Plaintiff has suffered loss and damage being the quantum of the debts being $95,000.*

And the Plaintiff claims against the Defendants:

i. *$95,000.00;*
ii. *Alternatively, $95,000 pursuant to s.588M(3) of the Act;*
iii. *Alternatively Damages;*
iv. *Interest pursuant to Statute;*
v. *Costs;*

vi.   *Such further or other orders as the Court deems fit.*

In addition, in the event the liquidator had previously issued and settled proceedings against my client regarding an alleged unfair preference payment by John Smith Pty Ltd (in liquidation), additional paragraphs could be included (or even by way of separate proceedings as applicable) in the above statement of claim in order to recover the settlement sum paid by my client company to the liquidator. Such additional paragraphs, by way of example, could be set out as follows:

11.   Further, the liquidator in County Court proceedings numbered CI.00.0000 commenced on 15 October, 2020, commenced proceedings against the Plaintiff seeking payment of the sum of $78,000.00 being alleged preferential payments received by the Plaintiff from the Company which it alleged was liable to pay to the liquidator pursuant to section 588FE of the Act.

Particulars
Details of the payments which were alleged to be preferential payments are set out in the liquidator's report.

12.   The County Court proceedings settled on the basis that the Plaintiff pay to the liquidator the sum of $55,000.00 in full and final settlement of the liquidator's claim.

Particulars
The settlement was paid to the liquidator pursuant to Terms of Settlement entered into on 10 January, 2021. A copy of the

Terms of Settlement is in writing and may be inspected at the offices of the solicitors for the Plaintiff by appointment.

13. The Plaintiff was required to settle the proceeding by reason of the fact that the Defendants continued to allow the Company to trade in circumstances where they were aware or ought to have been aware or there were grounds of suspecting that the company was insolvent or would become insolvent at the time of:

a.　incurring the debts which were the subject of the preference payments; and

b.　at the time when the preference payments were made.

14. By reason of the matters referred to in paragraph 13 herein, the Plaintiff has suffered loss and damage.

Particulars
$55,000 being the settlement sum paid to the liquidator.
And the Plaintiff claims against the Defendants:

i.　$150,000.00 ($95,000 & $55,000);
ii.　Alternatively, $150,000.00 pursuant to s.588M(3) of the Act;
iii.　Alternatively Damages;
iv.　Interest pursuant to Statute;
v.　Costs;
vi.　Such further or other orders as the Court deems fit.

The issue now faced by the former directors of the company now in liquidation was, in the absence of any agreement to settle, they faced a judgment order being entered against them, allowing the plaintiff to commence enforcement proceedings to recover the judgment amount. Such enforcement proceedings could include a warrant to seize property, an attachment of earnings and, of course, bankruptcy.[83]

However, directors of a company in liquidation do have some safeguards in place that they could fall back on. I say this on the basis that, whilst section 588G of the Corporations Act creates onerous obligations on company directors to not trade whilst insolvent, making them personally liable for any debts their company in liquidation incurred under their watch, they still do have a protective course of action available to them.

In late 2017, the Corporations Act was amended to include under section 588GA a course of action to provide relief protection for company directors from personal liability for debts incurred by their insolvent company. Commonly referred to as a "safe harbour" protection, the onus is on each director to be seen to take a course of action which is deemed to lead to a more preferred and better solution for, not only their company, but its creditors.

This course of action is then pitted against the option of the appointment of a liquidator due to insolvency, leaving them open to proceedings not only by creditors, a liquidator and even ASIC, but also civil pecuniary penalties.[84] In the event of any dishonest conduct, a director can be pursued by way of criminal charges and, if proved, can result in imprisonment.[85]

In order to fall back on the safe harbour relief and from being personally liable for company debts, section 588GA of

---

83   for instalment orders see *Judgment Debt Recovery Act 1984* (Vic).

84   see Division 4 of the Corporations Act.

85   see generally Part 9.4 of the Corporations Act.

the Corporations Act allows such debts to be incurred during a period what is deemed to be a "restructure period", reasonable in the circumstances, in order to turn the company around and prevent insolvency. During this period, what could be considered a time for reflection and the best way forward for the company, its directors must ensure they take a reasonable course of action to ultimately achieve a better outcome for their company and its shareholders, as against the traps of falling into liquidation.

In facing this dilemma and to access the safe harbour preferred outcome, the directors need to first consult with their financial advisers and even those specialising in restructure situations, to make sure they are properly advised on the profit and loss situation of their company and certainly the current position in respect of creditor debts. At the same time, they need to put in place a proper business plan for the safe way forward out of their current quagmire and ensure they maintain, for production as required, proper financial and business records of the company. It goes without saying that in looking for safe harbour protection, they need to ensure all employees and their entitlements, including under the *Superannuation Guarantee (Administration) Act 1992*(Cth), are adhered to without fail.

If, in the event a company is placed into liquidation as the only viable outcome, company directors will suffer some repercussions in any event, even if they can avoid creditor anguish, personal debt recovery and civil and criminal sanctions. Their credit rating, like bankrupts, will be flagged not only with ASIC, but also various business–creditor information entities such as Dun and Bradstreet.

If they are a director of a company now in liquidation, it is normally believed that will prevent them from taking a position of a director with another company. That is not the case and, provided they are not disqualified by ASIC for breach of the Corporations Act, they can still be appointed as a director.[86] Financial lenders will, of course, take into account the director's previous history and provided their own financial position is secure, that will not automatically disqualify such director from obtaining finance.

This chapter is by no means an exhaustive discussion on the perils of liquidation for directors. It does, however, identify a number of traps for directors, particularly those regarding their bona fide fiduciary duties as a director, which they must comply with,[87] including other relevant legislation and of course common law principles.

---

[86]   see section 206B of the Corporations Act.

[87]   see sections 180-185 of the Corporations Act.

7
INDUSTRIAL ACCIDENTS

Unfortunately, workplace accidents are a common occurrence and can result in death and injury to both employees and members of the public, such as the tragic accident at the Brisbane Eagle Farm Racecourse in October 2016, when two workers were crushed to death after a concrete slab fell on them when being moved by a crane. The responsible company was fined on appeal the sum of $625,000.[88] In the same month, four members of the public died as a result of a faulty water ride at the Gold Coast Dreamworld Theme Park with the owner fined a total of $3.6 million.[89]

In Victoria, issues of health and safety are governed by the *Occupational Health and Safety Act 2004*(Vic) (OHS Act) and its Regulations (OHS Regulations). The main premise of the guiding legislation is to:

    (a) secure the health, safety and welfare of employees

---

[88]   *Steven John Reynolds v Criscon Pty Ltd* [2019] QDC 252.

[89]   *Aaron Guilfoyle and Ardent Leisure Ltd* [2020] QMC 13.

and other people at work and importantly to (b) eliminate, at the source, risks to the health and safety of employees and other persons at work, including, not placing the public at risk.[90] In regards to workers employed by the Commonwealth of Australia, their health and safety is regulated by the *Work, Health and Safety Act 2011*(Cth).

As early as 2002, the Australian Capital Territory became the first Australian jurisdiction to legislate for industrial manslaughter, initially under section 49C of the *Crimes Act 1900*(ACT) and now section 34A of the *Work Health and Safety Act 2011*(ACT). This was followed by Queensland in 2017 in response to the tragic deaths at Eagle Farm and Dreamworld and now regulated under section 34C of the *Work Health and Safety Act 2011*(Qld) (WHS Act).

Its first industrial manslaughter conviction was a result of the successful prosecution of Brisbane Auto Recycling Pty Ltd in June 2020, following the death of an employee who was struck and killed by a reversing forklift. The company was fined a total of $3 million with two of its directors sentenced to 10 months imprisonment, wholly suspended for 20 months, for negligent conduct which the sentencing judge noted:

The defendants knew of the potential consequences of the risk, which were catastrophic. Steps to lessen, minimise or remove the risk posed by mobile plant were available. These steps were neither complex nor overly burdensome. [91]

In 2022, a further successful prosecution against Queensland business owner, Jeffrey Owen, followed as a

---

[90] see section 2 of the OHS Act.

[91] *R v Brisbane Auto Recycling Pty Ltd & Ors* [2020] QDC 113.

consequence of the death of his friend who was unfortunately killed helping him to unload a generator from the back of a truck with a forklift considered to be inadequate for the task at hand. Owen was convicted of industrial manslaughter due to his workplace negligence, but the issue for the jury was whether the deceased was deemed a "worker" under the provisions of the WHS Act.

The jury, however, accepted the prosecution submissions that for the purposes of the legislation, such negligence caused the death of another person in a workplace and, therefore, he was, for all intents and purposes, a worker. Owen was sentenced to five years imprisonment but suspended for a period of five years after serving 18 months, subject to any appeal by Owen. Judge Cash QC noted that whilst Owen had no prior convictions and had now implemented proper documented procedures for workplace health and safety, at the time of the accident he was not licenced in any event to operate a forklift.[92]

Other Australian states and territories to legislate industrial manslaughter laws include the Northern Territory and Western Australia, with the latter in 2021 successfully prosecuting Mark Withers, a director of MT Sheds (WA) Pty Ltd who was sentenced in the Esperance Magistrates Court to a two-year two months term of imprisonment. This prosecution under the *Occupational Safety and Health Act 1984 (WA)* and the *Occupational Safety and Health Regulations 1996 (WA)* was a result of the death of a young employee with another seriously injured. The charges included gross negligence and driving a crane whilst unlicensed and also saw fines imposed totalling $607,250. In 2020, the WA Government legislated the *Work Health and Safety Act 2020(WA)* and its implementation in 2022

---

[92] *R v Jeffrey Owen* [2022] QDSR 168.

replaced the original Act and associated work health and safety elements of associated legislation, bringing all workplaces, including mining and petroleum, under one single Act.

The Northern Territory under its *Work Health and Safety(National Uniform Legislation)Act 2011(NT)*, included the indictable offence of industrial manslaughter replacing such a provision under its *Criminal Code Act 1983*(NT).The 2020 amended legalisation, in order to commence a prosecution following a breach of duty in respect of health and safety resulting in death of a person, covers all workplaces regardless of size and, of course, includes such reckless or negligent conduct. Their first industrial prosecution was commenced in March 2020 against a construction company following the death of a worker during an excavator towing operation, but was subsequently withdrawn, however, the company still faces a charge of failing in its duty to comply with health and safety in its workplace.

In Victoria, the offence of workplace manslaughter was introduced in July 2020 pursuant to section 39G of the OHS Act and now provides for a maximum penalty of 25 years imprisonment for any individual convicted of such a crime and a fine up to 100,000 penalty units ($19.23 million) for such negligent employers, noting previously companies would only be fined if found to be negligent in causing a workplace death. The Victorian Minister for Workplace Safety, Jill Hennessy, in announcing the new offence of workplace manslaughter said:

If an employer's negligence costs someone their life, they will be prosecuted and may go to jail- that's now the law... Broadening the definition of a workplace fatality will help better identify and address the true extent of workplace health and safety issues in Victoria.

This encompassing legislation was enacted after numerous workplace deaths over many years and following the deaths of 25 people in workplace accidents in the first half of 2020 and has a broad interpretation. In that regard, it not only applies to employers and self-employed people, but also officers of the employer in the event of any negligent conduct causing death of a member of the public. The prior legalisation for example could result in a prosecution under section 26(1) of the OHS Act in that:

> *A person who (whether as an owner or otherwise) has, to any extent, the management or control of a workplace must ensure so far as is reasonably practicable that the workplace and the means of entering and leaving it are safe and without risks to health. Penalty: 1800 penalty units for a natural person; 9000 penalty units for a body corporate.*

Such a prosecution, prior to the enactment of the offence of workplace manslaughter, resulted in Keilor-Melton Quarries Pty Ltd being convicted and fined a total of $230,000.[93] This was a consequence of the death of a worker at its quarry when a truck tipped over, killing its driver. His Honour, Judge Lyon, whilst taking into account the seriousness of the incident resulting in death, also took into consideration submissions from both defence counsel and the Crown that the gravity of the offence was not at a high level, despite a workplace death.

---

[93] *Director of Public Prosecutions v Keilor- Melton Quarries Pty Ltd* [2018] VCC 2139.

The company did not have overall management or control of the work site and the likelihood of a repeat breach was unlikely. His Honour made a relevant point, however, in that the breach was 'self-evidently high and that in turn means that the potential gravity of the consequences was high.'

Judge Lyon was also mindful of the High Court decision of *Chiro v The Queen* [2017] HCA 37 and that the company should be sentenced, taking into regard the facts most favourable to it. What was also favourable to the directors of the company on sentencing was they were people of excellent character, were community-minded with a long history of generous community support. His Honour was also referred to the Victorian Supreme Court of Appeal decision in *Di Aldo DiTonto & Anor v The Queen* [2018] VSCA 318 in which an appeal by the company and its director on the severity of sentencing in respect to breaches of sections 23(1) and 144(1) of the OHS Act was upheld, reducing total fines from $480,000 to $240,000. Keilor- Melton Quarries Pty Ltd subsequently sought leave to appeal which was refused as the court determined that the company failed to do what was reasonably practicable, in order to eliminate a risk to the safety of its workers.[94]

The first person charged in Victoria with workplace manslaughter under section 39G (1) of the OHS Act was a stonemason company director following a fatal accident at its Somerton factory in October 2021. The accident was as a result of the alleged negligent conduct of the director, who was operating a fully loaded forklift when it unfortunately fell sideways onto an unsuspecting sub-contractor. Two Melbourne companies have also now been charged with workplace

---

94   *Keilor- Melton Quarries Pty Ltd v The Queen* [2020] VSCA 169.

manslaughter under section 39G (1) including failing to provide employees with adequate supervision while performing the work[95] and failing to ensure other persons and not just employees were not exposed to risks in respect of their health and safety.[96] Both matters are ongoing and currently before the court.

Fortunately, incidents involving forklifts, such as in Somerton, Victoria and in Brisbane, Queensland, resulting in death are not a common occurrence. However, a worrying factor is that more workplace deaths and not just injuries will occur if employers fail in their duty of care to ensure the safety of their workers and others while operating a forklift. By way of example, in Victoria in 2022 a total of 142 Workcover claims were accepted by WorkSafe Victoria in relation to injuries caused by a forklift, with on average of around 400 people injured in Victoria alone.

More troubling is that since 1985 in excess of 55 Victorian workers have died as a result of a forklift incident. The common trend was, the deaths and injuries were caused to workers as a consequence of poorly secured forklift loads that fell off. In some instances, the load was supposedly secured by a wire cage, all to no avail and an accident waiting to happen, as the load was too heavy and simply fell off or tipped the forklift over.

One of my steel company clients, Bloggs Steel Pty Ltd (not entity's real name), were certainly fortunate not to be charged with a section 39G workplace manslaughter offence following an incident at its factory when one of their workers was seriously injured following a heavy load falling off a forklift. While he suffered life threatening injuries and most likely

---

95   see section 21(1) and 21(2(a) of the OHS Act.

96   see section 23(1) of the OHS Act.

would never work again, somehow, he survived after a lengthy stay in hospital. As a consequence, my client was charged with a section 21(1) breach of the OHS Act in that:

An employer must, so far as reasonably practicable, provide and maintain for employees of the employer, a working environment that is safe and without risks to health.

Bloggs Steel Pty Ltd was further charged with a section 21(2)(e) offence as an employer it failed to:

provide such instruction, training or supervision to employees of the employer as is necessary to enable those persons to perform their work in a way that is safe and without risk to health. Penalty: 1800 penalty units for a natural person; 9000 penalty units for a body corporate.

In addition, the client copped a hamburger with the lot and was also charged under the OHS regulations for allowing an unlicensed employee to perform high risk work, which carried a further fine of 500 penalty units and 100 units for a natural person.[97]

The event could also have resulted in other employees being injured, as the closed-circuit television (CCTV) footage of the incident showed a number of other employees in the work area, but luckily, they escaped harm. The problem for my client was they had no safety system in place and no traffic management plan, despite having a number of forklifts operating in the same confined area and in close proximity to their employees. The other damning factor was the driver

---
97   see section 129 of OHS Regulations.

of the forklift, as mentioned above, was operating without a licence, was not in training and, even if he was, he needed to be enrolled in a training course and operating such forklift in close proximity to a licensed operator. It's fair to say that WorkSafe Victoria has a zero-tolerance policy in respect to the unsafe use of forklifts and certainly in respect to one being operated by an unlicensed driver.

After obtaining instructions from the client, it was obvious that such wilful blindness was an accident waiting to happen. To make matters worse, when the employee was first employed, he simply told the client at interview that he held a heavy-duty forklift licence. Now you would think the client would have at least obtained a copy of such licence and placed same on his employee file, but alas, no they didn't and employed him in good faith. In view of all the circumstances and given the serious incident was captured on CCTV, on my advice, a guilty plea was really the only sensible option. Fortunately for the client, a charge under section 21(1) of the OHS Act, although an indictable offence, could be heard and determined summarily in the Magistrates Court.[98]

The matter proceeded in the Dandenong Magistrates Court and, after the prosecutor presented a detailed summary, including the viewing of the CCTV, I commenced my plea submission. For some reason, I also called the director of my client to give evidence before His Honour to explain what had now been put in place following the incident in order to mitigate against any further serious incidents. The prosecutor, of course in cross examination, put to my witness their overall management failures, including allowing an unlicenced forklift driver to operate in a dangerous environment. It certainly

---

98   see section 28 of the *Criminal Procedure Act 2009*(Vic).

begged the question of why the defendant company had not put in place proper traffic management plans, including training and supervision of their employees.

The presiding magistrate was also quite scathing and simply put to my client's director that they should have known of the overall safety risks in such an environment, in loading and unloading heavy duty steel. Further, why had they not checked to see if the employee was in fact licensed to drive a heavy-duty forklift? Also, the client was very fortunate they were not facing a charge of workplace manslaughter. I tried my best to submit a plea in mitigation including:

> *My client pleads guilty at the first opportunity, has no prior convictions, has now rectified and put in place an appropriate traffic safety plan and to ensure its operation of forklifts includes a check list procedure to ensure they are not overloaded and the operators are fully licensed.*

As my client company was operating a business which, to say the least, was quite profitable, I chose not to submit evidence of yearly profit and loss as the concern was, of course, that the fine imposed would be quite high. The magistrate took into account the client company had departed from its statutory duty and the extent to which it resulted in a serious injury to one of their employees and fined the client a total of $100,000 with conviction. The magistrate also indicated if it had not been for a guilty plea, the aggregate fine would have been $175,000.[99] To make matters worse, being quite a costly day for the client, I asked the magistrate for three months to pay the fine which,

---

[99] see section 6AAA- Sentence discount for a guilty plea- *Sentencing Act 1991*(Vic).

rightly, copped a scathing response from His Honour in that a company must pay such a fine within 28 days and I certainly had no grounds to request further time, let alone three months.

Employees are also required to take reasonable care for the health and safety of other employees and can be prosecuted in cases of breach. One particular client, who I will call Reg (not his real name), thought it would be a bit of a lark to terrorise an apprentice. Along with two fellow workmates, they locked the unsuspecting young man in a toilet and then proceeded to throw lighted cigarettes and rolls of toilet paper over the top, as he was screaming to be let out. Fortunately, he wasn't seriously injured but Reg would appear in the Frankston Magistrates Court on two charges under section 25 of the OHS Act. I tried to downplay the incident before the presiding magistrate, saying it was just 'boys having a bit of fun', but Her Honour was not impressed. It was put, in no uncertain terms, that the consequences of injuries to their victim could have turned out to be very serious.

Well, Reg was certainly going to learn the consequences, as he was fined $3,000 and walked out of court a lot poorer, as he had my account to pay as well. What was also waiting for him were a number of media outlets and he appeared on the news bulletin that night. His two accomplices were also fined but the employer was not prosecuted for what took place. They had, as all responsible employers should, previously disciplined Reg and the other two for similar behaviour, obviously to no avail. The only positive outcome in this matter was that WorkSafe, for the next few months, would run a television advertisement recreating the workplace incident, warning that any similar conduct would result in heavy fines.

The lesson to be learnt from all of this and certainly to avoid serious injury to its employees and members of the public, is that company directors must ensure they have efficient safety systems, governance, proper diligence and training in place. If there is a serious criminal breach, they could be exposed to personal liability which may well have serious implications, particularly if a death occurs as a consequence of the conduct of their business. The bottom line is, of course, and company directors please take note, to undertake a risk assessment of workplace operations, which may well identify any business activities that could cause injury or death, including identifying applicable employees who do not possess high risk licences.

8
DON'T DRINK, TAKE DRUGS, THEN DRIVE

As far back as 1909, Victoria, well ahead of the times, had the dubious honour of being the first Australian state to prohibit driving motor vehicles under the influence of alcohol[100]. Police were certainly not blessed with such devices as portable breathalysers for random breath testing and would have to rely on the driver's behaviour, including any slurred speech, dishevelled clothing and, of course, the smell of alcohol. If found guilty in those days, the offending driver would be fined the sum of 10 pounds for a first offence and any repeat offending would result in a 25-pound fine and the potential of three month's imprisonment.

Blood testing of drivers began in the late 1950s, but the suspect driver had to consent to the taking of a blood sample. In 1965, Victoria again being the leader, was the first state in

---

100   see *Motor Car Act 1909* (Vic).

Australia to pass legislation that resulted in an offence to exceed a certain blood alcohol concentration with a further amendment to the Motor Car Act. In the 1970s, police introduced portable breath testing stations which would ultimately and affectionally be known as "booze buses", with random breath testing (RBT) being carried out at roadside checkpoints.[101]

The governing law in respect to driving offences in Victoria is now the *Road Safety Act 1986* (Vic) (Road Safety Act) and applicable regulations such as the *Road Safety Drivers Regulations 2009*(Vic), which are constantly reviewed towards imposing tougher penalties. Our laws certainly impose such heavy penalties for any drink or drug driving infraction and determine that any person in control of or attempting to drive a motor vehicle, can be subject to a RBT for blood alcohol content (BAC); this includes sitting in the driver's seat of a stationery vehicle, supervising a learner driver and following a traffic accident where police are required to attend. A driver can refuse any police request for a breath sample and strict penalties will apply for not blowing correctly or intermittently, including two years loss of licence.

If the breath test determines that you are under 0.05% and not the holder of a probationary licence and subject to a zero BAC, then you may continue on your merry way, but if over 0.05%, you will be arrested without a warrant for further testing at either a mobile van, police station, or even at a hospital for a blood test. A zero BAC also applies if the driver is on a learner permit, relicensed following a previous drink or drug driving conviction and those driving a commercial passenger vehicle such as a bus and also any vehicle, such as a truck, greater than 4.5 tonnes. The penalty in these types of zero BAC offences

---

[101] see *Motor Car (Breath Testing Stations) Act 1976* (Vic).

requires the presiding magistrate to cancel your licence and disqualify you from driving for a minimum of three months. If your BAC exceeds 0.10%, police have the power to immediately suspend your licence, until your court appearance pursuant to s. 85-s.85W of the Road Safety Act which was previously known as a s.51 notice, prior to November 2020.

Immediate licence suspension also applies in a myriad of other readings, including drug driving or high speed and if a P-plater exceeds a BAC of 0.07% or more. The only saving grace in respect of immediate licence suspension, is that any time off the road must be taken into account regarding the period for the loss of licence.

Victoria certainly has a reputation for being the most stringent state in respect of penalties for drink driving. As from 30 April, 2018, the penalties for drink driving were increased courtesy of the *Transport Legislation Amendment (Road Safety, and Other Matters) Act 2017* (Vic) and Part 5 of the Road Safety Act (as amended), noting Part 5 contains seven categories of drink driving type offences. The most serious being driving under the influence (DUI) (s.49 (1) (a) of the Road Safety Act), in other words, a driver whose ability to drive a vehicle is adversely affected by the consumption of alcohol.

I was to find that a police informant would often include a DUI in cases where 0.15% had been exceeded, together with a charge pursuant to s. 49(1) (b) of the Road Safety Act, being a charge of exceed the prescribed content BAC limit. It is possible to contest this latter charge, but only on the basis of expert evidence in that police did not comply with the drink driving legislation. Good luck with that as most of these contested matters generally fail.

With a drug driving offence under s. 55A (1) of the Road

Safety Act, Victoria is again at the forefront and will impose strict penalties for driving while drug impaired (s.49 (1) (ba)), refusing such an assessment and if required, refusing to provide a blood or urine sample following an assessment (s.49(1)(ca). The types of prescribed illicit drugs include cannabis, methamphetamine and ecstasy and the only proof required is that a drug was in fact present, followed by a second but more thorough test.

Penalties for drink driving can also include a mandatory loss of licence with a minimum of three months for a BAC between 0.05 and 0.69%, then increasing per month based on the reading after 0.69%. If there is a second and subsequent offence within 10 years, then the penalty is doubled with loss of licence, accompanied by a fine, and an interlock device to be fitted for a minimum of six months, courtesy of the *Road Safety Amendment Act 2014*(Vic). A behaviour change program must be completed before any restoration of licence and there must be a zero BAC when driving for the next three years.

More severe penalties apply if caught both drug and drink driving, including harsh fines and the possibility of a term of imprisonment, especially for repeat offenders. In addition, police can impound your vehicle without making an application to a court, including for exceeding a BAC reading of 0.10% or above for a first offence, or any reading regardless, for a second offence. Depending on the type of offence, impoundment can be between 30-45 days and the costs involved for a vehicle to be released are around $1,100.

Tragically, there has been a number of incidents resulting in the death of, not only the driver, but passengers due to the level of intoxication or drug affected driver. The sentence for a charge of culpable driving causing death will usually result in a term of imprisonment noting the maximum penalty is 20 years and/or a fine up to 2400 penalty units,[102] with a standard sentence of around eight years[103] for standard sentences. As of April 2023, a Victorian penalty unit was $184.92, noting such penalty units are subject to re-assessment each year and may increase/decrease accordingly.

The consequences of drink driving causing death was certainly evident when a drunk driver on the Mornington Peninsula crashed into a tree killing his passenger friend and seriously injuring two others. The offending driver recorded a BAC reading of between .209 and .229 and the sentencing judge, on imposing a prison sentence of 12 years and nine months with a non-parole period of eight years and nine months said:

> *A young man with a bright future and loved by family, was killed by your actions that night. Their heartbreak and sorrow is palpable. They will never recover. Their lives will never be the same… It's frustrating to police and the courts, the message just doesn't seem to be getting out, particularly to young drivers, of the devastating effects of driving at speed and under the influence of alcohol.*[104]

On appeal, the sentence was reduced to 11 years with a non-parole period of seven years on the basis the original sentence was deemed to be manifestly excessive.[105]

One anomaly though, to this day, is a disparity between

---

[102] see section 318 of the *Crimes Act 1958* (Vic).

[103] see sections 5A and 5B of the *Sentencing Act 1991* (Vic).

[104] *DPP v Phongthaihong* [2020] VCC 294.

[105] *Phongthaihong v the Queen* [2021] VSCA 317.

first time drink and drug driving offenders. A first-time drink driver faces a much harsher penalty compared to first offence drug driver; the latter only facing a maximum 12 penalty units with a fine, whereas a drink driver, under the Road Safety Act, can be fined up to 20 penalty units, but both with a loss of licence. Another anomaly I found was regarding supervising driving instructors of learner drivers. Section 3 of the Road Safety Act defines such a person, other than a commercial driving instructor, who is sitting beside a learner driver. As a supervising instructor from 14 December 2011, s.49C of the Road Safety Act was brought in to ensure that supervisors were not impaired by alcohol in order to ensure a learner driver received adequate instructions and to send a message that drink driving is totally unacceptable.

I appeared before His Honour, Graeme Keil, at Frankston Magistrates Court in such a situation for my client, Don (not his real name), who drove to his son's football training. After Don consumed a few beers at the club, his son drove home as a learner driver, displaying the mandatory L plates, but was pulled over for a breath test. Recorded as the supervising driver, Don showed a reading of 0.08 % BAC. Police chose not to issue him with an on-the-spot fine, which incurred only 10 penalty units, but to present him before the Frankston Magistrates Court.

The disparity was, there was no mandatory loss of licence under s. 49c of the Road Safety Act as the maximum penalty at the time was only 10 penalty units. On this occasion, the police prosecutors were pushing for loss of licence and His Honour was in the frame of mind to accept their submissions. As far as the prosecutor was concerned, there had to be a mandatory loss of licence and I believe if Don had appeared unrepresented, he would have.

I was able to refer His Honour to s.49C which stated the maximum he could impose was only 10 penalty units with no loss of licence. Magistrate Keil accepted my submission and only imposed a fine with conviction. However, now under section 89A (1) (a) of the Sentencing Act, magistrates do have a discretion to suspend or cancel a driver's licence for any offence regardless. It is also worth noting that in addition to supervising driver legislation, it is also an offence to consume alcohol whilst driving, which was initially inserted pursuant to the *Road Safety Amendment (Drinking while Driving) Act 2011* (Vic). It now carries a maximum penalty of 10 penalty units under section 49(B) of the Road Safety Act and, like the supervising driver legislation, does not carry a mandatory licence suspension, unless of course your BAC exceeds the prescribed limit.

Our laws in the state of Victoria are, for all intents and purposes, the strictest in Australia, but it was not always like that. Prior to 1999, if your licence was suspended and you were caught for drink driving in Victoria, you could just obtain a driver's licence in another state. In addition, if your reading was between 0.05% and under 0.10% BAC, providing there were no other offences committed, such as speed or careless driving, it was possible to obtain a good behaviour bond (GBB).

I appeared on many occasions at Frankston Magistrates Court regarding these low-level types of offending and making successful submissions for a GBB. I would tender character evidence, refer to a prior good driving record and my client's reliance on needing to continue to drive in respect of employment. In addition, prior to January 2018, if you held a Victorian driver's licence and committed a drink driving offence in any other state, the offence was not treated as being committed in Victoria. That has now changed so if you are caught drink or drug driving in another state, it is now be considered as the offence being committed in Victoria and vice versa under cross–jurisdiction, providing the respective state authorities correspond with each other accordingly.

For a drink or drug driving matter, there was one particular magistrate at Frankston who we didn't want to appear before. His Honour, Rodney Crisp, who was appointed to the bench in 1985, was particularly tough on drink/drug drivers and rightly so. However, in the early days at Frankston, numerous local legal practitioners, including I dare say, yours truly, would go "magistrate shopping" and, if the drink/drug drive matter was listed before Mr Crisp, we would seek an adjournment of not less than four weeks, hoping on the return date we would appear before another magistrate. His Honour, in due course, certainly became aware of this. I would often sit in court waiting for my matter to be heard and with a grin on my face, listen to non-local lawyers applying for an adjournment or transfer to another court before His Honour, with most being generally unsuccessful.

One thing about Mr Crisp, he was tough but, at times, rather entertaining. On one particular occasion he had an application before him for an alcohol interlock device (AID) to be removed from a vehicle. There are a number of requirements when making such applications; one being that there were no failed attempts to start the vehicle due to the detection of alcohol.

In this matter, the police prosecutor was concerned as to why the AID had registered a fail and the applicant motorist submitted to His Honour that it was due to a "Bubble O' Bill ice-cream" that he had consumed before starting his vehicle and blowing into the device, which recorded a BAC of 0.018%. To his credit, Mr Crisp stood the matter down, so the applicant could run a test with police overseeing him consuming a Bubble O' Bill and then reporting back to the court. Sure enough, the motorist was right and, after being tested, recorded the same reading. His Honour accepted the test and granted the application to have the interlock removed.

One such "bubble user" was not so lucky when he appeared before His Honour at the Moorabbin Magistrates Court. On this occasion, the defendant, when looking at Mr Crisp, blew a bubble, in fact a rather large chewing gum bubble, which popped. His Honour was offended and jailed him for 30 days for contempt. He spent 12 hours in custody before he was granted bail on appeal against the sentence being manifestly excessive and also against his treatment and conviction. Such sentence was subsequently quashed by the Supreme Court on appeal, with Judge Jack Forrest saying, 'The Supreme Court did not condone acts of contempt, but firmness must be accompanied by fairness.'

I did have one unsuccessful matter before Mr Crisp and had to appeal the manifestly excessive sentence to the County Court. My client was charged with careless driving pursuant to s. 65 of the Road Safety Act as a consequence of an accident early one morning in Mt Eliza. There was no suggestion of any alcohol or drugs in his system and it was largely due to the sun being in my client's eyes when he rear-ended a stationery vehicle.

Unfortunately, a driver about to leave for work was seated in the stationary vehicle and he suffered some minor injuries, requiring an ambulance. My client had no prior convictions, indeed he had no previous traffic matters and, in my view, if he lost his licence at best, it would be for one month. I made a submission to Mr Crisp that it was an unfortunate accident due to the sun blinding my client as he drove up a hill. He was not speeding and he simply didn't see the stationary vehicle.

Unfortunately, Mr Crisp took a rather strict approach and despite my submission, fined my client $1500, nearly the maximum of 12 penalty units at the time. He suspended his licence for 12 months and warned him of the penalties that applied if he was detected driving during the suspension period. His Honour then turned to me with a final comment, 'No doubt, knowing you Mr O'Neill, you will lodge an appeal.'

Quite shocked with the penalty, my response was, 'I will obtain my client's instructions in that regard,' then left the courtroom.

I don't recall turning and bowing, as we are required to do, before leaving and entering a court as a sign of respect to the court.

After receiving instructions from my shocked client, I immediately lodged an appeal then went back to appear before Mr Crisp to make an application to allow my client to drive, pending the outcome of his appeal in the County Court as too "manifestly excessive". As I entered his courtroom, ensuring I bowed this time, His Honour stopped talking on a video link with a prisoner in custody who was applying for bail, turned to me and said, 'Mr O'Neill, no doubt you have appealed my sentence and your client wants to drive in the interim. Sit down and I will get to you in due course.'

I took a deep breath, sat down and waited until the video link was completed, noting, not unexpectedly, that bail was not granted to the applicant prisoner. I then spent at least 15 minutes convincing Mr Crisp to allow my client to drive in the interim, including there being no alcohol or drugs involved, the lack of local public transport, being the sole bread winner in the family, licence needed to transport children and so on. The end result was, he reluctantly allowed my client to drive and subsequently, on appeal before the County Court, my client only lost his licence for one month, not 12.

I have acted for many clients who have exceeded the prescribed BAC, but the highest reading in a matter was 0.28%, which is a big drink. It seems my client had a history of drink driving and this was his third time committing such an offence. Given he was detected following a t-intersection collision, I had no doubt he would be sentenced to a term of imprisonment and rightly so. Certainly, if it was before Frankton Magistrates Court and in particular Mr Crisp, his feet would not have touched the ground on his way to the cells.

Fortunately for my client, the matter was listed at the Melbourne Magistrates Court before a magistrate we would sometimes refer to as "Father Christmas" and I certainly don't say that with any impropriety, as said magistrate was always a pleasure to appear before. On this occasion, in an all-out effort to keep my client out of prison, I called his brother to provide some character evidence. My client's sibling was a well-known journalist who performed very well in the witness box. So well, that my client stayed out of jail, but lost his licence for a total of five years with a heavy fine. Sometimes you get lucky and certainly all my client's Christmases had come at once.

If you are the holder of a probationary licence and detected with any alcohol in your system, then heavy penalties follow. In one matter, my client, the holder of a probationary licence, thought he was fit to drive after downing three Jack Daniels cans with a meal, then sleeping for six hours. He recorded a

BAC of 0.078%. Unfortunately, while driving, he fell asleep and ran off the road into the scrub causing minor damage to his motor vehicle. His licence was immediately suspended and, on a guilty plea to a charge of careless driving which resulted in the accident, he was placed on a bond to be of good behaviour for 12 months without conviction, providing he completed a road trauma awareness seminar.

In relation to drink driving whilst a probationary licence holder, he lost his licence for 6 months, had to complete a drink driving program, fined $500 and of course an interlock device would be fitted to his vehicle on getting his licence back on application to the Court for a licence eligibility order, pursuant to section 31B of the Road Safety Act.

Roadside drug testing, often referred to as the "lick test", gives Victoria Police the right to drug test a driver at any time for traces of illicit drugs, namely methamphetamine, tetrahydrocannabinol (THC) and MDMA (ecstasy). This is usually carried out by police requesting a preliminary saliva sample by placing a small absorbent pad on the tongue of the driver. This sample will then be analysed and, if the test is positive, a further evidentiary sample will be required for laboratory testing to ascertain if the subject has been driving with a prohibited drug in their system. Roadside drug tests are not there to detect such drugs as prescription and even non–prescription medications, but on the odd occasion such medication has been detected. Unlike alcohol, the taking of drugs can remain in your system for some time and the fact you may have smoked pot some days before is not a defence.

One matter involved a client who was charged with driving a motor vehicle with a prescribed concentration of a drug, being a breach of section 49(1) (bb) of the Road Safety

Act and also driving whilst suspended pursuant to section 30(1) of that Act. In respect of the latter charge, his lift to work failed to pick him up so, in a panic, he used his vehicle even though he knew his licence was suspended. The medicinal cannabis was consumed some 48 hours prior to driving but was still present in his system. The drug had been prescribed to treat his medical condition and I submitted a medical report in that regard from his treating medical practitioner.

The medical use of the drug did not give him any excuse for driving, but it was to demonstrate to the court the reason why he took such prescribed medication. On being charged by police, his vehicle was impounded for 30 days at a cost of $1,010. He received little sympathy from the court, was disqualified from driving for a further 12 months and received a heavy fine.

In another particular case, my client had allegedly consumed medicinal cannabis which he stated was at least a week before, yet on being pulled over while riding his Harley motorcycle, he was still a bit concerned that he might be detected. When police returned to his vehicle to retrieve a test sample, he reached up to a eucalyptus tree hanging overhead and started sucking on some gum leaves, hoping this would cover up any drug saliva sample in his system. Of course, his "gum sample" failed and he was now seeking my assistance to avoid a heavy fine and a further extended period off the road. He received a s.85 immediate suspension notice under the Road Safety Act in any event as a repeat drug drive offender and despite that, he attended our appointment with his motorcycle helmet in hand. In other words, he took no notice of the suspension of his licence.

A few weeks later, "Blinky Bill", as he was now nicknamed,

was once again in trouble but this time it was not due to sucking on gum leaves but using his daughter's saliva to try and avoid detection. On being pulled over once again by police, who no doubt had checked his motorcycle registration and now knew his chequered history and driving while still suspended, he had his daughter, who was his pillion passenger, provide him with her saliva before being tested. Again, all to no avail. He now had further serious drug driving charges, was to appear in court in due course and his motorcycle was impounded. I suggested the outcome for Blinky Bill was not going to be to his "licking", sorry "liking" and his licence was ultimately cancelled. As we were leaving court, he told me he would take his bike for one last spin, which I suggested was not a good idea.

There is a push by the recently elected Legalise Cannabis MPs and supported by the Victorian major parties, to allow drivers with traces of cannabis to continue to drive. This is providing they are not high on the drug and have a medicinal cannabis prescription, noting that THC can remain in the human body for some weeks after use. The *Road Safety Amendment (Medicinal Cannabis) Bill* was introduced into the Victorian Parliament in February 2023, to amend the Road Safety Act, which would bring such use in line with other prescription drugs such as antidepressants. However, it was suspended for further consideration by the Victorian Government.

In 2016, they did legalise the use of medicinal cannabis, but it still continues to be an offence under the Road Safety Act if detected driving. Despite 41% of drivers and motorcyclists killed since 2018 having drugs in their system, the Andrews-led state government proposed to trial the use of medicinal cannabis by drivers without fear of prosecution, but on the basis they only drive without being impaired. I suggest this will only result in more prosecutions of drug-impaired drivers who will, of course, use the excuse, 'I thought I was okay to drive.'

Driving while affected by alcohol and/or drugs also has a number of other repercussions, including possible loss of employment in the event your job requires you hold a current licence. You may also be subject to a degree of social and public embarrassment, especially if you have a high reading and court outcomes are accessible to the media with resultant publicity. It would be quite common in court to see a local journalist sitting there taking down notes, which would then appear in the local paper on the court outcome for drink/drug driving.

Most insurance policies will not cover you if, at the time of an accident, your BAC exceeded the legal limit or you were driving under the influence, including drugs, or you refused a breath test. In some situations and depending on the insurer, a conviction may even result in a higher premium or excess for anywhere up to five years, and an insurer may not provide cover for a certain period following conviction. Regarding a benefits payable to an injured person in the event of a traffic accident, if the injured party was the driver and is charged and/or convicted of drink or drug charges, sections 39 and 40 of the *Transport Accident Act 1985* (Vic), benefits may be limited. In many circumstances, the injured driver will not receive any benefits unless such driver can satisfy the Transport Accident Commission's (TAC) requirements that the concentration or presence of alcohol and/or drugs did not contribute in any way to the traffic accident.

A number of my clients, charged with either drink or drug driving offences, failed to understand when you lose your licence for a period of time, there is no such thing as a "work licence", which allows you to drive your vehicle for work purposes only. They also found it difficult to understand that if you are caught driving while suspended or disqualified, severe penalties will follow. Section 30 of the Road Safety Act provides that any person charged with driving while suspended or disqualified can be fined up to 240 penalty units, two years imprisonment, or both; the latter in particular if you have a history of driving whilst disqualified.

In a further effort to reduce the number of road toll deaths in Victoria due to drink driving, which currently stands at one in four drivers dying, new laws from October 2024 means every person caught drink driving, regardless of the blood alcohol reading, will be subject to a mandatory three-year zero blood alcohol content on completion of a court mandated Alcohol Interlock program. The vehicle breath testing interlock device must be fitted for a minimum of six months and, depending on the level of the reading and offending, could be extended for up to four years.

Greg Harper, the mastermind behind the TAC revolutionary advertising campaign to increase awareness of the strict liability perils of drink and drug driving, was correct when he coined the iconic slogan, 'If you drink, then drive, you're a bloody idiot.'

9
FAMILY VIOLENCE AND INTERVENTION ORDERS

On 5 January, 1976, the Australian Parliament enacted the *Family Law Act 1975* (Cth) (Family Law Act) to replace the *Matrimonial Causes Act 1959* (Cth), the latter determining fault and separation after five years as the only ground for divorce. The new legislation now introduced the concept of "no fault" in that, the only ground for divorce was based on the presumption that the marriage had "irretrievably broken down".

The law in relation to parental responsibility was amended by the *Family Law Reform Act 1995* (Cth), for dealing with children's matters and also introduced the term "parenting orders" and "parental responsibility". This was followed by a further amendment in 2006 to change the terms "residences" and "contact" to more acceptable wording such as "living and spending time with". A specialist Family Court was established in 1975 which included a counselling service as part of the overall procedure, with emphasis by this new "caring" court for any marriage break down and dispute to be determined and, with some sensitivity, as quickly as possible.

The subsequent amendments to the Family Law Act meant the legalisation allowed the Family Court to deal with matters involving divorce, property, maintenance, parenting orders involving children and to obtain protection by way of injunctions to prevent disposal of marital property, including de facto and same sex relationships. If any dispute cannot be settled by conciliation or counselling, particularly for child disputes, it will, at some stage, progress to a contested hearing before a judge.

My initial and brief exposure to family law as a legal practitioner quickly determined that to practice in this area with some expertise, a person needs, at least, a postgraduate qualification. In effect, they would need to practice it solely without delving into other areas of the law. It also became apparent, the only real winners in disputed proceedings will, in many cases, be the lawyers. I always made a point of telling my clients that they needed to settle their separation dispute as quickly as possible and without the need for time-consuming and costly litigation. Some clients took this advice, whereas others didn't. Unfortunately, in one case, the custody of the family pet was the only thing left to reach an agreement on and it became a very expensive point of contention.

I initially appeared as the duty lawyer at the Family Court at Dandenong and, to put it bluntly, it was a nightmare. It was even worse than my duty time at the Dromana Magistrates Court. I then acted for a client who, for some unknown reason, blamed me for the outcome, or lack of outcome, in gaining access to his children which, given his demeanour, I completely understood. Becoming extremely angry with me, his other half and the rest of the world, he drove around in his kombi van, which had swastikas and comments lambasting the Family Court of Australia and me, scribbled all over it, as well as threats to get me.

He was subsequently determined as a vexatious litigant under the *Vexatious Proceedings Act 2014* (Vic), after repeatedly issuing court proceedings without any reasonable chance of success, because he believed he had been wronged in some way by our court system. This Act replaced existing similar provisions under the *Supreme Court Act 1986* (Vic) and gained some prominence with the 1987 Hoddle Street killer, Julian Knight, who continually remained in the public eye as he launched something like 40 hopeless separate legal proceedings, before he was finally declared a vexatious litigant for life by Supreme Court Justice Jack Forrest in 2016.

Whilst I would not for one moment put my former Kombi van client in the same category as Knight, at the same time, I had to treat the threats against me seriously. For example, in 2006, a fellow family law practitioner, David Robinson, was shot dead by a disgruntled client over a divorce settlement. His client was subsequently sentenced to a 28-year term of imprisonment.[106]

There was one moment, which I must admit made me think there was also a funny side to family law, but only for one fleeting moment. My client had separated from her de facto partner and there was an issue with the ownership of some property. We proceeded to a mediation with an elderly, but well credentialed, barrister as the mediator. On arrival at

---

106   *The Queen v Glascott* [2008] VSC 236, which was reduced to a minimum of 24 years on appeal (*Glascott v The Queen* [2011] VSCA 109).

the mediation centre in Collins Street, Melbourne, her ex had come well prepared, or should we say, well accompanied.

On his arm was a very attractive, blonde lady who he insisted was his support person at the mediation. After the mediator explained the rules and stated that anything said was without prejudice, he then turned to my client's former partner to ask for his side of the story. He didn't hold back when he announced the real reason they had separated was because he found out my client was having "hoosh ma goondie" (sexual relations) with his brother. Before he could finish his story, my client yelled back at him, 'Certainly did and you wanna know something? He was the best fuck I have ever had.'

I am not sure who fell to the floor first with shock or was it laughter, but it's fair to say the mediator was rather flabbergasted and our attempt at settling the dispute was over very quickly, as was my short tenure into this area of family law. Waiting for me, though, was the job of acting for clients with incidents of domestic violence and the likelihood of an intervention order.

For some time, violence against women in particular, has highlighted a problem in our society, ingrained with what can only be termed as male privilege. Prejudice followed by violence. Such domestic violence can include, not only physical, but sexual, psychological, verbal and emotional abuse, together with financial pain, all as a means of either pay back or controlling behaviour. In some cases, completely terrifying the victim and leading to a total emotional breakdown.

This type of coercive control is all too common in a controlling relationship and, unfortunately, can take place over a period of time so may be difficult for some victims to identify, even though their daily activities are being constantly monitored. It can include the victim being isolated and denied freedom and autonomy, name-calling, bullying and coercive control identified under the term "gaslighting". This is when the abusive perpetrator makes his intimate partner doubt herself and her own sanity, being continually told he knows what's best for her.

Domestic violence, unfortunately, is nearly always, but not exclusively, perpetrated by men against women and children, either being subjected directly or exposed to such behaviour, making them fear for their safety and that of their loved family members. Sadly, in a number of situations, such domestic violence has escalated to murder and the number of males guilty of committing family violence has dramatically increased in Australia. The 2021 domestic violence statistics, released by the Australian Institute of Health and Welfare, also determined that whilst one in six women have experienced physical or sexual violence from a cohabiting or previous partner, one in 16 men now experience such acts of domestic violence by a partner, with one woman murdered every day and one man every 29 days.

Unfortunately, Vicki Cleary was a victim of domestic violence when she was stabbed and murdered in August 1987 by her former partner, Peter Keogh, after she had left him some months earlier. Subsequently, in 1989, Keogh was to be found guilty of the lesser charge of manslaughter, after he successfully argued a legal loophole in that he was provoked and would only serve one month shy of four years in prison.[107]

Keogh was also named as a significant person of interest by Deputy State Coroner, Caitlin English, for the stabbing

---

107 *R v Keogh* (unreported, Supreme Court of Victoria, Hampel J 15 February 1989).

murder of Maria James in Thornbury in June 1980, which sadly still remains unsolved to this day. Vickie's brother, Phil Cleary, a former prominent Australian rules footballer and coach, would subsequently become an activist against violence against women, in honour of his sister and the injustice of the court system, even raising the previously deemed taboo subject of family violence when he was elected to the Australian Parliament in 1992, replacing Bob Hawke in the seat of Wills.

The same legal loophole of provocation as a partial murder defence was subsequently abolished after John Ramage was also acquitted of murder but found guilty of manslaughter after a history of bullying, assaulting and emotionally intimidating his then separated wife, before strangling her to death in 2003. Even though Ramage had "confessed" to police, including his efforts to conceal his despicable crime, he still relied on the defence of provocation and was sentenced to only 11 years imprisonment, with a minimum of eight years, by Judge Robert Osborn. His Honour commented that the law, as it then stood, was a "crock" in applying the current law but also said:

> *I have no doubt that you feel regret for your actions and the consequential disintegration of your former way of life, but I am not persuaded you have felt or expressed genuine remorse for the brutal killing of your wife.*[108]

Phil Cleary even authored a book in 2005 titled, *Getting Away with Murder*, about Ramage, in his further efforts for campaigning against domestic violence against women. Thankfully, his tireless pursuits and the public outrage closed any such partial defence as relied on by cretins like Keogh and

---

[108] *R v Ramage* [2004] VSC 508.

Ramage. As aptly put by The Age journalist, John Silvester, on the release of Ramage after only serving eight years, 'Ramage should be shunned like a rabid dog.'

Domestic violence again reared its ugly head and it's hard to describe the despicable acts of John Sharpe, a Mornington resident, when he murdered both his pregnant wife and 20-month-old daughter with a spear gun to their heads. In describing his actions to police, he stated it was because of an unhappy marriage and that his wife was, in his words, 'too controlling'. He later told a forensic psychiatrist, trying to justify the murder of his daughter that he felt "threatened" by her.

Justice Bernard Teague recited the reasons alluded to by Sharpe as "totally irrational", further describing the events surrounding both murders as 'too awful to contemplate'. His Honour sentenced Sharpe to two consecutive terms of life imprisonment with a non-parole period of 33 years, meaning he will be 70 years old before he can be considered for release.[109] In the interim, he remains in protective custody as, unsurprisingly, there have been a number of threats on his life by fellow prison inmates.

Rose Batty, another advocate for survivors and victims of domestic violence, campaigned vigorously following the death of her 11-year-old son Luke, who was murdered by his father, Greg Anderson, at the Tyabb cricket ground on 12 February, 2014. At the inquest into this sad loss of life, Coroner Ian Gray made a point of referring to the missed prior opportunities, as Anderson was the respondent in two intervention orders, with

---

109   see *R v Sharpe* [2005] VSC 276.

a total of four arrest warrants that had not been executed by police.[110]

During a 10-year period commencing in 2004, Ms Batty made many allegations against Anderson that included physical assaults and threats to kill her. Following an incident with Anderson involving a knife in April 2013, an interim intervention order was granted, preventing him from having any further contact with his son, with Ms Batty also named as a protected person. The interim order was contested and, unfortunately, Anderson was granted access to Luke, but only in public areas when he was playing sport, only to murder him.

Pursuant to section 53 of the *Family Violence Protection Act 2008* (Vic) (FVP Act), interim intervention orders can be granted by a Victorian Court on the basis that, on the balance of probabilities, such an interim order is necessary, pending a final order to ensure the safety of an affected family member (AFM), including a child, as a protected person. Any family member, including immediate and extended family alleging domestic violence, can apply online or in person, for a family violence intervention order (FVIO) and there is no filing fee. A family member also includes, not only a current or former spouse, but a domestic partner, a person who has/had an intimate personal relationship with the respondent, which does not have to be sexual in nature, boyfriend-girlfriend relationships, including same sex and even close platonic friends. Police can also apply and do not have to first obtain consent from the AFM under a family violence safety notice.

A final intervention order can be made under section 74 of the FVP Act and as set out in section 81, can include, not only prohibiting the respondent from carrying out any form

---

110   *Batty, Luke* COR 2014 0855[2015] Vic Cor C 23285.

of family violence, but contacting the AFM by any means, including through a third party, revoking any firearms licence permit and generally an exclusion condition regarding the protected person's residence.[111]

In addition, it is possible to apply in person at a Magistrates Court for a personal safety intervention order (PSIO) as a protected person for stalking including cyber stalking, pursuant to the *Personal Safety Intervention Orders Act 2010* (Vic) (PSIO Act), which generally covers a broad spectrum of behaviour to protect a person from physical or mental harm from a non-family member. Police can also make an application for a PSIO if they form the view a person needs to be protected.[112]

Such orders under each Act are, however, only civil in nature and are put in place to restrict and prevent the respondent carrying out prohibited acts in breach of the legislative provisions and will only become criminal if breached. Some breaches, such as coercive controlling behaviour, are not stand-alone type offending and will only give rise to a criminal charge in the event of a breach. There are calls for Victoria to not only have hybrid orders available for women as needed, but the requirement for legislation also in place that criminalises certain family violence coercive behaviour, such as adopted by New South Wales in November 2022,[113] followed by the Queensland Government introducing in February 2023 the *Domestic and Family Violence Protection(Combating*

---

[111] see sections 5,6 & 7 of the FVP Act for meanings of family violence, emotional and psychological abuse.

[112] see sections 5-10 of the PSIO Act for meanings of prohibited behaviour and conduct.

[113] see *Crimes Legislation Amendment (Coercive Control) Act 2022* (NSW).

Coercive Control) and Other Legislation Amendment Bill 2023 which, when enacted, will set out the basis for a standard alone offence of coercive control. Tasmania is, however, a leader in criminalising non-physical acts of family violence, such as economic and emotional abuse when it brought into legalisation the *Family Violence Act 2004*(Tas).[114]

I recall my first appearance with my client's application for a FVIO which was at the Melbourne Magistrates Court. It was taken out against a very distant family member who had been making threats and demands. The final order was being contested and, after taking evidence from my client, the respondent entered the witness box to give his side of the sorry saga. At this point, I felt the magistrate had not been completely satisfied that a full order was required as my client, despite being a lovely man, was not very convincing in giving his evidence. I should not have worried as the respondent for the next 10 minutes ranted and raved and even made threats against my client from the witness box, despite the magistrate telling him to stop. At the conclusion of his evidence, His Honour, with a sly grin on his face said, 'Mr O'Neill, I take it you have no cross examination?'

'No, Your Honour,' and I immediately sat down at the bar table. I believe at the time I held the record for the duration of a full FVIO of 10 years, with all eight conditions, including the respondent to attend counselling.

Although an intervention order is considered to be the easiest and most effective way to provide protection, on many occasions, either acting for an AFM and more particularly a respondent, I would encourage my respondent client to consider entering into a written undertaking to not commit family

---

114   see Part 2 for definition of family violence offences.

violence. The undertaking would normally be for 12 months only but, with the right of reinstatement, contain all the usual prohibitive conditions and required consent of the other party. The only problem with written undertakings, notwithstanding they are without any admission of wrongdoing, is they are not enforceable and police have no jurisdiction. What this means is, if the undertaking is breached, the AFM who initially applied for a FVIO would need to recommence proceedings to reinstate the original application.

In one matter acting for the respondent, I tried to convince the applicant AFM, who had taken out an interim order, to agree to a written undertaking, all to no avail. It was obvious my client still had very strong feelings for her and their young child and he had hoped at some point in the future they would be able to work out their differences. I obtained further instructions from my client to consent, without admission of any wrongdoing, to a full order containing the usual eight conditions, including approach or remain within five metres of the protected person, which extended to their child and not go to, or remain within, 200 metres of any premises where they lived, worked or attended school. We tried for a full order of one year, but the applicant was adamant that it had to be two years, which was subsequently made by the court.

The court is required, pursuant to section 57 (interim order) and section 96 (final order) of the FVP Act, to explain to both the respondent and the AFM the purpose, terms and effect of the order, including penalties that apply if there is any breach.

Regardless, after any FVIO or PSIO is made, my standard practice is always to explain to my client that any breach of the order is a criminal offence and can result in arrest, with significant fines and any persistent breach can result in a term of imprisonment of up to two years. One of the many misconceptions is that as long as the AFM consents, the order can be breached without any repercussions, even if the parties were to advise both the police and the court they had reconciled, as the court order first must be altered or revoked.

I always reinforce this with my clients and, on this occasion, I gave him an example when I said, 'I don't care even if she invites you around to have a cuddle, or more explicitly a "hoosh magoondee", don't fall for that.'

Unfortunately, my advice fell on deaf ears and, within a matter of a few weeks, my client received text messages from the AFM requiring assistance with their child, followed a few days later by further text messages from the AFM telling him of her love, asking him around for the night and 'hoping we can have a shower together.'

Of course, he instantly took up the invitation, had an enjoyable night and left her a loving message in that they, 'would get back together and live happily ever after.'

For reasons only known to the AFM complainant, she notified police of the breaches and my client was charged pursuant to s.123 of the FVP Act, which carries a maximum of two years imprisonment or a level seven fine of 240 penalty units, or both.

I appeared before His Honour, Julian Ayres, and tried to explain to the court the extenuating circumstances and then went into some detail, tendering the text messages and invitations received. Mr Ayres was not impressed because in Victoria, a protected person cannot be held liable for any offence that encourages, permits and authorises a defendant to breach a FVIO. All the prosecution has to prove is the defendant was subject to a FVIO, the order was served and explained and the defendant then subsequently breached the order.

In other words, the defendant is wholly to blame despite the mitigating circumstances that led to the breaches and, effectively, based on the concept of strict liability, or as I would say to my clients in these types of situations, 'You do the crime, you do the time.'

The only solace for my client was that he was not convicted but sentenced to an 18-month CCO with a fine, including 150 hours of community work, together with attending a Men's Behaviour Change Program. Unfortunately, my client still did not a learn a salutary lesson as, four months later, we were back in court and again before His Honour Ayres. Regarding this latest breach, he had received a text message again from his former AFM partner wishing him a happy birthday to which he replied, thanking her and hoping they can catch up at some point for dinner. No threats, just forlorn text messages without any criminal intent, except he was still in breach. The court allowed him to continue with his CCO, but he was also fined the sum of $1,000 but this time with conviction.

The utilisation of FVIOs has certainly placed Victoria Police in a situation where they must adopt a cautious approach with no limits, in protecting a victim being allegedly subject to domestic violence. Pursuant to the FVP Act, any police officer who responds to, or is made aware of any family violence incident, can act as the applicant for the issuing of a family violence safety order (FVSO). The police officer must form the view that such an order is necessary to ensure the safety and wellbeing of the AFM, to preserve any personal property and to protect any child caught up in incidents of family violence against the AFM.

Police now have no choice but to become actively involved when intervening in domestic violence, to a degree that they can urgently apply online for an interim order outside of the usual sitting hours of the court, including by way of an application and warrant for an intervention order. This means, at any time of the day or night, seven days a week, an interim order can be obtained by police. In addition, following an incident in order to protect a family member, a police officer of at least the rank of sergeant can also issue a family violence safety notice (FVSN), which lasts for up to five working days until a court determines the application for an intervention order.

In effect, the FVSN has the same impact as an interim order but certainly provides immediate protection to any family member under threat, once served on the named respondent. The FVSN usually contains the same conditions as an interim notice but can also include a condition that the respondent must immediately leave the family home and cannot visit or return until a magistrate makes a determination. In the event a respondent refuses to leave, or returns to the family home, police have powers to forcibly remove the respondent and any breach is also subject to criminal sanctions which can include bail conditions.

Police are really in a "no win" situation and any breach, regardless, must be treated seriously and, in most cases, they do not hesitate to charge a respondent with any s.123 FVP Act contravention. This was very obvious in a matter involving a client who I will call Brian (not his real name). He was served by police with an interim FVSN after allegations of domestic abuse and despite having the usual standard prohibitive conditions explained, he committed two breaches the day after service.

On the return date, seven days later, I submitted to the court that Brian was confused about what he could or could not do. He sent a photo of him crying and professed his love for the AFM and, of course, his children. He also mentioned he needed to pick up some clothes and asked when he could at least visit his kids. I tried to convince the magistrate it was a technical breach, just a loving husband and father who had to leave the family home, following police taking out the notice. My submissions to the court received some leniency and the matter was adjourned by way of a good behaviour bond for 12 months and that he complete a Men's Behaviour Change Program. In addition, without admissions, he consented to a 12-month full intervention order, where he was not to communicate with the AFM or his children.

The phrase in condition five of any FVIO, states that the respondent must not 'contact or communicate with a protected person(s) by any means.'

By any means is obviously far reaching and covers nearly every type of situation and usually only provides for such communication through lawyers. For example, two months later, Brian, after finishing work, was running along the beach, being one of his regular pastimes, when he saw his children in the company of their mother. He sent them a friendly wave, returned to his car and left. Some days later, when completing a delivery for his employer and seated in his vehicle, he saw his children walk past with his estranged wife. Once again, he acknowledged them with a friendly wave. The delivery address was two streets from where his estranged wife and children lived.

All very innocent but, yes, he was in breach as he should not have acknowledged his estranged family in any way. Police charged Brian with two section 123 FVP Act contraventions and, despite submitting to the court that the appropriate disposition would be to extend his good behaviour bond by a further six months with an appropriate monetary contribution to the court fund, Brian was fined with conviction. The only redeeming factor for Brian was that consent was finally reached separately between the respective family lawyers for Brian to have access to his children on a regular basis.

Whilst I completely accept in numerous situations police have little choice but to issue a FVSN and adopt a zero-tolerance approach, one particular matter had far reaching consequences for both my client, Robert (not his real name) and his de facto partner, Anne (not her real name). Robert and Anne had been in a loving relationship for nearly 30 years and, although they had slept in separate beds for over 20 years, the relationship for all intents and purposes was quite amicable. Anne, however, had a drinking problem and had previously spent a number of months in hospital for serious physical and mental issues and, despite Robert's best efforts to control her alcohol consumption, it was all to no avail. Robert also had a major depressive disorder and was on medication.

On one particular night, after Anne had consumed far too many drinks and fell out of bed, hitting her head, she then had an argument with Robert. After screaming at him, he initially placed his hand over her mouth to stop the noise and try to calm her down. Police were called in the early hours of the morning by Anne and, although they observed she had suffered no injuries and despite Robert initially denying he had harmed her in any way, he was placed under arrest.

After interviewing Robert some hours later over the allegations of assault, in which he made an admission to placing his hand over her mouth to stop her screaming profanities at him and then slapping her, they issued and served an FVSN, as they were told by Anne she was frightened for her safety. This meant Robert had to leave the home and Anne was left to look after herself and, of course, continued her heavy drinking at will.

Five days after the incident, the court approved an interim intervention order confirming Robert was unable to return home and effectively look after Anne. When Anne was made aware Robert was charged with assault and not allowed to return home, she tried desperately to have the interim order, at the very least, amended and the charges withdrawn. All to no avail.

It would appear to be a common misconception that, particularly in domestic violence matters, the alleged victim can seek to have the charges withdrawn by way of making a statement of no complaint. Police laid the assault charge based on Robert's admissions and it was entirely at their discretion not to proceed in such cases. In the interim period, Anne continued with her drinking, despite having National Disability Insurance Scheme (NDIS) carers supposedly appointed to look after her and, unfortunately, some months later died of ill health, caused by her alcoholic lifestyle.

I was not initially instructed by Robert to act in this matter as he was represented by another law firm after being charged with unlawful assault. On my appointment, the assault matter had only proceeded to a summary case conference without resolution. Section 54 of the *Criminal Procedure Act 2009* (Vic) (Criminal Procedure Act) defines such a conference as without prejudice between the defendant's lawyers and police prosecutors. They discuss the merits of the case, issues in dispute and the way forward by negotiation, including, where applicable, charges(s) being withdrawn or to proceed by way of a contest mention or summary guilty plea. It is considered essential that any competent lawyer would have read the police brief, listened to the record of interview and obtained their client's version of events, prior to such conference. No plea had been formally entered by the previous lawyers and, unfortunately, no issues in dispute were raised. Before I was able to consider Robert's plea options and advise him accordingly, I needed to listen to the police record of interview.

In that regard, an accused has the right to silence, in other words, the common law privilege against self-incrimination and generally with some statutory exceptions in certain situations. For example, the *Major Crime (Investigation Powers) Act 2004* (Vic), to only provide your name and address, fingerprints, if requested, to be photographed for identification purposes only and a suspect is not obliged to take part in any identification parade.

My advice to any client in custody, when telephoned after hours and if I previously had not obtained full and frank instructions, was to advise them to only state their full name, address and date of birth and then, in response to any further questions and I would emphasis this, 'On legal advice I make no further comment.'

In those situations, after providing the client with that advice, I would always notify the police informant, out of courtesy, that my client on legal advice would be making a "no comment" record of interview.

There are a number of arguments for and against a lawyer attending a police record of interview. On the one hand, such presence allows the lawyer to determine any client's special needs and to protect their best interests and, overall, ensure their legal rights are upheld. However, a lawyer who is present during a record of interview, can also be subpoenaed as a witness for the prosecution in the event of any dispute over the conduct of the interview and the answers provided. On that basis, it was always my practice not to be present during a record of interview, unless I felt it was in my client's best interests and the benefits outweighed the negatives.

Police must advise the suspect of their right to speak with a lawyer, interpreter, relative or friend who also, if requested by the suspect, may be present at the record of interview. Another important requirement is to allow the suspect, if required, to obtain medical attention or to rest and recuperate and certainly, if drunk, allow a period of time to be sober enough to be interviewed.

I have listened to and considered many police records of interviews and, overall, most have been conducted appropriately. However, the record of interview conducted by police with Robert was a failure in every aspect. It was clear right from the outset that Robert was sleep deprived, having been arrested at 2am and held in a cell pending interview some four hours later. He was confused and even told police he had not taken his daily medication.

Further, on being advised he could contact a lawyer, relative or friend, he indicated that he needed to make his daughter aware he was under arrest and also wanted to speak with a lawyer. The police informant then said if he chose to, he could make a no comment record of interview. It was obvious this only confused him more, but then police stopped the record of interview as Robert had exercised his right to speak with a lawyer.

One minute and fifty seconds later, the record of interview recommenced with the informant confirming Robert had agreed to waive his right to contact his daughter and speak with a lawyer as, evidently, according to the informant, Robert 'didn't want to waste the police members' time.'

I later queried Robert what had taken place during this short time lapse, but he couldn't remember and, given his confused and sleep deprived state, that was understandable. All through the interview it was readily apparent though he was totally confused, shaking and clearly in need of some medical assistance.

Regardless, police continued with the interview with Robert making admissions he had placed his hand over Anne's mouth to stop her yelling and that he had slapped her when she slapped him in her drunken state. Nonetheless, it was obvious Robert would have confessed to anything put to him by police and some 45 minutes after recommencing the interview, police said he may be charged with unlawful assault, took his fingerprints, which he consented to and then released him pending any charge.

It was my view the FVSN should never have been issued by police and the charge of assault should have been withdrawn on the basis that the record of interview was clearly inadmissible and they now didn't have a complainant, because, sadly, in the interim period, Anne had passed away. In respect of the latter, there is an exception to hearsay evidence, courtesy of section 65 of the *Evidence Act 2008*(Vic) (Evidence Act), where a statement may be admitted into evidence if the person who made the statement is unavailable, in this case, as the complainant had died, now only supported by hearsay police evidence of what they were told. If, of course, Anne had been alive, she could not in any event have been compelled to give evidence as section 18 of the Evidence Act provides a privilege for a married spouse, de facto and children to not testify against the accused person.

At a further mention before His Honour, Julian Ayres, I made submissions in order to have the matter listed for a contest mention. I did refer to the issues in dispute, including the admissibility of the police record of interview and the absence of the complainant. It was listed for a contest mention, but His Honour did indicate to the police prosecutor that it would appear they had some difficulty with the admissibility of evidence, given the concerns I had raised.

Within a matter of a few days, I received an email from police prosecutors advising it was my "lucky day" as they would agree to withdraw the charge of unlawful assault, if there was no application for legal costs. With respect, I didn't think it was my lucky day but on instructions from my client, we agreed that if the charge was withdrawn, there would be no application for costs.[115]

The charge was ultimately withdrawn but in a final email to police prosecutors, I did suggest, with no discourtesy, that perhaps the record of interview should be sent to the Police Academy, so recruits could be instructed in how not to conduct an interview. In the interim, Robert, of course, had been unable to return home to live with Anne and look after her before she died.

In 2014, Rose Batty created a foundation named after her son to assist victims of family violence and she was also awarded Australia's National Courage Medal. In order to

---

[115] see section 401 of the Criminal Procedure Act– costs in the Magistrates Court.

further honour Luke and raise issues of family violence, to assist those affected by his sad passing, Tyabb Cricket Club now play the Luke Batty Memorial T20 Cricket match every year. Ms Batty's profound suffering, following the murder of her son, together with a number of other similar family violence deaths, was also instrumental in the 227 recommendations following the 2016 Victorian Royal Commission into Family Violence. The role of the royal commission was to explore ways to, not only prevent family violence, but provide ongoing support for victims of such violence and to bring the perpetrators before the courts.

The Victorian Government gave a commitment to implement all the 227 recommendations and, as part of their Public Safety Package in the 2016-17 budget, include the introduction of police body worn cameras (BWC) in order to improve responses to incidents of family violence. This was also in line with recommendation 58 of the royal commission, namely the 'Development of resources to improve the identification and understanding of "systems abuse".'

As a consequence, an amendment was made to the *Surveillance Devices Act 1999* (Vic), which meant police could overtly record a person and/or incident using a BWC without any need for consent.

Whilst it is fair to say the jury is still out on the use of a BWC by police, with the report by the Victorian Auditor General in 2021 finding many "missed opportunities" with cameras not being activated, a number of family violence court cases showed their use as an effective evidence tool in bringing the perpetrator to justice. Police are required to also provide the footage within seven days in respect to an indictable offence and when disclosed, access to the full brief can be obtained by a legal practitioner on behalf of a client on request to the police informant pursuant to section 39-Criminal Procedure Act.[116]

On one such occasion, police BWC footage actually assisted, with the charges against my client being withdrawn. My client was charged by police for being in breach of an FVIO, which he had previously consented to without admissions, following a drunken argument with his then estranged partner, now the AFM, in respect to childcare arrangements for their daughter. On the night in question, the AFM, after seeing a family counsellor, had consumed a number of drinks before the argument erupted. On receiving a number of text messages accusing him of being a coward and stating she felt like punching my client in the face, he simply responded by saying he was thinking of ending his own life.

Police were called by the AFM after she left the premises and it was obvious from the BWC footage I obtained from police, my client was totally rational and had fully cooperated with them. A number of the conversations between the two attending police constables had been muted, except one in which one police member stated that the AFM was 'clearly the instigator, was drunk and if anyone should be charged it should be her.'

In complete disregard to the overwhelming evidence that my client was not the instigator of any family violence, he was still charged with a section 123 breach of the FVP Act.

Despite my initial best efforts to have the charge withdrawn, police prosecutors at first said he had breached the FVIO by committing 'emotional abuse' in advising the AFM he would kill himself. In other words, if my client would plead

---

[116]   refer Part 3.2- Division 2–Pre-hearing disclosure of prosecution case-Criminal Procedure Act.

guilty to that reduced charge, police would amend the brief and the matter could proceed by way of a summary plea. It was not until the day of the contest mention, as my client had no intention of pleading to any alleged breach, common sense prevailed and the matter was resolved by way of withdrawal, providing we did not seek legal costs against police.

Any relevant conduct in breach of an interim order may also be a criminal offence. I acted for a client who was charged with stalking (section 21A (1) of *Crimes Act 1958* (Vic)) together with a second charge of using a carriage service in a harassing manner as per section 474.17(1) of the *Criminal Code Act 1995*(Cth). In this matter, police charged my client with these offences which occurred prior to the AFM taking out a final FVIO, some two weeks after the offence.

The charge of stalking related to the ownership of a dog, collecting personal items, including a car and, at the same time, still professing his love and wanting to resume their relationship. The only problem for my client was he sent over 400 text messages including phone calls and emails over two days, so it's fair to say the stalking and using a carriage service to menace obviously occurred. My client was of good character with no prior convictions; he fully cooperated with police, made full and frank admissions and expressed his regret for his unacceptable conduct. The magistrate, who was not impressed with the number of calls he made, still agreed to place him on a good behaviour bond for six months without conviction, together with a fine of $600. While at court for the plea, my client also agreed to a further 12 months for the FVIO as it was now due to expire.

I acted for many clients over a number of years, either as an AFM instigating a FVIO or PSIO, or a respondent in particular to the allegations of breaching such an order, whether it be an interim or final order. All my clients as an AFM, in the first instance, were female being subject to family violence and the respondents were all male, either opposing a full order or the subject of allegations of family violence in breach of any existing order. This does not suggest that males are not subject to family violence, but from my own experience, males were certainly the main instigators or alleged to be. However, on one occasion I did act for a young woman in her early twenties who was the subject of a police investigation, or lack of, relating to an alleged sexual assault of a young girl, aged five.

I had known the family of my client for many years and, although you must keep an open mind as a lawyer, I could not believe that Sally (not her real name) would have been involved in any of the alleged conduct. However, the Sexual Offence Crime Investigation Team (SOCIT), perhaps proceeding with caution in the first instance, initially took out an interim personal safety intervention order against Sally, with a return mention date six months later due to the court backlog following the first COVID-19 lockdown. This meant that regardless, the interim order would remain in place until the first court return date.

The interim order was taken out by police and served on Sally in which it was alleged that the named person, being the young child as the AFM, needed to be protected from Sally, who was known to her family as a social acquaintance. The interim order was taken out despite there being no active police investigation because the father who made the initial complaint to SOCIT, did not want his daughter subjected to a visual audio recorded evidence procedure (VARE). Such evidence is used with vulnerable witnesses, such as this young child, in order to improve access to our criminal justice system and to provide testimony other than in an open court. A VARE statement is usually obtained from children who are witnesses in an offence of either sexual or physical in nature.

So, it seemed in this case, a person could go to police, make unsubstantiated allegations of sexual assault involving a young child without providing any particulars to the date(s) and location(s) where such alleged assaults occurred, name the suspect, but then refuse to allow the alleged victim to be interviewed. Police, obviously acting with some extreme caution, then took out the interim order pending any investigation. The only investigation the police did in the initial stages was to obtain a medical report, which they subsequently obtained many months later, where it was confirmed the young girl had been sexually interfered with and that she named Sally as the alleged offender.

We initially objected to the interim order and the court was advised it would be vigorously contested as the allegations were baseless. My initial thinking at the time was any consent to a full order, regardless of whether it was without admissions, could still be construed that the allegations might have some substance. However, the court had no choice, as is their usual procedure in contested matters, but to list it for a further directions hearing, being months down the track and the interim order would, in any event, remain in place in the meantime.

It was at this point and five months after the interim order had been issued, that I determined there was no point in contesting it as we needed to concentrate on the criminal allegations. As a consequence, Sally consented to a final personal safety intervention order being made but, of course, without admissions to any wrongdoing. Although it was agreed with police prosecutors that the final order would only be for a period of two years, Her Honour made an order for a total of five years, referring to the allegations as 'very serious and the best interests of the child were paramount.'

Apart from the 10-year final order at Melbourne Magistrates Court many years prior, a duration of five years in my view was simply without merit. I did make submissions to the court that there was no active police investigation, the VARE procedure was refused by the father of the child and, indeed, one of the officers from SOCIT, initially involved, had now been the subject of disciplinary allegations. On leaving the court after the final order was made, I noticed the father of the child sitting there with a smirk on his face. I subsequently forwarded a scathing letter to the Officer in Charge of SOCIT advising that, 'their handling of the matter was totally unsatisfactory,' as they had failed to conduct any investigation, other than to obtain a medical report. Further, our client had not been given the opportunity to defend the allegations at the first available opportunity and that this 'inexplicable delay was having a damaging effect on our client and her well-being.'

I also asked them to advise 'if there was a police investigation…If not, why not and did they at any point intend to interview my client?'

I even told police we welcomed an investigation stating, 'which we have no doubt will determine that our client, for reasons unknown, has been unjustly accused.'

I also requested they respond as matter of urgency, but it was some four months later when I was advised they now wished to interview my client. This meant the so-called investigation did not include a VARE, but SOCIT determined that perhaps they should now interview my client as the alleged person of interest. I suspect they were hoping Sally would make full admissions, but I can assure you that was not going to happen as she had not committed any such abhorrent assault on the young girl.

I considered it was not in the best interests of Sally to be subject to a police record of interview as, understandably, she was already suffering from episodes of depression and anxiety on being wrongly accused. To be placed under arrest upon attending the police station, then subjected to a lengthy record of interview with the "good cop and bad cop scenario of questioning" was certainly not in her better interests.

However, I proceeded to draft and have Sally sign and date, a written typed statement which set out how she came to know the family, her interaction with the young child and, of course, denying the unsubstantiated allegations. What was also included in the statement was reference to a conversation Sally had with another person, who had now provided detailed information to her of what in fact had occurred regarding the alleged sexual assault.

Although hearsay, this person was named and I invited SOCIT to at least conduct an interview with, what appeared to be, a very credible witness. Some eleven months after police first issued and served the interim order wrongly accusing Sally, they finally determined that Sally was no longer a person of interest and, in fact, were now concentrating on an unnamed family member. The PSIO was struck out before the same magistrate who initially made it for five years, leaving Sally, unfortunately, still suffering from being wrongly accused.

This was quickly followed by another matter in which another of my clients, in breach of a FVIO, assaulted his former wife in a drunken state after consuming too many beers at a local pub, which just happened to be around the corner of her home. He was located, by responding police, hiding in the front yard of the newly purchased place of residence. Somehow, I was able to keep him out of prison following charges of assault and in breach of the order. I reiterated to him, in no uncertain terms, that he needed to stay away from his ex and certainly not commit any further breaches. I explained to him that jail was not a very nice place and that is where he would be residing if he continued with this type of unacceptable conduct.

It was obvious to me, after acting in many intervention order matters, that domestic and family violence is a crime in a realm on its own. It is a complex area of the law and it is very apparent that police spend an extraordinary amount of time and resources in responding and investigating incidents of alleged family violence.

Many of my clients, in committing such offences, were either highly intoxicated or drug affected which, of course, was no excuse. Others would be in such an emotional state following the breakdown of a relationship and missing, not only their now ex-partner, but in some cases their children. They were not thinking clearly and would make contact either by text messages or email in breach of an existing intervention order. Of course, such conduct was brazen, particularly when sending literally hundreds of messages professing their unrelenting love for the other party.

Following the 227 recommendations contained in the 2016 report of the Royal Commission, the Victorian Government subsequently released its 10-year reform plan titled, *Ending Family Violence*, with a $2.9 billion investment allocated in various successive budgets to meet the needs of victims and reduce family violence incidents. Importantly, on 25 November 2017, as a consequence of the agreement reached by the Council of Australian Government (COAG), the National Domestic Violence Order Scheme (NDVOS) was introduced providing for any court domestic violence order to be automatically recognised and enforceable by police in any other Australian state or territory.

The Domestic, Family and Sexual Violence Commission is also a new national body which commenced on 1 July, 2022, being established under the *Public Service Act 1999*(Cth). The commission will coordinate policy and associated services in assisting victims and survivors subject to such acts of violence and Australia will be one of three countries to have put in place such a body. This was followed in October 2022 with the announcement by the Australian, State and Territory governments of a 10-year *National Plan to End Violence against Women and Children 2022-2032*, which will be proactive towards ending such unacceptable violence.

To a degree, much has changed and there has been untold progress in altering the behaviours and attitudes that give rise to family violence, but it is not an easy task and police are often faced with difficult situations. On some occasions, the police response and subsequent filing for an order could be viewed as a "knee jerk reaction" and questionable. However, police really have no other viable alternative and must adopt a safety-first conservative approach, as such incidents of family violence, unfortunately, continue to rise with one person dying every two weeks in Victoria as a consequence, with over 93,000 family violence incidents reported on average each year, which is nearly one every six minutes.

The Australian Bureau of Statistics (ABS) determined

that one in three reported murders in Australia were related to family and domestic violence with 50 women killed by such acts during 2022. In Victoria, by way of further example, for the 12 months ending to 30 September 2022, the Crime Statistics Agency (CSA) reported a total of 91,500 family incidents out of an overall criminal offences total of nearly 344,000. Of these, youths aged between 10-14 years committed a total of 66 family violence offences, which was an increase of 94 per cent, compared to 2021.

Another disturbing trend revealed by the CSA in its latest 2023 statistics is it is more likely now in Victoria for acts of family violence to be committed by ex-partners as compared to those carried out by current partners and in the previous five years, 52 women and 13 children have been murdered in family violence incidents and overall, in the past three years, a massive 60 per cent increase in breaches. The NSW Domestic Violence Death Review Team set up under the *Coroners Act 2009*(NSW) in its 2022 report, stated there were 31,775 incidents of domestic violence-type assaults during a 12-month period up to June 2022, with a staggering total of 137 domestic-violence related murders during the period 2016-2021.

The issue of domestic violence in Australia was unfortunately highlighted once again with the brutal murder of Samantha Harris by her estranged husband, Adrian Basham in July 2018, when he waited in the garage of her Cowes home in Victoria. This planned execution and leaving her body as though she had committed suicide, was in response to their separation and Samantha was about to give evidence against him for allegedly submitting her to marital rape. On sentencing Basham to a term of life imprisonment with a minimum of 30 years, Supreme Court Justice Lesley Taylor stated, 'You subjected her to a beating in which she sustained multiple injuries... (it was) selfish in the extreme and displays an extraordinary degree of entitlement.'

Her Honour also made a damning statement condemning domestic violence and summed it up in no uncertain terms in that it was:

Often invisible in public life and disproportionately committed by men who held reputations as hardworking, reliable fathers and community minded citizens. It was the ultimate act of family violence.
The lasting aftermath is, there are now three children left without a mother and, for them, the lifelong legacy of their remorseless father in prison for her murder.[117]

On International Women's Day 2021, a so-called loving husband made reference to his adored wife by way of an Instagram tribute describing her as 'strong creative and hilarious... who gives me the privilege of being around her every day...'

Some 12 months later in 2022, in what the court described as a savage and sustained attack, Adam Brown stabbed his wife Chen Cheng to death, all over a silly argument about childcare arrangements. His Honour, Supreme Court Justice John Champion, in sentencing Brown, who pleaded guilty, to 24 years with a non- parole period of 17.5 years and said such murder was once again a 'regrettably common' example of an Australian male murdering his female partner.[118]

Evidence that more needs to be done in respect of domestic

117　*The King v Basham, Adrian James* (Sentencing) [2023] VSC 79.

118　*DPP v Brown, Adam* [2023] VSC 311.

violence was again very apparent in the sad and shocking murder of Hannah Clarke and her three children at Camp Hill, Queensland on 19 February, 2020. Hannah was fatally set on fire, as were her children, by her estranged husband, Rowan Baxter. He had a chequered history of all types of controlling behaviour during their relationship, including being the named respondent in a domestic violence order (DVO) under the *Domestic and Family Violence Protection Act 2012*(Qld). The DVO was initially made after he kidnapped one of his children. It then varied some weeks before the fatal incident, allowing Baxter unrestricted contact with his children. This access was then revoked by police in early February 2020, leading to his rampage. This included Baxter stabbing himself to death shortly after the murder of his estranged family.

Hannah's family then set up the foundation known as "Small Steps 4 Hannah" in recognition of the mother and her children, with the aim to HALT (named after **H**annah, **A**aliyah, **L**aianah and **T**rey, incidents of family violence and trauma in Australia. Their Small Steps 4 Hannah foundation provides short-term quality crisis accommodation for affected family members to escape and be safely housed from the perpetrators committing violent and abusive behaviour.

A domestic violence survivors refuge named "Hannah's Sanctuary" was subsequently opened in May 2023 in honour of Hannah and her children and is now one of nine such much-needed safe house facilities in Brisbane. The Queensland Government also introduced, in their commitment to end coercive control in domestic violence situations, the enactment of the *Domestic and Family Violence Protection (Combating Coercive Control) and Other Legislation Amendment Act 2023*(Qld). From July 2024, similar legislation will apply in New South Wales, courtesy of the *Crimes Legislation Amendment (Coercive Control) Act 2022*(NSW). Initially, Tasmania was the only jurisdiction in Australia to legislate against coercive controlling offending under section 7(ii) of the *Family Violence Act 2004*(Tas), and now both Queensland and NSW have followed with similar legislation, which should encourage other states and territories to follow their lead.

A fatal attack in Bayswater North, Victoria, in October 2021 again brought home the issue of domestic violence, when a young pregnant mother of two children was bashed and stabbed to death by her estranged partner, Benjamin Coman. This was all over his previous drug-affected behaviour and her pregnancy, which he wanted aborted. This poor, suffering young woman moved out taking her children with her, only to be murdered. At a pre-sentence hearing in the Supreme Court of Victoria, the victim's mother made an impact statement which demonstrated the trauma she faced at the loss of her daughter. She stated in court, fighting back tears:

I will make sure your boys know you are a cold-blooded murderer and I will make sure that they will hate you forever for depriving them of a life without their loving mother and their little brother or sister.

Coman was subsequently sentenced to a term of imprisonment of 25 years with a 20-year non-parole period with Justice Tinney saying:

Your crime was carried out by reasons of anger and resentment. I'm satisfied you had it within yourself to control your actions.

You knew full well what you were doing when you attacked Michelle.[119]

Similar terrible circumstances surrounded the murder of young mother Ju Zhang by her killer Joon Seong Tan, who had only known his victim for a month, stabbing her to death in a fit of jealousy and rage when she rejected him. Tan had no remorse and disposed of her body in a wheelie bin in February 2021, with her remains being found at a local tip some four months later. The prosecution, prior to a jury trial in which Tan pleaded not guilty, first made application to the Victorian Supreme Court to rely on an exception under the Evidence Act to hearsay evidence regarding two representations involving the relationship between Tan and his victim, as detailed in a witness statement of a friend of the deceased.

Both representations of admissibility were opposed by the counsel for Tan, saying they were irrelevant and not recognised under the hearsay exception and should be excluded.[120] The court dismissed the first representation as not relevant, but allowed the second one as admissible hearsay evidence pursuant to section 65(2)(c) of the Evidence Act in respect of Tan accessing the mobile telephone of the deceased.[121] After being found guilty and on sentencing Tan, who made a last minute self-serving confession, Supreme Court Justice Amanda Cox remarked:

You took her life because you felt rejected…all your actions were taken with the single selfish aim of protecting yourself and

---

119   *DPP v Benjamin Coman* [2023] VSC 159.

120   see section 137 of the Evidence Act.

121   *DPP v Tan, Joon Seong* (Ruling No 1) [2023] VSC 296.

escaping punishment... One troubling aspect of this case, after a relationship of only one month, you became so jealous... that when faced with rejection you were capable of murder...'[122]

Tan will most likely be deported after serving a minimum of 23 years non-parole period, which is no consolation to the victim's family, particularly her eight-year-old son Jack, who still cries out for his mother in his sleep. Special mention, however, must be made of Detective Senior Constable Samantha Russell, who left no stone unturned in the search for the victim's remains and bringing Tan to justice. She was subsequently named in 2021 by Victoria Police as Detective of the Year.

One coward who, unfortunately, escaped a more severe term of imprisonment was Paul McDonough sentenced to 11 years and six months, after pleading guilty to the 2019 manslaughter of his partner who was hoping to bring their relationship to an end. Despite Supreme Court Judge Fox being aware that the fatal assault was committed on the day McDonough was released from custody on bail, noting he had an extensive criminal history and limited prospects for rehabilitation, he will be eligible for parole after serving a mere eight years and six months.[123]

The New South Wales Police Force must be commended for putting in place Domestic Violence High Risk Offender teams (DVHROT), supported by other specialist teams operating under Operation Amarok One, with the sole aim of bringing to justice their most dangerous offenders who commit

---

122 *DPP v Tan, Joon Seong* [2023] VSC 416.

123 *DPP v McDonough, Paul Philip* [2023] VSC 352.

family violence. Over half the murders in the state are domestic violence related.

During a period of three days in January 2023, the Amarok specialist police units made a total of 648 arrests, which included 164 of those listed as being wanted for committing acts of domestic violence. They also served 655 outstanding Apprehended Domestic Violence Orders (ADVO). Police also detected drug related offences and seized prohibited firearms and weapons, laying a total of 1153 charges. A further Amarok blitz over four days in July 2023 resulted in nearly 600 domestic violences perpetrators being arrested with 1100 charges laid, not only for offences involving acts of domestic violence, but also for possession of prohibited weapons.

NSW Police have also now made available what has been termed an "Empower You" app, to enable victims to secretly record incidences of domestic violence, as well as enabling access to appropriate support services. In introducing the new technology, Police Assistant Commissioner Stuart Smith said:

The "Empower You" app was designed to be user friendly, intuitive and interactive… the diary feature allows a victim to collect…photos of injuries and property damage… screen shots of emails or messages…document an incident when it happens, no matter how minor or whether report it to police at that time…the abuse is clearly demonstrated and the power comes back to the victim.

Consideration is also being given to obtain Supreme Court orders under the *Crimes (Serious Crime Prevention Orders) Act 2016*(NSW), against persons over the age of 18 years and convicted of serious offences of domestic violence.

This would be in situations where the police consider, unless drastic action is taken against the offender, such conduct may further result in a family violence homicide. Such orders up to five years duration contain specific provisions, which include excluding the offender from the vicinity of specific addresses, a curfew and being in contact with nominated persons. Further conditions can also include restrictions of a person's finance, personal property, employment and even use of certain items.

The West Australian Government, in a further dedicated response to address domestic violence, has set up a new taskforce as an advisory group, in addition to its ministerial portfolio for the Prevention of Family and Domestic Violence. The taskforce will hopefully compliment their government's commitment to address ways to assist and improve the safety of domestic violence victims.

Victoria Police established a new family violence taskforce and in 2015 began a series of investigations into an identity they later called the "Son of Satan", one of the most despicable perpetrators of family and sexual violence ever seen in the state. Andrew Males was charged with over 130 offences and, after being found guilty of rape and even a charge of false imprisonment, he was sentenced in 2022 to 25 years and six months.

In a first ever combined 500 police effort under Operation Enforceable, commencing in August 2023, Victoria Police concentrated on bringing to account an estimated 3,100 family violence offenders, who had escaped the claws of justice. Of these, there were at least 1100 outstanding warrants with over 640 FVIO orders still to be served. Thankfully, over 450 FVIO orders have now been served with 460 offenders arrested. A worrying trend, though, is some of these perpetrators were also believed to be in possession of illegal firearms, with another 500 in breach of their stringent bail conditions.

In an attempt to further assist victims of family violence, the Commonwealth Government has made amendments to the National Employment Standards (NES) with the legislation of the *Fair Work Amendment (Paid Family and Domestic Violence Leave) Act 2022* (Cth), increasing the entitlement from five days unpaid leave to 10 days paid leave for all employees, including casuals, suffering from family and domestic violence. The changes were applied from 1 February, 2023 for employers with 15 or more employees and for small businesses with less than 15 employees from 1 August, 2023. Such leave will cover emergency-type family domestic violence situations requiring crisis accommodation, accessing police assistance, attending court hearings, appointments for medical and psychological counselling and also consultation for financial and/or legal assistance.

Despite the Federal Government's good intentions, it remains to be seen if these leave provisions are workable. I say this on the basis that many victims of domestic violence have, understandably, some difficulty in even discussing their plight with family and friends, let alone their employer. I know from my own experience in acting for clients who were the subject of such violence, they were very guarded in even discussing what had taken place with their lawyer and were, in some cases, very reluctant to even make a complaint to police for fear of repercussions from their violent partner. The other issue is, if employers will be responsible for the paid domestic violence leave, they most likely will request evidence of the legitimacy of the application, which, once again, will put untold stress on the employee seeking such paid leave.

In any event, despite all these initiatives, our community is still faced with many challenging issues regarding family violence, resulting in serious assault and domestic related murders. Already in the first four months of 2024, 32 women have lost their lives, which included 28 allegedly murdered by either a current or former partner. The problem still remains and it is obvious our courts, particularly in Victoria, that we really need to toughen up and stop just fining the perpetrators for breaching family violence orders, given the maximum that can be imposed is prison.

In other words, any perpetrator with a history of family violence, whether it be coercion, emotional or physical, should not in any way have a presumption of bail. Lock them up and let their lawyers try and convince the court they should be released back into the community. Hopefully, the planned reforms announced in late May 2024 by the Allan-led Victorian Government, in particular to provide for a tougher sentencing regime for family violence breaches, will have a much-deserved impact in providing better protection for victims.

10
COWARD'S PUNCH

The sad and often fatal consequences of what is now known as the "coward's punch" had an innocent beginning, which was then often referred to as a "sucker punch". This was in reference to the victim, often in a boxing match when the unsuspecting opponent would be punched with either their back turned or often when the referee was breaking apart the two fighters and one would suddenly lash out without warning. Of course, this was deemed against the rules and incurred a penalty.

I can recall in my early days at school when two students in a fight would result in one, without warning, being punched by the other. One of my favourite tricks was to show a clenched right fist and, whilst my opponent was staring at that, belt him unmercifully with my left fist.

How times have changed and the sucker punch cannot now be tolerated especially in law. It has graduated from a sucker punch, a king hit or one punch attack, and, rightly so now, to a coward's punch. As a consequence, such a crime started to gain prominence in the Australian media in 2004 after the death of former well-known Australian Test cricketer, David Hookes, when he died following a punch by a hotel bouncer and falling to the ground hitting his head. The perpetrator was charged with manslaughter but subsequently acquitted by a jury.

Such type of deaths became more prominent and over the previous decade to 2012, 91 persons had died from brain trauma after being punched in the head in drunken, unprovoked but lethal violence. In July 2012, a young teenager with his whole life ahead of him had it cut short, when he became the victim of what was more commonly becoming known as a coward's punch. Thomas Kelly was felled by a single punch in Sydney's King Cross, being struck by 18-year-old Kieran Loveridge, who was initially sentenced to a mere five years and two months non-parole period.[124]

Following a public backlash and an appeal by the Crown, the result was Loveridge's sentence nearly doubled to a 10 year and two months minimum, with the Court of Appeal finding the original decision was 'manifestly inadequate' and said further:

The use of lethal force against a vulnerable, unsuspecting and innocent victim on a public street in the course of alcohol-fuelled aggression... called for express and demonstrable application of the element of general deterrence as a powerful factor on sentence in this case.[125]

---

124   *R v Loveridge* [2013] NSWSC 1638. Also see the sentencing regime and factors to be taken into account under *Crimes (Sentencing Procedure) Act 1999*(NSW).

125   *R v Loveridge* [2014] NSWCCA 120.

Loveridge subsequently had his appeal, as put by his counsel as a 'crushing sentence', rejected by the High Court of Australia. In a further unthinkable tragedy for the Kelly family some four years after the loss of their eldest son, his younger brother committed suicide, unable to cope following the death of Thomas. Loveridge initially applied for parole in June 2023, which was rejected by the parole board. However, a further application in April 2024 was approved, apparently after making positive progress while in custody. He is now able to resume his life in the community after serving more than 10 years in prison, but subject to strict parole conditions.

As a consequence of the death of Kelly, there was also further dissent from the community following the one punch death of Daniel Christie on New Year's Eve in 2013, again on the streets of Kings Cross, Sydney. The coward puncher was Shaun McNeil who was found not guilty of murder but convicted of the lesser charge of manslaughter. He was sentenced to a minimum of seven years and six months with Justice Robert Hume stating that, whilst his conduct was alcohol related it 'gave vent to a perceived, but grossly mistaken need, to violently punish an innocent young man.[126]

The deaths of both young innocent men again accelerated a push in New South Wales to stop the coward's punch, which provided a response by the government enacting the *Crimes and Other Legislation Amendment (Assault and Intoxication) Act 2014*(NSW). This legislative amendment provided for a minimum eight-year sentence linked to deaths following an alcohol related assault.[127] In a further attempt to reduce such fatal assaults, the NSW Government in 2014 provided for

---

126   *R v Mc Neil* [2015] NSWSC 1198.

127   see further sections 25A and 25B of the *Crimes Act 1900*(NSW).

10pm bottle shop closures until January 2020 and also 1.30am lockouts with a 3am closing time for all CBD and Kings Cross venues, save for the Star Casino, to March 2021.

However, police also had the power to conduct a search of any persons suspected of carrying out offences either drug or alcohol-related. The first person convicted under the widely accepted NSW coward one-punch legislation was Howard Garth, who was convicted in 2017 of unlawful assault occasioning death of Raynor Manalad in May 2014 and sentenced to a non-parole period of eight years. District Court Judge Townsend noted on sentencing Garth that he had exhibited no remorse, did not take any responsibility for his conduct and his rehabilitation prospects were not favourable.[128]

The coward's punch approach was also adopted by Queensland in 2014, courtesy of the *Safe Night Out Legislation Amendment Act 2014*(Qld), which provided for a 15-year minimum term of imprisonment for unlawful striking causing death. In order to prove such an offence beyond reasonable doubt, it had to be shown the assault was unlawful, it was to the head or neck and it resulted in death. The new legislation amended the *Criminal Code Act 1899*(Qld) under section 314A, in addition to a number of amendments to the *Penalties and Sentencing Act 1992*(Qld) and the *Bail Act 1980*(Qld).

Western Australia adopted a specific homicide offence in 2008 supposedly to address the problem of a one-punch death. Under section 280 of the *Criminal Code Compilation Act 1913* (WA), manslaughter carries a maximum life imprisonment term and section 281 for unlawful assault causing death is a maximum term of 20 years. However, the sentence of seven years and six months handed down for manslaughter, following

---

[128] *R v Garth* (No 2) [2017] NSWDC 471.

the death of nightclub manager, Giuseppe Raco, in 2020, who was hit from behind by Jaylen Dimer, has seen calls for a more specific and tougher coward's one-punch law, following the dismissal on appeal by the state due to the sentence being manifestly inadequate.[129]

The Northern Territory Government in 2012 implemented a one-punch homicide offence under section 161A of the *Criminal Code Act 1983*(NT), which will even apply in a death that was not intended and the conduct was not reckless or negligent. The legislation also provides for such an offence in situations of consenting adults engaged in a physical fight. This new coward's punch law followed a public outcry following the death of an off-duty police officer when he was fatally punched in a nightclub in Katherine. The perpetrator was initially sentenced for manslaughter to only three years and eight months with a minimum of one year and 10 months, but on appeal by the Crown the sentence was increased to five years with a minimum of two years and six months.[130]

In Victoria, a coward punch resulted in the death of Shannon McCormack in 2007 when he was punched and fell to the ground hitting his head. His attacker remains at large despite a $1 million reward but hopefully advances in DNA technology may eventually lead to the perpetrator. Sadly, in 2009, the death of Cain Aguair was as a consequence of a fatal blow by Jacob Polutele outside a suburban Victorian hotel. Polutele was found guilty of manslaughter and sentenced to 10 years with a minimum of seven years. On sentencing, Victorian Supreme Court Judge, Katherine Williams, labelled his conduct as:

---

129 *The State of Western Australia v Dimer* [2022] WASCA 148.

130 *The Queen v Martyn* [2011] NTCCA 13.

> *Unacceptable...you are responsible for the death of an innocent young man....He fell striking his head on the kerb ...he did not give any indication of having seen you coming. In that cowardly way, you delivered a punch of such force that it rendered him unconscious ...represents exactly the sort of unthinking or misguided reaction which must be denounced and from which you and others must be deterred for the safety of the community.[131]*

A sentence for manslaughter under section 5 of the *Crimes Act 1958*(Vic) (Crimes Act) and affray (section 195H of the Crimes Act) was handed down to coward Dylan Closter, who punched and killed David Casaai in Rye on the Mornington Peninsula in 2012. Closter was only sentenced to a maximum of nine years and three months, noting the maximum penalty for manslaughter is 25 years imprisonment and his non-parole sentence of six years left a lot to be desired.[132]

Understandably, what brought further angst from the victim's family and the Victorian community was also the manifestly inadequate sentence handed down to a mate of Closter who randomly assaulted friends of Casaai, with one suffering a broken jaw. Martial arts fighter, Tyrone Russell, was originally charged with affray, recklessly causing serious injury and recklessly causing injury.[133] The original sentence imposed was a paltry 15 months with a minimum of eight months[134] but was increased to three years with a non-parole period of one year and nine months. The appeal judges, in calling on the state

---

131   *R v Polutele* [2011] VSC 381.

132   *DPP v Closter* [2014] VSC 484.

133   sections 17 and 18 of the Crimes Act.

134   *DPP v Tyrone Steven Russell* [2014] VSC 292.

government to get the unacceptable street violence message through to the public, said:

> *Random street violence is a scourge on our society… Typically the violence is brief and unpremeditated, but it has profound and enduring consequences…Innocent people are killed or seriously injured; their families are left devastated… communities disrupted.*[135]

Following the death of Casaai, his mother started a campaign called "STOP. One Punch Can Kill" and with more than 11,000 signatures in support, the Victorian state government was encouraged to at least consider a mandatory jail term to apply in respect of a coward's punch. Danny Green, four times world boxing champion, also founded the "Stop the Coward Punch Campaign" in 2012, which spreads awareness, together with education and safety, throughout Australia trying to eliminate such unacceptable behaviour.

In Victoria, between the years 2000 to 2015 a single punch, resulting in death, saw 20 male victims and two female victims, with the majority of the offenders committing the coward's punch sentenced under the existing legislation for manslaughter. In 2014, these ghastly coward's punch deaths finally led to the Victorian state government imposing a minimum mandatory jail term under the *Sentencing Amendment (Coward's Punch Manslaughter and Other Matters) Act 2014*(Vic) to amend both the Crimes Act and *Sentencing Act 1991*(Vic) (Sentencing Act).

This provided one punch attacks, as manslaughter caused by a single punch or strike that the offender punched the unaware victim to the head or neck deliberately with intent

---

[135]   *DPP v Tyrone Steven Russell* [2014] VSCA 308.

(requisite mens rea), with a statutory minimum jail term of not less than 10 years.[136] Further, the amendment to the Crimes Act provides under section 4A (3) and (4), that the punch can also be a series of punches and not just a single punch and, if the victim dies from another injury such as impact when hitting the ground, the initial punch or punches is still determined to be the cause of death. In other words, manslaughter due to a dangerous act.

Although the intention of the Victorian state government was to impose a mandatory 10-year term of imprisonment for a coward's punch causing death, the legislation is not without some issues. This was apparent in the death of Patrick Cronin in April 2016, who died following a single punch to the head in Diamond Creek. His assailant, Andrew William Lee, was initially charged with murder but it was downgraded to manslaughter on his plea of guilty. Lee was not sentenced to the statutory 10 year minimum as His Honour Justice, Lex Lasry, was not satisfied beyond reasonable doubt that Lee did intend to coward punch Cronin and that such punch was targeted at another person. This was also agreed to by the DPP as not falling under the legislation and, as a consequence, Lee was sentenced to eight years with a minimum of five years before being eligible for parole.

On sentencing, His Honour also took into account a number of mitigating factors favourable to Lee, including good prospects of rehabilitation and added:

On any view, you acted violently and that violent act had a dreadful consequence...your actions were spontaneous... you made a terrible mistake...your plea of guilty has avoided

---

136   see section 9C (2) of the Sentencing Act.

the need for a trial and the trauma connected with it... I am satisfied that you are remorseful...I do not regard you as someone from whom the community needs to be protected...[137]

Lee subsequently appealed the sentence as manifestly excessive and whether Justice Lasry erred by not determining the offence should be considered in the lowest possible category of seriousness, thankfully such leave to appeal was refused.[138]

The parents of Cronin were quite rightly disappointed and upset that Lee could possibly only serve a paltry five years, despite killing their son in a coward punch. In memory of their much-loved son, they established the Pat Cronin Foundation with the catch cry, 'How do we end the coward punch?'

In this call for a tightening of the mandatory sentencing and, supported at large by the community, it was the fervent hope that such laws would result in no escape for such perpetrators. It was obvious, the sentencing of Lee a prime example, the imposing of a minimum 10-year sentence had a number of "get out of jail" provisions, in view of the high threshold the prosecution must establish beyond reasonable doubt.

This also appeared to be the case in the fatal punch inflicted on Jaiden Walker in May 2017, following an assault by Richard Vincec in the Melbourne CBD while under the influence of alcohol and drugs. On sentencing Vincec to eight years imprisonment with a minimum of just five years, His Honour Justice Riordan was not satisfied beyond reasonable doubt of the victim's failure to take evasive and protective action on falling to the ground was due to the punch by Vincec, it was more likely due to his excessive consumption of alcohol. Regardless, the

---

137 *The Queen v Andrew William Lee* [2017] VSC 678.

138 *Lee v The Queen* [2018] VSCA 63.

fatal punch rendered Walker unconscious suffering a fractured skull and brain damage. Counsel for Vincec, Robert Richter KC, contended in his written submissions that the defendant's fatal punch could not be classed as a coward punch and further, that it was not a severe blow to the head, notwithstanding Walker did not survive. The prosecution had originally filed a requisite section 9G notice under the Sentencing Act in order to seek the mandatory 10-year minimum sentence, but it was subsequently withdrawn following the plea of guilty by Vincec.[139]

Vincec appealed his sentence on six spurious grounds, which failed in any event, with leave to appeal refused. In fact, His Honour Justice Riordan said:

Placed excessive weight on the campaign for more severe sentences for the offence of manslaughter involving alcohol and drug consumption and the need for general deterrence (ground b); Placed excessive weight on the nature of the offence being a circumstance where one punch has been delivered in the consumption of alcohol and drugs and the need for general deterrence(ground d); insufficient weight to the obvious fact that this offence fell into the less serious category as an example of the offence of manslaughter(ground e) and Placed insufficient weight on the need to moderate the sentence when considering the applicant's personal circumstances and the impact upon him of his removal from his young family).[140]

Finally, the first person appropriately sentenced in Victoria under the coward's punch 2014 legislation was Joseph Esmaili,

---

139   *R v Vincec* [2017] VSC 602.

140   *Vincec v The Queen* [2018] VSCA 18.

when in May 2017, he king hit respected heart surgeon Patrick Pritzwald-Stegmann outside the Box Hospital. This coward punch death was all over Esmaili being told by the good doctor not to smoke in a non-smoking zone in hospital grounds. Supreme Court Justice Hollingworth completely rejected the claim by Esmaili, as submitted by his counsel, that he was acting in self-defence, sentencing him to 10 years and six months with a non-parole minimum of 10 years. To add further insult, it was suggested the death was not as a result of the coward punch, but more associated with and, as a consequence of, the distraught family turning off the victim's life support some four weeks later. Her Honour had no sympathy for the defendant, but certainly for his family, in particular his twin five-year-old daughters saying:

> *The trial was also traumatic for them, in particular, because you accepted no responsibility and contained to blame Mr Pritzwald-Stegmann for what happened at the hospital.*[141]

There was, however, no similar sentencing outcome in the death of victim, Luke Francis, leaving his family both appalled and gutted when their son's assailant, Tyson Armstong, who attacked Francis at Crown Casino in March 2022, escaped the mandatory sentencing and was only imprisoned for a maximum of 10 years, but with an eight-year non-parole minimum. This means he will be released from prison when he is just 37 to continue his life and, once again, enjoy family time with his children. This can't be said for his victim who leaves behind three innocent kids who have now lost their father.

To make matters even more galling, Armstrong had a significant and troubled criminal history for similar violence

---
141   *DPP v Esmaili* [2019] VSC 218.

and exhibited poor rehabilitation prospects. The learned judge in handing down his sentence, relied in part on section 5(3) of the Sentencing Act, often referred to as the principle of parsimony, in that the sentence should be no more severe than what is deemed necessary. In determining the sentence His Honour said:

I take into account, in your favour, the steps you have taken in recent years to get your life on more of an even footing. I also take into account, in sentencing you, the anguish which I know you will feel at the prospect and the reality of being separated from your children and partner while serving the term of imprisonment.

His Honour did reflect on the type of coward's punch and the concern by the legislature about the prevalence of such a dangerous act, describing Armstrong's conduct as those of a violent thug. In referring to the 2014 legislation, incorrectly referring in paragraph 162 of his judgment to the *Crimes Amendment (Coward's Punch Manslaughter and Other Matters) Act 2014*, His Honour further determined under section 6AAA of the Sentencing Act, if it was not for his plea of guilty he would have sentenced Armstrong to a maximum of 13 years, with a 10 year non- parole period.[142]

It would be remiss of me not to let the distraught family of Francis have a final say. When outside the Supreme Court after sentencing, his mother, who was hoping for a sentence of 15 years told the waiting media that:

I think what sickens me the most is the way he was taken out

---

142 *DPP v Armstrong, Tyson* [2023] VSC 374.

> *by a coward, doing nothing… Armstrong's just nothing but a coward who likes to hit from behind and that makes me sick, sickens me.*

One client and his family I also felt much empathy for was a young man who was assaulted and effectively left for dead after a brutal attack by two offenders. He was left in a coma after he was coward punched to the ground from behind, kicked and then repeatedly stomped on. The vicious attackers even left a cigarette butt between his buttocks, which was subsequently their downfall, following identification by way of a DNA sample and they were further identified from CCTV footage. My client's injuries were so serious he was not expected to survive and his parents were told to brace themselves for the worst possible outcome. Thankfully, he did survive but with an acquired brain injury to a degree that his chances of remaining in employment were very unlikely. The two offenders were committed to stand trial in the County Court of Victoria on serious charges, including intention to cause serious injury.

It is plainly obvious that bringing an end to the cowards' punch is going to be difficult, despite the legislature prescribing a 10-year mandatory minimum sentence for such an attack resulting in death. Technically, there is a high bar the prosecution must overcome to achieve such a desired outcome, to ensure the perpetrator receives the maximum 10 years without parole. In essence, the prosecution must prove, beyond reasonable doubt, four main key elements. They are: that the punch was to the head or neck; the victim would not have expected it; the attacker most likely was aware the victim was not expecting to be punched and that such a punch was deliberate, in other words, intentional.

Victims' families continue to encourage the Victorian State Government to at least amend the current legislation as it currently stands, to ensure the coward punch will see the imposition of a mandatory 10-year imprisonment sentence. Such mandatory sentencing, however, is not largely supported by the legal profession, according to the 2018 Monash University *'Legal Response to One- Punch Homicide in Victoria; understanding the Impact of law Reform'*. What needs to be taken in to account though is that 175 Australians have suffered fatal consequences in the past 22 years as a consequence of a coward's punch and those that did not suffer such an outcome, 83 per cent suffered neurological damage.

Nothing could be further from those terrible statistics but the example of a South Australian father who suffered lifelong injuries after being punched in the head for no reason by his daughter's former boyfriend, Thomas James Short in 2022. His victim requires round the clock care and is confined to a wheelchair and most probably will never walk again. Short was not so unlucky as he can resume his life after only serving a short sentence of just under three years, following his plea of guilty to one charge of recklessly causing serious injury, which carries a maximum sentence behind bars of 15 years.[143]

The notable Coward Punch campaigns, as instigated by the Cronin family and Danny Green, has seen since 2013, funding by the Commonwealth Government under the *Proceeds of Crime Act 2002* (Cth), with such funding initiative also distributed to various law enforcement and crime prevention bodies. It is fervently hoped that such funding will further reduce the harmful and sometimes fatal consequences of the coward's punch.

---

143   see section 29 of the *Criminal Law Consolidation Act 1935* (SA).

It is also goes without saying the current Victorian legislation needs to be tightened to ensure such cowards serve at least a minimum of 10 years imprisonment.

11
ISSUES WITH THE NDIS

It is a sad fact that over time, people with a disability have largely been ignored and disappointingly the subject of some ridicule and contempt. By way of example, history suggests the method used in dealing with the then burden of disability was simply to place such person in an institution and, in some cases, in prison. There is also the example of seeing sterilisation of disabled women as a means of treatment which was largely accepted by the community. At the turn of the 20th century, the Australian Government enacted the *Invalid and Old Age Pensions Act 1908*(Cth) which provided a means-tested disability pension for those over 16 unable to work, in addition to a pension to men over 65 and women over 60.

This first recognition and acknowledgement of people with a disability as worthy members of our society was then followed by government-funded rehabilitation programs and employment services for our soldiers returning from both world wars, who were now living with an impairment, in order for them to hopefully resume a decent life. The Commonwealth Rehabilitation Service (CRS) operated in each capital city and followed the enactment of the *Disability Services Act 1986* (Cth) and the *Disability Act 2006* (Vic) to further the needs and rights of people with a disability. The CRS, now known as CRS Australia, adopted a more case focused management role. The *Disability Discrimination Act 1992*(Cth) (Disability Discrimination Act) also protected the rights of Australians from discrimination due to a disability.

In 2008, the United Nations *Convention on the Rights of Persons with Disabilities* (UN Convention) was acknowledged by over 160 world member states to 'promote, protect and ensure the full and equal enjoyment of all human rights and fundamental freedoms by all persons with all types of disabilities.'

In 2009 a National Disability Agreement (NDA) was reached between the Australian Commonwealth Government and states and territories in order to reform and provide government support, including advocacy and specialist assistance for people with a diverse range of disabilities. The key objective of the NDA was to contribute to and measure the progress of 'people with disability and their carers (and that they) have an enhanced quality of life and participate as valued members of the community'.

Disability Care Australia was the original statutory body, now known as the National Disability Insurance Agency (NDIA), when the Gillard-led Labor Government brought into legislation the *National Disability Insurance Scheme Act 2013* (Cth) (NDIS Act). Its role was to put in place the National Disability Insurance Scheme (NDIS) to take over the responsibilities and services proved by CRS Australia, with eligible recipients not subject to a means test and not required to contribute any fees towards their care, pursuant to a NDIS plan.[144]

The service, amongst other things, implemented by the NDIA under the NDIS is to provide a funds subsidy to Australian citizens over the age of seven and under the age of 65, who need such on-going support because of their level of disability. In addition, it was hoped this would lead to outcomes that would allow people living with a disability to achieve economic participation, together with social inclusion and to enjoy greater choice with the opportunity to remain living as independently as possible. Such family-type individualised living environments became an option and a preferred choice against an aged care or residential group residence.

In situations where a disabled participant was receiving NDIS benefits prior to turning 65, such disability benefits can continue after reaching that age. For those not on benefits and requiring disability assistance after turning 65, they can access My Aged Care, but it is means-tested, requires contribution towards fees and, in any event, does not consider the needs in respect of requisite care for each applicant. A class action has now been instigated against the Commonwealth Government by Mitry Lawyers for persons over the age of 65 and suffering from a disability. The class action will allege discrimination of such exclusion is a potential breach of human rights and the Commonwealth 'has acted beyond their constitutional power', due to the age exclusion as set out in the NDIS Act. As at March 2023, over 800 Australians had joined the class action.

NDIS plans, depending on the recipients' needs, can

---

144   see *National Disability Insurance Scheme (Becoming a Participant) Rules 2016* (Cth).

include a wide range of funded services, such as assistance by authorised NDIS service providers with personal care and may include, as necessary, access to medical practitioners, assistance with daily personal activities, household tasks and modifications, transport, gardening, cleaning and necessary mobility aids. This then provides a degree of autonomy under a personalised goal and aspirations plan. It is important to note the NDIS will not provide funds not related to a person's disability support needs. In 2022, it was a widely held view that the NDIS, while assisting over 500,000 Australians including 80,000 children, needed vast improvements.

This was recognised by the Australian Government and the NDIS Act was amended from 1 July, 2022, to allow much easier access for eligible participants and their authorised representatives. This also includes situations needing to vary the existing NDIS plan, without having a complete review of the existing plan.[145]

Prior to the recent amendments, it was fair to say those in most need were overcome and frustrated with delays and the plethora of paperwork requiring full financial disclosure, together with a comprehensive analysis of their medical issues. Substantial delays even saw one eligible person having to wait nearly two years to have a wheelchair funded which, unfortunately, was not an uncommon occurrence across the board. The much-needed change will be most welcome, particularly by those seeking a reassessment of the support they urgently need.

Participants still have the right of appeal of any decision through either a NDIA internal review process and, if needed,

---

145   *(National Disability Insurance Scheme Amendment (Participant Service Guarantee and Other Measures) Act 2022* (Cth).

an external review by the Commonwealth Ombudsman or the Administrative Appeals Tribunal (AAT), the latter being set up in 1976 by the Malcom Fraser-led coalition government. It is noted that as of March 2022, a total of 4,656 NDIS appeals by eligible participants had been lodged with the AAT for the 2021/22 financial year, which was effectively double the number for the previous financial year, with a third on average being vigorously defended by lawyers representing the NDIS.

The AAT is, of course, not without its critics and, as announced in December 2022 by Attorney-General Mark Dreyfus, this 'irreversibly damaged body… had a very real cost…(on) decisions such as whether an old Australian receives an aged pension… a veteran is compensated…or whether a participant in the NDIS received funding for support', will be axed and replaced by a new entity as soon as possible.

The effectiveness of the recent amendments is still to be tested but it is clear there remains many issues still to be addressed in respect of the administration and integrity of the NDIS, including a history of fraudulent claims by some registered service providers. This includes approved disability services which, in fact, were never provided by a registered NDIS provider, following a joint investigation by the Australian Federal Police (AFP) and the NDIA called "Operation Persei". The AFP charged a Melbourne crime syndicate with defrauding the NDIS and the Child Care Subsidy in excess of $800,000, by establishing personal disability plans and then exploiting such participants for profit. This meant that up to six people living with a disability never received the level of entitled care they desperately needed.

This AFP joint investigation also resulted in the deregistration of another three registered NDIS providers and the charging of a Melbourne western suburbs disability service provider for fraudulently claiming in excess of $23,000 from NDIS for domestic nursing disability services that didn't exist, including a claim for a so called "support nurse". This led to the then opposition Labor member, Bill Shorten, as NDIS spokesperson saying, 'Sadly, it is not overstating things to say that in 2021 the NDIS has the front door padlocked to the genuine needy and the back door wide open for crooks and profiteers.'

When elected to government in 2022 and now as NDIS Minister, Shorten not only gave an assurance there would be a new appeals body other than the AAT, but ordered a complete and thorough review of the NDIS referring to the scheme as a 'black box where providers came up with fees, but you don't know the magic of how they're coming to it.'

Hopefully, the review will uncover and address the systematic rorting and waste it has been subjected to and bring the rogue registered and unregistered providers before the courts.

The scale of these fraudsters, masquerading under the banner of registered NDIS providers, eventually brought the Chief of the Australian Criminal Intelligence Commission (ACIC), Michael Phelan, to say in August 2022, 'You've got to wonder how far down the scumbag scale you get before you start ripping off our most vulnerable people.'

This damning comment came as a consequence of police condemning such rorts by assorted crime syndicates and con artists falsely claiming illegal payments from the NDIS since its establishment in 2013. In other more serious cases, there was even evidence of participants being exploited and having their entitlements stolen after being involuntarily put in psychiatric care.

Such bogus claims have led the ACIC to form the view that the NDIS was far too easy to commit fraud against, by extorting our most vulnerable living with disabilities. Such fraudulent activity amounted to currently around $30 billion, which is 20 per cent of its overall budget, and expected to be as high as something in the order of $60 billion by 2030.

A subsequent investigation by *The Age* and *60 Minutes* confirmed that these NDIS registered fraudsters also claimed further fees, called a "NDIS surcharge", for additional disability services, which, of course, had never been provided. The Herald Sun also revealed that price gouging was a common theme, with claims lodged under the scheme, for example, home renovations far in excess of what you would normally pay for such services, or even wheelchairs purchased for $395 but the provider charging in the order of $1700.

Access to exploit the lucrative NDIS funding packages had also seen a rise in a number of "pop-up" private suburban residences housing people with disabilities, being veiled attempts to develop properties and then seek to have them leased under NDIS funding. As a consequence, Victoria's Office of Public Advocate (OPA) brought their concerns over such exploitation and neglect to the attention of the NDIS Quality and Safeguards Commission (NDIS Commission). It was the independent body established in 2018 to, not only regulate NDIS providers, but also the body to oversee complaints and reportable incidents, including the abuse and neglect of participants.

My involvement with the NDIS and its registered providers or, more loosely described by some as "commercial vultures", became a reality when I acted for the Jones family (not their real name) on behalf of a deceased family member who was a loving partner and mother. On the material before me, I formed the view that there had been a fraud committed claiming NDIS funding, particularly when Mrs Jones was incapacitated whilst in hospital. The other allegation was that on my instructions, these registered providers had failed to deliver the necessary daily care required by Mrs Jones over a period of some 10 months, which was the period of care, contributing to her death from chronic alcoholic liver disease.

Despite initial funding from NDIS of around $120,000, as family members were unable to provide the level of care needed, a significantly higher amount in the order of $350,000 was paid to select NDIS providers by a court appointed trustee from separate funds held in trust for Mrs Jones. Representatives of the family had previously raised their concerns of the expenditure with the trustee in relation to the on-going monthly payments of approximately $35,000, all to no avail. In addition, the family were receiving separate invoices from the selected NDIS providers for payment of 'medical care and services of Mrs Jones', other than those to be paid from trust.

I had initially raised my clients' concerns with a letter of demand to each provider, firstly regarding their claim for payment during a number of periods whilst Mrs Jones was hospitalised due to her then current state of ill health. However, the NDIS had issued a short notice cancellation policy at the start of the COVID pandemic which initially provided for 10 business days' notice of any cancellation, which then as from 1 July, 2020 reverted back to two business days.

This, in effect, meant Mrs Jones' providers could be paid for her residential care in the absence of the cancellation notice, notwithstanding she was in hospital and such care was not needed. However, such policy also requires that 'providers can only claim for a cancellation if in the event they have not found billable work for the relevant carers', noting many of these workers were in fact casual employees, and the 'provider is required to pay the carer for any time that would have been spent providing such support'.

Whilst one provider pleaded they looked after her needs whilst she was in hospital, I wondered how that could possibly be the case when Mrs Jones would have been cared for by hospital staff, they all still argued they were entitled to payment under the NDIS cancellation policy. Interesting though, not one provider gave any evidence they were unable to find billable work during the period Mrs Jones was hospitalised. They simply submitted their weekly or fortnightly invoices and gleefully accepted such payments from the court trustee.

The other main concern also set out in each letter of demand, was that a number of the providers were allowing Mrs Jones unfettered access to alcohol. There were instances where they even accompanied her to licenced venues to consume alcohol at will. In essence, this access could hardly be described as for her medical care and quality of life, noting that she was already an alcoholic. The issue of her alcohol consumption was previously raised on a number of occasions by family members with both the NDIS, court trustee and the providers, all to no avail. The NDIA, in fact, advised they were precluded from allowing any funding treatment for alcohol addiction, whilst none of the providers addressed the question of access to alcohol by Mrs Jones.

Following the death of Mrs Jones, a subsequent autopsy as a reportable death under the *Coroners Act 2008* (Vic) (Coroners Act), determined that the cause of death was decompensated alcoholic liver disease, noting she had consumed excessive amounts of alcohol over a number of years, despite numerous detox attempts by her family.

After a subsequent autopsy, the family requested the coroner to hold an inquest pursuant to section 52(5) of the Coroners Act given the circumstances that led to her death, particularly the action by the providers in continuing to allow Mrs Jones unlimited access to alcohol. This request was denied by the coroner as it was determined that the cause of death was not in dispute and could be determined without the need to hold an inquest,[146] and the actions of the NDIS providers were not sufficiently connected with the cause of death.

It also came to light that the providers were relying on various sections of the NDIS Act (as amended) and the *National Disability Insurances Scheme (Restrictive Practices and Behaviour Support) Rules 2018* (Cth) (RPBS Rules) which, amongst other things, sets out the rights of a person with a disability as the same rights as other members of our society 'to realise their potential for physical, social, emotional and intellectual development'.[147] In regards to the definition of what is meant by restrictive practice, it is any 'practice or intervention that has the effect of restricting the rights or freedom of movement of a person with disability'.[148] Further, under section 17A(1) of the NDIS Act, there are a number of principles relating to the participation of people with a disability to a degree that 'so far as reasonable in the circumstances, to have capacity to determine their own best interests and make decisions that affect their own lives'.

By relying on the NDIS Act and its accompanying

---

[146] see section 67 of the Coroners Act.

[147] see section 4 of the NDIS Act.

[148] see section 9 of the NDIS Act.

RPBS Rules, the providers argued they were not permitted to implement any restrictive practice without authorisation by a medical practitioner and that the purchase of alcohol was a basic human and legal right. On that basis, they saw no reason why they could not accompany Mrs Jones to the bottle shop for her personal safety. Even if they had put in place an authorised restrictive practice, they argued Mrs Jones would have simply purchased alcohol herself with or without assistance from support workers, therefore, not only compromising her safety allowing her to walk to and from the bottle shop, but her human rights. I subsequently lodged a complaint with NDIS Fraud Reporting and the NDIS Commission against the actions of the providers. The jury is still out on that complaint and I suspect it will be dismissed.

In another matter, the NDIA relied on the NDIS Act and, in particular, the RPBS Rules to deny an application by the family of a severely disabled teenager for funding a security fence around their home. The young boy suffered from severe autism with extreme difficulty in both verbal and nonverbal communication. His degree of autism required not only ongoing family support, but with NDIS funding and an approved plan in place.

One issue the family faced was their son would often leave the home environment and climb over a small brick fence to wander onto a very busy public road. The family applied for further funding under the NDIS to erect a security fence around their house, which would prevent the young lad from the risk of injury, even death, if he ventured onto the roadway. The application was refused on the principles of the RPBS Rules in that such a security fence 'would restrict the rights or freedom of movement of a person with disability'. This matter was subsequently appealed to NDIA internal review and may ultimately finish up by way of further appeal to the AAT, or its replacement body.

Hopefully, such an appeal will be successful in view of other appeals determined and approved by the AAT, including finding the NDIS should fund extensive independent living area renovations to a family home for their family member with cognitive impairments. The AAT, in another appeal, even suggested though that funding for a disabled person to engage the services of a "specialised sex therapist" would be in line with the NDIS legislation,[149] noting such guidelines, despite stating that any services provided must be "reasonable and necessary", allow other alternative therapies such as tarot cards, sound baths and even crystal wands. This led to NDIS Minister Shorten questioning why these types of sex services were being funded by taxpayers as reasonable and necessary.

It is therefore appropriate that the NDIA and the NDIS Commission continue to protect and authorise appropriate restrictive practice decisions which at the same time, as far as reasonable in the circumstances, fully support the human rights of those living with a disability. However, the case examples I have referred to above alone certainly raises concerns that the NDIS and its administration has issues that hopefully would be addressed with some common sense.

The NDIA 2021-22 Annual Report refers to its Fraud and Corruption Control Plan, which sets out in some detail how they are addressing their responsibilities under the *Public Governance, Performance and Accountability Act 2013* (Cth) and the Commonwealth Fraud Control Framework 2017, in addition to its external audit program in conjunction with

---

[149] *National Disability Insurance Agency v WRMF* [2020] FCAFC 79.

the Australian National Audit Office. Further, the federal government has now replaced the existing NDIS fraud taskforce with a newly named "fraud fusion taskforce" to address alleged NDIS provider fraud and serious cases of non–compliance.

The taskforce has now uncovered a number of providers submitting 'falsified and inappropriate claims for payment to the NDIS for services not delivered', resulting in a 'serious adverse effect on NDIS participants' mental health and wellbeing'. Notably, during 2021-22, the NDIA received a total of 9,230 tip-offs on its fraud and scams reporting helpline, mostly concerning overcharging by providers, resulting in 35 active fraud investigations with 14 matters currently being prosecuted before the courts. "Operation Ivory" carried out by taskforce members raided a number of premises in June 2023 and reportedly seized evidence which it will be alleged demonstrates fraudulent claims in the order of $11 million since 2018. Apparently, the mastermind behind these frauds encouraged and enabled around 112 participants to be granted NDIS eligibility and then allegedly claimed for services not provided.

NDIS Minister Shorten in a 2GB radio interview and with further comments to other media outlets, again warned unscrupulous providers rorting the system that amendments would be made to prevent grossly inflated invoices, stating:

> *We are right now upgrading the invoices so you can't simply put in the invoice without scrutiny…There is a lot of inappropriate and undesirable conduct happening…I give fair notice to the price–scourgers, the rent seekers, the opportunists that you may have had a business model which involved inflated prices*

exploiting vulnerable people. We are going to crack down on this, we are going to out you, you will be shamed.

Such scrutiny of fraudulent conduct has already resulted in a NDIS fraudster being sentenced to three years imprisonment for dealing with the proceeds of crime in the order of $10 million.[150] Another player in defrauding the NDIS copped a five-year sentence for similar offending in dealing in the proceeds of crime and obtaining a financial advantage by deception.[151] The AFP, thanks to "Operation Pegasus" they set up in 2020 to investigate what they believed to be fraudulent activities by NDIS providers, ultimately saw three people jailed in October 2024 for more than a combined 12 years, after pleading guilty to various counts including conspiring to dishonestly obtain a gain from the Commonwealth. Some of these counts included providing false medical reports in order to obtain NDIS funding.

It is, of course, a pity that this compliance crackdown was not already in place in respect of those so-called providers, who ostensibly were looking after the better interests of my client, Mrs Jones. It is fervently only hoped that those most in need in our community suffering from disabilities not only continue to receive access to proper NDIS funding support, but the care and compassion they deserve. It is simply not just a blank cheque for some unscrupulous providers.

We can take some comfort, however, that on balance, the NDIS has markedly improved the lives of its participants giving them, not only greater independence, but certainly an improved quality of life they richly deserve. We now see 16 per

---

150   see section 400.3 of the *Criminal Code Act 1995* (Cth).

151   see section 134.2 of the Criminal Code Act.

cent of children as NDIS participants with the majority for autism and currently overall, approximately 200 participants are being accepted every day by the NDIA with a budget for 2022/23 of $35 billion, increasing to $56 billion by 2026/7, with suggestions of up to $60 billion by 2027.

The final 2023 report of the Disability Royal Commission made 222 recommendations, including the enactment of a Disability Rights Act to enshrine the principles set out in the UN Convention, together with much needed amendments to the Disability Discrimination Act. It was hoped the Australian Government would accept the recommendations in the final report and that of the Independent NDIS review, in order to strengthen the rights of people living with a disability so they wouldn't simply be seen as some sort of human commodity by unscrupulous providers, many of which still remain unregistered. In the interim, unfortunately, the lack of proper care and the rorts would simply continue.

After also receiving nearly 7,000 submissions to how best the NDIS could be improved for participants and to bring in to line the providers who continually 'make money while the sun shines', updated NDIS laws came into effect on 3 October, 2024 and will be followed by further amendments. In announcing the legislative changes courtesy of the *National Disability Insurance Scheme Amendment (Getting the NDIS Back on Track No 1) Act 2024*(Cth) (the Bill), NDIS Minister Shorten said:

> *…We found that whilst the scheme is working really well for a lot of people, the lack of clarity has led to some scams, rorts, non-evidence-based therapies and the exploitation of participants…I can't keep driving by something which ultimately undermines the sustainability[and] the trust in the scheme…*

Truer words could not be said and the now new definition of what constitutes NDIS support, puts what can be provided to participants under funding and what can't and won't be allowed. In turn, this will provide for a more detailed but rigorous scheme, which will hopefully continue to provide proper support to those in need, but also bring into line the unscrupulous providers. The first part of the bill was subsequently passed by parliament into legislation, effective from 3 October, 2024 with the improvement to the existing legislation also clarifying how NDIS participants will access the scheme, budget allocation and spending and the further strengthening of the NDIS Commission.

The second stage of the bill, when eventually passed into legislation, will further impose much needed stricter regulations to ensure compliance by NDIS providers, with heavy fines for those who continually rort the scheme. Hopefully, this will in some way deter such conduct and improve the overall quality of the services provided to those with a disability, noting by late October 2024 a total of 126 NDIS providers had been struck off and banned for life.

12
FIREARMS AND OTHER WEAPONS

Prior to the 1980s, violent crime in Australia, when compared to the United States of America, was reasonably low and, for want of a better term, arguably at an acceptable level. Unfortunately, between 1984 and 1996 it began to rear its ugly head with a series of multiple gunshot killings, causing understandably much public concern. The 1984 Milperra murders, which involved outright war between outlaw motorcycle gangs, witnessed the deaths of seven people with 28 injured.

The "Milperra Massacre" resulted in seven counts of murder with a total of 43 members of the Comancheros and Bandidos being charged. The trial outcome saw five Comancheros receiving life sentences for murder with 16 Bandidos members sentenced for manslaughter. As a consequence of the massacre, the New South Wales Government amended its legislation only allowing firearms licences for registered owners and a right to carry such a firearm had to be with "good reason".[152]

Unfortunately, multiple shootings resulting in death were to continue in 1987 in Victoria with the Hoddle Street massacre at the hands of Julian Knight, when he shot seven people dead and wounded many others.[153] Knight was sentenced to seven life terms and will never be released, unless the Victorian Parole Board is satisfied that he is in imminent danger of dying or seriously incapacitated and, as a result, does not have the physical ability to harm any person.[154]

Russell Street bomber, Craig Minogue, who became eligible for parole in 2016, also appealed similar legislation amending the Corrections Act to keep him in prison,[155] which was rejected by the High Court of Australia.[156]

Hoddle Street was followed, some months later, with the Queen Street massacre by perpetrator, Frank Vitkovic, shooting to death eight innocent people, highlighting the flaws in Victorian gun laws. About two months prior to this massacre, Vitkovic submitted an application to obtain a gun licence stating on his application form that he needed such licence for 'hunting purposes' only. After paying a deposit for an M1 carbine, he then came into possession of such a weapon on 21 October, 1987, with around 250 rounds of ammunition. Whilst hindsight is a wonderful thing, it beggars belief that he was able to obtain such

---

152 *Firearms and Dangerous Weapons Act 1973* (NSW).

153 *R v Knight* [1989] VR705.

154 *Corrections Amendment (Parole) Act 2014* (Vic); section 74AA- *Corrections Act 1986* (Vic)-*Knight v Victoria* [2017] HCA 29.

155 *Legislation Amendment (Parole Reform and Other Matters) Act 2016*(Vic); section 74AB- *Corrections Act 1986* (Vic).

156 *Minogue v Victoria* [2019] HCA 31.

a lightweight semi-automatic weapon, which has an effective and accurate firing range of up to 300 metres and was the standard type of firearm used by American soldiers in numerous conflicts, including the Vietnam War. What followed on 8 December, 1987 could have been much worse with many more deaths, if it had not been for a problem with his weapon that only allowed single bolt shot action, as compared to its normal rapid automatic firepower dispensing many rounds.

As a consequence, many Australian states and territories amended their firearm laws to the effect that all guns needed to be registered with a restriction on self-loading rifles and shotguns. Despite this, supervision and enforcement of such amendments and subsequent firearm breaches remained lacking, to say the least. Up until April 1996, our federal government effectively played no role in the legislation of firearms, leaving such regulation control to the state and territory governments, save for them regulating under federal law the importation of firearms into Australia.

This was, however, to change following the Port Arthur Massacre on 12 April, 1996 when crazed lone gunman, Martin Bryant went on his murderous rampage killing 35 unsuspecting civilians and wounding another 23, many of who were lucky to survive. The murders occurred at the historical site of Port Arthur, Tasmania, when he used two semi-automatic rifles shooting dead 20 bystanders in a gift shop followed by shooting and killing a number of other victims, including innocent children, in an adjacent car park. Bryant was subsequently arrested by police but only after he shot dead two other people and setting fire to a property. He was subsequently sentenced to 35 life terms and he will never be released from prison.[157]

---

157 *The Queen v Martin Bryant*-22 November 1996-comments on passing sentence for multiple murders.

The Port Arthur Massacre would radically change our national firearms laws under a *National Firearms Agreement* (1996) (NFA), between the Commonwealth Government and its states and territories, establishing a non-binding national approach with comprehensive restrictions on the registration, licencing and use of automatic and semi-automatic weapons. The NFA also put in place a gun buyback scheme with the voluntary surrendering of firearms under federal funding and state and territory government amnesties. Credit must be given to Walter Mikac who, in unimaginable grief, after losing his wife and two children to Bryant's murderous rampage, wrote to Prime Minister Howard some weeks later imploring him to urgently amend Australia's gun laws when he said:

As the person who lost his wife and two beautiful daughters at Port Arthur, I am writing to you to give you the strength to ensure no person in Australia ever has to suffer such a loss… all I can say is there must be enough of a penalty against possession of such horrific weapons…

As a consequence, in excess of a million firearms of all makes and sizes were handed in with no questions asked, to be destroyed by local authorities. The NFA was, however, not without its critics, in particular the Sporting Shooters Association of Australia who claimed a membership of over 50,000 and slammed the NFA ban with its President, Ted Drane, rebuking Mr Howard, saying he was a fool because it was 'one of the greatest infringements on the liberties of individuals in Australian history'. However, Mr Howard remained steadfast in his total commitment to a national reform of Australia's gun laws.

I received instructions in one matter when a client, who had been subjected to domestic violence, confiscated her now ex-husband's .22 rifle without his knowledge as she was very concerned about his outbursts of anger and gave it to me to hand to police under the amnesty. I delivered the weapon to the local police station, making sure, of course, I telephoned the station before hand over. Whilst there was effectively a national ban on automatic and semi-automatic rifles, the Victorian State Government, at the time, were successful in convincing their federal counterparts to put in place an exception in order to allow farmers restricted access, provided they were able to convince regulating police that such weapon was based on their "farming needs". In other words, such applicants would only need to demonstrate that such a weapon was needed on their property in the case, for example, of pest control.

The handgun shooting death of two students at Monash University in October 2002, where the perpetrator of the mass shooting, Huan Xiang, was armed with five loaded handguns legally registered to him, prompted Prime Minister John Howard to again review Australian gun laws. Further agreement was reached between the Australian, state and territory governments for the reform of current legislation, courtesy of a *National Handgun Control Agreement* (2002) for a national handgun buyback scheme funded by the Commonwealth, which ran for the last six months of 2003 with the enactment of the *National Handgun Buyback Act 2003*(Cth). The new restrictions also established a maximum for calibre and shot numbers for handheld guns and a minimum length for barrels of single shot guns, semiautomatics and also revolvers.

Overall, the resolutions reached were particularly focused on restricting, not only the availability but the overall use of handguns, with additional diligence on persons who were members of sporting gun clubs. This was followed by an agreement between all parties under a *National Firearms Trafficking Agreement* (2002), which further reiterated a requirement to put in place substantial penalties for the illegal trafficking trade of firearms. The national approach to firearms registration and licensing now requires a firearms licence holder, who wishes to possess and/or use a firearm, to demonstrate a genuine and lawful reason for such possession and use, the latter limited to (i) lawful employment; (ii) the active participation in a lawful sport, recreation and entertainment and (iii) the legitimate collection, display or exhibition of weapons.

In particular, in Victoria, our gun laws and the use of firearms is legislated by the *Firearms Act 1996* (Vic) (as amended) (Firearms Act) and the *Firearms Regulations* (2018) and is certainly more complex when compared to some other states. Such requirements determine that, in order to obtain a licence to hold and possess a firearm, there are a number of eligibility provisions, which include: not only must you be a resident in Victoria, but over the age of 18 years (adult licence) or between 12 and 18 years (junior licence); you must be a fit and proper person and have and can maintain a genuine reason for the need to hold a firearms licence. If your application for a licence is approved, it will be reviewed every five years and stringent requirements will apply for the storage of any firearms, where they must be stored in a purpose-built locked steel storage container.[158]

In order to obtain a licence, all applicants must have attended and completed a designated relevant firearms safety

---
[158] see sections 121-123 of the Firearms Act.

course and produce such certificate with an application. All applications, together with 100 points of identification, are then determined by the Licensing and Regulation Division of Victoria Police and no licence can be issued until 28 days have expired from the date of the application.

Heavy penalties apply if someone is found in possession of an unregistered firearm[159] and also in possession of a firearm without a licence.[160] In addition, failure to store a firearm in accordance with the Firearms Act, pursuant to section 121, is now punishable by 60 penalty units and up to 12 months imprisonment. However, sentences can be as high as up to seven years imprisonment depending on what type of illegal firearm is found in possession. It is also illegal in Victoria to have in your possession cartridge ammunition without a licence.[161]

Prohibited weapons are also legislated by the *Control of Weapons Act 1990* (Vic) (CW Act) and its applicable regulations. Such weapons deemed prohibited include: imitation firearms, knives of varying types, tasers, swords, knuckle dusters, extendable batons and even sling shots and body armour, noting this list also includes other types of weapons.[162] If, indeed, it is considered someone has a lawful excuse to carry a prohibited weapon, exemption must be first obtained from the Chief Commissioner of Police prior to bringing prohibited weapons into Victoria, including selling or possessing such weapons. Controlled weapons, such as cattle prods and spear guns can be

---

159   see section 7B of the Firearms Act.

160   see section 6 of the Firearms Act-generally see Division 1–Offences under the Firearms Act.

161   see section 124 of the Firearms Act.

162   see section 3 of the CW Act.

carried, provided it is for a legitimate purpose and lawful excuse such as for work, sport or recreation.[163]

In Victoria, under section10D (1) of the CW Act, police can declare a designated area over a nominated day between the hours of 1pm-11pm, where they are authorised, without warrant, to search any person in that area for weapons, together with anything in the control of that person or in their vehicle. Police also have powers to order any person to leave the designated area if they reasonably believe someone intends to engage in conduct that would be deemed an affray, or violent disorder.[164] This has resulted in police, under these special powers since 2019, seizing a record number of knives and in the 2021/22 financial year, under Operation Omni, a total of 36 designated areas were subject to searches without warrant.

Despite such legislation in respect to weapons, unfortunately, stabbings in Victoria continue to rise. According to the 2022 Monash University Victorian Injury Surveillance Unit statistics, over the past 10 years, there has been an increase of nearly 140 per cent of stabbing victims attending at emergency at public hospitals. This has led to suggestions that the overall efforts to reduce knife attacks has not resulted in any real downturn in such crimes, in particular those related to incidents of family violence. It seems carrying knives, especially by youths, is now widespread and the main reason given is allegedly because of "fear" and the need for such a weapon in self-defence. This is despite heavy penalties if a person is found in possession of a prohibited and/or controlled weapon.[165] Despite such penalties, all sorts of dangerous and

---

163 see the CW Act and *CW Regulations 2021*(Vic).

164 see sections 195H and 195I of the *Crimes Act 1958* (Vic).

165 see sections 5 & 6 of the CW Act.

deadly weapons including machetes,[166] axes, hunting daggers and swords can simply be purchased on social media and retail websites. You don't have to prove your identity and eligibility, pending any legislation amendment long overdue, being over the age of 18 years.

Queensland recently amended its *Police Powers and Responsibilities Act 2000*(Qld), removing the expiration date of its scanning(wand) provisions making such provisions permanent. This will allow their police officers to detect, by way of a wand search, in designated areas, such as public trains, trams and buses, any person in possession of weapons. This legislative amendment was brought about following the stabbing death of 17-year-old Jack Beasley in 2019 and, in recognition of his sad passing, is now known as "Jack's Law". His killer, who was 15 years of age, was subsequently sentenced to 10 years in custody, but with a minimum of only seven years.

The Jack Beasley Foundation conduct, on an annual basis, a commemorative Ride for Jack. Following the 2023 ride, it called on the Queensland Government to totally ban the sale in supermarkets of knives to teenagers. Police conducted an initial trial on the Gold Coast between May 2021 and November 2022 and detected 241 weapons, including flick knives, machetes, screwdrivers, knuckledusters and even a replica gun.

The Northern Territory Government now has also introduced similar wand powers based on Jack's Law and is also proposing to amend its *Control of Weapons Act 2011*(NT), for the definition of knife to include axes and machetes as controlled weapons. Heavy penalties will apply if there is no reasonable

---

166   The Victorian Government has now put in place an interim ban on the sale of machetes as from 28 May 2025. Machetes will be banned outright as from 1 September 2025, unless the holder has a valid exemption.

excuse to be carrying a weapon. A maximum of 12 months imprisonment and 24 months if the offence is committed at night can apply.

The NSW Government is also proposing amendments to its *Crimes Act 1900* which will, in effect, increase the maximum term of imprisonment for knife crimes from two years to four years. If a person is detected in possession of a knife in a public place or school, the penalty by way of a fine will increase from $2,200 to $4,400.[167] The Minns-led Labor Government will also follow Queensland's lead and introduce wand powers in designated areas, together with legislation banning the sale of knives to children under the age of 18 years.

Victoria's strict legislation to the licensing and possession of firearms also extends to those persons considered to be "prohibited" from having and/or using a firearm.[168] This means a person will be deemed prohibited if found guilty of an indictable offence within the previous 12 months, including any conviction for an indictable crime outside Victoria. A person sentenced to a current term of imprisonment, including any prison sentence over five years in the previous 15 years, is also deemed to be a prohibited person. An individual, defined in section 3 of the *Criminal Organisations Control Act 2012* (Vic), will also be declared a prohibited person.

The term "prohibited person" also applies under the Firearms Act to family violence respondents subject to an intervention order made under the *Family Violence Protection Act 2008* (Vic) (FVP Act) or the *Personal Safety Intervention*

---

167 see current offences set out in section 11C and 11E of the *Summary Offences Act 1986* (NSW).

168 see section 3 (1) of the Firearms Act.

Orders Act 2010 (Vic) (PSIO Act). This, in effect, means if an intervention order is made, including similar orders in other states and territories, a person will not be permitted to possess a firearm including five years after the date of expiry of the order made by the court.[169]

The court can revoke, cancel or suspend any licence permit to carry or use firearms, including any weapons approval,[170] unless the respondent makes a section 189 application under the Firearms Act to reverse the prohibited person order. In the event an interim intervention order is made, it can also include a condition suspending any firearms or weapons authority, pending a final intervention order. If the court determines it will cancel the respondent's authority to possess firearms or weapons by way of the final order, the respondent will be precluded from having the status of prohibited person reversed.

Police, rightfully, adopt a very stringent approach when attending reported incidents of alleged domestic violence and, prior to police attending the incident, will usually be aware, from their Law Enforcement Assistance Program database (LEAP), if there are any firearms licence holders prior to attending at the premises, the subject of any domestic violence report, including any previous incidents of family violence. In that event and depending on the circumstances giving rise to the alleged incident of domestic violence, police may issue an interim Family Violence Safety Notice (FVSN) under the FVP Act and will seize any firearms, ammunition, licence documents and weapons as a matter of due diligence.

In respect of one matter I acted in for a client by the name of Phil (not his real name), police responded to a call from his

---

169   see section 81 and 95 of the FVP Act.

170   see sections 67-69 of the PSIO Act.

wife, Judith (not her real name), alleging she had been assaulted by Phil during a drunken argument. Both had been drinking heavily and, although Judith told police the assault was only a push, police had no choice but to immediately issue and serve on Phil an interim FVSN. He was then required to hand over his registered firearms, which were locked in a compliant home gun safe.

A 12-month duration final Family Violence Intervention Order (final FVIO) was then granted by the court a week later, which included a number of conditions consented to by Phil without admission of liability, including attendance at a Men's Behavioural Program. The final FVIO now deemed Phil as a prohibited person under section 3(1) of the Firearms Act. This meant, as a prohibited person, his firearm licence was suspended for a period of five years after the expiry of the final FVIO (period of prohibition). As a consequence, section 5 of the Firearms Act meant that if Phil was detected, during the period of prohibition, possessing, carrying or using a firearm, he would be liable for a maximum penalty of 1800 penalty units (over $200,000) or 15 years imprisonment.

As Phil lived with Judith on a semi-rural farming property, which was subject to serious pest problems from rabbits and foxes and also being an active sporting shooter for over 35 years, he had a genuine and legitimate reason to want to possess firearms. As a consequence, I submitted an application to the Magistrates Court which made the final FVIO, under section 189 of the Firearms Act, together with an accompanying affidavit sworn by Phil, to reverse the prohibition order and have the suspension lifted, noting such application had to be made within three months of the final order. If the application is not made within three months, then the prohibition order remains and this meant Phil's firearm licence would be cancelled.[171]

The supporting affidavit set out Phil's history, including his employment, his loving relationship with Judith, the fact the secured firearms on the property were not in any way involved in the incident which gave rise to the FVSN, the fact he was a responsible owner of firearms, always abiding by the rules as set out in the Firearms Act and its applicable Regulations, and that he had a legitimate need to retain his licence and have the prohibition order lifted. The Chief Commissioner of Police (CCP) opposed the application and, despite my request for further information why the CCP intended to rely on in support of the position that Phil should remain a prohibited person, it was not until the application proceeded before the court that we became aware of his previous firearm conviction some 30 odd years earlier, for which Phil could not recall.

Fortunately, I had briefed counsel on this matter and his six-page submission for the court, that Phil be not deemed a prohibited person, was certainly persuasive. In particular, counsel relied on the matter of *Pickford v Chief Commissioner of Police* [2002] VSC 435 in which Justice Nettle in a section 189 application under the Firearms Act noted:

> *Unguided by authority, however, it appears to me that the section was to enable a person to be relieved of the consequences of being a prohibited person when, viewed objectively, the circumstances which gave rise to that status, or developments since, or both in combination, impel the conclusion that it is not appropriate or desirable that the person be afflicted with the consequences of being a prohibited person....*

---
171   see section 49 (4) of the Firearms Act.

The learned magistrate certainly took a pragmatic approach and described Phil in his sworn evidence before the court as being very sincere and noted he was supported by his wife, Judith. An order was subsequently made deeming Phil not to be a prohibited person and his firearms were subsequently returned to him by police. Despite an application for costs against police, this was refused, leaving Phil with, shall we say, a very expensive chapter in his life in order to continue to hold a firearms licence.

Our strict firearm laws in Victoria extend to members of sporting gun clubs, requiring handgun target shooters to be licenced and one of the many conditions requires that the licence holder, based on the number of classes of handguns owned, must participate in a designated number of handgun target matches or shoots (events). This will include events over each calendar year at an approved handgun sporting pistol club shooting range (the participation requirements). The Firearms Act does provide a discretion to the CCP to either exempt or alter the licenced holder's participation requirements, depending on the genuine reason offered by the holder. In the absence of any genuine reason, such as a medical condition, in meeting the bare minimum annual participation requirements, the CCP will take enforcement action including cancelling the holder's licence for a period of 12 months.[172]

This strict enforcement was readily apparent when acting for a member of a local gun club by the name of Sam (not his real name), when he failed to meet the minimum member participation requirements over a calendar year. I requested a review of the decision by the CCP to cancel his handgun licence and submitted two statutory declarations: one from Sam

---

172 see sections 123A- 123G and 179A of the Firearms Act.

and the other from another same club licenced handgun holder. The evidence relied on for the review set out the number of handgun shoots allegedly attended by Sam, further supported by dairy entries and firsthand witness accounts of the supposed shoots undertaken by Sam.

Unfortunately for Sam, the so-called diary entries and witness accounts did not align in any way with the record keeping of the gun club, who, under the Firearms Act, have a legislated duty to maintain strict record keeping in respect of the recording of member shoots. Nice try Sam! His handgun licence was cancelled requiring him to make a further provisional licence application after the cancellation period of 12 months. In the interim, he was required to handover to the CCP the hard copy of his gun licence and surrender his handguns to a licensed firearms dealer. If, in the event, his application for a provisional licence is refused by the CPP, the only available review recourse open to Sam is the Firearms Appeal Committee[173] and failing that, the Victorian Civil and Administrative Tribunal (VCAT).[174]

It is very evident that Australia, along with other countries such as the United Kingdom and Canada, have put in place radical changes to their firearms laws, but more needs to be done. Our potential for mass shootings still remains and we were again reminded of the inherent problems regarding gun control with another shooting in the Melbourne CBD in June 2007. The perpetrator, Christopher Wayne Hudson, was a member of the Hells Angels Motorcycle Club and, after assaulting his girlfriend, shot dead a member of our legal

---

173   see section 167 of the Firearms Act.

174   see sections 34(2), 44(2), 50(2), 112L, 112M and 182 of the Firearms Act.

profession, Brendan Keilor, who came to her assistance, and also wounded two others. Some days earlier, Hudson had also fired his weapon at police. He is currently serving a life term with a minimum of 35 years.[175]

Fears of an underbelly war erupted in August 2013, in which a drive-by shooting in Lygon street, Carlton, resulted in three deaths, including the patriarch of a well-known Melbourne crime family. We also witnessed an attack by terrorist, Man Haron Monis, on bail at the time for attempted murder and other offences, at the Sydney Lindt Café (the siege) in December 2014. This lone gunman held, at gunpoint, a number of patrons and employees, with one shot and killed by Monis. Police stormed the café killing Monis but, unfortunately, Sydney barrister, Katrina Dawson, was also shot and killed in the gunfight, with three other hostages and a police officer suffering injuries.

It was particularly noted that prior to the siege, Monis was bailed on a number of occasions relating to numerous charges of assault, including as an accessory to murder. It raised, quite rightly, a number of questions of his right to bail, noting a Sydney magistrate who had granted Monis this privilege, was never advised he had previously breached bail. Indeed, if the magistrate had been advised of the breach, in all likelihood, Monis would have had his bail refused.

A subsequent federal-state review of the siege resulted in the New South Wales Government establishing an illegal firearms reward scheme for information resulting in any conviction for the possession and use of illegal firearms. In addition, a maximum of 14 years imprisonment would now apply for any offenders convicted of possessing a stolen firearm.

---

[175] *R v Hudson* [2008] VSC 389 VSC.

Another sad and tragic shooting also took place in Osmington, Western Australia in May 2018, in which a husband and father, before committing suicide, shot dead six members of his family, including his wife, daughter, and four grandchildren. This shooting was the worst in Australia since the Port Arthur massacre and, despite the mental health issues of the murderer, he still had unfettered access to firearms. It was noted WA's *Firearms Act 1973* (WA) was not amended like other states and territories, following the Port Arthur massacre. This was also apparent following a shooting incident allegedly perpetrated by a teenager at a school in Perth in May 2023 in which, fortunately, no one was injured but leading its police minister to say:

That was a bit of American gun culture right here in the Perth suburbs… There are 360,000 or so licensed firearms in Western Australia… They are too easily accessed.

The Western Australian Government, as an Australia-first initiative, did introduce mandatory mental health checks for all state gun owners following the Osmington shooting. In their commitment to reassess their outdated firearms laws, WA Police Minister, Paul Papalia, noted of the 20 people shot dead in their state in 2022, at least half of the deaths were due to mental health issues. Following further requests from the WA Police Force, they also proposed by 1 July, 2023 to outlaw dangerous high-powered firearms by strengthening the state's gun and weapons laws to further improve community safety and, in particular, target outlaw motorcycle groups and organised crime gangs.

In addition, the WA Government introduced in February

2023, a $64.3 million buy back scheme for high powered weapons and just prior to the 30 June 2023 deadline, three quarters of the "very high-powered" firearms have been surrendered with a further 70 still outstanding. In a complete revision of their gun laws, the government will also ban and revoke gun licences from holders who have been either subject to a violence restraining order or convicted of a serious criminal offence. In an Australian first, they will also limit the number of firearms owned by one person, which will affect a number of the 90,000 firearms licence holders who currently possess around 360,000 firearms. The proposed 2024 legalisation amendments will also put in place stricter storage requirements and compulsory standards, regarding training, which will include mandatory and on-going mental health checks.

Australia does, however, pale into insignificance when compared to the United States of America. Recent statistics reveal that an estimated 90 people a day are murdered in the USA by the use of a firearm, with over 690 mass shootings in 2021 and 640 in 2022. The American Gun Violence Archive defines a mass shooting as four victims being shot and either killed or wounded, and a mass killing as one where four people are killed, not including the armed offender.

The 2022 mass shootings included the Robb Elementary School in Texas with 21 innocent people, including 19 students, fatally gunned down in May of that year. This brought the total number of children killed by guns in 2022 to 1,680. In 2023, a total of 754 people were killed with 2,443 injured from a total of 604 mass shootings. It is an understatement to say it was perhaps their bloodiest year yet with 16 mass shootings at their schools alone, with 25 mass killings and a total of 21,928 related firearm deaths. July 4th is the country's annual Independence

Day and is considered to be at most risk for mass shootings. However, already by April 2024 a total of 4,138 deaths have been connected to acts of gun violence and of those killed, 355 were children.

Unfortunately, they have no easy answer as the Second Amendment to the USA Constitution allows '…a well-regulated militia, being necessary to the security of a free state, the right of the people to keep and bear arms, shall not be infringed', meaning they have a constitutional right to possess firearms. In fact, in the state of Arizona, you are allowed to walk around the streets with a gun on full display strapped to your belt. In 2015, the Bureau of Alcohol, Tobacco Firearms and Explosives(ATF) recorded over 64,000 licenced USA gun dealers meaning easy access to registered gun outlets by its citizens. President Joe Biden had once again tried to pressure congress to pass into legislation a ban on assault weapons, but no doubt, there was untold resistance from the powerful gun lobby and lack of support from the Republican opposition. There was a limited ban in place in 1994, led by Biden, banning semi- automatic assault and high-capacity type weapons, with such legislation expiring in 2004. Congress did put in place legislation allegedly encouraging its states to put in place "red flag laws" enabling a court order to be placed temporarily over individuals with mental health issues but, clearly, that is not the answer.

Most states, in any event, still do not have any laws in place which stipulates that owners of guns must secure such weapons if there are children in the household. One possibility though, as espoused by the Senate Judiciary Committee, is to at least put in place proper background checks and the safe storage of weapons for those applying for gun licences. The issue, of course, for the American people is that many seek to obtain guns as a means of self-protection as per their constitutional right, particularly following further incidences of mass shootings. Perhaps there is a way forward with the September 2023 establishment of a federal gun violence prevention office in a further attempt to resolve or, at least, limit their epidemic of mass shootings.

We need to remain very vigilant and continue with our ground-breaking radical gun reforms. The significant initiative by the Victorian Government in 2018 was the amendment to the Firearms Act, which introduced the making of firearm prohibition orders (FPO) to target 'illegal guns, organised crime and drive-by shootings.'

This amendment, courtesy of section 112D of the Firearms Act, provides the CCP, or as delegated with authority, to declare any individual prohibited from gun possession in the event the CCP deems such a person to be a danger to our community and is in the public interest.[176] Such person must be over the age of 14 years and pursuant to section 112(b) of the Firearms Act, it will be an offence to 'acquire, possess, carry or use a firearm or firearm related item' if a FPO is in place. The penalty for any infringement is 10 years imprisonment.

In effect, the right to impose such an order is to target organised crime and drive-by shootings, with a particular emphasis and focus on outlaw motorcycle gangs, including Middle Eastern and mafia organised crime groups. Given the number of drive-by shootings in Victoria, the power given to police to make a prohibited order, to further protect our community, is another welcome addition in the fight against crime and to limit the dangerous conduct of certain individuals.

---

[176] see further section 112E of the Firearms Act.

Since 2018, a total of 669 FPOs have been served by Victoria Police, together with the seizure of over 770 firearms alone in 2021.[177] Despite such anti-gun measures by Victoria Police, a recent judicial review appeal on behalf of Colin Patterson in the Supreme Court regarding a 10-year prohibition order, upheld a decision by VCAT overturning the order.[178] This was on the basis it would "to some degree"' impinge on the applicant's basic human rights, noting the original *Firearms Amendment Bill 2017* acknowledged such prohibition orders were, to a degree, inconsistent with the *Charter of Human Rights and Responsibilities Act 2006*(Vic).

This was despite police alleging such order was needed to prevent access to guns following concealment of an unregistered handgun with a silencer. It seems, on appeal, Patterson alleged, amongst other things, that the prohibition order also prevented him from being on any property that possessed a gun, meaning he could not visit his local family and neighbour friends.

The war on illicit firearms in Victoria continues regardless and, in a further bid to reduce organised crime by preventing the trafficking of firearms, has also been further enhanced with the setting up in September 2020 by Victoria Police of a special squad known as the Illicit Firearms Unit (IFU). The IFU has a total of 22 experienced officers with the specific aim to carry out specialised investigations into the manufacturing and trafficking of firearms, which also features heavily in, not only homicides, but the illicit drug trade. Police Minister, Lisa Neville, in announcing the creation of the IFU, stated:

---

177 see *Websdale v Chief Commissioner of Police* (Review and Regulations [2019] VCAT 666- first application for review of a firearm prohibition order).

178 *Chief Commissioner of Police v Cameron Patterson* [2023] VSC 172.

Whether its shootings, accidental shootings or the use of weapons to undertake criminal activities, like carjackings, home invasions and robberies, [these are] things that cause serious harm within the community and cause serious concerns within the community about their public safety.

Victoria Police also established the VIPER taskforce in July 2022 in a further bid to address organised crime and the possession of illegal firearms, following a number of shootings in Melbourne. In its first year of operation, it carried out 560 FPO searches and, in addition to issuing a further 37 such orders, also seized a number of prohibited imitation weapons, including firearms, together with making 342 arrests and laying 1372 charges. There are also plans being considered to amend legislation in order for police to have additional powers in respect of FPOs.

Caches of illicit firearms, however, may in some way assist the perpetrators when arrested and charged by police. Often described as "hand-ins", they can lead to a sentencing discount which was clearly apparent regarding gangland identity, Omar Tiba. On being sentenced for a drive-by shooting by the Victorian Supreme Court, he pleaded guilty to intentionally causing serious injury in circumstances of gross violence.[179] Justice Beale referred to the co-operation of Tiba in surrendering a number of weapons, all of which were in good working order. This was despite potential identifying marks being removed, which may have led police to other crimes. His Honour said:

There is, of course, a benefit to the community in those weapons

---

179   see section 15 A of the *Crimes Act 1958* (Vic).

> *being surrendered. The mere fact that functioning weapons are off the street. I consider it appropriate that there be some reduction of your sentence by reason of surrender. But that discount will be a modest one due to the fact that I have no idea of the provenance of the weapons.*

His Honour then went onto say:

> *You indicated to police that no-one would be upset by their surrender. That indicates to me that you have not taken any significant risk in surrendering the weapons. A member of your family facilitated the handover of the weapons. For all I know, the weapons could have been acquitted by your family solely for the purpose of trying to buy a sentencing discount.*

Whilst it could be argued the hand in of weapons has some benefit to the community in these types of circumstances, it begs the question, what else has been gained when no other crimes have been detected from such recovery of weapons, other than perhaps reducing gun violence between organised crime gangs? In any event, Tibar was sentenced to seven years and six months and, if not for his plea of guilty and, of course, the weapons hand over, according to Justice Beale, pursuant to section 6AAA of the *Sentencing Act 1991* (Vic), he would have received a total of nine years imprisonment.[180]

Despite the measures in place, particularly in Victoria, the domestic, illicit firearms and other weapons numbers across Australia remains undetermined, with estimates by the Australian Criminal Intelligence Commission (ACIC) as high as between 300,000 and 600,000 firearms alone. The

---

180   *The Queen v Tibar Omar* [2021] VSC 515.

Australian Gun Safety Alliance formed along with a number of organisations, including White Ribbon and the Alannah and Madeline Foundation, has estimated there is in excess of 3 million firearms, both legal and illicit, currently throughout Australia. Indeed, the ACIC, in its 2016 report, determined that firearms, including pen guns and submachine guns, are still being manufactured illegally in Australia. The Australian Firearms Information Network is overseen by ACIC, but it has its fair share of critics as has the National Firearms Identification Database, with the Australian Federal Police Association (AFPA) describing the network as 'slow, clunky and only tracked people who had gun licences.'

The AFPA has been lobbying governments for a national firearms registry for some years now, but initially it fell on deaf ears, citing overall costs as it seemed such a registry was too difficult to put in place. If a national registry was established, it would allow for a firearms record of each gun, together with its technical details and history, and also allow for tracking of such throughout our state borders.

A permanent national firearms amnesty was, however, agreed to by all Australian governments commencing on 1 July, 2021, providing for members of the public to anonymously surrender, without fear of prosecution, any unwanted, illegal or unregistered firearms, including parts and ammunition and even crossbows and tasers, in their possession. In the first year of the amnesty, around 18,000 firearms and weapons were surrendered to be destroyed, including gel blaster-type weapons and even a Vietnam War-era flamethrower. One troubling aspect is, from numbers released by the Crime Statistics Agency (CSA), an increase of 65 percent in 2022, as compared to 2021, of youths aged between 10-14 committing weapons and explosive offences. Multiple deaths by firearms in Australia are still considered low in comparison to other international incidents and we can thank our strict gun laws in that regard.

However, we obviously cannot rest on our laurels as was certainly witnessed by the incomprehensible shooting deaths of two young police officers and an innocent civilian in the rural town of Wieambilla, Queensland in December 2022. These unfathomable murders brought our nation to its knees in utter shock and disbelief given the high-powered cache of weapons found at the crime scene, suggesting there was still a requirement for even more stricter legislation in respect of firearms and other weapons.

Finally, a comprehensive review determined that there was a need for a more consistent approach throughout Australia, including establishing the National Firearms Registry of all persons holding firearms and licences, such database being long overdue. In early December 2023, our National Cabinet finally agreed to put in place such a register, which will be administered by ACIC and will result in establishing a totally effective firearms risk policy for all states and territories.

13
BAIL OR NO BAIL

The concept of bail was initially based on the presumption that when charged with an offence, a person is deemed innocent until proven guilty. In theory, the person charged will be released from custody on their own undertaking to appear in court and, for the more serious offences and depending on the accused's previous criminal history, either on a surety, usually in the form of a deposit of a stated value, or other conditions, including being remanded in custody.

Other conditions may also include reporting daily to a nominated police station, attending drug rehabilitation, a curfew, not to consume alcohol and also not contacting any prosecution witnesses. Bail is not usually required for the lesser minor offences such as traffic matters and the person charged will be brought before the court at a later date by way of charge(s) and summons to appear.

The *Bail Act 1977* (Vic) (Bail Act) in its initial form applied to offences under state law and also in respect of certain Commonwealth offences.[181] Bail could be granted by police following an arrest and, failing that, by a bail justice or magistrate. Bail justices are appointed under section 14 of the *Honorary Justices Act 2014*(Vic) and are used in after-hours bail applications as well as remand hearings for defendants held in custody by police. In addition to hearing bail applications, bail justices can also witness documents under the *Evidence (Miscellaneous Provisions Act 1958*(Vic). Other bail decision makers are defined in the Bail Act (section 3), giving power to either grant, extend, vary and, of course, revoke bail.

In the event of any breach of bail, including its conditions, committing more offences and/or failing to appear at a court return date, the person on bail can be arrested and charged with the breach. Significant penalties for a breach of bail conditions and committing an indictable offence whilst on bail include up to three months' imprisonment. Failure to answer bail is punishable by up to two years imprisonment, noting the defendant does have a defence, providing it can be demonstrated on the basis of reasonable grounds for failure to appear.[182]

Following the minor 2013 legislative changes to bail conditions, significant amendments to the Bail Act took place in 2018. This included expanding the presumption against bail which was certainly not in keeping with the *Charter of Human Rights and Responsibilities Act 2006* (Vic), in particular section 25 in relation to the right to be tried without unreasonable delay.

These subsequent amendments were as a consequence of the Bourke Street massacre, which took place on 20 January

---

181   see section 68(1), 79 and 80 of the *Judiciary Act 1903* (Cth).

182   see section 30 of the Bail Act.

2017, in which six people were deliberately run over and killed, with 27 seriously injured. The perpetrator of this sad event was James 'Dimitriuos' Gargaslouas, who some three days earlier and despite police opposing bail to charges alleged during a police pursuit, including speeding on the wrong side of the road, was granted bail by a bail justice with a return date being the day of his murderous rampage.

The community was quite rightly outraged, which led to a review headed by Paul Coghlan QC, as ordered by the state government with subsequent reforms, including increasing the sitting hours of the Melbourne Magistrates Court to operate after hours between 5pm to 9pm, seven days a week. Gargaslouas was subsequently imprisoned on six counts of murder with a non-parole period of 46 years, meaning he will be at least 75 years old if he is ever released.[183]

What then followed were legislative reforms in two stages known as the *Bail Amendment (Stage One) Act 2017*(Vic) and the *Bail Amendment (Stage Two) Act 2018*(Vic), inserting a framework under section 1A as to when a person, accused of a criminal offence, should be entitled to bail and what conditions would apply. This was followed by a further amendment under section 1B, setting out guiding principles to maximise to the greatest extent possible for the safety of the community and persons affected by criminal acts.

The Bail Act, following the amendments, now provides for a "reverse onus test" which will require the accused to demonstrate that bail should be granted competing with police having to provide reasons why bail should be refused. A court will refuse bail if the accused is an unacceptable risk in that they will not appear on the court return date, will commit

---
[183] *DPP v Gargaslous* [2019] VSC 87.

further offences, are an "unacceptable risk" to the community or will obstruct the course of justice.[184] If, of course, the person in custody is charged with certain serious offences and unless they can demonstrate "exceptional circumstances" (section 4A) or are subject to a "show compelling reason" scenario (section 4C), they will be refused bail and remanded in custody, pending any further bail application. In addition, police officers of the rank of sergeant or above were given the power to remand a person in custody for up to 48 hours (section 10 AA).

In effect, the amendments to the Bail Act now made it more onerous for an accused to obtain bail, due to the reverse onus provisions of demonstrating either compelling reasons or exceptional circumstances. Whilst the aim was to make it increasingly more difficult for those deemed serious and violent offenders to obtain bail, there is a broad range of low-level offending, such as shoplifters, now caught up in the amendments. Indeed, according to the 2022 Victorian Aboriginal Legal Service report on the key changes to our bail laws, there is at least 100 offences which now fall under the presumption against bail.

Applications for bail are available during various stages of a criminal matter and the timing of such applications are crucial, including the preparation for the bail hearing. An accused in custody who has been refused or had their bail revoked, prior to the hearing of the charge(s) as alleged, can make a further application for bail, but such application can be heard by a court providing now, of course, there are new facts and circumstances since the bail refusal. In addition, if the accused was unrepresented at the time of refusal of bail or such bail was heard and refused by a bail justice, such an application can be

---

[184] see section 4E of the Bail Act.

made under the Bail Act (section 18AA), and an application to vary a bail condition is also available (section 18AC).

My first matter involving a bail application under the Bail Act, prior to the 2017 and 2018 amendments, was before a magistrate at the Frankston Magistrates Court in respect of a client allegedly assaulting police whilst on bail. Joe (not his real name) was initially charged with causing damage to a number of golf course greens at a popular Mornington Peninsula Golf Club. As part of his bail conditions, he had to report to Rosebud Police Station and, on arrival, he was advised by Senior Detective Peter Butland that he needed to speak with him over other matters.

To say Joe was unimpressed is an understatement and he resisted arrest before being quickly subdued. It's not a good idea to resist arrest and take on a number of police officers in the foyer of a police station, but that's exactly what he did. After I was called down to the station as his lawyer by police who were opposing bail, he was taken to the Frankston Magistrates Court to appear in an out of court session.

I appeared before His Worship, introduced myself and then listened to the evidence from S/D Butland. On completing his evidence, I was told by the presiding magistrate to proceed with cross examination. I politely informed the magistrate that there was no cross examination and sat down. Only being in my second year of practice, I was not sure what I had said was wrong, but the Magistrate exploded.

'What do you mean there is no cross examination, Mr O'Neill?'

I stood up and said, 'Because there is no bail application at this point,' and then sat down.

Perhaps His Worship was having a bad day and as it was

around 5.30pm, he may just have been tired. Then again, it might have been me at fault.

'I am sick and tired of you lawyers relying on the Bail Act, so I suggest you get further and better instructions from your client. I should lock you up for contempt.'

To say I panicked is an understatement, because there I was in court with the magistrate, for some unknown reason, threatening to lock me up in the cells.

My, shall we say, then "limited" understanding of the Bail Act in Joe's case was, we would only get one go at applying for bail, unless we could then submit new facts or circumstances. The likelihood of getting him bail, after being previously refused, is unlikely. There was the basic presumption then that any accused person is entitled to bail, unless there is an unacceptable risk. In Joe's case, the problem was he had committed further offences whilst on bail, to wit, assaulting police when he went berserk in the police station and was deemed to be an unacceptable risk and in a "show cause" situation.

Prior to the 2018 amendments, the onus would be on the prosecution to then establish unacceptable risk.[185] In determining unacceptable risk, it must be seen as against circumstances in favour of bail, such as a right to bail due to lengthy delays.[186] In the matter of *Mokbel v DPP* (No 3) [2002] VSC 393;133 a Crim R 141, bail was granted under exceptional circumstances due to the indefinite delay in the committal and trial.

In my view, it was best left for another day to apply for bail. I also needed to put some material together if we were to

---

185   *R v Paterson* [2006] VSC 268 A Crim R122 (also see Re Asmar [2005] VSC 487).

186   *Hildebrandt v DPP* [2008] VSC 198.

succeed in any bail application. I quickly told Joe in a shaky voice, 'Don't worry, I know what I am doing.'

Well, I was not so sure about that, but I told the magistrate, 'On my instructions, there was no application for bail'.

Expecting to be again jumped on, I was surprised when he simply said, 'Well, what do you want me to do?'

'Please remand my client in custody, Your Worship, pending any consideration to a bail application in due course.'

His reply was, 'I will remand him overnight and suggest you come back tomorrow and we will sort this out.'

The plan was to brief barrister, Chris O'Grady KC, put together some material and then run a proper bail application within the next seven days. In the interim, Joe would remain in custody.

On appearing the following morning, I took fellow lawyer, Louise Luke, with me to sit at the bar table and take notes, given what had happened the night before. First case up and as Joe was led into the dock from the cells, the magistrate asked me, 'Why has your client got a black eye and cuts all over his face, Mr O'Neill?'

I politely informed His Worship that he had those injuries the afternoon before when he appeared, as a consequence of him resisting arrest.

'I didn't realise that, Mr O'Neill. What is happening now with your client?'

I replied, 'There is no bail application, Your Worship, and I ask that you remand my client in custody.'

Without exaggeration, the magistrate responded, 'Now I see why you didn't cross exam Detective Butland, given there is no application for bail.'

With no disrespect to the court and certainly none to

His Worship, I suggested the magistrate must have not been listening to me the night before, as I told him there was no cross examination and there was certainly no application for bail. Given his response, that he would lock me up for contempt, I had a sleepless night thinking my very short and somewhat inexperienced law career was about to come to an embarrassing end. In any event, after I briefed barrister, Chris O'Grady, a bail application was proceeded with some days later with bail being granted. Joe would go on to plead guilty to the golf greens saga and also to a number of other charges, to be sentenced to an intensive corrections order, with, of course, a conviction.

Following the 2018 amendments to the Bail Act, I acted for a client who was charged with offences, including possession of an imitation firearm and an extended baton without an exemption.[187] At first glance, it seemed all rather low-key offending and, given the client had no prior convictions, I determined a good behaviour bond without conviction would be the probable outcome.

My client, Charlie (not his real name), was bailed on his own undertaking in respect of the possession of weapons breaches, to appear in court at a later date. What I didn't know at the time was what would eventuate in due course regarding his further offending, resulting in him being in a show exceptional circumstances situation, to be entitled to bail. I appeared in court on behalf of Charlie in a plea of guilty and, after the police prosecutor detailed the summary of alleged facts, it would be fair to say the presiding magistrate was not impressed.

Charlie's conduct arose when a drug deal went wrong, when he attempted to purchase a prohibited drug from a drug

---

187   see sections 8B and 8C of the *Control of Weapons Act 1990* (Vic).

dealer. A fight then ensued over money with one of Charlie's mates being stabbed by the dealer and he was lucky to survive. Charlie's excuse for buying drugs, when in the possession of prohibited weapons, was that it was just in case something went wrong. Well, it certainly did go pear-shaped, but not the way Charlie had envisaged with police attending at the hospital, searching his vehicle and locating the weapons. I had some good antecedent material to present to the magistrate, including references of Charlie's good character.

Before I could even start my submissions, I was asked by His Honour, 'What are you seeking as to penalty Mr O'Neill?'

I knew the court was busy, but this was certainly what we called "supermarket justice" – where cases are in and out like a revolving door, dealt with within five minutes then on to the next case – so I simply said, 'Thank you, Your Honour. Given all the circumstances, may I respectfully suggest a good behaviour bond without conviction?'

His blunt reply was, 'Try again, Mr O'Neill.'

Okay, that got me nowhere, so I tried again and this time got it right.

'Perhaps a community corrections order (CCO) without conviction?'

His Honour agreed and sentenced Charlie accordingly, placing him on a CCO for a period of 12 months.

Now, you would think Charlie would have learnt a salutary lesson, but he hadn't and was again charged some months later with a number of drug related possession offences, for which he was brought before the night court at Melbourne that same evening and fined with conviction and released. However, some days later, he was at it again, this time being charged with further drug related offences including trafficking[188], handle stolen goods (section 88A) and proceeds of crime (section 194) and, of course, in breach of his CCO. He was somehow deemed by police not to be in a show exceptional circumstances or compelling reasons situation, released on bail on his own undertaking to appear in court at a later date.

It would only be a matter of time, though, and lo and behold, two months later, Charlie was charged with further similar offending and, also under the Bail Act for breach of his earlier bail (section 30B). This time he was deemed to be in a show exceptional circumstances/compelling reasons situation, refused bail and remanded in custody overnight. Somehow, the following morning, after a protracted appearance before His Honour, Tim Gattuso, I was able to obtain Charlie's release from the police cells later that evening under certain bail undertakings, including his place of residence to be back with his family, not to use a drug of dependence, a strict curfew and to undertake a drug rehabilitation program, pending his next court appearance. Interesting though, one other condition was he could only be released from custody to a nominated member of his family, to ensure he didn't go back to his previous rented accommodation and mingle with his so-called mates. I waited at the police station until around 7pm and he was finally released into the custody of his family member.

Charlie complied with his bail undertakings to a degree, but a month before his scheduled court return date, committed further similar offending, namely trafficking a drug of dependence, resulting in a total of 15 charges including a section 30B bail breach. This offending was detected by police when he was observed, along with his co- accused leaving a

---

188   see section 71AC of the *Crimes Act 1958* (Vic).

retail car park in the early hours of the morning, which was not a good idea, particularly when the retail premises are closed. In fact, I would also act for a number of clients who fell into the same trap, as police would simply sit off the car park when they had nothing else better to do in the early hours of the morning, knowing they would detect drug-related crooks plying their trade.

Charlie was once again in a show exceptional circumstances situation with the police informant stating in the preliminary brief:

> *The accused has a disregard for the judicial system. The accused is on bail and has an active Community Corrections Order yet continues to offend. The accused has a history of drug and deception related offences. It is unlikely that the accused will cease offending if granted additional bail. If the accused were to be granted bail, police do not believe there are conditions the court can impose on the accused to prevent him from further offending.*

It was obvious Charlie did not learn from his past mistakes and, as his court return date was only a matter of a few weeks off, in consultation with his family and, of course, the client, it was felt any further application for bail would be a complete waste of time. We did, however, have a number of telephone conversations with Charlie, whilst he was held in remand at Melbourne Assessment Prison (MAP), pending his scheduled court date.

At the court return date, Charlie was represented by budding and very competent young lawyer, Ayla Dodson. I had been acting as her mentor for some months. It was felt at the time that perhaps a new and fresh approach with Charlie might be warranted. In addition, the sentencing would be before His Honour Gattuso, who we always found to be very fair, but would impose appropriate sentences as the occasion warranted.

The submission by my colleague was outstanding and, as a consequence, Charlie received an aggregate sentence of two months' imprisonment on all charges, including the breaches of his CCO with His Honour stating, 'But for the plea of guilty, the sentence I would have otherwise imposed is a term of six months imprisonment.' [189]

With time served, Charlie would be released from MAP the following morning.

In addition, His Honour also put in place a number of other orders, including a further CCO of 18 months with 100 hours of unpaid community work and a requirement for drug treatment and rehabilitation. His Honour also required a judicial monitoring hearing in three months to review Charlie's progress and his compliance with the sentencing conditions.[190] Hopefully, Charlie has now seen the errors of his way and I think the two odd months in prison might just have been the turning point for him.

The significant amendments to the Bail Act were in response to combat acts of extreme violence, such as the Bourke Street massacre and to take into account the type of offending as set out in the example of my client Charlie, when bail is breached. Already, many legal advocates are calling for such bail regime to be overhauled, citing the Bail Act silently discriminates against women, in particular those of Aboriginal and Torres Strait Islander descent, people of a young age and

---

[189] see section 6AAA of the *Sentencing Act 1991* (Vic).

[190] see section 48K of the Sentencing Act.

those with a disability, being remanded in custody for low-level offending that, in most situations, would not result in a term of imprisonment.

Recent data released by Corrections Victoria highlighted that at present 53 per cent of woman and 89 percent of Aboriginal and Torres Strait Islander women remain in prison and are yet to be sentenced after being denied bail, with a prison population increase of 30 per cent as at 2019. This meant, with the 2018 bail law amendments the number of Aboriginal women in custody had increased two-fold.

Coroner, Simon McGregor, in his January 2023 damning findings in respect of Veronica Nelson, an Indigenous woman who died in custody whilst on remand, instead of being released on bail for alleged minor shoplifting offences and outstanding warrants, said that police had predetermined such refusal of bail, even before completing the record of interview. When brought before the Melbourne Magistrates Court she was also unrepresented, yet the presiding magistrate still determined she was not entitled to bail.

This was followed by her repeated calls for medical assistance, whilst held in maximum security at the Dame Phyllis Frost Centre, which were largely ignored by prison staff who subsequently found her dead in a prison cell. The Department of Justice and Community Safety carried out two separate internal reviews into the circumstances surrounding the death of Nelson. These reviews were referred to by the coroner as being 'grossly inadequate and misleading.'

The coroner further stated, in calling for urgent changes and in his view, the Bail Act was clearly an 'incompatible unmitigated disaster,' with a person's right to liberty, in particular regarding First Nations people, was infringed under the Charter of Human Rights. He went onto say, it had resulted in people being charged with low-level-type offending and accused of bail breach offences, although they posed no risk to our community, but were still repeatedly remanded in custody.[191]

This was also despite federal and state governments not implementing the recommendations set out in the *1987 Royal Commission into Aboriginal Deaths in Custody* and, if they had been in place, Nelson would not have died in terrible circumstances. One of the main recommendations in its final report, released in 1991, was that imprisonment of First Nations people should only occur as a "last resort", in addressing the dilemma of the number of Indigenous people dying in custody. Since 1991, 525 Indigenous Australians have died whilst held in police or prison custody, yet the majority of the recommendations have not been legislated.

In a recent *Jailing is Failing* report, as released by the Justice Reform Initiative, it determined that the prison population in Victoria had risen by 32 per cent in the last 10 years, with those in prison on remand doubling from 20 percent to 42 per cent. These disproportionate rates were obvious in respect to, not only First Nations people, but also children in out-of-home care, those suffering from a disability and mental health issues and recently arrived refugees and migrants.

The disproportionate bail laws were further summed up by the Law Institute of Victoria President, Tania Wolff, when she said, in highlighting that changes to such bail laws were long overdue:

The changes in 2018 responded to the actions of a violent man in

---

[191] *Nelson, Veronica* COR 2020 0021 (2023) Vic Cor C 28312.

> Bourke Street but these changes have impacted our community's most vulnerable people ... For our community to be safe, the Bail Act must be amended to ensure that only those who pose a specific and immediate risk to the physical safety of another person or pose a demonstrable flight risk, can be denied bail.

In response to the overwhelming tide of criticism in respect to the bail laws, including calls for the presumption that bail must favour all offences at the discretion of the courts, Victorian Premier, Daniel Andrews, on 31 January, 2023 gave a commitment to such justice system reforms, stating, 'We will not waste a moment. It will be done as soon as possible' and that it was 'not right children, as young as 10, were being incarcerated.'

The proposed amendments and the "reverse onus test" would, at first glance, be applicable to only the most serious offending, meaning low-level type offenders only needed to demonstrate they did not pose a safety risk to the community and were not a flight risk to avoid prosecution for the event they were to be granted bail. This would also apply to the unacceptable risk test and the risk of offenders committing repeat minor offences would not be a sufficient reason to deny bail. This meant many accused juveniles, including repeat offenders, unless charged with serious offences such as murder, would not be remanded in custody.

Victorian Attorney-General, Jaclyn Symes, in an exclusive interview with the Sunday Age, but whilst not apologising for the 2018 restrictive bail law amendments hastily made in response to the Bourke Street massacre, stated:

> There's no denying that there are consequences of the changes

we made. We know that they've had a disproportionate impact on a lot of groups, particularly Indigenous people, people with disabilities and women. It's become clear that... we cast the net too wide...the reforms (will) address the most urgent changes needed to our bail system...

However, the Victoria Police Union, in response to bail law reform, then proposed by the Victorian Greens political party, vehemently stated their opposition to any weakening of such laws. Police Association Secretary, Wayne Gatt, said at the time:

Keeping our community safe does come at a price. If laws are wound back to once again let violent criminals, like sex offenders and drug traffickers act with impunity, the cost to community safety will be far greater.

It then remained to be seen whether Victoria's current strict bail laws and any proposed overdue amendments would be proportionally balanced accordingly. This would be particularly regarding those deemed vulnerable and to at least remove remanding those in custody accused of low-level offending, together with young offenders and First Nations people, leaving such remand for only those accused of violent crime and considered a danger to the community. The proposed amending legislation under the Bail Amendment Bill 2023 was subsequently passed, given the State Opposition was always in favour, providing they were "sensible".

These amendments came into effect on 25 March, 2024 relaxing and modifying the unacceptable risk test, changes to Schedules 1 and 2 of the Bail Act and certain offences for which bail cannot be refused, in addition to the amendments in respect to children and First Nations individuals. In effect, when anyone applies for bail in Victoria, the type of offence as charged will determine what test is applied by the court, noting there are currently three different thresholds to bail applications. Exceptional circumstances would apply to Schedule 1 offences, terrorism type charges and any offences committed while on bail applicable to both Schedules 1 and 2. A compelling reason threshold would still apply in certain situations and the prima facia entitlement to bail created, of course, a presumption in favour of bail if the charges did not fit the exceptional circumstances and show compelling reason threshold.

In respect to juveniles, they were usually only remanded in custody as a last resort.[192] As an extra tool to try and enforce bail compliance with juveniles, as part of the Victorian Government's proposed *Youth Justice Bill*, a trial would also be undertaken, involving 50 young offenders charged with a serious crime in Victoria. They were to be fitted with ankle bracelets and monitored by police. If a bail condition, such as a curfew was broken, they would be hauled back before the Children's Court for breach. The only problem there, of course, was they would most likely be released once again on further bail conditions, so the merry go round would continue, but we wait with interest for the outcome of electronic monitoring as part of an optimal bail condition.

However, in a surprising turnaround, the government then foreshadowed strengthening the bail test for juveniles, including a new crime of committing a serious offence when on bail. Hopefully, this means violent offenders won't be sent back into the community to continue their offending. On 21

---

192   see section 3B of the Bail Act.

March 2025, the Victorian Parliament finally announced the passing of the first tranche, of what they see as the toughest bail laws in Australia. The Government now agrees community safety is paramount and will be the overarching principal in bail decision making. It will now no longer be necessary to place a juvenile on remand as a last resort. What will also come into immediate effect is providing police with the power to bring a person detained for breaching bail immediately before the court, as against waiting for a bail justice.[193] The second tranche under the *Tough Bail Bill* will be introduced into Parliament around July 2025.

Meanwhile, the age of criminal responsibility in Victoria will be increased by the Labor Government from 10 to 12 years of age, despite the current youth crime wave in Victoria, with a further proposal to increase it to 14 by 2027, which has since been discarded. This means Victoria Police will not charge young children up to the age of 12, other than in respect of serious crimes, such as homicide or rape, preferring that they are given a caution and provided with rehabilitation support services.

Given the current climate, though regarding violent crime, including domestic violence related offending, perhaps the only solution is if by chance an offender is granted bail and then commits a further breach, bail would be automatically revoked and the offender placed on remand with no further chances, pending a final hearing. Then again, we can only wish.

---

[193] See further for the significant amendments in the first tranche of the *Bail Act 1977*(Vic), inter alia, which includes a new section 1B(1AA) in respect of community safety; section 3b(1)(a) removes remand as a last resort and also a section 3B for the offence of committing an indictable offence while on bail.

14
VICTIMS OF CRIME

A form of compensation for victims of crime was introduced as far back as 1958 when provisions were included in the *Crimes Act 1958* (Vic). This allowed sentencing to include an order that the convicted offender make restitution to a victim by way of a compensation payment. The only issue was, of course, the difficulty for the victim in trying to obtain such compensation, particularly if the offender had no financial means to comply with the order of the court.

Victim financial assistance schemes, brought into play by legislation, were initially introduced in a number of overseas jurisdictions in the early 1960s. The first such state-funded compensation by way of statute was enacted in New Zealand in 1963, followed by the United Kingdom, Canada and the United States. Under the initial scheme in New Zealand, such victim applications for compensation were determined by a three-person tribunal. Such determinations for pain and suffering, including medical shock, were a maximum amount of 1500 pounds and dependents of murder victims were eligible for weekly payments of nine pounds for a maximum of six years.

In Australia, compensation payments for victims of crime were first mooted as early as 1964 when the Commonwealth Government attempted to obtain agreement from the states and territories for a compensation scheme. It was not until the *Criminal Injuries Compensation Act 1972* (Vic) was legislated, that state-funded financial assistance would be provided to victims of crime. To a degree, this was not only to provide financial support for victims, but to also encourage the reporting of criminal incidents.

In 1985, the United Nations made a declaration in respect of the "Basic Principles of Justice for Victims of Crime and Abuse of Power". The declaration defined such a victim as:

Persons who, individually or collectively, have suffered harm, including physical or mental injury, emotional suffering, economic loss or substantial impairment of their fundamental rights, through acts or omissions that are in violation of criminal laws…

The Declaration also further defined victims where appropriate to include:

The immediate family or dependants of the direct victim and persons who have suffered harm in intervening to assist victims in distress or to prevent victimisation.

The establishment in Victoria of the Criminal Injury Compensation Tribunal and as a consequence of the Hoddle Street shootings in August 1987, resulted in excess of 170 victim applications for compensation. The tribunal initially awarded more than $1 million, followed by a further ex-gratia payment of $1 million for the victims, as determined by the John Cain Labor Government.

By the early 1990s, the overall operational costs of the compensation payments were the subject of much conjecture, as they had grown financially crippling with such schemes also becoming too legalistic and prone to technical issues. Some jurisdictions then introduced maximum-type payments and redefined the types of injuries that could be compensated.

In 1996, the Victorian Government then enacted the Victims of Crime Assistance Act (VOCA Act), which replaced the Criminal Injury Compensation Tribunal, by setting up the Victims of Crime Assistance Tribunal, commonly now referred to as VOCAT. In addition, in order to further assist victims of crime, a service known as Victims Referral and Assistance was established. This service provided various types of assistance and resources, for not only primary victims of crime but also for secondary victims who witnessed a crime and related victims, such as dependants.

In 2000, a subsequent amendment to the VOCA Act, was significant as it reinstated victim compensation for pain and suffering, notably now known as "special financial assistance", particularly for victims who suffered significant adverse effects as a direct result of an act of violence.[194] Importantly, victims were no longer limited to only making application for medical expenses and loss of earnings. In addition, a victim did not have to prove a diagnosable injury, provided they could demonstrate distress and/or trauma.

By 2001, VOCAT provided for magistrates to hear such

---

[194] *Victims of Crime Assistance (Amendment) Act 2000* (Vic).

victim applications at the majority of Victorian Magistrates Courts, which meant victims living in regional areas no longer had to travel to Melbourne to have their application considered by the tribunal. Paramount to the new scheme, primary victims of a crime, committed on or after 1 July 2000, could now apply for special financial assistance up to a maximum of $7500. In addition, they were not limited to just compensation for loss of income, medical expenses and counselling.

The *Victims of Crime Assistance (Amendment) Act 2007* (Vic) then increased special financial assistance to victims of crime committed on or after 1 July 2007, from $7500 to $10,000. In addition, VOCAT could also award up to $60,000 to primary victims for financial assistance for medical expenses, including counselling, safety initiatives needed as a consequence of the criminal act and funeral expenses. Loss of earnings up to $20,000 were also compensable.

The types of violent crimes covered under the VOCA Act include offences such as homicide, armed robbery, burglary with aggravating circumstances, assaults, sexual offences and making threats to kill. It does not apply to such offending as obtaining financial advantage by deception and fraud-related offences. There is also an amount that can be awarded, up to $50,000, for secondary and related victims, also with financial assistance available to a relative of a victim that dies, following the committing of a criminal act. Funeral expenses, on application, are also available to any person who pays for the funeral of a primary victim who died as a direct consequence of the violent crime.

The applicant's reasonable legal costs, including disbursements, are paid at the discretion of the tribunal, pursuant to section 48 of the VOCA Act and can be considered by the tribunal for payment, even in situations where an application has been dismissed. Generally, a lawyer cannot charge a client for any legal costs except as allowed by the tribunal on application.

The VOCA Act, in distinguishing primary and secondary victims, determines that a primary victim of a crime is a person who is injured, either physically or psychologically (the requisite injury), or dies as a consequence of a violent criminal act, including acting to place a person under arrest, attempting to prevent such violent act and even aiding a victim of violent crime. A secondary victim, pursuant to section 9(2) of the VOCA Act, defines that such person must have been present at the commission of the violent crime or as a witness to such act and suffered the requisite injury. Further, on becoming aware of the violent criminal act, if they are to be eligible for crime compensation as a parent or guardian of a primary victim, such victim must be under the age of 18 years. Related victims at the time of the commission of the violent criminal act resulting in death under section 11(1) of the VOCA Act, are only eligible if they are a close or dependant family member, or in an intimate personal relationship with the primary, but now deceased, victim.

An interesting aspect of the VOCA Act, which is generally not considered or indeed known by some victims, is that a victim of a violent criminal act that occurs during the course of employment, for example an armed robbery or assault, can apply for compensation. Such victim can still proceed with a crime compensation application, notwithstanding they have also made an application for Workcover. The tribunal will, however, take into account any other award of compensation received by a victim applicant.[195]

Members of Victoria Police are not precluded in making such an application and I acted for a member following an incident in which he was attempting to place an offender under arrest. Unfortunately, my client suffered a serious fracture requiring a period of hospitalisation to undergo surgery, including insertion of two titanium rods. An application was made to VOCAT as a primary victim and he was awarded significant compensation, including under special financial assistance, together with an interstate holiday and gym membership, the latter to assist in his recovery. His loss of wages of some months was, of course, covered under Workcover.

An application was also made on behalf of his family members who, to put it mildly and understandably, were simply traumatised by what had taken place, even to the degree they would become very upset each morning after he finally recovered and returned to duty. Unfortunately, section 9(2) of the VOCA Act overrode any such application, which was subsequently refused by the tribunal.

If you are a victim of culpable or even dangerous driving and suffered an injury, in addition to compensation under the *Transport Accident Act 1985* (Vic), you still may be entitled to a crimes compensation payment and special financial assistance up to $10,000. This is particularly important also if the victim is deceased as a result of the culpable act, enabling a secondary and related victim to make such an application. A victim of crime may also be eligible for payment from WorkSafe Victoria in the event they suffered an injury at work during the commission of

---

[195] see section 16 VOCA Act - also see overall Relevant Review Cases -Victims of Crime Assistance Tribunal-June 2020.

a crime and, in the event a victim was injured whilst assisting police, the *Police Assistance Compensation Act 1958* (Vic) provides for compensation to be paid for any personal injuries suffered.

It is also important for victims of crime to understand and accept that VOCAT is generally precluded from making any award of compensation by way of financial assistance if the criminal act is not reported to police within a reasonable time or in situations where the victim did not assist the police investigation. In that regard, there are a number of factors that the tribunal will, however, take into account under special circumstances, including the age of the victim and whether he/she was under any disability at the time of the criminal act(s). Intimidation and threats by the offender are taken into account, as is the primary victim being under an overriding influence of trust and power from the offender.[196]

This was very relevant in one application I made for a client which was not submitted until 11 years after the offending, noting applications must be lodged within two years.[197] There is, however, a provision under this section which allows applications out of the time limit, if the criminal act took place when the victim was under the age of 18 years.

In this particular case, my client between the ages of five and 10 years old was sexually abused by her domineering male cousin who, at the time of first committing the offences including rape, was aged 13 years old. His offending stopped some five years later when he was 18 years old. My client subsequently received counselling for depression and eventually revealed to both the counsellor and her parents what had taken

---

196   see *Arnold v CCT* (unreported VSC–10 December 1992- special circumstances).

197   see section 29(1)- VOCA Act.

place many years before. The offending was then reported to police.

As a consequence and given the special circumstances, VOCAT accepted the application and, given it was not a straightforward claim that could be made administratively,[198] an appearance before the tribunal was requested. At the appearance, I made submissions including filing a two-page summary which set out, in some explicit detail, what had transpired over the five years of offending. His Honour handled the matter very well and it was apparent he had much empathy for my now tearful client. The award of compensation, together with special financial assistance, included an overseas holiday, a video camcorder for such trip, gym membership and further counselling.

It should be noted that VOCAT usually notifies the alleged offender in victims of crime applications, for example, where an offender was found not guilty, a police brief was not authorised or even when the victim had not filed a complaint with police. A victim usually has 21 days to respond to VOCAT before a determination of all the facts is made and whether any alleged offender notification is necessary. This does not mean the victim must sit in the same tribunal room if the alleged offender, on subsequent notification, elects to appear and the matter proceeds after a further directions hearing. The tribunal can elect under section 42 of the VOCA Act to close the hearing to any member of the public, if it is satisfied the applicant victim is likely to suffer distress or feel humiliated.

Pursuant to section 54 of the VOCA Act, the tribunal will also take into consideration, any criminal history of the applicant when determining any award for assistance and

---

[198] see section 33 of the VOCA Act.

compensation. This was readily apparent in one matter I was instructed in by an applicant who was assaulted as result of an attempt to steal his motor vehicle. It is fair to say, he gave "as good as he got" in the scuffle with the assailants, but did suffer some facial injuries. The matter was reported to police and I made a victim of crime application on his behalf.

Not for one moment did I think to ask if he had any criminal priors and the first I knew about his three-page list of convictions, including assaults, was when the tribunal advised by letter that they would be taking such prior criminal history into account in their determination of assistance, if any. I took the view that in all the circumstances, his chances of receiving even a reduced amount were unlikely and, on his instructions, the application was withdrawn.

To his credit, though, he continued to cooperate with police and the Office of Public Prosecutions (OPP) by way of a victim impact statement, resulting in the offender, on appeal, still being sentenced to a term of imprisonment. The lesson to be learnt though was, when acting for victims of crime, you should make them aware that any personal criminal history may impact on any award of financial assistance.

I made a victims of crime application for a client who was coward punched from behind and lucky to survive. He subsequently received the maximum payment for special financial assistance, including loss of earnings of $20,000 and medical expenses. We also tried to claim an amount for special leg braces that could assist him in the event he returned to work, given the nature of his type of employment. For some reason, the tribunal refused any assistance for this part of the application.

A decision made by VOCAT can be the subject of an

appeal to the Victorian Civil and Administrative Tribunal (VCAT), provided any such application is made within 28 days of the determination by VOCAT. This is in situations where the tribunal refuses to make award of financial assistance, the amount of assistance being awarded or simply refuses to vary an award of financial assistance.[199] In the end, we determined any application to VCAT would be a complete waste of time.

Whilst the client under section 60 of the VOCA Act is eligible to make a further application for assistance by way of varying the original award of compensation, any application for a variation cannot be made after six years from the original award. In other words, victims of crime are effectively statute barred in seeking compensation after an act of violence, regardless of them experiencing problems with a recurring initial injury.

Under section 17, a loss of earnings payment is for a maximum of up to two years and limited to $20,000, which my client had already received. This, in effect, means he had no further entitlement for loss of earnings and whilst he could seek a variation for additional financial assistance, it was limited to medical and related expenses, including counselling. My client, as any victim, is entitled to compensation for pain and suffering under sections 85A-85M of the *Sentencing Act 1991*(Vic) (Sentencing Act), providing, of course, guilt of the offenders is first determined and any such application is made within 12 months of the decision by the court. The compensation order can also include, for an offender to pay to the victim, related medical and other expenses, including counselling. Although the court is required to take into consideration the financial circumstances of the offender, any order still remains difficult

---

199   see section 59 of the VOCA Act

to enforce, especially if the offender(s) has no assets or financial means.

As a victim, my client also had the right to commence civil proceedings for damages against the offenders, following the criminal act and particularly resulting in his serious injuries. The same problem exists though, if the offenders have no viable financial means and any civil litigation commenced will incur legal costs for the plaintiff victim, which also may never be recovered from the defendants.

In 2004 in Victoria, a Victims of Crimes Register was established in respect of offenders sentenced to a term of imprisonment. This provided for victims of a violent crime to be notified when an offender, for example, is to be released from prison, or even due for parole. The latter then allows a victim to make submissions to the Adult Parole Board in respect of the application for parole. The problem though, is many victims of crime have no knowledge of such a register and that they have to make application to be registered before the can be advised of any prisoner release from custody.[200] The consequences of not registering became very apparent in respect of Bekkie-Rae Curren-Trinca, who was bashed to death by her former violent partner on the day he was released from prison. Perhaps, if she was automatically made aware of his pending release, the sad outcome may have been different.[201]

Notification does follow to registered victims of crime if an offender, whilst in prison, receives a payment of $10,000 or more from the State of Victoria, following a negligence claim for any injuries suffered during the period of incarceration by way of damages. A victim, listed on the register, is notified,

---

200   see further Victorian Victims Register- offender information.

201   *DPP v McDonough, Paul Philip* [2023] VSC 352

together with an advertisement in both the Government Gazette and daily newspapers. The compensation payment is placed in trust into the Prisoner Compensation Quarantine Fund for an initial period of 12 months to allow the victim to determine whether civil proceedings should be commenced against the offender.[202]

Of course, even in the event a plaintiff victim is successful in a civil proceeding and obtains damages against the offender after an award is made by VOCAT, section 62 of the VOCA Act requires the amount of compensation assistance awarded be refunded, if such assistance, as paid, is less, equal to or greater than the damages awarded. In other words, a victim can't, as we say, "double dip" by obtaining compensation from two different sources. A victim can lodge an appeal under section 62 to VCAT in respect of any refund but would certainly need to have an arguable legal basis.

Sadly, the bottom line for the client, who suffered terribly when he was coward-punched from behind at the hands of his two assailants, was his chances of at least recovering damages from them was very limited and really, in all the circumstances, not financially viable. Overall, the best he could hope for was a further, but limited compensation variation from VOCAT and, as necessary, Centrelink payments.

With a view to providing more support and recognition for victims, the 1985 United Nations Victims of Crime Declaration was ratified into law by the Victorian Government under the *Victims Charter Act 2006* (Vic) (Victims' Charter Act). The Victims Charter Act, as legislated, enshrined principles in law to ensure victims and persons adversely affected by crime

---

[202] see further *Corrections Act 1986*(Vic)–Part 9C-Division 2–Award of damages to prisoners.

were provided with all necessary support, in addition to being acknowledged and respected as such a victim. Its main aim was to introduce a coherent framework and combine all existing legislation and compensation rights for victims of crime.

Such victims would also now have another avenue by way of complaint or concern with the appointment in 2015 of a Victims of Crime Commissioner under the *Victims of Crime Commissioner Act 2015* (Vic). The commissioner was established in order to promote and represent the rights and recognition of victims of crime in our justice system and certainly in respect of such government recognition. Part of the commissioner's role was to also consider complaints from victims about victims' services organisations and their compliance with the principles of the Victims' Charter Act.

Despite such measures, the Victorian Law Reform Commission determined in 2016 that victims overall still felt 'marginalised and disrespected.'

In the Victims of Crime Commissioner's Annual Report of 2018-19, it was noted at page nine that two of the most common complaints in respect of VOCAT was (1) the length of time the tribunal took for applications to be assessed and (2) the victims lack of understanding of the processes of the tribunal.

A lack of respect for victims of crime rears its ugly head even in situations where a court has no choice but to seal a verdict where a defendant dies, prior to the rendering of such verdict. The anguish felt by such a victim's mother was in the case of Leisl Smith, who was allegedly murdered in 2012 by James Church. The day before a judge-alone trial verdict was to be handed down, Church committed suicide, meaning at common law the case against him was extinguished as the judge has no alternative but to seal the verdict, given there was now no accused. This left Leisl's mother as a secondary victim with no answers, not knowing what may have happened to her daughter, whose body has never been found and whether Church was responsible. This led to the New South Wales Attorney-General, Michael Daley, saying, 'this is a tragic situation for the victim's family- the circumstances are complex and raise difficult legal issues.'

In a show of respect for victims and, in the interest of justice, the law needs to be amended by legislation that will allow verdicts to be rendered in such circumstances when a trial has been completed and in the absence of the accused, due to death.

With unwarranted delays and being made to feel marginalised and disrespected was, unfortunately, very real for one of my clients. This client suffered terrible injuries as a consequence of being physically and mentally abused by her then partner, causing horrific injuries to her body, in particular her face and damage to her gums and teeth. The original VOCAT application was for psychological counselling and, importantly, remedial dental work and restorative healing skin treatments, in the total sum of around $18,000. The remedial work was in addition to the surgery she underwent for burns to her skin and a broken jaw, the latter requiring a metal plate.

Despite the application, which also included a counselling report from her treating psychologist setting out in some detail the client's untold distress and self-consciousness of the scarring and damage to her face and teeth, the tribunal was still not satisfied. Indeed, their written response was from the presiding tribunal member who considered the dental and skin work, as proposed, was simply for cosmetic purposes only.

In addition, such presiding member also required a further two medical reports, one from my client's dentist and one from her general practitioner that supported such treatment as not purely cosmetic. The tribunal required these two reports within four weeks or my client's application would be struck out. Whilst an extension in obtaining the reports was subsequently granted by the tribunal, my client was so dismayed about the time delays and the lack of sensitivity and compassion shown by them, the claim for dental and skin restoration was withdrawn.

I really took issue with the attitude of VOCAT and the presiding tribunal member in this instance. The Victims of Crime Assistance (Special Financial Assistance) Regulations 2021(SFA Regulations) defines very serious physical injury as 'actual physical bodily harm to the body of a permanent or long-term duration that involves (a) loss of body function'; or (b) disfigurement of a part of the body; or (c) total or partial loss of part of the body…'

There was no question my client indeed suffered a severe disfigurement as, every time she looked in the mirror, the injuries she suffered were seen as a constant reminder of the trauma she was subjected to. Yet the tribunal, in its wisdom, completely ignored the intent of the SFA Regulations and made her feel somewhat vain for wanting to look the way she did before the abuse, wanting to repair the damage that was caused to her appearance through no fault of her own. The tribunal's attitude was very disappointing to say the least.

In the 2020-2021 Annual Report of the Victims of Crime Commissioner, reference was again made to a plethora of consistent complaints by victims who, not only felt unsafe in our community, but felt they should be treated as fairly with equal rights as those enshrined for alleged offenders. Victims of crime, under the Sentencing Act, do have a right to make a victim impact statement, which can be by way of either a statutory declaration or sworn evidence in court. Such a statement also provides for details to any injury suffered, loss or damage and a medical report can also be included.[203]

The victim does have the option for another person to read the statement during sentencing, if they are too traumatised to make it,[204] but victims can be cross examined by defence counsel who have been previously provided with a copy of such statement.[205]

The question of fairness and rights of victims compared to offenders, came to public attention, following the sentencing in the County Court of former AFL Collingwood cheer leader, Jeffery 'Joffa' Corfe. Corfe received a 12-month jail sentence wholly suspended, for sexual assault in 2005 of a juvenile. Whilst the victim was required to provide a victim impact statement by way of a statutory declaration, the lawyers for Corfe were allowed to submit written character references that were either "undated" or had been obtained at least six months before Corfe pleaded guilty. Further, the referees had no knowledge that their old references were being used as evidence of the so called "good character" of Corfe.

These questionable references were obtained and subsequently tendered to the court, following previous sentence indication hearings which provide the court an idea of the sentence to be imposed if Corfe was to plead guilty. Such indication was, he would not be sentenced to an

---

203   see sections 8K, 8L and 8M of the Sentencing Act.

204   see sections 8Q and 8R of the Sentencing Act.

205   see section 8O of the Sentencing Act.

immediate term of imprisonment.[206] Corfe should certainly buy a Tattslotto ticket as, not only were his character refences questionable, but suspended sentences were abolished in Victoria for serious and significant offences committed on or after 1 May, 2011.[207] A suspended sentence enables the court to either suspend all or part of a sentence from imprisonment for a specified operational period, allowing the offender to reside in the community as normal, but providing that they do not commit any further offence which is punishable by a term of imprisonment.

In addition, intensive corrections orders, combined custody and treatment orders and home detention were also abolished as a sentencing or post sentence options on 16 January, 2012.[208] This was followed by a further amendment for all types of offences committed on or after 1 September, 2013.[209] Given the offending by Corfe was carried out in 2005 and the amended legislation was not retrospective, this was his only saving grace in receiving a suspended sentence.[210]

This so called "good character" system of references and a question of balance during a sentencing hearing, led to a scathing comment from the Victorian Victims of Crime Commissioner, Fiona Mc Cormack, saying:

---

206   see Part 5.6 of the *Criminal Procedure Act 2009* (Vic)–Sentence indication.

207   *Sentencing Amendment Act 2010* (Vic).

208   *Sentencing Amendment (Community Correction Reform) Act 2011* (Vic).

209   *Sentencing Amendment (Abolition of Suspended Sentences & Other Matters) Act 2013* (Vic).

210   *DPP v Corfe* [2023] VCC 253.

While victims have to submit victim impact statements as statutory declarations and abide by strict evidentiary rules, offenders' good character references are seemingly submitted without any real checks and balances...character references should be subject to the same stringent requirements...defence counsel can offer numerous mitigating factors seemingly unchallenged, while the court can rule as inadmissible the whole or any part of a victim's impact statement.

The question of the admissibility of Corfe's outdated character references, as submitted by his lawyers, who stated they followed correct process, was not challenged by the OPP, let alone ruled inadmissible by the court. The OPP, when questioned by the media, said it was 'not their job to check references.'

I found this rather perplexing as it went without saying that any character references submitted to the court, needed to be, in my view, at least dated just prior to the sentence hearing and clearly indicate that the reference is made with the full knowledge of the referee as to the matter before the court. In obtaining such letter of good character, with a copy always provided to the prosecutor, the pro forma letter to the referee that I used always included that, *the reference should state that it is given with the knowledge of the charge(s) and that our client is pleading guilty.*

In the event my client provided letters of reference that were undated and/or dated many months before the court hearing, including without the knowledge of the charge(s) as laid, they were simply not acceptable. However, it seemed the Corfe letters of "good character" escaped scrutiny, leading to the Victorian Premier Andrews calling for stricter rules. In the interim, the victim of Corfe was left to wonder about the inadequacy of our system of justice. At least victims of such offending in New South Wales can look forward to their government reviewing legislation regarding court character references, following the errors in the Corfe matter. Hopefully, Victoria will do the same in all jurisdictions and we won't see another Corfe repeat. In the interim, the County Court quietly and without any fanfare, changed its procedures covering the use of character references, which hopefully will eliminate the type of outdated references used in the Corfe hearing.

Victims of paedophile Anthony Hutchins also had the right to be aggrieved and felt let down by our justice system when he was sentenced in late May 2023 to a wholly suspended term of imprisonment, following his repeated indecent assaults of two young boys. These victims only came forward after he was sentenced to jail in the 1980s for previous abuses he committed against children when he was working with young volunteers at the Ferntree Gully "Puffing Billy" tourist attraction. It was most likely his long list of medical ailments, old age and obesity that kept him out of prison. Cold comfort for his victims.[211] Another convicted paedophile attracted to Puffing Billy was Robert Kinglsey Whitehead who, despite being convicted of offences against children in 1959, committed more disgusting acts before being convicted in 2015 on 24 child sex offences.[212] His offending resulted in a 2018 report to the Victorian Parliament by the Ombudsman pursuant to the *Ombudsman Act 1973*(Vic), in response to his victims wanting to know how he escaped justice for so long, given his predatory involvement

---

211   *DPP v Anthony John Hutchins* [2023] VCC 738.

212   *DPP v Whitehead* [2015] VCC–CR-15-00645.

with the tourist attraction and other railways went back as early as 1961, following his initial release from prison.

One of my clients, who had every right to also be disillusioned with her treatment in the criminal justice system, was in respect of a victim of crime application for special financial assistance to cover the cost of a taxi to and from her counselling sessions with a psychologist. These sessions had previously been approved by the tribunal by way of an interim award following threats by a former partner, who even fitted a tracking device to her vehicle. Police were so concerned for her safety, an intervention order was in place. As the client could not now drive due to a spinal injury, compounded further understandably by her mental health and anxiety symptoms, the only obvious transport means she had in the absence of family was by way of taxi. This was supported by her psychologist in a report to the tribunal so she could attend counselling.

Whilst I understand and accept that VOCAT does not allocate funds to victims without just cause, it seemed on this occasion they were being petty. The first application for travel expenses was refused on the basis that the client's taxi driver used a tollway, which was included as part of the reimbursement for taxi fares. In the tribunal's guarded opinion, the travel expenses should have been less, as there were back roads that could have been used as against the expense of a toll.

In a short letter in response, I advised VOCAT the toll freeway was, in fact, the shortest and most economical route compared to back roads. I further indicated, given the attitude of the tribunal, this matter should be listed before a magistrate so I could make further submissions. The tribunal responded, wanting to know what the issue was to bring it before a magistrate for hearing!! This matter was finally settled after some 11 months from the application for special financial assistance, with my client's travel expenses being approved, all except $50.

In another statement by Commissioner McCormack, she said victims repeatedly told her, 'There is a need to raise the bar for how victims are treated in the justice system.'

The bar was again certainly not raised by His Honour, Richard Pithouse, who was counselled after he made comments about an alleged rape victim in a VOCAT hearing in October 2018 as her having "buyer's remorse". He then went on to say, in further reference to the victim's alleged conduct, 'Intoxication is not an excuse for the purposes of the tribunal,' that the victim, 'put herself in that position…there is an old adage you can't profit from your own malfeasance.'

In a separate matter some six months later, it was reported in the media by journalist, Nino Bucci, that Mr Pithouse sent a highly offensive tweet. It was alleged he stated, 'It's the same situation when the legal representatives in a VOCAT matter, preparing a case by reading the police material which necessitates even further delay for alleged victim. People who live in glass houses…'

In response, Commissioner Mc Cormack, also made the comment that victims:

> …*should never have their experience trivialised…to increase these victims' trust in the justice system, it's critical that those who interface with victims are trained so they have a comprehensive understanding of the challenges victims face… There is a need for a continued focus on requiring legal professionals, including judicial officers, to undergo training to improve attitudes and understanding of victimisation, trauma*

and the ways in which the justice system can cause additional harm to victims of crime....

Unfortunately, Mr Pithouse has a number of strikes against him for his attitude to victims. In one matter, involving a victim who was subject to a brutal assault, the learned magistrate rejected the evidence before him, including the injuries inflicted and sentenced the perpetrator without conviction to a donation of $250, of all things, to the RSPCA. The victim did send a letter of complaint to the chief magistrate, after naturally being upset with her treatment and even stated to the media it felt she, 'was being treated like a dog and made me feel like I was some hysterical bimbo.'

The media even labelled him the "wrong way magistrate" after he drove to Ararat instead of the court at Ballarat and then refused to accept a victim impact statement from a sex assault victim who had flown from Queensland, invoking criticism from victims' rights groups. To make matters worse, he was also named in two other complaints, one by a welfare entity and the other by police. There was also another allegation made against him in September 2017 when Mr Pithouse failed to stop and report a traffic accident. In this matter, the Judicial Commission of Victoria determined that he made a conscious decision to keep driving and 'failed to respect and observe the law.'

It was also reported in the Herald Sun by journalist, James Campbell, that Mr Pithouse refused to grant an application by police for an urgent intervention order against a violent prisoner accused of stalking his wife. According to His Honour, to him the police were conducting a vendetta against the prisoner, even though there was evidence of threats by letter. Unfortunately, the victim was then attacked by her husband when he was released from prison, resulting in two black eyes, severe bruising with strangulation marks around her neck. So much for the so-called vendetta, as clearly it was in respect of the victim. To his credit, though, Mr Pithouse did accept the criticisms and his shortcomings after he was counselled and mentored by both Ian Gray, Chief Magistrate, and also by a retired County Court judge on the basic need to exercise 'sensitivity, courtesy and respect towards all court users, including victims.'

However, a further complaint was then made by Victoria Legal Aid (VLA) against His Honour to the Judicial Commission of Victoria (the Judicial Commission).

The Judicial Commission is a body legislated by the *Judicial Commission of Victoria Act 2016*(Vic) (JCV Act), with the principal functions of assisting the courts to reach consistency in sentencing, providing and supervising a scheme for the on-going education and training of the courts' judicial officers and lastly, to investigate complaints against such court officers. Following its setting up in 2017, a total of 1110 complaints making allegations against judicial officers has been filed with the Judicial Commission.[213]

A further complaint against Mr Pithouse was over his alleged conduct concerning a single mother he placed in custody overnight as he didn't like her "attitude", leaving her special–needs child stranded in court, before being released the following morning. The VLA complaint alleged that he:

> *used the threat of immediate imprisonment to terrify the woman ...He failed to demonstrate respect or courtesy towards the defendant at any point during the hearing, or to respect*

---

213   see Part 3 of the JCV Act-Investigations by the Judicial Commission.

> *her dignity... The officer demonstrated a lack of impartiality and integrity in that he appeared to prejudge the matter before hearing from the VLA lawyer... his decision making was dictated by his emotional state of anger rather than application of the law... allowed himself to become angry and aggressive as a result of taking the defendant's behaviour personally. In remanding the defendant in custody overnight (Mr Pithouse) made use of his judicial power to assuage his own anger.*

Mr Pithouse was stood down from court duties in early February 2023, to allow a further investigation of the allegations. He subsequently resigned from the magistracy on 14 March, 2023, but vehemently denied the allegations. Following his resignation, it then came to light that there was a further allegation against him for sexually harassing a junior solicitor in an 'unprofessional and inappropriate manner'. The Judicial Commission subsequently determined that the 'alleged conduct could be characterised as sexual harassment'. However, the panel appointed by the Judicial Commission dismissed both complaints against Mr Pithouse on jurisdictional grounds as they now no longer referred to a judicial officer, following his resignation.[214]

It was subsequently reported by the Herald Sun newspaper that Mr Pithouse allegedly topped the list of complaints for the previous five years to the Judicial Commission. He wasn't on his own though, with reserve Magistrate Crisp being ordered by the Judicial Commission to be counselled after his bullying behaviour of a solicitor after mocking his submissions and allegedly threatening to refer him to the office of the Attorney-

---

214 see section 16(2)(b) of the JCV Act.

General. The Judicial Commission described his actions as 'rude, sarcastic, discourteous…'

It is fair to say that the 'jury is still out' in respect of the rights of victims and to ensure they are treated fairly with empathy and a compassion in our justice system, whether it be civil or criminal proceedings. Indeed, the September 2021 Victorian Law Reform Commission report, *Improving the Justice System Response to Sexual Offences* (VLRC report), set out a number of measures that should be immediately introduced to make our legal system fairer, in particular for victims of sexual assault.

In further support of the comments by Commissioner Mc Cormack for judicial officers to undertake specialised training to improve their understanding of victims of crime, the VLRC report also makes particular mention of this urgent need. Whilst the report focus is on victims of sexual assault, such report emphasises, not only providing independent advocates in support of victims at all stages of the criminal process, but the training of judges and magistrates on how best to conduct such criminal trials for the benefit of both the accused and alleged victim. Whilst the Victorian Government has already implemented some of the recommendations contained in the VLRC report, to ensure equality for all in our justice system, all the recommendations need to be implemented. As reported in an earlier study of best practice communication with victims by the OPP, such equal rights should also include the active participation of victims in the prosecution process, instead of simply being told by the OPP of their decision to downgrade a charge in order to resolve a matter quickly and without the need for a lengthy trial.

The Victorian Government, in an apparent further

disregard for victims of crime, introduced a two phase *Spent Convictions Act 2021* (Vic) (Spent Convictions Act), which provides a scheme from 1 December, 2021 to automatically have minor specific convictions removed from a criminal record,[215] or by further application to the Magistrates Court from 1 July, 2022. The application to the court was required in respect of serious offences where a term of imprisonment is 30 months or more but less than five years, or no term of imprisonment for the conviction was imposed for sexual assault or a serious violent offence.[216]

The only reference to a victim is under section 19(2)(a) in that the court must consider the impact on a victim by allowing the conviction to be spent. Victims have no come back as the hearings are closed to the public, unless the court determines circumstances dictate an open hearing (section 16(2)). In any event, any hearing only requires notification to the applicant, Attorney General and the Chief Commissioner of Police (section 16(3)). Rightly so, Commissioner McCormack was again totally frustrated when her call for violent and sex offenders to be banned from making any application was totally ignored by the law maker. The bottom line was that once again victims really had no say.

The equal rights of victims of crime, or lack thereof, once again came to the attention of the public in the case of Frankston serial killer Paul Denyer, who was sentenced on three counts of murder and, on appeal, to a non-parole period of 30 years.[217] Denyer became eligible for parole after serving his full sentence, but his initial application to the Victorian

---

215 see Division 1 of the Spent Convictions Act.

216 see Division 2 of the Spent Convictions Act.

217 see *R v Denyer* [1995] 1VR 186.

Parole Board was refused. The Parole Board has jurisdiction under Division 5 of the Corrections Act to make such decisions to grant parole after prisoners serve their non–parole period.[218]

In the case of Denyer, the victims' families and friends, quite rightly, want him never to be released and fail to understand why the Victorian Labor Government refused to enact legislation, similar to that used for Julian Knight and Craig Minogue. Such legislation would amend the Corrections Act and Denyer would be prevented from making any further application to be released from prison unless totally incapacitated or about to die. Premier Daniel Andrews initially adopted the position that in his so-called educated view, it would be 'highly unlikely' any further parole application would be granted by the Parole Board. This questionable position once again left victims in a state of limbo and was aptly summed up by Liberal Democratic MP, David Limerick, when he said:

> *Every new parole application was traumatic (for the victims). Having faith in the Parole Board ignores the fact that friends and family of victims have been re-traumatised and will be dreading this happening again. The people of Frankston are clear about this. They want to ensure Denyer never gets a chance to hurt another woman.*

The Andrews-led Government continued to maintain their steadfast position and the proposed *Corrections Amendment (Parole) Bill 2023* to amend the Corrections Act, introduced into parliament by the opposition, was voted against by the Andrews Government, the Greens and Legalise

---

218   also refer *Children, Youth and Families Act 2005*(Vic) and Sentencing Act for jurisdiction of the Parole Board.

Cannabis party. Given the lack of empathy for the victims of Denyer, it left his imprisonment still not beyond doubt, leaving him open to making further parole applications as he sees fit, bringing further trauma to his victims' family and friends. Such a rejection of the bill in the Upper House led to them making a joint statement:

> *Today has been one of the worst days of our life since Denyer was granted a parole application... We have been fighting since 2021 to keep the public safe from Denyer... we have not been granted peace today. We walk away with no closure and still no idea when we will have any.*

However, Andrews, in an apparent back flip after supposedly listening to family members of the victims of Denyer, then suggested his government may give consideration to imposing a five-year ban on serial killers reapplying for parole. This was, of course, questionable whether it would give any comfort whatsoever to those victims left behind to pick up the pieces, knowing parole applications could still be made. However, newly appointed Victorian Premier, Jacinta Allen, finally listened and will now throw away the key in respect to Denyer, with proposed legislation which will ensure he remains behind bars on the same conditions as Minogue and Knight.

The trauma inflicted on such victims, regarding the initial legislation impasse over Denyer would also cause further anguish for the victims of serial rapist, William Craig Forde. He was sentenced to an indefinite jail term in 2006 but, as required under section 18A (3) of the Sentencing Act, the court must set a nominal sentence which they originally did, imposing 17 years, meaning he could have applied for release in 2023.

Forde has an appalling history with four prior rape convictions dating back as early as 1989 and had previously served 15 years for rape, including that of a 13-year-old victim and would repeatedly reoffend shortly after being released. Again, some three months after being released from jail in 2006, he raped a young mother at knifepoint and, as described by the sentencing judge, 'Offences of a gravity and extent rarely seen' and described the victim's experience as 'a prolonged ordeal of physical and mental pain, degradation, humiliation and despair.' Judge Wodak went on to say, regarding the power to impose an indefinite sentence, that there:

was very little indication of remorse ... I am satisfied that this is such a clear case (to impose an indefinite sentence). I consider that if an indefinite sentence was not imposed, there is a risk of serious danger to members of the community.[219]

Indefinite sentences were introduced in 1993 under the *Sentencing Amendment Act 1993*(Vic) and the sentence imposed on Forde of 17 years is one of four handed out to Victorian sex offenders since the inception of the amendment. Such indefinite sentences are imposed if a court is of the view that the person to be sentenced poses a serious danger to the community and, as such, it will impose a prison sentence, with no set release date.

Forde, after serving 17 years, was granted funding by Victorian Legal Aid to challenge his indefinite sentence with no release date, which gives little comfort to his victims, with

---

219   *R v Forde* [2007] VCC 1610

his 2006 victim being advised of his pending application and that he may well be granted parole. However, in September 2023 his indefinite sentence was discharged and he was ordered to be the subject of a five-year reintegration program and would be imprisoned for a further five years.[220] What was in Forde's favour was the 2015 Court of Appeal decision in respect of another convicted rapist and paedophile, Anthony John Carolan, who won his appeal against his indefinite sentence. The court determined that under the *Serious Sexual Offender (Detention and Supervision) Act 2009*(Vic), there were sufficient safeguards in place in determining that Carolan was not a threat to the community.[221]

The then Andrews-led government was again subjected to some further well-deserved criticism on their response regarding Forde and the protection of the community and victims of this depraved habitual offender. If the County Court hears his review appeal to be released, they will, of course, take into account his appalling history, that he still poses a risk, his apparent nil prospect for rehabilitation and, of course, the ongoing trauma still being experienced by his victims. Hopefully, he will be left to rot in his prison cell, noting the powers given to the Parole Board now look likely to be increased regarding serial sex offenders like Forde and he may face a further 10 years before he can apply for parole.

The other remaining on-going difficulty for all victims of crime at the moment is that our judicial system and no thanks to the COVID-19 pandemic, now has a bigger back log of cases with a reported 44 per cent of criminal matters in the Magistrates Court finalised in established time frames in 2022

---

220   *DPP v Forde* [2023] VCC 1763.

221   *Anthony John Carolan v The Queen* [2015] VSCA 167.

as compared to 90 per cent in 2014. This means protracted delays for, not only the accused, but also victims and, as such, will also apply to matters before VOCAT. There remains a total of 70,000 criminal cases still to be determined in the Magistrates Court compared to 54,0000 prior to the pandemic, whilst in the higher courts the backlog in criminal cases is still very obvious.

I note that judicial registrars who have delegated powers under the *Magistrates Court (Judicial Registrars) Rules 2015*(Vic), are able to deal with victims of crime applications under the VOCA Act in respect of both primary and secondary victims, other than applications involving sexual assaults, family violence or related victim applications. Such registrars are legally qualified and since 2006 have brought to our justice system a wide range of expertise and experience, but there is to date no exclusive judicial registrar jurisdiction.

Given the existing back log of criminal matters and VOCAT applications, perhaps the government could have considered the appointment of a number of additional judicial registrars with extended powers under the existing rules, whose sole exclusive function is the hearing and determination of all VOCAT applications. This would remove the need for magistrates to also hear such applications and provide more dedicated and experienced VOCAT members. This would certainly raise the bar for victims and it might be the right way to go, instead of the wrong way. The bottom line is though, as I would always inform victims of crime, there is 'not a pot of gold at the end of the VOCAT rainbow.'

One initiative that I do have some initial reservations about in respect of assisting victims of crime, is the Restorative Justice Program (RJ program). This program takes a different approach to justice for victims of crime, by trying to get offenders to take responsibility for their criminal actions and, at the same time, assisting victims with some form of closure and will involve a respectful mediation meeting between the victim and the offender. A similar program was implemented by the South Africa Government in 2012 known as the Victim–Offender Dialogue programme. The RJ program is, of course, voluntary, remains confidential and the participants are ably supported by not only program staff, but wider representatives of the community. One of the goals is to also challenge the offender to take responsibility for their criminal conduct and explore ways to reduce and eliminate such future behaviour.

I fully accept and understand that many victims of crime that I have acted for, did not want to be involved in such a program, let alone be recorded on the Victorian Victims Register. In many cases, the last thing they needed in their life was a face-to-face meeting with the offender that caused them so much pain. Alternatively, for some victims, it has proven to be a useful tool in reducing their levels of anxiety, giving them a chance to be heard in such a face-to-face meeting and, hopefully, some satisfaction that the offender has ultimately taken responsibility for their conduct and its implications for their victim.

A 2024 extensive and scathing report of some 516 pages by Victims of Crime Commissioner McCormack, aptly titled *Silenced and Sidelined*, after speaking with many victims of crime, brought further pressure on the government to make some urgent changes to further reduce the trauma inflicted on them. The report makes a number of recommendations to the Victorian Government to give victims a voice and to take away their lack of choice and, in particular, that the Victims Charter Act should be amended to:

> *...include victims' rights to be a protected witness, to be treated with respect, to be protected from unreasonable trial delay and noted as a participant in court.*

The Victorian Government did indeed listen to put in place a more victim-centric justice system thanks to the 2021 VLRC report, following the recommendation by the Royal Commission into Family Violence. The *Victims of Crime (Financial Assistance Scheme) Act 2022* (Vic) will take effect from 18 November, 2024 replacing VOCAT. This means victims of crime can apply online to access payments under a new financial assistance scheme. In addition, some primary victims of crime can receive an extra $25,000 in compensation, which was initially set at a maximum of $60,000. The practice of pooling and capping financial assistance at $100,000 for bereaved families has been removed, which means each family member can apply and access up to $50,000. There are also a number of other amendments in respect of secondary and related victims.

The winding up of VOCAT, to ensure victims of crime are righty treated with respect, dignity and compassion, was certainly overdue. This means victims of crime are no longer faced with the added stress of having to appear before a Tribunal Magistrate. I think some lawyers may also breathe a sigh of relief now not having to appear in VOCAT.

15
COURT DIVERSION PROGRAM

The Criminal Justice Diversion Program (CJDP) allows first time low-level offenders with the possibility of avoiding a conviction and is legislated by section 59 of the *Criminal Procedure Act 2009* (Vic) (Criminal Procedure Act). It provides an opportunity for defendants, in order to avoid a criminal record with a plea of guilty, to agree to certain conditions which normally include a letter of apology to a victim, paying compensation by donation to a nominated charity and, in some cases, to undertake counselling and any other conditions as imposed by the Magistrates Court.

It first began as a pilot program in the Broadmeadows Magistrates Court in 1997, followed by courts at Sunshine and Mildura. Its noted success followed a review some three years later when it determined that there were favourable completion rates with low-level repeat offending and in 2003 it was formally approved, following an expansion to all Victorian Magistrates Courts. The legislation for a diversion requires, under section 128A of the *Magistrates Court Act 1989*(Vic), that the defendant must acknowledge responsibility for the offence, which does not mean pleading guilty by way of a formal plea but provides for the person charged to recognise that their conduct was wrong. This is important as providing the person placed on a diversion order completes the requirements, they are then discharged at a court completion hearing without any record or finding of guilt.

Prior to proceeding by way of diversion, it must be an offence that is triable summarily in the Magistrates Court and must be agreed to by both the police informant responsible for the filing of any charge and police prosecutors before consideration by the presiding magistrate, or a judicial registrar. In the event the diversion is not approved, or the conditions not completed, it will be referred back to the court mention list for further determination by either a plea of guilty or not guilty. In situations where a diversion has been rejected by the court, there is a process of appeal to a judge sitting in the County Court of Victoria.

The Children's Court, under its Youth Diversion Service, also provides for a diversion option based on similar principles to the mainstream court requirements as set out in the *Children, Youth and Families Act 2005* (Vic) (CYF Act). Such diversion is a pre-plea option and is available to young offenders with little or no criminal history and is a further limb to a formal police caution, or a one-day interactive education program known as "Ropes" and also a range of activities to reduce the risk of reoffending. Such diversion option also requires consent from not only the accused but police prosecutors. The Children's

Court Youth Diversion Service program should be applauded as recent figures indicate that it has seen a reoffending reduction by diverting over 6,000 juveniles along another path outside the criminal justice system.

Victoria also has two types of diversion programs for drug offenders and, if a caution is not applicable, the offer of a diversion requires police consent and the quantity of drugs must be a small amount as set out in the *Drugs, Poisons and Controlled Substances Act 1981*(Vic). An offender will not be eligible for a diversion order in circumstances where they already have a criminal record, although, in some limited cases minor prior offending may not exclude diversion consideration, such as a careless drive or shop theft.

The usual procedure at court, either prior to or on the first mention date and providing police have consented, is making an application to the Diversion Coordinator for an interview, completing a questionnaire and, in some instances, the court may speak with the victim as to the appropriateness of a diversion.

In response to the coronavirus pandemic (COVID-19) to limit the face-to-face attendance at court, many applications for diversion were, as a consequence, submitted "on the papers". This involved filing an application for consideration by the Magistrates Court complete with police consent, a copy of their brief, a diversion information sheet signed by the applicant, which included antecedents such as reasons why the offending took place, family history, including the applicant's financial situation, a short outline of any defence submission in dot form, together with any matters relied on in mitigation and with good character references.

Whether it was an appearance in person before the court,

or applications on the papers, in my view, there are some inconsistencies in the diversion program, mainly involving the police informant and, on one occasion in particular, the presiding judicial officer sitting in determination to grant the diversion. I say this with no disrespect to police or the court, but in respect of police, it is open to personal bias and, on many occasions, the informant's own assessment of the bona fides of the offender or taking some offence to a suggestion that perhaps their brief was rather lacking and incomplete in a number of areas.

In one matter, my client, Fred (not his real name) was charged with a minor unlawful assault, had no priors and, on discussing the question of a diversion with the informant, it was obvious the police informant viewed Fred with some disdain and refused to agree to a diversion notice. In a summary case conference with police prosecutors, they initially took the view that in the absence of consent by the informant, it would have to proceed to court for determination. A summary case conference only applies to summary offences and not indictable offences unless the charge(s) is being heard summarily in the Magistrates Court. Generally, it is a discussion between police prosecutors and the defendant's legal representative as to the merits, or lack of, in respect of the police brief and the way forward to resolution.

I appeared before His Honour, Magistrate Tim Gattuso who, following a well-credentialed criminal law background, was appointed to the bench in November 2015. In my plea of guilty, I submitted to His Honour that the minor offending took place in a drunken pub fight for which my client took full responsibility. He had no prior criminal background, supported by a number of glowing references and I failed to see why the police would not agree to a diversion. His Honour agreed with my submissions and suggested to the police prosecutor that they needed to reconsider their position, because in his view it was most suitable for diversion. The matter was stood down and on return, a diversion was agreed to with a letter of apology to the victim and a donation to a nominated charity.

In another matter before His Honour, I was highly embarrassed as, for some reason, I never filed or tendered any character references on behalf of my client. To make matters worse, well-credentialed lawyer, Tony Hargraves, who was acting for the other co- offender had tendered a total of five references on behalf of his client in the application for a diversion. I can't say it was an oversight, as I normally always tender references regardless of the type of plea, but on this occasion my thinking at the time was that oral and written submissions would be sufficient as my client's exemplary background spoke for itself.

Clearly, His Honour was not impressed and rightly so as he could not understand why I had no references in further support of my diversion submission. At one stage, I asked His Honour "with cap in hand" to adjourn the matter, part heard, in order for me to obtain very quickly, supporting references, but after he gave me a dressing down, the diversion was granted. Not one of my better appearances to say the least and lesson learnt.

Another client, charged with three counts of unlawful assault following an incident at a northern suburbs market, finally resulted in police agreeing to a diversion, but not without a protracted "bun fight", so to speak. The client, on my instructions, on carrying out a work delivery was assaulted following an argument over illegal parking in a loading zone. He finished up in hospital with injuries but before he was transported to hospital by ambulance, police took a statement from him in which he said he had no idea who threw the first punch. This only came to light after repeated requests to the informant for a copy of his body worn camera (BWC) field interview with my client, noting the preliminary police brief didn't even include any such reference by the informant, other than in the brief summary.

In addition, police did not canvass the scene for any independent witnesses. This included not taking a statement from a security guard who allegedly witnessed what took place. I subsequently obtained a court order for a copy of all material police intended to rely on, as previously requested, however, the informant still failed to comply. Following a summary case conference again, all to no avail, an application was then made pursuant to section 401 the Criminal Procedure Act for an order for costs due to the negligence of the police informant. However, in the interim, the informant finally provided a proper brief, including his statement as informant that they intended to rely on.

It was obvious from the BWC and the subsequent statement by the informant, why he was reluctant to cooperate as he said to my client, 'Bro, you are now starting to piss me off,' in response to my client's confused and concussed state.

Unfortunately, the client, with the words used in the informant's statement, didn't do himself any favours. He had made some racially abusive comments about the other alleged victims, who had now also made supporting statements that they were indeed assaulted and only acted in self-defence, which resulted in placing my client in hospital.

The police brief was still embarrassing, to say the least. However, my client, by this stage, due to a number of mitigating personal factors, agreed to a diversion plan, which police now also consented to. One of the four conditions included completing an anger management course, donating $500 to the court fund, to be of good behaviour for 12 months and to also write a letter of apology to the victims. The original letter of apology, drafted by me, gratuitously said words to the effect, 'If my actions on the night in self-defence were deemed to be unacceptable then I apologise.'

As I was to find out, there was no way this letter was going to be accepted by the court as the diversion legislation requires the defendant to acknowledge responsibility for the offence and to recognise that their conduct was wrong. The saga was finally laid to rest when his letter of apology was amended to, 'I acknowledge my retaliatory actions and sincerely and genuinely apologise.'

I was faced with a similar situation of not accepting responsibility in another matter, but this time it involved an alleged theft and use of a credit card to the value of under $40.00. Despite my client, Gina (not her real name), explaining the circumstances of how she came into possession and use of the card, it was all to no avail. After a night of heavy drinking with her flat mate, she went to a local store the following morning and thought she was using her personal credit card. However, it was a credit card she mistakenly took from her friend's wallet. Despite even calling this person on her mobile to see if she wanted anything from the store, it was still deemed by police to be a theft.

A further mitigating factor was a week later, when she found the credit card in her car, knowing the alleged theft had now been reported to police, she attended at the local station, handed the card in and attempted to detail how, in her hungover state, it had initially come into her possession. Despite making no admissions of any criminal conduct, Gina was charged with, not only handling stolen goods, but also dealing with the proceeds of crime and obtaining property by deception and theft.

There were errors in the brief with a wrong amount, incorrect reference to the goods purchased as belonging to a bank and, in my view, the record of interview was also inadmissible, given her state of confusion due to sleep deprivation when interviewed. The matter proceeded to a summary case conference and, despite my client continuing to plead her innocence, like many clients, the protracted saga simply wore her down to a degree that she wanted it to be resolved and agreed to a diversion notice. The problem I was then faced with, in making the application for a diversion hearing on the papers, my dot point defence submission with suitable references in support failed to acknowledge responsibility and was worded, shall we say, incorrectly, when I simply said, 'Defendant inadvertently used complainant's credit card by mistake.'

This certainly was not accepting guilt despite my following statement, 'Pleads guilty at the first opportunity.'

Judicial Registrar, Julian Bartlett, who I had appeared before on other occasions and also knew quite well when he was a court registrar, understandably, was not impressed there was no acknowledgement of committing the offences and, on that basis, would not agree to the diversion. On being called in before him with Gina and, after further submissions by me, all to no avail, he suggested the matter be stood down whilst I obtained further instructions for accepting responsibility for the offending. I subsequently received such instructions and the matter was resolved with, of course, a proper letter of apology.

In another alleged assault matter and despite police agreeing to a diversion plan, the Presiding Magistrate, Richard Pithouse, flatly rejected the application and it was referred back to the court mention list. The client was charged with two counts of unlawful assault, initially only one charge pursuant to section 23 of the *Summary Offences Act 1966* (Vic), then a further charge under section 24, an assault involving a female. The latter charge was subsequently filed after I raised a number of issues with the two statements by the complainant female. Her first statement was recanted, which clearly contradicted the closed-circuit footage of what had taken place.

Not for one moment would I criticise His Honour, but it was obvious he was now doing a complete u-turn and raising the bar a lot higher for female victims. In my view, if the complainant had not been female, I suggest the diversion plan would have been a formality. Indeed, given the latter charge of assault female was withdrawn, in any event, the only charge proceeding was the initial unlawful assault, which involved my client knocking a mobile phone out of the hands of the woman who was filming him. He had no prior convictions and I also tended two excellent character references.

Of all the diversion applications I have made as the instructing lawyer, this was one I had no doubt was at the "bottom end of the scale" and the only diversion program condition police wanted was a donation to a charity, despite my client offering to provide a letter of apology. I subsequently received a telephone call from a very embarrassed court registrar advising me that His Honour had refused the diversion with the comment, 'The less I say about this, the better.'

To say my client was very unimpressed is an understatement and, of course, it was all my fault.

The diversion was not approved and he withdrew my instructions.

I did appear before His Honour Pithouse, shortly after in another minor assault of an antagonising male, by a client who was a well-known, but former neo-Nazi extremist who had a very chequered criminal history, to say the least, with a number of pages of convictions, including terms of imprisonment. Diversion was certainly not an option given his prior convictions, but on this occasion His Honour was very accommodating and only fined him, with, of course, a further conviction.

In my discussions with other lawyers about the diversion program, the consensus view held was, it was a viable option on most occasions that are deemed suitable. The problem was, in many instances it was difficult to obtain proper instructions from clients to admit to the offending as in the absence of this they would not qualify for a diversion.

Overall, the most common offences that will give rise to diversion eligibility are property offences, minor dishonesty and assault, sometimes referred to as "street offences". I still hold the view though that police maintain a degree of control and discretion whether they will agree to a diversion, which has unfortunately led to a number of inconsistencies. In addition, many clients would rather accept a diversion even though they have a very arguable defence, rather than proceed to a contested hearing with associated legal costs and, of course, face the risk of being found guilty with a higher penalty.

16
VIRTUAL COURT

COVID-19 in March 2020 also resulted in a disruption to normal court procedures with a back log of matters that left our court system in temporary disarray, together with a level of frustration for all concerned. Many criminal matters listed for mention in the Magistrates Court were simply adjourned to a later date. This included defendants on bail, provided they didn't breach their bail conditions, as in-person hearings were considered totally unsafe, certainly during the Andrews Government unprecedented lockdowns.

Our courts were left with a dilemma and, in order to overcome the mounting back log, electronic virtual court hearings were introduced across most jurisdictions, either by zoom video link, telephone, for example for civil pre-hearing conferences, and in the case of the Magistrates Court for criminal matters and particularly for a guilty plea, by way of Cisco Webex from October 2020.

In order to participate in such a virtual court hearing, we

were required to provide an email address and internet access to receive the virtual hearing link. All that was needed to join was either a computer, laptop, tablet or even a mobile smart phone. The other main requirement was that at least three days before the online hearing, it was a requirement to contact the court, usually by email, confirming my attendance and the client defendant. A link would be sent notifying of the block time, normally two hours, for the matter listed. It could be a morning or afternoon block. Once the party joined the link, they would wait in the virtual court waiting room until the matter was called.

On some occasions, we were provided with an exact time the matter would be called and on others we simply sat, albeit virtually, in the body of the court usually around 15 minutes beforehand, waiting for our matter to be called. Some matters were still listed for in-person hearings, such as urgent family violence, but unless you were advised by the court registrar that an in-person attendance was required or approved, such hearings would be conducted online.

It was an important requirement for all those participating in a virtual court hearing, that in effect we had to conduct ourselves, including defendants, as if we were physically in court. As a lawyer, I certainly had to appear in my usual court attire, a suit with collar and tie and the client at least in smart casual. The judge or magistrate was still to be addressed as "Your Honour" and we also had to be courteous and polite to opposing counsel and police prosecutors. The location of all those appearing should be in a quiet area, free of interruptions. Mobile phones and other devices needed to be switched off and, of course, we could not consume food and/or drink for the entire duration of the hearing, save for a glass of water. In addition, all virtual hearings could not be recorded and if we required a transcript in any event, they would be provided in the usual way in typed form on request.

In my criminal matters, by way of virtual hearing, I would always reiterate to my client to treat the hearing as if they were in court in person and dress appropriately. During lockdown, I would conduct the virtual hearing from my home office and would dress accordingly, albeit sometimes in track suit pants but, of course, with a suit jacket and tie, which was all that could be seen on the computer screen. Prior to the hearing and usually some 30 minutes before, I would contact the client and go over what was about to take place and ensure they understood what rules of court etiquette they had to follow. To say this fell on deaf ears on some occasions was an understatement.

It even fell on deaf ears with a lawyer I was mentoring at the time. He appeared in the virtual hearing in question, only to observe the matter. On being introduced to the presiding magistrate and despite Her Honour being told he was only there to observe, the Magistrate pointed out to me, in no uncertain terms, he was inappropriately dressed to appear in court. Mind you, he was wearing a collar and tie but no suit coat. I explained to Her Honour he was only observing with no active role but was told very bluntly, 'Mr O'Neill, any lawyer appearing in my court, albeit virtually, will still dress appropriately. I suggest he leaves now and doesn't return until he is suitably attired.'

In one drink drive matter, my client, Clint (not his real name), was sitting in front of his computer and dressed quite smartly. When I finished my plea submission, the Presiding Magistrate turned to Clint to address him about his conduct and advise of the penalty. Unfortunately, at this point, the client was sitting there with a can of beer in his hand and quietly sipping away. His Honour was most unimpressed and told me, understandably, that such behaviour was unacceptable. Whilst Clint made sure the can of beer disappeared very quickly, I have no doubt the fine may well have been increased and he was lucky the period off the road was in accordance with his blood alcohol content (BAC) reading at the time.

In another matter, I sat in the virtual court waiting room for an application for costs against police, which was listed for hearing at 2.30pm. An hour later and on not being heard, thinking the court was simply still hearing other matters before mine, I telephoned the court registrar only to be told, as I did not appear at 2.30pm, the application had been dismissed. I told the registrar I did remotely connect with an appearance, my virtual presence acknowledged by the court clerk and I was placed in the virtual court waiting room, which was standard procedure. Somehow the court clerk forgot about me and, when my matter was called, I was not connected to the applicable court. Oh, the joys of virtual court, but at least the magistrate understood it was not a technical glitch at my end and the matter was relisted to be heard some two days later.

I was certainly experienced, prior to the pandemic, in conducting telephone conciliations in the Fair Work Commission (FWC), but certainly not in contested matters. This virtual hearing, for want of a better word, was conducted by telephone and, I think, using the AAPT teleconferencing platform, for an unfair dismissal application filed out of time. I was acting for the respondent employer and, whilst the applicant was giving her evidence, I objected as, clearly, what she was saying was inadmissible. My usual experience in contested matters when appearing in person, if I had some issue with opposing evidence, I would normally stand in making my objection. When I interrupted, the commissioner admonished me and said, 'Mr O'Neill, if you are going to object, then you say "objection".' Obviously very hard to object by telephone, but lesson learnt.

One problem that also reared its ugly technical head, so to speak, in conducting virtual hearings, albeit by telephone, is when going into a private session, the FWC conciliator needs to ensure the telephone connection to the other party is disconnected. On this occasion, after completing our opening submissions in a joint session in which, shall we say, I had a real crack at the respondent employer for their conduct, the conciliator advised he would now discuss the matter in private session with first myself and the client, who we alleged had been unfairly terminated, before then having a private session with the respondent.

My learned opponent, on thinking their telephone connection was now disconnected, then made the comment that I was nothing but a "cockroach", to be heard by not only me, but the conciliator. To say the conciliator was not impressed is an understatement, giving the lawyer a right dressing down for her unsavoury comments. I have been called a few things by opposing lawyers, but a cockroach was a first. To her credit though, this particular lawyer did call me after completing the conciliation to apologise for her conduct.

His Honour, Julian Ayres, was also not impressed on a number of other occasions with technical glitches, particularly when he berated me for turning pages over during a submission, as it seemed the feedback was quite loud. The court was also not without its problems and again, before Mr Ayres, the feedback at the court's end and not me on this occasion, resulted in him leaving the bench abruptly and telling his clerk to fix the problem.

I also found some clients would appear in virtual court in their motor vehicle and, on one occasion, a client pulled over in his work truck with the engine still idling away, all to the disdain of the magistrate. Another client could not be seen no matter where he moved to and I also had some technical glitches, to such a degree I missed the first 30 minutes of one hearing. When I finally gained access, the magistrate welcomed me and simply said, 'Better late than never, Mr O'Neill.'

It became very obvious that I could not continue with Court Webex hearings, particularly for a guilty plea from my home office with various technical issues and with the client connecting to the virtual hearing from their place of residence or work vehicle. My thinking at the time was that I needed to be at least present with the client in the same room to ensure it proceeded appropriately, as if physically in court. Thankfully, on 2 August, 2020 during the second COVID-19 lockdown, the Victorian Government introduced a permit system to allow travel to work outside the five-kilometre radius restriction.

In order for the client to attend at my normal office for a virtual hearing, they would be provided with a letter on the firm letterhead, which set out why they were travelling outside the radius restriction. In addition, as part of the virtual hearing for a guilty plea, I initially made it my practice to submit written plea submissions, together with any references for placing on the court file with a copy to police prosecutors and the informant. Generally, the plea material would be perused by the presiding magistrate prior to the virtual hearing. However, this was not always the case.

In one matter, I was acting for a member of Victoria Police who had been detected driving at a high speed in a manner dangerous whilst off duty, such speed being in excess of 45 kilometres of the speed limit. As the guilty plea was proceeding by way of a virtual hearing, I submitted for filing at least a week before it, a three-page typed submission, but also with five annexures, including a psychological report and character references, in order that the magistrate could peruse them prior to the plea.

As my client was a serving police officer, the Office of Public Prosecutions (OPP) was appearing on behalf of the police informant by way of counsel they had briefed. If convicted, in all likelihood, the client would be terminated by Victoria Police where she had served diligently for some 10 years. Unfortunately, at the remote hearing, the magistrate had not read my submissions and the material attached, which I was now finding was quite a common occurrence and probably due to the heavy workload judicial officers were under.

The matter was stood down for 15 minutes and then resumed after the presiding magistrate had perused my plea submissions. Interesting though, as I was seeking a non-conviction, noting her licence would be suspended in any event, counsel for the OPP, on being asked her thoughts of a non-conviction, objected on the basis that my client was at the time on Workcover and made the following gratuitous comment, 'The defendant should be convicted as, in all likelihood and being on Workcover, won't be returning to employment with Victoria Police in any event.'

The fact my client was on Workcover was due to a number of traumatic incidents witnessed as a serving police member and was in no way related to the traffic charges before the court. I, of course, immediately objected to such a "without proper basis" statement. Whilst it was somewhat difficult in a virtual court hearing to voice my displeasure, the magistrate agreed with me that such a comment by learned counsel was baseless and certainly inappropriate.

Indeed, if I had been in court on the day, I suggest I may well have had a "quiet chat" with counsel outside the confines of the court on her ill-founded statement. I reiterated to Her Honour that my client, given she was a serving member with Victoria Police, would be terminated if convicted and stated that, 'such an outcome is unfair over and above any other member of the public would face.'

I then referred to the relevant sentencing considerations[222] whether to record a conviction, taking into account the factors in the *Sentencing Act 1991*(Vic) (Sentencing Act) namely, the nature of the offending, the character and past history of my client and the significant impact a conviction would have on her employment.[223] In my written submissions I reiterated that:

The concept of punishment and deterrence cannot overshadow some of the compelling matters in mitigation present here. The defendant is a mature age first offender. The public does not need protection from her and, indeed, Victoria Police have already suspended her right to drive a police vehicle. The defendant will, in any event, lose any licence to drive for a considerable period but such a suspension will not impact on her career with Victoria Police. It is respectfully submitted that a conviction is a poor avenue through which to deter others. Given her lack of antecedents and, indeed, the punishment that has already flowed from the conduct itself, she is specifically deterred. Overall, her prospects for reform and to teach others that such conduct is

---

[222] *Sentencing Act 1991* (Vic) section 8(1).
[223] Ibid.

> *unacceptable, is exceptional. The defendant has facilitated the course of justice through her plea.*

When making this type of submission in a virtual court hearing, it is difficult to emphasise each point you are making as, unlike being physically in court, you are seated and looking at a large screen which has, not only the magistrate in focus, but also the court clerk and the prosecutor. Also in view, is the defendant and any supporting family members. In my opinion, a virtual appearance makes it so much more difficult to assess the impact of the arguments being made. Nonetheless, a good outcome was achieved as the client only lost her licence to drive for 12 months with a fine, but without conviction.

My most "memorable appearance", for want of a better word, in a virtual court hearing occurred for a client I will simply call Will (not his real name), who was charged with a number of offences as a consequence of a road rage incident. Prior to taking his instructions, incidents of road rage were starting to rear their ugly heads, from tailgating to verbal abuse and even assaults and, in some incidents, with motorists being hospitalised. Tailgating, which could result in rear end collisions, is an offence under the *Road Safety Act 1986*(Vic) as is touching, tampering and/or interfering with another person's motor vehicle without lawful excuse. However, there is no specific road rage legislation and each incident must be assessed on its merits before any charge(s) is laid.

In this particular matter, Will consented to a guilty plea on three charges, namely damage property pursuant to section 197(1) of the *Crimes Act 1958* (Vic) and two other charges under the *Summary Offences Act 1966*(Vic), all occurring from the same incident. The two latter charges were for an unlawful assault and throwing a missile, to wit, a can of drink at the driver of another vehicle being a young woman aged in her early twenties. Unfortunately, she made the mistake, according to Will, of flashing her lights at the vehicle he was a passenger in, parked by the side of the road, when she observed him throwing a can out of the car window.

The innocent driver then regrettably stopped on the opposite side of the road to pick up the discarded can, when Will approached her in an aggressive manner, kicking and damaging the side mirror on her vehicle and then grabbed her, shouting, 'Fuck you, I'll fucking get you.'

Will's mother, who was driving their vehicle, tried to intervene and pull him away, but he still carried on snatching the victim's handbag and emptying the contents out. Still in a rage, he then threw a can at her car, causing further damage.

Will had a substance abuse problem, being a user from an early age and first came to the attention of police in his early twenties. He had previously been sentenced to a 12-month CCO for drug related offences, including trafficking, but for some years since this offending he had managed to stay out of trouble. There was also a separate police brief before the court, again for a drug related matter, and I decided to consolidate both matters and make a submission for a further CCO with conditions.

Prior to the virtual hearing, I also filed two drug assessment reports which underlined the cause of his offending with treatment recommendations, together with an exceptional character reference from a former employer. In my view and given that his mother would also appear in support of her son, I was reasonably confident that the disposition would be a CCO, together with attending a Men's Behaviour Change Program.

However, what I didn't even consider was, he may also lose his driver's licence, noting he was only a passenger in the vehicle at the time of the offending.

In June 2013, courts were provided with amended legislation, courtesy of the Sentencing Act, which allowed for the cancellation or suspension of a driver's licence for any 'conviction or finding of guilty for any offence'. This meant that the offending did not just have to be related solely to driving and the publicity given to the new powers, suggested it was in a bid to crack down on cases of road rage.

This legislation amendment went further than the recommendations to combat road rage as set out in the 2005 Victorian Government parliamentary report and, as such, was loudly criticised, in particular by the Law Institute of Victoria, as being too broad. Its president, Renay Tang, said at the time, 'If you are going to lose your licence, it should actually be related to driving offences and not to things like littering or swearing in public or offences that have no relationship to driving.'

On the other hand, Brian Negus from the RACV did say it might be appropriate for a road rage related assault but then said further that it was 'not appropriate for other assaults that have no connection to driving.'

Prior to the virtual court hearing, on Will's arrival at our office with his mother, it was obvious he was highly agitated and I suspected he may well have consumed an illicit substance prior, given his erratic behaviour. In any event, the plea proceeded before His Honour, Julian Ayres, and for all intents and purposes, I was overall reasonably happy with my submission, which basically referred to his agitated state on the day of the road rage incident, his substance abuse and interaction with drug treatment case management, including his efforts to overcome such addiction, together with difficulties in finding employment due to COVID-19.

In respect of the minor drug related matter, he was fined without conviction and, in respect of the three charges tantamount to road rage, albeit as a passenger, he was convicted and ordered to undertake a nine-month CCO, which included 50 hours of community work. His Honour also agreed that Will needed to complete a Men's Behavioural Change Program and, at this point, I was satisfied with the court's disposition and Will had also somewhat accepted the outcome.

His Honour, however, then stated that in line with section 89A(1)(a) of the Sentencing Act, 'I will also suspend any driving licence held for a period of three months'.

I am the first to admit that at no stage did I even remotely consider Will may also have lost his licence, given that, at the time of the offending, he was only a passenger, notwithstanding it was a road rage incident. It followed that I never advised him of such a possibility and it certainly came as a shock to both of us.

What followed next was also a first for me. I have acted for many miscreants over the years and, at times, they have become, shall we say, quite pissed off at the sentence dispositions imposed by the court. On this occasion, Will let loose with an outburst by standing up and yelling at the magistrate, 'You cunt!' He then proceeded to storm out of our board room continuing to yell obscenities. His Honour, probably in shock as we all were said, 'Mr O'Neill, what did your client just say? I am minded to impose a licence suspension of 18 months if he is going to carry on like that.'

I quickly apologised and, at this point, I really thought His Honour would stand the matter down as part heard and require my client to appear before him in person the following day, where I had no doubt he would be placed in the cells for his conduct. I also considered that if the hearing had been in person at the court and not virtual, Will would have been quickly marched out by court security after being sentenced to 30 days imprisonment, as was Bubble O' Bill for his contemptuous carry on before Mr Crisp. Mr Ayres did not increase the licence suspension, however, and did not require my now former client to appear before him. I notified the court the following day that I had ceased to act and that was one idiot I would no longer have the "pleasure" to act for, noting he never paid my account.

In my view, it remains to be seen of the benefits of virtual hearings in our judicial system. As a practitioner who has appeared in many in person court hearings during the past 25 odd years, I personally found it very difficult appearing remotely compared to actually being in court. I also think initially there was some scepticism amongst legal practitioners and other court users and we all thought such virtual court hearings would only be a short-term temporary strategy and, after the pandemic, it would revert back to normality with in-person hearings.

It has been suggested, however, that virtual or remote court hearings are more efficient, provide greater flexibility and allow hearings to be resolved with less time-consuming banter and discussions between opposing counsel, than what generally occurs in a physical court. There is also the suggestion that the reduction in travel results in a cost savings but compare all these benefits against the behavioural problems I sometimes experienced in those attending virtual court, as opposed to physical court, I wasn't so sure.

Following the easing of the pandemic lockdowns and with a large back log and significant delays in matters being heard, particularly in the Magistrates Court, there is now a choice offered whether a hearing will be held in person, but only on application, virtually or perhaps even using a combination of the two. Whilst being very much old school, I certainly preferred appearances in person, but love it or hate it, virtual court hearings are here to stay.

17
FOOL FOR A CLIENT

In my early days' foray into law, my then principal, John Hall, introduced me to the saying, 'That a man who is his own lawyer, has a fool for a client', and he wasn't just referring to me as the April Fool's Day lawyer. This English proverb was first believed to have been referred to in a novel as far back as 1814 by Henry Kett titled *The Flowers of Wit*. There is also some suggestion that a few years earlier in 1809, it was used by a prominent legal scribe by the name of Bryan A Garner, when he said, 'He who is always his own counsel will often have a fool for his client'.

Self-representation, whilst generally viewed by lawyers as, shall we say, 'not a good idea', is allowed in Victorian courts in both criminal matters under section 328 of the *Criminal Procedure Act 2009*(Vic) and also in civil matters, courtesy of section 100(6(a) of the *Magistrates Court Act* 1989 (Vic), *County Court Act 1958*(Vic) and *Supreme Court Act 1986*(Vic) and including their Rules and Practice Notes. It is also not uncommon for a court to allow an individual or organisation to act as a friend of the court, known in Latin as "amicus curiae", to assist the court with their particular expertise and, as stated by Lord Salmon in *Allen v Sir Alfred Mc Alpine & Sons Ltd* [1968] 2 QB 229 at page 266:

I had always understood that the role of amicus curiae was to help the court by expounding the law impartially or, if one of the parties were unrepresented, by advancing the legal arguments on his behalf.

In the United States of America, it is also referred to as an intervenor under what is termed an "amicus brief", whilst in Canada the concept of amicus curiae is usually a lawyer who can make proper legal submissions on behalf of a self-represented litigant to assist the court in reaching a decision.

In Australia, in matters involving either family violence or allegations of sexual offending, respondents and defendants may be precluded from self-representation and will need to engage a lawyer to act. The Federal Circuit and Family Court of Australia allows unrepresented litigants to appear in their own right, but generally in highly contested divorce applications, which also involves property and child custody issues, it is not a good idea to self-represent as the outcome might well not be what is hoped for.

In the Victorian Civil and Administrative Tribunal(VCAT), a person may need to seek leave to have a lawyer act and, in goods and services cases under the value of $15,000, a person is generally precluded from having a lawyer or other type of professional person to appear on their behalf.[224]

---

[224] see section 62 of the *Victorian Civil and Administrative Act 1998* (Vic).

In the Fair Work Commission (FWC), if a lawyer is engaged to act, such lawyer would need to seek leave to appear, which is not always granted.[225]

There is also the concept of what is known as a "McKenzie friend" which, with leave of the court, such a person can assist a self-represented accused by taking notes, making suggestions and such a friend does not need to have legal qualifications.[226] Such a concept has also been allowed with leave of the court, where appropriate, in complex matters for the friend to make oral submissions on behalf of a self-represented accused.[227]

A court does have complete discretion whether to allow the use of a McKenzie friend[228] and will generally take into account the complexity of the evidence and issues in dispute. It should be noted that an accused's decision to not accept legal aid is one very important factor in determining whether to allow such a friend.[229] In criminal trials, it is common for judges to refuse to grant leave as it is generally considered the hearing will become prolonged and could result in a fair trial or even a miscarry.

Understandably, the difficulty many people face regarding legal matters, leaving them with little choice but to self-represent, is the financial burden they are confronted with as "lawyers do not come cheap".

That financial burden may well certainly increase if, for

---

225   see section 596 of the *Fair Work Act 2009* (Cth).

226   see *McKenzie v McKenzie* [1970] 3 All Er 1034; Collier v Hicks (1831) 109 ER 1290.

227   *Li v So* [2021] VSCA32; *Nepal v Minister for Immigration and Border Protection* [2015] FCA 366.

228   *Smith v R* (1985) 159 CLR 532.

229   *R v Burke* [1993] 1 Qd R 166.

example, a costs order on either the court scale of costs or on an indemnity basis is made against the unsuccessful self-represented litigant. In some cases, unrepresented civil litigants may face an application prior to judgment by the other party for security of costs to be paid, as directed by the court.[230]

Such an application usually applies in situations where it is believed the unrepresented party is financially lacking in funds but is at the discretion of the court.[231] Security for costs in unfair dismissal matters may also apply in the FWC and, if granted until the amount ordered is placed in trust, the case before the commission will be adjourned.[232]

There is, however, available to those contemplating self-representation, a number of local community legal centres able to assist with free legal advice and determine eligibility for assistance based on a number of factors, which does not include means testing. Assistance may also be available from Victorian Legal Aid (VLA), depending on the applicant's financial situation, as they cannot provide legal representation in all court matters. Any assistance, including legal advice and appearing in court, will depend on a means test in determining eligibility. In addition, VLA has duty lawyers available at many courts and tribunals to assist most people who are unrepresented,

---

[230] see regulation 62.02 of the *Supreme Court (General Civil Procedure) Rules 2015 (Vic)*, the *County Court Civil Procedure Rules (2018)* (Vic) and the *Magistrates' Court General Civil Procedure Rules 2010*(Vic).

[231] see for example *Livingspring Pty Ltd v Kilger Partners* [2008] VSCA 930; *Spiel v. Commodity Brokers Australia Pty Ltd (In Liq)* (1983) 35 SASR 294.

[232] See section 404 of the *Fair Work Act 2009* (Cth) and Rule 55 of the *Fair Work Commission Rules 2013*(Cth) also see for example *O'Reilly v. SA Waste Management Pty Ltd* [2011] FWA 4229.

but again conditions still apply. The Law Institute of Victoria (LIV) also provide a free 30 minute, no obligation, consultation with a selected law firm on application.

I found people representing themselves, particularly at the Frankston Magistrates Court in criminal matters, did so for a variety of reasons and excuses. With no disrespect, mention day, which was usually a Wednesday at Frankston was what we lawyers would sometimes refer to as the "zoo". It would usually be very busy with many unrepresented defendants from different backgrounds and some, sadly, still affected from substance abuse. It was not uncommon for police protective services officers (PSOs) on duty to escort some from the court precinct or separate those for whatever reason in dispute.

The presiding magistrate would certainly encourage such self-represented person to seek legal advice before the next adjournment date or stand down the matter in order for advice to be obtained from the duty lawyer. Leniency, for want of a better word, was certainly given to those who were unrepresented and it was not unusual for a defendant to request a further adjournment, even for example, on the third mention date. This allowance was never afforded to those represented by lawyers though and the best we could hope for was adjoining the first mention date without an appearance. We would then have to appear in court with some good excuse at the next mention date as to why the matter could not proceed, either by way of a guilty plea or by way of a plea of not guilty and listed for a contest mention.

It was not uncommon to be approached by those unrepresented, to see if I would act for them whilst at court or at a later adjourned date. I recall when one rather dishevelled middle-aged chap approached me after I had finished a guilty plea in a criminal matter and asked for my business card. It seems, he was rather impressed by my plea submissions and the outcome I obtained for the client and wanted me to act for him in respect to a number of criminal charges he was facing. As I was leaving court, he politely asked what my hourly charge out rate was and, understandably, that was the last I heard from him. I did of course encourage him to seek advice from the duty lawyer or make a VLA application.

Self-represented clients have to be very careful when appearing without legal representation, particularly in criminal matters where they are facing the distinct possibility of imprisonment. Such defendants should really consider what alternate options are available to them and whether they have the ability, not to mention the resources, needed to navigate our complex legal system. It is not just a matter of standing up in court and having your say, but the requisite skills to argue points of law with police prosecutors and make proper submissions to the court. Most magistrates don't tolerate fools and that also applies to lawyers, particularly those just recently admitted to the legal profession.

Some lawyers, me included, have, at times, struggled to remain clear-headed and not be intimidated by an opponent or the presiding judicial officer. Courts are generally open to the public and the body of the court room can be crowded of with attendance by school pupils undertaking legal studies. I have seen many a lawyer in certain situations become very rattled and I can recall in my early days many a time that would happen with me. All I could do in that situation was trying to refocus or request the matter be stood down, whilst obtaining 'further instructions' from my client.

I can understand self-represented litigants would

certainly have similar difficulties in those sorts of situations, keeping in mind they need to know the law and the legal process, including, as applicable, paying court fees, the filing and service of documents, subpoenaing witnesses, all very time consuming and costly. The Victorian County Court has on its web page detailed information to assist those thinking of self-representation in both civil and criminal matters. The court also has self-represented litigant case managers who can provide necessary support to guide people through court procedures.

There are also a number of other alternatives available instead of court proceedings, including Dispute Settlement Victoria and the Resolution Institute. The bottom line is, though, self-represented litigants really need to think carefully about taking such a path as they may well have a fool for a client, namely themselves.

18
A BLIGHT ON THE LEGAL PROFESSION

In order to practice law in Victoria, you must first be qualified with a Bachelor of Laws from an approved university and then make application, deeming yourself as a fit and proper person and eligible for a practising certificate. In the event you do not have an offer from a law firm or other approved entity to practice law, you are unable to apply. All new lawyers admitted to practice with their first practising certificate will then be under supervision as part of the legal practice requirements.[233]

Our profession is governed by the Legal Services Board and Commissioner (LSBC) established on 12 December, 2005 under the *Legal Profession Act 2004*(Vic) and as of 1 July, 2015, courtesy of the *Legal Profession Uniform Law Application Act 2014*(Vic) (LPULA Act). The legislation and its uniform rules impose strict requirements on lawyers as officers of

---
233   see further *Legal Profession Uniform Admission Rules 2015*.

the Supreme Court and that the administration of justice is paramount, followed by acting in their best interests when representing clients, adhere to their lawful instructions and, of course, complete the legal work not only competently and promptly but at all times acting in an ethical manner.[234]

The introduction of the legislation also saw the broadening of volunteer practicing certificates in Victoria. Such practising certificates only allowed the holder to practice as a community legal service volunteer. From 1 July, 2015, any Victorian lawyer, the subject of a volunteer practising certificate, was allowed to practice, not only as a volunteer at a community legal service, but also on a pro bono basis. The Latin phrase is "pro bono publico", in other words for the good of the public in the provision of providing legal services for free and generally viewed as assisting the disadvantaged in our community to access our system of justice without the additional burden of legal costs.

One practitioner who was on a restricted practising certificate and I have no doubt he meant well, unfortunately, was subject to the wrath of the LSBC for contravening the restrictions placed on his practising certificate. He was the subject of 10 charges of misconduct for condition contraventions when he was a local community legal centre volunteer. The disciplinary charges alleged that on his application for a practicing certificate, he provided false information saying he was only a volunteer on a limited practicing certificate. At the same time, he had continued to conduct himself as a legal practitioner with a full certificate, including appearing before

---

[234] see further *Legal Profession Uniform Law Australian Solicitors Conduct Rules 2015; Legal Profession Uniform Legal Practice (Solicitors) Rules 2015*, noting there are separate Rules applicable to barristers.

judges in certain courts. Whilst I considered his intentions were most likely not meant to be dishonourable, such false declaration led to him being found guilty of unsatisfactory professional conduct.

As legal practitioners, we have two main duties, amongst others, and if there is any conflict between the two, our responsibility to a client comes second behind our paramount duty to the court. As a legal practitioner, we have a duty to not only be competent but totally frank and open when appearing before the court, including in criminal and civil matters, which also extends to our opponent.

Lawyers have an overarching obligation to their clients in civil matters and such stringent conditions are set out in the *Civil Procedure Act 2010* (Vic) (Civil Procedure Act). Such obligations extend to all parties, not only when pursuing a civil claim, but also defending a civil action, which must have a proper basis by filing such certification, including to disclose all discoverable documents in a timely manner as each party 'has a paramount duty to the court to further the administration of justice…'.[235] Any contravention of such overarching obligations can have significant cost sanctions against the lawyer and/or client and rightly so.[236]

Unfortunately, our legal profession has been tarnished over time by not only lawyers but also legal clerks acting unethically and committing acts of professional misconduct, including misappropriation of client funds held in trust. This blight on our profession is disgraceful as are those fools masquerading

---

235 see overarching obligations under sections 16-27 of the Civil Procedure Act.

236 see sections 28-31 of the Civil Procedure Act.

as lawyers, with no legal qualifications whatsoever, acting and appearing in court for their unsuspecting clients.

One such miscreant came to the attention of the public in the form of David Jensen. Jensen pretended he was a qualified and registered lawyer, acting for unsuspecting clients in the Gippsland region. Despite warnings from the LSBC and a 2018 court injunction banning him and his associated entities from posing as a lawyer,[237] this charlatan continued to provide legal advice without any concern whatsoever for his clients. Not only did he act without any legal qualifications, he also posed as a health professional and treated cancer patients.

Jensen was subsequently banned by the Health Complaints Commissioner after one of his patients died of cancer, so he then turned to his other profession, masquerading as a lawyer, even representing clients in court. Jensen was subsequently sentenced in the Supreme Court in October 2022 for contempt of court[238] to a three-month term of imprisonment, wholly suspended for one year. Any breach by again offering legal services would see him jailed. His Honour, Justice Dixon, stated that, 'Mr Jensen's contempt should be regarded as most serious.'

It remains to be seen whether Jensen will see 'the errors of his ways'.[239]

Another embarrassment and blight on our legal profession was the circumstances and publicity surrounding the conduct of Sara Grasso. Her actions, under the guise of being a qualified

---

[237] *Victorian Legal Services Board and David Jensen & Ors* [2018] VSC 740.

[238] see Order 75 of the *Supreme Court (General Civil Procedure) Rules 2015* (Vic).

[239] *Victorian Legal Services Board and David Jensen & Ors* [2022] VSC 603.

and registered lawyer with fake degrees and scholarships, conned not only her family and friends, but all and sundry who would listen. However, it was all a sham. Grasso had everyone believe she had now been admitted to the Victorian Bar, posing in her barrister's wig and gown before 70-odd guests, including lawyers, telling them 'This is what I have to wear in court,' and that she was also a member of the Law Institute of Victoria.

As a consequence of her charades, including giving so-called legal advice to unsuspecting family members and cheating them out of $660,000, Grasso was ultimately convicted after pleading guilty to theft and related offences, including obtaining financial advantage by deception.

At the time of her committal, Geoff Wilkinson of the Herald Sun reported that even after Grasso received legal advice to plead guilty from 10 different lawyers, her unwavering belief in her own legal abilities resulted in her sacking the lawyers and representing herself at the committal. Grasso was subsequently convicted and sentenced in 1995 to three and half years' imprisonment. One of the police investigators made the comment that although her legal knowledge was flawed, she was 'good enough to rip off gullible naïve people.'

Hopefully we have seen the last of this fake lawyer.

Criminal prosecutions from law firm trust account deficiencies are another poor reflection on our profession, which has not just involved lawyers committing thefts, but also law clerks, with one paralegal, during the period 2013 to July 2017, misappropriating client trust funds in the order of $1.56 million, resulting in a guilty plea to a total of 16 indictable charges. Another paralegal, by the name of Domenic Mak, stole $2 million from his firm's property clients by falsely representing his personal bank account to be the law firm's trust account. This offending took place over some eight months and in August 2020, Mak was sentenced in the County Court to a four-year term of imprisonment.[240]

In another theft from a solicitor's trust account, involving an employee of the law practice, this brazen conduct led to a contract killing in May 2000, resulting in the murder of solicitor, Keith Allan. In this unfortunate turn of events, law clerk, Julian Clarke attempted to cover up his theft of large sums of money by having Allan murdered. His body has never been recovered. Clarke and his two accomplices were ultimately convicted and sentenced to lengthy terms of imprisonment at the third trial for the murder of Allan.[241] This followed two earlier trials in the Supreme Court of Victoria, with a Victorian Court of Appeal annulment of the jury verdict in the first trial, followed by a hung jury in the second trial.

Despite the sad circumstances, this case was significant at the time as the Court of Appeal held that the judge in the first trial, should have better explained to the jury the standard of proof and meaning of the criminal standard of "beyond reasonable doubt" for a guilty verdict, which cannot be expressed in percentage terms.[242] This is unlike in civil jurisdiction where the term "on the balance of probabilities" is analogously described by most lawyers as "more likely than not" or a percentage of greater than 51.[243]

---

240 *DPP v Domenic Mak* [2020] VCC 1233.

241 *DPP v Cavkic, Athanasi, Clarke* [2004] VSC 158.

242 see section 141 of the *Evidence Act 2008* (Vic).

243 see section 140 of the Evidence Act- also refer *Briginshaw v. Briginshaw (1938)* HCA 34 60 CLR336 at 362 – also referred to as the Briginshaw Principle in that the common law recognises two different standards of proof.

In 2017, the LSBC released a statement in which they named a person with 14 aliases, in an attempt to stop her brazen fraudulent conduct, in which she embezzled at least $1.5 million from her employer's law trust account. Unfortunately, the law practice was not aware of her criminal background when they employed her some years earlier; such crimes resulting in convictions for theft and even terms of imprisonment. It was most likely her use of fake names, such as "Athena Bouzas" and "Teena Zissiadis", that allowed her to continue with these unrelenting criminal escapades. This, now former, paralegal, Athena Razos, was sentenced in the County Court by His Honour, Judge Kelly on 19 July 2024 to five years and three months imprisonment with a non- parole period of two years and nine months.[244]

An alleged ethical breach by local solicitor, Francis McGrath, was brought to my attention by a client who he previously represented. In my view, I had no choice but to report the alleged breach to the LSBC. As a matter of courtesy, I advised this particular lawyer that I was now acting for his former client and, on the instructions provided to me, I had to report his alleged misconduct. I did receive a response from this practitioner to the effect that the allegations simply had no basis.

The alleged improper conduct then extended criminally to a fascination with child pornography, when first acting in an incest trial. On sentencing, after pleading guilty to possessing child pornography between 1 July, 2007 and 8 February, 2008 contrary to section 70(1) of the *Crimes Act 1958*(Vic) and using an online information service to publish child pornography, contrary to section 57 of the *Classification (Publications, Films*

---

[244] *DPP v Athena Razos* [2024] VCC 1077.

and Computer Games)(Enforcement) Act 1995 (Cth), he was sentenced to 12 months imprisonment on each charge to be served by way of an intensive corrections order. McGrath was subsequently sentenced, after pleading "not guilty" for again possessing child pornography in February 2009, to 290 days imprisonment with 90 days suspended, which he appealed. Such despicable conduct was described by Magistrate Keil as looking 'into an amphitheatre of hate...I look at these children and see their innocence destroyed...'

McGrath was also registered as a sex offender for life. In addition, and rightly so, the now retired solicitor was struck off the legal practitioners roll in 2010 by Supreme Court Chief Justice, Marilyn Warren.

Her Honour stated he was:

> *not a fit and proper person to be on the roll... He allowed his criminal conduct to germinate from his professional practice without recognising the deviance of his sexual interest, the seriousness of his offences, or controlling urges that the court and the community regards as callous, predatory and exploitive in the extreme... [his conduct was] completely inconsistent with his membership of the legal profession.*[245]

I am not aware of the result of the appeal or the jail sentence, by the now disgraced former lawyer, nor was I advised by the LSBC of the outcome of my complaint.

Another local solicitor, Michael Kesik, who I knew reasonably well, also ran afoul of his ethical obligations but this time it was regarding trust account deficiencies, such offending being committed over a long period. His misconduct

---

[245] *LSB v Francis McGrath* (No 2) [2010] VSC 332.

was mainly to use his clients' trust monies, in the order of $500,000, to support his legal practice and, as a consequence, he was sentenced to three years imprisonment, with a non-parole period of 18 months.[246] Unfortunately, Kesik also had a previous misconduct matter in 1995, in which he was referred to the Legal Services Board for overcharging clients for his professional costs. For that breach, he was fined $4,000 and ordered to repay the sum of $20,000.

Theft from a solicitor's trust account was also committed by the principal of law firm Coulter Roache Legal (now known as Coulter Legal) when Kevin Roache stole in the order of $420,000. What made his conduct more appalling was the monies were taken from two deceased client estates. Following his plea of guilty to seven counts of obtaining property by deception, the lawyer for Roache made pre-sentence submissions that his client's perilous financial situation, to support another ailing business venture, was the main reason for his offending. This former, now bankrupt, lawyer,[247] now suffering from dementia and mental health issues, was subsequently sentenced to 28 months imprisonment with a non- parole period of 12 months with His Honour Chief Justice, Peter Kidd, saying:

> *While the courts often see higher sums involved in solicitor frauds, the sums here, in total, were not small. You committed these offences while occupying a position of trust and responsibility as a legal practitioner…responsible for administering the deceased estates.*[248]

---

246   *R v Kesik* [2006] VSC 493.

247   also see *LSBC v Kevin Roache* VCAT J50/2021.

248   *DPP v Kevin Roache* [2023] VCC 1034.

Mario Condello was also once an infamous lawyer with a sordid reputation as a member of the "Carlton Crew", alongside such other convicted criminals as Alphonse Gangitano and Graham Kinniburgh. Condello had a crime background, included convictions for arson and fraud and was allegedly involved in a number of murders. Like Kinniburgh, he met his maker when he was shot dead in the driveway of his home in February 2006. This led to Robert Richter KC, advising the trial judge the next morning that Condello would not be appearing in court over a conspiracy murder charge as he 'was murdered last night...he died confident of his acquittal.'

Condello was, however, somewhat popular with over 700 people attending his funeral with a number of Melbourne identities acting as pallbearers, including "mediator and debt collector", Mick Gatto.

One other very high profile, flamboyant lawyer, Andrew Fraser, acted for many criminal identities, including Lewis Moran, Dennis "Mr Death" Allen and even corporate magnate and fraudster, Alan Bond. On one occasion, he was also wrongfully accused by Jason Moran, who pulled a gun on him, of being a police informer. Fraser simply told him he was a friend of his father, Lewis, and to basically 'piss off home' and behave himself.

Fraser was certainly held in high esteem by the legal profession and also represented the alleged 1988 Walsh Street police killers who were found not guilty. Unfortunately, Fraser, formerly a tenacious criminal defence lawyer but now a drug addict, was to join some of his clients in jail, being sentenced in December 2001 to a minimum of five years after he pleaded guilty to trafficking and importing cocaine to the order of a street value of $2.7 million. To his credit, Fraser turned his life around after serving his period of incarceration, being released in September 2006, first by turning Crown witness after convincing the Director of Public Prosecutions of what he knew about convicted double murderer, Peter Dupas' involvement in the then unsolved 1997 murder of Mersina Halvagis at Fawkner Cemetery.

After two trials, Dupas was also convicted of that murder, largely thanks to the evidence of Fraser from what his former cellmate had told him.[249] Whilst Fraser was a former blight on our legal profession, he then went on to become a best-selling author and his film, *Murder in the Outback*, won an Australian Academy of Cinema and Television (AACTA) award in 2020 for best factual documentary. Fraser passed away in 2023.

The theft of over $250,000 from six unsuspecting clients saw solicitor, Michael Bakhaazi, jailed in December 2006 for three years and three months. He blamed such stealing on his rampant gambling habit and a failed marriage.[250] In the matter of *R v Gabriel W* [2006] VSC 397, this recalcitrant solicitor pleaded guilty to a total of 13 charges, including theft and obtain financial advantage by deception, after stealing more than $1 million in client trust monies. Once again, a gambling excuse was part of his plea which fell on deaf ears, being sentenced to nearly six years on the top with a bottom of three and half years before being eligible for parole.

In another misconduct prosecution in the Victorian Civil and Administrative Tribunal (VCAT), the Law Institute of Victoria (LIV) sought a 50-year ban against a solicitor to not hold trust monies. This particular lawyer had taken $75,000 of monies held in trust for clients. This ban was deemed manifestly

---

249   *R v Dupas* [2006] VSC 481.

250   *R v Bakhazzi* [2006] VSC 496.

excessive by the presiding VCAT member, who only ordered a suspension for holding trust monies for the next 20 years with a two-year ban in applying for a practicing certificate. The LIV had also, unsuccessfully, sought for him to be referred to the Supreme Court to be struck off the roll of legal practitioners.[251] In any event, County Court judge, Lex Lasry, had already sentenced him to 18 months imprisonment wholly suspended, due to his mental illness.

Corporate lawyer, Andrew Nguyen, was also struck off on August 2013 following a VCAT recommendation as it was determined he was 'not a person of honesty', after he was found to be guilty of professional misconduct, which involved lying to a judge in a separate disciplinary hearing. Nguyen was found to be engaged in legal practice and holding himself out as such, whilst he was not qualified nor entitled to do so.[252]

Bentleigh lawyer, David Chapman, after being arrested with a loaded weapon and charged with drug trafficking and possession and perverting the course of justice, spent 47 days in custody before receiving a suspended sentence of 20 months wholly suspend for two years.[253] Chapman was struck off the Supreme Court roll for legal practitioners in June 2019. Another lawyer, Kim Blackberry, spent seven years evading arrest, following the theft of over $200,000 from his conveyancing clients and was sentenced to two years imprisonment after his run from police finally came to an end.[254]

Another disgraced solicitor, in order to fund his opulent lifestyle and renovate his luxurious Balwyn home, stole over

---

251   see *Law Institute of Victoria v DSS* [2008] VCAT 1179.

252   *LSC v Nguyen* [2013] VSC 443.

253   *DPP v David Chapman* [2013] VCC 2139.

254   *DPP v Kim Charles Blackberry* [2019] VSC 279.

$1.75 million from his clients from monies held in trust. His written and signed guilty plea, pursuant to section 216 of the *Criminal Procedure Act 2009*(Vic), proceeded in the County Court in 2020 and Judge John Champion noted that his blatant offending had 'brought the entire legal profession into disrepute.'[255]

Hopefully his four-year minimum sentence will give him time to think about the error of his ways, noting his appeal against sentence failed.[256]

All that offending though, pales into insignificance when compared to jailed former lawyer, Hisam Mahmoud Sidaoui, who holds the record for damaging the legal profession and thieving from unsuspecting clients, when he swindled a total of $16.8 million from financial institutions in the names of, not only his friends and acquaintances, but also family members.[257] The LSBC in 2019, paid out in the order of $5.2 million for 17 claims, including to victims of Sidaoui and he was struck off the roll of practitioners in November 2018.

Victims of such despicable crimes might get some limited satisfaction for such periods of incarceration and from the Victorian LSBC Fidelity Fund (the fund), which also provides for compensation to be paid to victims due to the dishonest and fraudulent shenanigans of lawyers, including paralegals. It remains as a reminder and example of the blatant corruptible misconduct of those few miscreants in our profession. There were a total of 24 new claims against the fund seeking compensation in 2021–2022 in the order of nearly $5 million.

Victoria is, of course, not alone with having its share

---

255   *DPP v Kotsifas* [2020] VSC 347.

256   *Kotsifas v The Queen* [2021] VSCA 368.

257   *R v Sidaoui* [2018] SCR 0220.

of disgraced and jailed lawyers, with Sydney solicitor and accountant, Dev Menon, being sentenced to a jail term of 14 years with a minimum of nine years. His criminality, from around June 2015, involved a payroll scheme that cheated the Australian Tax Office (ATO) of $105 million. Justice Anthony Payne, in sentencing Menon in the New South Wales Supreme Court in respect of conspiracy to dishonestly cause a loss to the Commonwealth and deal with the proceeds of crime, was scathing of his conduct and said he 'abused his position' (as a solicitor) and also relied on his legal skills to:

> *derail the proper administration of the law for the benefit of the criminals in which he acted in concert. He was involved for long hours and exercised his legal skills to give effect to the conspiracies. His behaviour in accepting funds…which should have been paid to the ATO is thoroughly discreditable conduct for a solicitor to engage in.*[258]

As further detailed in the 2022 Annual Report of the Victorian LSBC, a total of 1,071 lawyer complaints were lodged with around 60% over costs and related negligent service matters, whilst 36% were possible lawyer professional conduct breaches. A total of 13 disciplinary matters were ultimately determined by the Victorian Civil and Administrative Tribunal, with one successful application made by the LSBC to the Supreme Court to strike off a lawyer from the legal practitioners' roll. In addition, the LSBC issued a direction to a total of 14 people, who were deemed to be unqualified in conducting a legal practice or were acting as a lawyer without a current legal practicing certificate.

---

258   *R v Dev Menon* [2023] NSWSC 768.

Unfortunately, our profession will continue to have a number of unscrupulous individuals as well as qualified lawyers acting without conscience. Of course, the "Lawyer X scandal" was another in a league of its own, bringing our legal profession once again into disrepute.

19
THE LAWYER IS A SNITCH

Our uniform rules require all lawyers with a practising certificate complete a minimum of 10 continuing professional development units (CPDU) in each year of practice, including at least one CPDU in ethics and professional responsibility, professional skills, substantive law and practice management and business skills.[259]

By the 31st of March each year, we must have completed the CPDU and are required to advise the Legal Services Board and Commissioner we have met this requirement when applying for a renewal of our practising certificate. If this obligation is not adhered to and, in the absence of any exemption to undertake 10 units, the LSBC can put in place a plan to rectify the non-completion.

---

259   see *Legal Profession Uniform Continuing Professional Development (Solicitors) Rules 2015*.

One of our CPDUs was specifically focused on a fundamental tenet of our profession that is, legal professional privilege, also known as client legal privilege. This English common law right in respect of a lawyer maintaining client confidentiality and disclosures, including providing legal advice to a client, was established as far back as the 16th century. Such client privileged instructions are sacrosanct and may only be disclosed with the direct permission of the client and underpins the proper administration of justice, unless such disclosure threatens the safety of the community.

These professional obligations were about to be trashed, as one CPDU particularly came about after the disclosure in 2019, involving barrister Nicola Maree Gobbo, with her identity initially supressed as "Lawyer X". Gobbo, unbeknown to her clients, was a registered police snitch (informer), providing confidential client instructions and communications from her clients to Victoria Police, despite at the same time, representing those clients in court.

In other words, Gobbo, with police informant registration number 3838 in 2005, was not only acting as a defence lawyer for her clients but simultaneously telling tales about them and their criminal acquaintances as a registered agent of police. Her involvement with police was prior to her 1996 admission in the Supreme Court as a barrister and solicitor, being the youngest female to be admitted to the bar. This had been in order to avoid a further drug conviction and she was first known to Victoria Police as informer G395 around 1995, which Gobbo later denied knowledge of any such registration.

It later came to light that in 2006, well known Melbourne gangland criminal identity, Carl Williams from his prison cell while waiting trial for four murders, complained to the Director of Public Prosecutions and the Law Institute of Victoria, alleging Gobbo was indeed a snitch that while acting for him was effectively dobbing him into police. Williams paid for the contract killings of Jason Moran and Pasquale Barbaro in June 2003, followed by the torching death of another criminal identity Mark Malia, some two months later in August 2003. Williams was also convicted of the murder of Michael Marshall, who was shot dead in 2003 in South Yarra in front of his young son, followed by the shooting death of Lewis Moran in March 2004. Williams was also implicated and pleaded guilty to conspiracy to murder former lawyer, Mario Condello. His sentences ranged, for all these murders, from life imprisonment to a 21-year non-parole period.

Williams was killed in prison by Mathew "The General" Johnson and the complaints by Williams about Gobbo obviously could not progress any further. However, in the 2011 trial of Johnson for the Williams murder, evidence was given by police that Williams was himself a police informant regarding corrupt police being implicated in several unsolved murders, with some even paying school fees for his daughter. They were even prepared to pay a $750,000 tax debt for his father. However, on legal advice the latter offer was withdrawn. One of his henchmen did turn Crown witness against Williams, being later identified in the McMurdo Royal Commission as "Mr McGrath".[260]

Johnson, following his sentence of life imprisonment for the bludgeoning murder of Williams, lodged an appeal for his murder conviction, which included grounds that Gobbo sat in on legal conferences and then allegedly informed on him to Victoria Police. He subsequently withdrew the appeal as

---

[260] *R v Johnson* [2011] VSC 633.

he'd had a "gutful" trying to obtain "discovery of documents" from Victoria Police. He remains in isolation since murdering Williams, despite being the boss of the Prisoners of War gang, who have an inherent hatred of police and their informants.

It was drummed into us at the CPDU seminar, in no uncertain terms, that any communications and instructions from our clients were protected by legal professional privilege and, as such, were strictly confidential. The only exception to such privilege was, for example, in the event a client was to tell their lawyer they were about to, or were planning to, commit a criminal offence. As I have previously said, our first obligation and paramount duty, in any event, was to the court and the administration of justice, as at all times we must act ethically and honestly.

I hasten to add I was never placed in a position where a client told me of a pending or planned criminal enterprise and, if I was in no doubt such escapade was to take place, I would have had no hesitation, as would most lawyers in reporting such 'probable commission of a serious criminal offence' to police.[261] However, there were a number of situations where clients would attend at my office for an appointment still driving their vehicle, despite having had their licence suspended and them telling me in confidence they would continue to drive, regardless. On the one hand, all that could be done in that situation was remind them of the serious consequences that would follow if they were detected by police driving whilst suspended. However, in a strict interpretation of Rule 9.2.5, I was arguably in breach of those rules if such client, for example, was involved in a serious car accident when driving whilst suspended.

---

261   see *Legal Profession Uniform Law Australian Solicitors Conduct Rules 2015*-Rule 9.

The Gobbo Lawyer X scandal was a defining blight on the legal profession and particularly placed lawyers in a very poor light. I became rather annoyed when the Lawyer X scandal first came to the attention of the public, when clients facing serious criminal charges would say to me with a grin on their face at our initial conference, 'You are not lawyer X, are you?'

I have no doubt my lawyer colleagues would have also been subjected to such a comment.

In 2015, Justice Murray Kellam launched an investigation on behalf of the Victorian Independent Broad-based Anti-Corruption Commission (IBAC) into the management of human sources by Victoria Police. Although Kellam determined that the management of certain informers by Victoria Police could be only described as negligent, such conduct was not unlawful. Overall, Kellam made a total of 16 recommendations, but they never saw daylight as they were not made public. Kellam did, however, request the Office of Public Prosecutions have a look at a number of police informer management cases as they had '… the potential to have adversely affected the administration of justice in Victoria… adverse effect of any prosecutions.'

The Chief Commissioner of Police and Gobbo then first sought an order in the Trial Division of the Victorian Supreme Court (Trial Division), to prevent the OPP from releasing material to certain individuals of their criminal convictions, which was dismissed by court order on 17 June 2017.[262] On further appeal, the Court of Appeal on 21 November, 2017 upheld the decision of the Trial Division.[263]

In affirming the Court of Appeal decision, the High

---

262   *AB & EF v CD* [2017] VSC 350 and *EF v CD* [2017] VSC 351.

263   *AB v CD & EF* [2017] VSCA 338.

Court subsequently in its judgment of *AB (a pseudonym) v. CD (a pseudonym); EF (a pseudonym) v CD (a pseudonym)* [2018] HCA 58, determined on further appeal that Gobbo's name should be disclosed and was formally revealed on 5 February, 2019, although her identity, by this time, was known to the public in any event. The High Court in its scathing judgment referring to Gobbo as EF said:

> *EF's action in purporting to act as counsel for Convicted Persons while covertly informing against them were fundamental and appalling breaches of EF's obligations as counsel to her clients and EF's duties to the Court.*

The High Court did not direct their scathing findings solely at Gobbo, but also Victoria Police when it said further:

> *Likewise, Victoria Police were guilty of reprehensible conduct in knowingly encouraging EF to do as she did and were involved in sanctioning atrocious breaches of the sworn duty of every police officer to discharge all duties imposed on them faithfully and according to law, without favour or affection, malice or ill-will. As a result, the prosecution of each Convicted Person was corrupted in a manner which debased fundamental premises of the criminal justice system.*

The names of the parties in the Supreme Court proceedings, due to overwhelming public interest, were then released, together with some redacted documents.[264]

As a consequence of the extremely critical comments of

---

[264]   AB–Chief Commissioner of Victoria Police; CD–Victorian Director of Public Prosecutions and EF–former barrister Nicola Gobbo.

the High Court, the Victorian Government in December 2018, sanctioned an enquiry into the Victoria Police liaison with Gobbo, aptly titled the *Royal Commission into the Management of Police Informants* (the Royal Commission). The four volume, 3000 page finding by Commissioner Margaret McMurdo AC, released in late November 2020, detailed at some length, following 129 days of evidence from in excess of 80 witnesses and making 111 reform recommendations, the overall extent of breaches aligned to Gobbo as a police informant source, contrary to the better interests of her clients. Commissioner McMurdo, in determining the conduct of Gobbo as 'inexcusable', made the recommendation for the appointment of a special investigator, not just to examine the conduct of Gobbo, but to determine whether current and former police should face criminal charges with over a hundred Victoria police officers being aware of the use of Gobbo.

It was particularly noted that Commissioner McMurdo stated, 'the police, generally including senior police, tolerated bending the rules to help solve serious crime' and that their conduct, 'had fallen short of their legal, moral and ethical duties.' The Royal Commission further referred to the convictions and findings of guilt of 1,011 people, which may have been compromised as a consequence of the 'conduct of Gobbo as a human source with 887 of those affected in a broad way and 124 in a specific way.'

The commissioner was particularly scathing of former Chief Commissioners of Victoria Police, Simon Overland and Graham Ashton as serving members, accusing them of failing in their legal, moral and ethical duties, contaminated by Gobbo. Overland was seen by some as the architect of the Gobbo arrangement and when he became chief in 2009 reportedly was warned by both Deputy Commissioner Sir Ken Jones and renowned homicide investigator, Ron Iddles, the latter even saying the use of Gobbo as a registered police informant would one day lead to a Royal Commission.

How right he was, with the Royal Commission pointing out that Overland, as head of the anti- gangland Purana Task Force in 2003, preferred not to obtain any legal advice in respect of the contaminated use of Gobbo with Commissioner McMurdo stating:

> *Having considered Mr Overland's contentions, the commission is of the view that the most likely reason that he did not obtain legal advice was that he feared it would limit the information he hoped to obtain from Ms Gobbo to help solve the gangland wars… once they knew of the grave risks of the situation and the questionable conduct of both Ms Gobbo and other police officers, they were obliged to either address it or satisfy themselves that others were appropriately doing so.*

This put to bed the argument allegedly from Overland that the taskforce needed to take action outside the normal boundaries to bring an end to the gangland murders that first started in 1998 with 11 unsolved crimes by June 2000 and continued unabated to 2010. This appears to suggest that the use of Gobbo was a necessary and important measure in dobbing in her clients' nefarious activities to police and bringing an end to the gangland war, which, of course, was rejected by the Royal Commission.

Ashton originally appointed Brendan Murphy KC, also widely known in our profession as "the barrister's barrister", as their legal representative at the Royal Commission in which

Victoria Police, on the grounds of public interest immunity, were challenging the disclosure of former clients of Gobbo attempting to have their previous and most likely compromised convictions overturned. This learned counsel, who over his career in criminal law, had been briefed in numerous high-profile cases, including the Faraday Primary School kidnappings and the Donald Mackay inquest, had his instructions to act subsequently withdrawn due to his legitimate concerns that the public interest claims by Victoria Police were not only onerous, but excessive. It is interesting that Murphy was, in fact, Victoria's first appointed independent Public Interest Monitor under the *Public Interest Monitor Act 2011*(Vic), to oversee and safeguard the interests of the public in applications by law enforcement bodies in the proper use of covert and miscellaneous coercive powers, including telephone intercepts.

Questions do remain though, as to whether other lawyers associated with, or aligned to Gobbo, knew of the conflict of her acting as a criminal defence barrister and, at the same time, acting as a police informer. What was revealed in the Royal Commission report, however, there were at least seven other Victoria Police informers who may have breached legal professional privilege, one of which was now deceased lawyer, Joseph "Pino" Acquaro who was shot dead in March 2016. His accused killer, Vincenzo Crupi, was on bail due to "exceptional circumstances",[265] regarding the lengthy COVID-19 pandemic delay in the matter coming to trial. Such trial has now been further delayed, following a High Court decision, which overruled the order of the Victorian Supreme Court requiring police to release documents which would have revealed the

---

265   see section 4A of the *Bail Act 1977*(Vic).

identity of a police informant.[266] The murder charge has since been dropped by the Office of Public Prosecutions.

Acquaro's alleged involvement gained ground following the Court of Appeal ruling, preventing Victoria Police from continuing to conceal details concerning one of his former notorious clients, namely Francesco Madafferi. Madafferi was sentenced to a term of 10 years imprisonment for the selling of ecstasy pills (tomato tins drug case) and believes his conviction and subsequent jailing was contaminated by the corrupt involvement of his then lawyer, Acquaro, in briefing Gobbo. Madafferi was denied bail pending the outcome of his appeal.[267]

Another client, drug kingpin Rocco Arico, who was sentenced to a term of 14 years in 2017,[268] subsequently reduced to a minimum of period of nine years, for extortion and other drug related offences, was hoping to rely on, as a get out of jail card, what he said was the snitching of his lawyer, Acquaro, with Victoria Police.[269] He will most likely be deported on his release.

Acquaro was referred to as "Lawyer A" with the registered numbers RFA06/08 and F710FDB to protect his identity, but according to Victoria Police, he was deemed not suitable as a registered informer. This was despite Acquaro providing valuable information to police about the "afterhours" activities of certain clients, but counsel acting for Victoria Police said, in respect of Acquaro as an informer, 'we cannot confirm nor deny.'

This position, however, seemed to be at odds when Victoria

---

266   *Chief Commissioner of Police v Crupi* [2024] HCA 34.

267   *Madafferi v The Queen* [2021] VSCA 332.

268   *DPP v Arico* (Unreported, County Court of Victoria, Judge Chettle ,10 November 2016 (conviction), 3 March 2017 (sentence).

269   *Rocco Arico v The Queen* [2018] VSCA 135; 272 A Crim R 450.

Police Chief Commissioner, Shane Patton, on being ordered by the Court of Appeal to release to the lawyers for Arico, all documentation between police and Acquaro, confirmed the only informing done by Acquaro had 'already been identified in another case.' Appeal judges were quite clear, though, in stating that Acquaro had 'two discrete sets of interactions with Victoria Police.'

The Royal Commission also made numerous other recommendations that should be considered to alter the scope of all police source management, the resultant miscarriage of justice and also the legal profession, as a whole, to be overseen by the LSBC. This would involve four main areas in implementing the further regulation of our profession and, in particular, restore and continue to promote trust and confidence for the public.

In the interim, a total of 24 of Gobbo's former clients launched appeals over her poisonous representation and 20 have current appeals before the court, with the Victorian Court of Appeal already setting aside the conviction of Faruk Orman , one of Gobbo's former clients, for the murder conviction of Walsh street police shooting suspect Victor Pierce,[270] noting the Director of Public Prosecutions conceded for Orman that there was a substantial miscarriage of justice.[271] Orman had previously served 11 years behind bars and will not be subject to a retrial.[272]

Orman subsequently reached a confidential settlement with Victoria Police in November 2024, in which they agreed to pay him in the order of $1 million in compensation due

---

270   *R v Faruk Orman* [2009] VSC 538 (Weinberg J).

271   *Faruk Orman v The Queen* [2019] VSCA 163.

272   see *Criminal Procedure Act 2009* (Vic) ss 276(1) (c),277(1) and 327.

to the Gobbo Lawyer X disaster. This means the civil trial set for 2025 will no longer be required and, no doubt, Victoria Police will breathe a sigh of relief as it means that none of their officers will now be required, at least in this matter, to testify about their connection with Gobbo.

Another client of Gobbo, Zlate Cvetanovski, also had his conviction for drug trafficking quashed and, like Orman, was freed from jail for his involvement in what was also known as the "Mokbel drug cartel". The Court of Appeal found in 2020, after he spent 10 years behind bars, that there was a further substantial miscarriage of justice in his irrevocably contaminated drug case, put together by Gobbo and Victoria Police, with the latter secretly paying $10,000 to a jailed alleged witness to convict Cvetanovski.[273]

There are also a number of further convictions in doubt for other clients represented by Gobbo, who are still in jail following their convictions in the much-publicised syndicate in the tomato tins drug case. This failed escapade was a drug conspiracy famous for its illegal importation of 15 million ecstasy pills loaded into tomato tins and imported from Naples in Italy in 2007. Whilst one client has now been released on bail following his successful appeal, namely, Salvatore Agresta, who was jailed in 2013, as he had almost completed his non parole period,[274] others, such as Mafia chief, Pasquale Barbaro, drug lord Robert Karam, former bikie gang leader John Higgs and Saverio Zirilli, still remain imprisoned, serving lengthy sentences, but are currently waiting on their appeals.

In regards to Karam, following his appeal in 2017, Justice Robert Osborn has now determined that Gobbo clearly acted

---

273 *Zlate Cvetanovski v The Queen* [2020] VSCA 272.

274 *Salvatore Agresta v The Queen* [2020] VSCA 334.

with a conflict of interest and that her information to police resulted in the seizure of the drugs in the tomato tins drug case.[275] Karam was waiting on a decision by the Court of Appeal to ascertain whether his appeal would be dismissed, either hoping they would quash his convictions with an acquittal or he would be retried. No such luck though, as his appeal was dismissed.

Zirrili, also represented by Acquaro and Gobbo, had already tried for bail to circumvent his maximum sentence of 26 years, such appeal bail being refused by the Court of Appeal as he failed to demonstrate "exceptional circumstances". The court did, however, say, 'there might be legitimate questions as to whether he (Mr Acquaro) provided independent and impartial advice', and made orders under section 317 of the Criminal Procedure Act, ordering Victoria Police to produce documents to determine if Acquaro was a police informer.[276]

One other syndicate member, John "Jan" Visser, failed in a bid to overturn his conviction, which was partly blamed on what he said was the alleged involvement of informer Gobbo, who acted for some of his co-conspirators and disclosed to police shipping documents commonly referred to as a bill of lading obtained from Karam. However, according to the Court of Appeal finding, Gobbo never acted for Visser who self-represented and there was no factual basis to determine his prosecution as malicious.[277] This decision should, however, not have any bearing on the other tomato tins drug case appeals, given that Gobbo acted for some of its syndicate members, so we will have to wait to see what transpires. A malicious prosecution

---

275 *Rob Karam v The Queen* [No 2] [2022] VSCA 163.

276 *Saverio Zirilli v The Queen* [2021] VSCA 2:287 A Crim R 407.

277 *John (Jan) Visser v The Queen* [2020] VSCA 327.

is deemed to be one without merit and no reasonable cause and any subsequent conviction should be quashed.

Convicted double murderer, Evangelos Goussis, also has an appeal pending in respect of his convictions and life sentence for the murders in 2004 of Lewis Caine[278] and Lewis Moran.[279] His appeal was based on the snitching of Gobbo and police misconduct in an attempt to overturn his 34 years and nine months non-parole period.[280]

One other very well-known criminal identity and drug kingpin, Antonios "Tony" "Big Wig" Mokbel, who was also represented by Gobbo during the 1990s to 2007, appealed his 2012 conviction, for which he pleaded guilty to drug offences, and was sentenced to 30 years with a minimum of 22 years. No doubt, Mokbel might have had some comfort at the time that any appeal for sentence might have been successful, given that Victoria's Court of Appeal in 2020 quashed his previous 2006 cocaine import conviction, as a consequence of Commonwealth prosecutors agreeing that Gobbo acted for him during her duplicitous arrangement with Victoria Police.

The other problem for Mokbel was his health, suffering a heart attack in 2012, not to mention he nearly met his maker when he was repeatedly stabbed in Barwon Prison in 2019. This attack followed a newspaper front page article which referred to Mokbel as a "prison big wig" and also a top enforcer, allegedly disrupting an extortion racket standover scheme by Pacific Islander prisoners. His non parole jail time was subsequently reduced from 22 years to 20 years,[281] with the Court of Appeal

---

278 *R v Goussis* [2006] VSC 168.

279 *R v Goussis* [2009] VSC 16.

280 also see *Evangelous Goussis v the King* [2022] VSCA 255.

281 see section 326E (3) of the Criminal Procedure Act.

also taking into account the COVID-19 restrictions whilst in prison and the attack that nearly killed him. Mokbel would have been eligible for parole in 2031,[282] subject to any further appeal.

In that regard, NSW Supreme Court Judge, Elizabeth Fullerton, was tasked with ruling on 24 questions regarding the drug convictions of Mokbel and the conduct of Gobbo. Others to face severe criticism in her 600-page judgment, handed down on 23 November 2024, included former chief commissioner Overland in which Justice Fullerton said:

> *His failure to take appropriate steps to ensure Ms Gobbo's use did not risk involving Victoria Police in illegal conduct or impropriety and resulting in potentially lasting damage to the administration of justice…nothing short of egregious…*

Her Honour also determined that other senior police actively played a role, and she was also damning in respect of the former director of public prosecutions, being current Victorian judge, John Champion. Mokbel's appeal will most likely be heard in 2025 and it will be interesting to see if it is before current Victorian or interstate judges. In the interim, Mokbel has been released on bail pending such appeal.

It will be interesting to see what also eventuates regarding any further claims for financial compensation, which will be at the sole discretion of Victoria's Attorney General, based on a wrongful conviction and subsequent imprisonment. In 1980, Australia initially ratified the 1976 International Covenant on Civil and Political Rights (OHCHR), courtesy of the Fraser Government, noting Article 14(6) which states:

---

[282] *Antonios Mokbel v The King* [2023] VSCA 40.

> *When a person has, by a final decision, been convicted of a criminal offence and when subsequently his conviction has been reversed or he has been pardoned on the ground that a new or newly discovered fact shows conclusively that there has been a miscarriage of justice, the person who suffered punishment as a result of such conviction shall be compensated according to law, unless it is proved that the non- disclosure of the unknown fact in time is wholly or partly attributable to him.*

Such ratification was thereafter declined in 1983, leaving Australia the only democratic nation worldwide not to agree to the OHCHR. To date, less than one third of those in Australia, who have been exonerated, have received compensation as there is still no statutory right to compensation for persons wrongfully imprisoned following a conviction, apart from the Australian Capital Territory. The ACT legislated the *Human Rights Act 2004*(ACT) (Human Rights Act) and section 23 supports the OHCHR, giving such a legal right for those exonerees to be compensated, providing they had such criminal conviction reversed or received a pardon based on 'the ground that a new or newly discovered fact shows conclusively that there has been a miscarriage of justice.'[283]

In respect of supergrass barrister Gobbo, the jury is still out, though it appears extremely unlikely as to whether any criminal prosecutions will ever be commenced against her and others. Former eminent High Court Justice, Geoffrey Nettle AC KC, as a result of the recommendations of the Royal Commission, was subsequently appointed with the enactment of the *Special Investigator Act 2021*(Vic) (Special Investigator Act) by the Victorian Andrews Labor Government as special

---

283   see section 23 (1)(c) of the Human Rights Act.

investigator with the Office of Special Investigator (OSI) which had the specific task of inter alia:

(1)(a) ... to investigate potential criminal conduct and breaches of discipline relating to the recruitment, management and use by Victoria Police of Nicola Maree Gobbo as a human source; and (1)(b) to enable access to all records held by the Royal Commission into the Management of Police Informants by the Office of the Special Investigator and the Independent Broad-based Anti-Corruption Commission.

Its role was somewhat impeded, however, as the OSI was largely not provided with any statutory powers, other than a somewhat "broad power" to:

do all things that are necessary or convenient to be done for, or in connection with, or as incidental to, the performance of its duties and functions.[284]

It cannot compel witnesses to answer questions other than provide their name and address[285] and/or provide documents as part of any investigation under a search warrant.[286] Such witness refusal, including by the Crown, is based on the doctrine of self-incrimination and legal privilege.[287] It then remained to be seen if the OSI would challenge such impediments by way of court proceedings and whether the OPP ultimately determined to

---

284   see section 10 of the Special Investigator Act.

285   see section 30 of the Special Investigator Act.

286   see section 31 the Special Investigator Act.

287   see section 36 of the Special Investigator Act.

proceed with prosecutions, based on any recommendations of the OSI.

The current attitude of the Victorian Director of Public Prosecutions, Kerri Judd, suggests, however, that despite the recommendation of Justice Nettle that five persons, including, no doubt, Gobbo, should be charged with perjury,[288] misconduct in public office and attempting to pervert the course of justice.[289] The OPP, faced with a difficult dilemma, acting as both "judge and jury" has rejected the OSI brief of evidence. This rejection was based on their view there was no reasonable prospect of conviction and it was not in the public interest to lay charges against Gobbo and police.

This is contrary to the opinion of the OSI, as the brief of evidence under the investigation known as Operation Spey was in excess of 5,000 pages of documentary evidence it considered admissible, together with a number of hours of audio recordings and supported by numerous witness statements. Justice Nettle, not surprisingly, on being advised of the OPP position, advised the Andrews Government that he was simply 'wasting his time' stating the probability of charges being laid were 'effectively nil' and suggested he would resign from the OSI and it be wound up. In respect of Operation Spey and, despite Justice Nettle's determination that the offending gave rise to a powerful prosecution case, Judd stated:

Much of this material was irrelevant to any likely facts in issue in the proposed proceeding or, if relevant, would have been inadmissible as a matter of law…my decision in relation to

---

[288] see section 314 of the Crimes Act 1958(Vic).

[289] see section 320 of the Crimes Act.

these matters should be interpreted as nothing other than the results of careful and realistic assessments of the evidence.

There was some suggestion, however, that the Victorian State Opposition may draft a bill to amend the Special Investigator Act to give prosecution powers to the OSI, but, no doubt, such bill would fall over in the lower house as it would lack the support of the Andrews Labor Government. In any event, Premier Andrews adopted a steadfast position in it would be highly inappropriate to provide separate powers to the OSI to lay charges and further stated on 28 June 2023:

There needs to be a separation (of powers). If you have investigated a matter, you are altogether too close to it to be making decisions about whether a conviction is likely. Investigators don't make good prosecutors...The only thing... that should guide that is the considered judgment of the Director of Public Prosecutions, Kerri Judd.

This incredulous view was, unsurprisingly, supported by Victorian Attorney General, Jaclyn Symes, who suggested that a lot had been learnt, despite no charges being laid and in support of the opinion of Judd, stated:

Not everybody gets the outcome that perhaps they want but the work has been completed...and the DPP has assessed that these cases would not make it through to a successful profession in the courts. She's an expert in her field.

The Andrews Government has also taken the view that after spending around $190 million from the taxpayers' purse on the Royal Commission, the OPP and Legal Aid, lawyers, Victoria Police responses and the implementation and investigations by the ÖSI, that have gone nowhere, the OSI will be wound up. This course of action was in response to the probable resignation of Justice Nettle and the rejection of the OSI brief by the DPP. The only winners, it could now be said, have been the lawyers assisting and acting for various parties and for want of a better expression, it certainly has been a "lawyers' picnic" in this taxpayer-funded bonanza.

The move to disband the OSI and not provide Justice Nettle with powers to, not only investigate but lay charges, led to a further scathing attack by Shadow Attorney General Michael O'Brien, when he lashed out at Premier Andrews and said:

Appalling decision...rotten lawyers and corrupt cops...By turning its back on former High Court Justice Geoffrey Nettle and closing down the OSI, Labor is giving a free pass to all those who engaged in what our highest court condemned as reprehensible conduct. The worst legal scandal in Victorian history will end with a whimper because a weak Labor government does not want to give the OSI the power to authorise charges. It is perhaps fitting that the scandal, which shockingly undermined Victoria's justice system, will remain unpunished because of the insipid weakness of the Andrews Government.

O'Brien then went on to say:

Many agencies, including agencies in his own government (Andrews) conduct investigations and then have the power to lay charges independently...IBAC (Independent Broad- based Anti-corruption Commission), councils, the Environment Protection Authority (EPA), WorkSafe and the RSPCA, all act as both investigator and prosecutor in many circumstances... Instead of trying to excuse the failure to prosecute those responsible for the Lawyer X scandal, the premier should give the Special Investigator (OSI) the power to test the evidence before a judge and jury.

This view, in respect of providing dual powers to the OSI, in order to be able to both investigate and prosecute, was also shared by Stephen Charles KC, being a former judge of the Victorian Supreme Court and board member for the Centre of Public Integrity, who stated it was:

Absolute nonsense... why on earth was he (Justice Nettle) asked to investigate the laying of charges in the first place? It's a nonsensical argument given the fact that plenty of other people and agencies have the ability to lay charges. The premier and his government are totally in thrall to police. They are allowing police to run the state. Justice Nettle has been treated unfairly and wasted two years of his life on this. He would be justified in feeling frustrated and furious.

It is, of course, correct that IBAC has a dual function as required with powers to identify, then investigate, public sector corruption and police misconduct. Its powers are legislated under the *Independent Broad-based Anti-Corruption Commission Act 2011*(Vic) (IBAC Act) and it can bring criminal charges after completing its investigation,[290] or it may alternatively

---

290   see sections 189 and 190 of the IBAC Act.

refer briefs of evidence to the Director of Public Prosecutions in matters it considers appropriate.[291]

Further to Premier Andrews' comments on 28 June 2023 and in support of the condemnation of his "learned opinion", a number of eminent barristers, including Robert Richter KC and Nicholas Papas KC, also signed a letter as exclusively revealed to the ABC's 7.30 program, demanding Mr Andrews redact and apologise for such confused comments. It stated:

> *We the undersigned barristers entirely reject the accuracy of the matters asserted in these statements. To the extent they purport to rebuke or criticise the Honourable Geoffrey Nettle AC KC, as 'being altogether too close' to the investigation or that he thereby lacks objectivity and capacity to form a reasoned and unbiased opinion, they are misguided, wrong and inappropriate.*

This extremely critical letter rebuking Mr Andrews continued:

> *These statements reflect little understanding of the separation of powers and the need for the Executive not to comment on or involve itself in the investigation and prosecution of criminal offences. They also reflect a lack of understanding of the extremely high level of skills and professional objectivity that a former judge of both the High Court and Court of Appeal is trained and more than well qualified, to bring to bear on all professional tasks.*

To make matters even more perplexing, it was subsequently revealed that Judd may indeed have a conflict of interest as she

---

[291] see section 74 of the IBAC Act.

previously acted as counsel representing Overland when he was the former chief of police in respect of the Tyler Cassidy coronial inquest.[292]

This young man, who was 15 years of age at the time, was shot dead in 2008 by police in an armed confrontation. The coroner, although finding that the safety of one of the police officers was apparent when Cassidy threatened him when armed with two knives, also determined that police had a basic lack of training in dealing with such a situation, leading to all police undergoing a two-day training course twice each year on how to appropriately deal with mentally ill persons. The use of tasers by police, other than just for specialised units, also received some further consideration and were initially under limited trial in Bendigo and Morwell in 2010. By 2016 they were more widely used by Victoria Police.

It appears the briefs submitted by Justice Nettle to the DPP, have apparently not recommended any charges be laid against Overland, naming other police handlers under his watch, although he was a key figure in the use of Gobbo. Therefore arguably, Judd does not have a conflict. The overall opinion is that Judd, in any event, has a perceived conflict of interest and on that basis needs to recuse herself with O'Brien saying:

> *To avoid any perception of a conflict of interest, the DPP should ask an interstate counterpart to review Justice Nettle's extensive brief of evidence and advise whether charges should be brought…justice must not only be done, (but) it must (also) be seen to be done.*

---

[292] Cassidy Tyler, COR 2008 5542 [2011] Vic Cor C 12.

This view was also shared by respected barrister and former Victorian Bar Council vice chair, Darryl Burnett, who said:

> *In contentious legal matters where local high profile identities are involved, it is not uncommon for the decision to prosecute potential criminal conduct to be delegated to an interstate DPP…(who) will have no professional relationships with the identities…no prior knowledge at all…in the Lawyer X case the delegated interstate DPP could be presented with the extensive briefs of evidence prepared by Mr Nettle in which he recommends prosecutions.*

Despite the condemning plethora of views and criticism and calls to amend the Special Investigator Act to be enshrined with the same powers as given to IBAC or at least obtain an independent DPP review of the Justice Nettle briefs of evidence, it seems that Gobbo and others may not ever face any criminal charges. To add further pain to this unmitigated disaster, in 2021 Gobbo instructed her lawyers to institute further legal proceedings against Victoria Police (2021 litigation), despite previously commencing proceedings in 2010 in the Supreme Court of Victoria, naming as defendants, not only the State of Victoria, but former Chief Commissioners of Police, Overland and Christine Nixon.

The lengthy statement of claim for undisclosed damages in that proceeding, alleges her security and safety as a witness had been compromised and that she was subject to inducements by police to make a statement implicating former drug squad detective, Paul Dale, regarding the double murder of Terrence and Christine Hodson. Dale was subsequently charged with the murder of Terrence Hodson and gangster Rodney Collins charged for both murders, with the charges later being dropped due to the bashing death in April 2010 of jailbird and important crown witness, Carl Williams. After he had spent some eight months in custody on remand, Dale was released on bail under exceptional circumstances.[293] Hitman Collins subsequently met his maker dying supposedly of natural causes in prison in 2018.

It seems that Gobbo, at the initiative of investigating police, agreed to wear a wire recording her conversations with Dale and her statement of claim also alleged that she was compensated with a $1,000 a week allowance and Victoria Police were very generous in paying for her rather expensive lifestyle. No doubt, at the same time, Gobbo would have been reaping the benefit of legal costs for representing her clients. As a footnote and whilst Victoria Police denied any agreement had been reached, they still agreed to pay her compensation in 2012 of reportedly nearly $3 million.

The murders of the Hodsons in May 2004 were particularly graphic, with both being executed by gunshots to the back of their heads. Terrence Hodson became a police informer, following his arrest in 2002 by corrupt Drug Squad Detective, David Miechel. In 2003, both Hodson and Miechel were arrested following a burglary and Hodson, being represented by Gobbo, also agreed to provide incriminating evidence against both Dale and Miechel. Miechel was subsequently charged with, not only burglary, but trafficking a drug of dependence which carried a maximum of 15 years imprisonment.[294] Miechel copped the maximum with a 12-year non-parole period[295] and

---

293   Dale v DPP [2009] VSCA 212.

294   section 71AC of the *Drugs, Poisons and Controlled Substances Act 1981* (Vic).

295   *R v Miechel* [2006] Supreme Court of Victoria, King J, 26 May 2006 (conviction) 18 August 2006 (sentence).

his appeal, including manifestly excessive and onerous prison conditions, was refused.[296]

The subsequent murders of Hodson and his wife led to the Victorian Labor Government in 2004 establishing a statutory independent police oversight body, known as the Office of Police Integrity (OPI).[297] Its main charter was to oversee the detection and investigation of police corruption and misconduct in office and, of course, the informer nexus between the underworld and Victoria Police. Interesting though, OPI assistant director was Graham Ashton who would later go on to be appointed as Chief Commissioner of Victoria Police and, while a number of its public hearings attracted some public interest, it was disbanded in in February 2013 following the establishment of IBAC.

The 2021 litigation, filed by Gobbo, is now seeking aggravated and exemplary damages believed to be in the order of $30 million, allegedly for negligence and that such negligent conduct has 'put her at a real risk of suffering harm by them and others', as a result of Victoria Police agreeing to use her services as an informer. The Writ's statement of claim also named a number of police officers, including Overland, drug squad detectives Paul Rowe and Steve Mansell(dec) and Purana task force detective, Stuart Bateson. The claim alleges the negligent exercise of power by Victoria police was an act of 'malfeasance in public office'. Overland's conduct as the then assistant commissioner of crime in allowing the use of Gobbo as a police informer, was invalid as he had no lawful authority because it, supposedly, subverted and insidiously weakened our

---

296 *David Anthony Miechel v the Queen* [2010] VSCA 225.

297 *Major Crime Legislation (Office of Police Integrity) Act 2004* (Vic).

criminal justice system and exposed Gobbo to the injury, loss and damage she now claimed.

In that respect, the claim makes interesting reading and certain paragraphs allege that Gobbo:

> *... was providing confidential and/or privileged information against her current and former clients who were being investigated or prosecuted for alleged criminal offences, which was contrary to obligations of a barrister as to maintaining confidential information and/or privilege... Those current and former clients were not informed that (Gobbo) was a Victoria police informer and providing confidential and/or privileged communications to the police pertaining to them, in breach of Overland's and police officer's duty of disclosure, which was contrary to law and gave rise to perverting the course of justice, a criminal offence.*

The claim also states that Gobbo, on consenting to act as an informer, was provided with a verbal undertaking of confidentiality and then goes on to allege that the police hierarchy:

> *...knew, or ought to have known, that (Gobbo) was vulnerable, being concerned about her health, scared for her welfare and/ or under pressure as a result of her gangland connections... by inducing (Gobbo) to assist the task force's investigations... (police) knew, or ought to have known, that they could not protect (Gobbo) from being exposed as an informer.*

Such claim in seeking exemplary damages 'to punish those Victoria Police officers and deter other police from doing what has been done to (Gobbo)', further alleges she now suffers 'distress, pain, insult, hurt and suffers from humiliation' and is now left with 'neurological, vascular, dermatological, orthopaedic and psychiatric injuries', due to police conduct that was 'high handed, insulting or reprehensible'.

Gobbo, separately, had also allegedly sought a prosecution indemnity and made a "can say" sworn statement of evidence to the OSI, effectively dobbing in certain police members of the Purana anti-gangland taskforce, her police source development unit handlers and even an OPP prosecutor in respect to her snitching escapades. Such a statement is the start of a formal process by a witness giving evidence against an accused, in exchange for prosecution indemnity from any criminal charges, or at least a lesser sentence in respect of any guilty plea. Such statement by Gobbo was initially set out in the following form:

> *I am making this statement of my own free will on the understanding that it will be used for the purpose of an indemnity/undertaking application on my behalf. I understand that there is no guarantee as to the success of that application... The contents of this statement constitute the evidence which I would be prepared to give in the event that I am called as a witness in any further proceedings in relation to this matter.*

Gobbo then goes on to say:

> *If Victoria Police were the only people that knew I was the source, in my mind, if I appeared for [client] in some sort of plea and nobody knew, apart from Victoria Police and they did not say anything, then it was morally wrong, but I did not believe that it was legally wrong. The handlers always said*

> *and/or inferred that there was no legal problem in what I was doing and inferred that the hierarchy in Victoria Police well knew what was happening…I recall saying that the ethics of me acting for people while informing to the police was fucked or words to that effect. This was said to the police many times.*

This part of the two statements she made beggars belief as, on the one hand, Gobbo said she did not believe it was legally wrong, yet then states that the ethics of informing was, in fact, in her words, 'fucked'. It was further reported in media releases that Gobbo, in her OSI statement, went on to describe her conduct as not only 'unheard of' but a 'perversion of the course of justice' and indeed, that she was involved in a 'giant conspiracy'.

Again in her own words, her conduct was 'immoral' for her involvement with Victoria Police, which even involved shredding or amending documents which is another breach of legal privilege. With respect, Gobbo was an experienced barrister with some standing at the time, being admitted to the Victorian Bar in 1998 and she well knew her informing to police was unethical and clearly in breach of lawyer-client sacrosanct privilege.

It remains to be seen whether Gobbo will be afforded any indemnity by the OPP, if indeed any charges are ever laid. In the interim, the public waits with some interest, the outcome of her 2021 claim, which is a protracted defended judge-alone hearing in the Supreme Court of Victoria held in October 2024, with a decision yet to be handed down. Her litigation, seeking a massive amount in damages has, however, been somewhat reduced, in the event judgment was determined in her favour, with the Victorian State Government passing legislation which limits such type of compensation to a maximum of $1 million, under its *State Liability (Police Informants) Act 2024*(Vic). Interesting, that under section 4 of the act it defines 'specified human sources' as (a) Nicola Maree Gobbo and (b) Joseph Acquaro. It was of no surprise though when on 13 June 2025, Supreme Court Justice Richards dismissed Gobbo's claim determining that there had been no breach of any duty by Victoria Police. In that regard, Her Honour stated:

> *Once Ms Gobbo became an informer, the risk of exposure was ever present...I consider that the risk of exposure was an inherent risk...the State could not be held liable in negligence for harm suffered by Ms Gobbo due to the materialisation of that risk...*[298]

Whilst Gobbo, since 2014, has not been registered with a legal practicing certificate, she was, however, struck off the Supreme Court Bar Roll in 2020. The final comment by a Supreme Court judge sums up this disgraceful episode in that her duplicitous conduct rendered her not being a 'fit and proper person to remain on the bar roll', and as a lawyer she was 'incapable of rehabilitation.'[299]

In August 2022, the Victorian State Government also announced that an 'aptly' titled *Human Source Management Bill* would be introduced into Parliament in 2023, to supposedly address a number of the recommendations set out in the Royal Commission to manage the human sources of Victoria Police. The bill would provide for the registration of a human source requiring police to make an application for approval by a senior

---

[298] *Gobbo v State of Victoria* (redacted) [2025] VSC 334 – paras 514- 515.

[299] *Victorian Legal Services Board v Gobbo* [2020] VSC 692.

officer, such registration only being approved by the Chief Commissioner of Police if such senior police officer considered it to be, not only justified, appropriate and the sourced information could not be obtained by other reasonable means. This would be in situations posing a major security threat to our nation's security, the community in general or in situations that imposed immediate personal danger to the life and welfare of any person.[300]

The bill would also establish robust management oversight of such human source registration by the Public Interest Monitor and IBAC, to ensure strict compliance by Victoria Police. Attorney–General Jaclyn Symes, on announcing the bill, said:

> *Human sources are extremely valuable for police, but we need clear laws in place to appropriately manage the inherent risks that go with it for both the person involved and Victoria Police. These important and nation- leading reforms achieve the appropriate balance between mitigating the risk of human sources and ensuring Victoria Police can continue to act on information to keep our community safe.*

The new law to be passed by the parliament would mean the Victorian Government would have then put in place 48 of the 55 Royal Commission recommendations, to hopefully provide for a clear framework for the management of police informants and we wouldn't again see a repeat of the Lawyer X snitch of unethical conduct in informing against their clients. However, on a first reading of the draft legislation, as introduced into parliament on 7 February, 2023, it seems

---

300   see recommendation 16 of the report of the Royal Commission.

despite the proposed oversight of human sources, particularly by IBAC, if the legislation proceeded without amendment, it would still provide for police discretion, allowing for lawyers to effectively snitch on their clients.

It also appears to, not only give apparent authority to police to use lawyers in such a way, but also obtain privileged and confidential information from journalists, priests, doctors and even children and politicians, all under the umbrella of apparently registered human sources. There was, however, some suggestion that one of the amendments being considered would not only require approval by the Chief Commissioner of Police, but the Victorian Supreme Court would need to be convinced of the paramount risk to our safety or national security.

The Law Institute President, Tania Wolff (LIV President), in response to what was being proposed put it succinctly when she said:

We welcome transparency that the Bill provides for the registration, use and management of human sources by Victoria Police. However, if we have learned anything from the Royal Commission, it's that lawyers should never be used as human sources. Despite Royal Commission findings and a High Court ruling that a lawyer who informs on their clients to the police while purporting to act for them is a clear breach of ethical obligations, this legislation in its current form would legitimise such conduct... We remain fundamentally opposed to a regime that allows lawyers to inform on their clients.

Victorian Bar President, Sam Hay KC, was even more direct when he said in response to what was initially being proposed as legislation, stating:

The registration of lawyers as informants will lead to precisely the same conduct that gave rise to the Royal Commission in the first place. The roles of informant and lawyer are fundamentally opposed. One person cannot ethically wear both hats at the same time.

The proposed legislation was further described by former Victorian Supreme Court judge Stephen Charles, KC, as:

... sloppy and incompetent. This is a terrible piece of legislation. The government should be thoroughly ashamed of putting it forward for enactment. It's doing more and worse than has happened in the Gobbo case. Our whole system of criminal law and its fairness depend on a number of things: the absolute right to silence, the right not to be tortured, the obligation remaining on the prosecution throughout and never on the defence, and the duty not to communicate what your clients told you to police or anyone.

Chris Winneke KC, who was counsel assisting the Royal Commission, also concurred saying that he had 'grave reservations of the registration of a lawyer in providing information to police. It raises so many problems, of the likes we saw in the royal commission'. Commissioner McMurdo, in supporting such concerns, indicated that she would have urgent discussions with the government on the proposed bill.

It then remained to be seen whether the state government would listen to the plethora of criticism. This was despite such critics including a number of influential groups consisting of the Victorian Bar, Australian Lawyers Alliance and Australian Medical Association, amongst others, all in mutual agreement that the proposed bill must be thrown out in its current form. It certainly begged the question whether the proposed legislation, which had initially passed the lower house in parliament, would provide the necessary oversight and diligent safeguards desperately needed regarding police informants. However, the proposed draft law was then placed on hold after the Victorian Government withdrew it from debate in the upper house, due to the overwhelming criticism of it from all and sundry in its current form.

The concern was the Victorian Government would still proceed despite such condemnation. What then followed was some cursory amendments to what was being proposed in the bill, which then received a nod of approval in the Upper House. It was rubberstamped in the Lower house and then enacted into law as of 30 September, 2024.[301]

These amendments with a number of, so called, safeguards, such as contravention oversight by IBAC, supposedly provide a clear legislative framework according to the Attorney-General. Such amended framework determines that lawyers can only inform on their clients for a maximum of seven days, following which, their registration as a human source must cease. In addition, police will be prohibited from 'requesting, procuring or inducing' children to act as a human source but, providing they act on their own free will and are accompanied by an adult, they can be registered as a human source.

In its current form and even with the cursory amendments, it suggests that we may well still see more Lawyer X type snitches once again acting without fear or favour, in breaching their professional and ethical obligations. On the upside though, the Lawyer X debacle may result in such potential police informers having second thoughts about detailing the nefarious activities of their clients to Victoria Police.

---

[301] *Human Source Management Act 2023* (Vic).

20
THE JURY IS STILL OUT

I was to find out very quickly as a lawyer that I would not only be an adviser to my client but also a mentor, front, mouthpiece, counsellor, shoulder to cry on and pleader. The list is never ending. What I would also discover is that my client's problem, or in many cases problems, somehow would become my problem and, if the outcome didn't turn out as well as could be expected, then the client would blame me as it was always the lawyer's fault. I would also say to a client charged with a criminal offence, in most cases more than one charge, 'Surely, you must have known that at some stage there would be a knock on the door by police with an arrest warrant?'

The answer always was, 'Nah, I thought I would get away with it.'

I would also be asked by clients, as I was to find out, 'What would you do if you were in my shoes?'

The simple answer was, 'I am not in your shoes and all I can do is advise you of your options. If you choose not to follow my advice, then that is up to you and I will give you the likely outcome.'

What I was also to discover was, clients facing serious criminal offences didn't understand, let alone accept, that as a lawyer, we are restricted regarding any defence arguments we can submit to the court. Often a client would tell you exactly what happened in the incident, in other words, guilty as charged, but then want us to run a not guilty plea. Whilst I can still act in that regard, my usual response was, 'Sorry, I am now somewhat limited, as my first duty is to the court and it would be in your better interests if you instructed another lawyer.'

After a few years of practice, I realised I should not second guess myself, as usually what comes into my mind, based on my legal training in the first instance, is most likely correct. In other words, don't second guess, which I unfortunately did in my early days, especially when on my feet in a court of law with a few "Dennis Denuto" moments.

What I did do for many years and even in my last year of practice, when returning from court and usually on the drive back to the office or after a virtual hearing, I would go over my appearance and submissions before the court and determine if there was anything I missed or how I could have done it better. This would even be in situations where I obtained a good result for a client, particularly in criminal guilty pleas for serious criminal offending. In some way, I suppose, this was a form of second guessing, but at least it showed I still had the passion, to some degree. It was also important to meet each week with other lawyers and senior staff in the practice for at least an hour to discuss difficult files and possible resolutions. I found these meetings invaluable and another form of continuing professional development unit in the making.

Importantly, as a lawyer we should always keep an "open mind" and not let first impressions of a client cloud your thinking. One good example was an elderly gentleman who came to our firm in a dishevelled state with tears in his eyes over a $300 excessive charge by a Telco provider. He appeared to me to simply be a struggling pensioner and I was more than pleased to quickly sort the matter out, which he was very happy about.

I didn't charge him a fee because I really felt sorry for him. He came back to see me some months later and, on this occasion, he wasn't quite so upset or dishevelled. I told him, before we discussed his latest issue, I would have to charge him a fee but would keep his costs down. There was no legal issue because this time he wanted me to draw up a deed of a gift to a local hospital. He was donating a sum well in excess of a million dollars to build a new wing with the only requirement for it to be named after him and his wife. His accountant confirmed his very strong financial position, so lesson to be learnt by all budding lawyers when dealing with clients, don't ever, as the saying goes, "judge a book by its cover".

Alternatively, one well-educated and successful business client needed to be made aware by me of 'a wolf in sheep's clothing'. Unfortunately, he fell victim to a Nigerian sweetheart scamster who promised him eternal love. He had lost his wife to ill health and couldn't believe his luck when this beautiful woman came into his life. Of course, she needed money to pay for her ill parents' medical bills, followed by air fares so she could come to Melbourne and live happily ever after with Michael (not his real name). Michael even went to Tullamarine

Airport to pick her up but then received another text saying her flight was cancelled and she needed additional money for an alternate, but more expensive flight. All up, it cost him over $100,000 and, sorry Michael, there was not much I could do trying to recover your lost savings.

On the other hand, many clients came to me already tarnished by lawyer jokes and I had heard them all. Winston Churchill's famous quote about men but altered to, 'Lawyers stumble over the truth, but most of them pick themselves up and hurry off as if nothing had happened.'

Bit rough, but what stemmed from that was the joke about the differences between a good lawyer and a bad lawyer. The bad lawyer makes your case drag on for years, but a good lawyer makes it last even longer!!

One client told me he was referred by his accountant and did I know the difference between an accountant and a lawyer? I hadn't heard that one so said, 'No, I don't know the difference.'

His reply, 'Accountants know their boring.'

I did tell a magistrate, jokingly, in one appearance when the matter was stood down, 'What do you call a lawyer with an IQ of 50?'

Now this particular magistrate, who I won't name for obvious reasons, responded with, 'A politician.'

He understandably wasn't impressed when I said, 'No, "Your Honour".'

Of course there was also the joke, 'You can tell a lawyer is lying because their lips are moving', or 'Do you know how to save a drowning lawyer? Take your foot off his head.'

I did have a laugh at one client joke though, when I was asked, 'What's black and gold and looks really good on a lawyer? A Doberman.'

I gave my pet Doberman a bit of a pat and hug when I got home that night.

Clients would always complain about their legal costs to a degree. One even said to me, 'If you see me in the street and say "hello" does that mean I will get a bill for that?'

Yes, we are known as sharks, but they don't attack us out of professional courtesy. Enough is enough and the bottom line is, 'There are only three lawyer jokes because the rest are true.'

I found many of the jokes to be in bad taste, indecent and bordering on obscene. Then again, they were talking about lawyers. I rest my case, Your Honour.

I was, however, to find, particularly in the first few years of legal practice, that I struggled to represent clients who had run afoul of the law. I had previously spent 19 years catching school crooks, yet here I was now appearing on behalf of defendants charged by police and some for a school burglary. I had an attitude that effectively meant I had no sympathy for them and in my view they should "cop their right whack", for their indiscretions.

As a lawyer though, I had to act in the best interests of my clients and the demeanour I initially had was certainly not ethical. I can understand many police officers, who subsequently enter the legal profession, would find it a lot more difficult in the initial stages of their law practice and would probably have a similar mindset. I am pleased to say, though, this reticent attitude didn't last long and, thereafter, I certainly acted professionally and provided the best legal advice and representation I could. I will admit, though, there were still a few clients who I had absolutely no time for and if they were jailed, then so be it, despite my best efforts.

One issue I did have during my time as a lawyer were

potential clients coming to me for a second opinion. I say "potential clients" as they had already provided instructions to another lawyer, but for a variety of reasons, usually they didn't like the advice initially given, they wanted to test that advice against another lawyer's opinion. There is nothing considered unethical in providing a second opinion, but solicitors are not bound by the "cab rank rule", unlike barristers. In other words, a solicitor can decline to provide such second opinion and not act for the client. Barristers are bound by the *Legal Profession Uniform Conduct (Barristers) Rules 2015* and rule 101 sets out the circumstances in which a barrister must refuse a brief of instructions and, in the absence of those grounds, accept the brief.

Our rules do allow us to provide such further opinion based on reasonable grounds that the matter is urgent and it would not be unfair, even though we know another solicitor is acting.[302] As a matter of fairness, though, if a solicitor was to take instructions, professional courtesy suggests it would be appropriate to advise the other solicitor of their client seeking a further opinion, even if the new client would prefer such a notification did not take place. Equally, if the other solicitor becomes aware of another solicitor providing a second opinion, that will allow just cause with reasonable notice to terminate any costs agreement entered into.[303]

One client of mine was not happy with the advice I was giving him regarding a number of police charges involving a home invasion and the theft of a dog, following a dispute with his now ex-girlfriend. He went to another local lawyer for a

---

302 see Regulation 33 – *Legal Profession Uniform Law Australian Solicitors' Conduct Rules 2015*.

303 Rule 13.1.3 of the Australian Solicitors' Conduct Rules.

second opinion and then played that advice against mine. I immediately terminated his costs agreement, refused to further act and, after he paid his account, transferred the file to his new lawyer.

There is obviously a raft of problems in providing second opinions. Whilst a client has every right to seek such further advice, I always declined to provide it. One of the problems faced with this is, I do not have access to all the relevant information, other than what was being told by the client, as the existing file with all the applicable documentation, will usually be on the other solicitor's file. In that event and even if such advice was provided with it being somewhat qualified, a lawyer could open themselves to a negligence claim if, for some reason, their advice was incorrect.

There is, of course, nothing unethical in acting for clients of other solicitors, if in the event they are referred by the other lawyer and in situations to provide specialist advice. In other words, the new client comes to the second lawyer with the blessing of his current solicitor.

Over a number of years, I did develop and have a professional working relationship with most police prosecutors, in particular, at Frankston Prosecutions. We had a mutual respect for each other and overall, the score would be even, well almost, with them agreeing to withdraw some charges and on one occasion, all charges, by determining the brief of evidence had no merit. Alternatively, with me agreeing with their submissions and arguments that certain charges and/or briefs left me with no choice but to run a guilty plea, if instructed by the client.

The jury is still out regarding my least favourite tribunal. Dare I say it, known as, and referred to by many lawyers as the "chook raffle", namely the Victorian Civil and Administrative Tribunal (VCAT).[304] VCAT is less formal than a court and can hear disputes in a diverse range of matters from goods and services, planning disputes, retail and commercial leases to guardianship matters, to name a few. I likened VCAT, on some occasions, more as a "crystal ball" and this was readily apparent in one matter in which I was acting for a respondent.

My client was a psychic reader and she gave a reading to a client who was at a very low point in her life. The reading advised that she would meet the man of her dreams within three months and they would have a very happy and long relationship. Feeling extremely sorry for this woman, my client did not even charge her the usual $100 fee for the reading. This psychic reading was very accurate about this woman's past and present trials and tribulations but apparently missed out on making the prediction for the future.

Unfortunately, the reading did not lead to the man of her dreams after three months, so she issued proceedings in VCAT for pain and suffering for misleading and deceptive conduct. I tried to convince the sitting member that one of the essential elements for a contract to be legally binding was consideration which, in this case, was no money paid by the applicant. Therefore, my client could not be bound. All to no avail of course as the tribunal member looked lovingly into a crystal ball and awarded a chook raffle prize of $750 in damages against my client. Really!

I appeared in a number of other matters in VCAT, particularly in guardianship applications and for elderly clients involving the State Trustees. I certainly agree with Victoria's Ombudsman, Deborah Glass in her 2019 findings that State

---

304   see the *Victorian Civil and Administrative Act 1998* (Vic).

Trustees often failed to act in the better interests of their clients. The report of Ms Glass found numerous examples in a number of complaints that doubled over three years to 2018, particularly their poor financial management which resulted in lost entitlements, increased aged care fees and neglect in not pursuing cases of fraud and financial abuse.

What I was to find in appearing before VCAT, involving matters concerning State Trustees as financial administrator, the tribunal lacked impartiality and appeared to favour their appointment regardless, despite my submissions to the contrary.

In one matter, when I was appearing for an elderly client by the name of Jack (not his real name), I encouraged the sitting tribunal member to meet with Jack in a private session, so he could explain why he did not want State Trustees reappointed, preferring a family member and that he wanted to relocate interstate to reside with his family. Jack had early onset dementia, but he was still very coherent and medical evidence confirmed he could provide me with proper instructions. The general principle that applies under the Guardianship and Administration Act 1986(Vic) (Guardianship and Administration Act) is the tribunal must give sufficient weight to the person's best interests wherever possible.[305]

Despite the member meeting with Jack in a private conference and, notwithstanding my lengthy submissions in his best interests, including the alleged financial mismanagement by State Trustees of Jack's affairs, it was apparent they would be reappointed. At one stage, the tribunal member asked me if I had any further submissions to make and I simply stood up and said, 'I really see no point Commissioner, as it is readily apparent that you have already made your decision.'

---

[305] see further *XYZ v State Trustees Ltd* [2006] 25 VAR 402.

To say the commissioner wasn't impressed with that comment is an understatement, but they still appointed State Trustees as financial guardian and the Office of Public Advocate as limited guardian for a further period of 12 months.

However, some months later, common sense finally prevailed and VCAT, albeit with some reluctance, finally agreed to the revocation of the earlier order with Jack's family member being appointed as both financial administrator and guardian. This would be on the basis that the guardian provided financial reports to VCAT on the administration of the funds for Jack, as and when required. I have no doubt, though, as Ms Glass determined, State Trustees do have a number of staff who are trying to act in the best interests of their clients with numerous examples of proper financial management and empathy for them. This became quite apparent in Jack's matter when the State Trustee's representative, with some embarrassment, apologised unreservedly to both Jack and VCAT for their negligent conduct and performance of the administration of his financial affairs.

I crossed paths once again with State Trustees in a separate matter, following a VCAT order for my client to be financial administrator for her partner, after their order had been revoked. Acting on instructions, I accused them of professional negligence on the administration of Bill's (not his real name) estate. In particular, it was alleged they failed to act in accordance with the Guardianship and Administration Act, did not act accordingly in the sale of Bill's house, were abusive and acted with a demonstrated lack of care and compassion in their personal interactions with Bill and the administration fees charged were unnecessarily incurred and exorbitant. The matter was finally settled with compensation being paid to Bill by State Trustees but, of course, without admission of liability.

Unsurprisingly, of the 30 State Trustee cases reviewed by Ms Glass, a staggering 23 files were found to display cases of financial mismanagement, including one where their client's worldly possessions were dumped at a local tip. In the interim, Ms Glass recommended the status of State Trustees be further considered to continue as a state-funded and owned entity and, in her own words, the complaints of those dealing on a regular basis with State Trustees, 'present a troubling picture'. The State Trustees who cooperated fully with the ombudsman acknowledged the findings and also apologised to their clients for their failings as detailed in the report.

VCAT was certainly not one of my favourite jurisdictions and now had a huge backlog of cases. In its 2021-2022 Annual Report, it listed a number of challenges, in particular, a 25 per cent increase in a backlog of cases as compared to the previous year, noting it was a very active Tribunal with over 80,000 cases filed each year. It was evident that tenancy disputes between landlords and tenants were now taking many months to be heard, with a delay on average of 22 weeks or more. Disputes involving building matters had an average delay of some eight months and, in one particular long running matter, was not listed to be heard until sometime in 2024, noting the original application by the landowner was made some three years earlier. The administrative division of VCAT, which also dealt with complaints against lawyers, now took an average of 8-9 months to come before the tribunal.

The report blamed these types of delays on improved accessibility, courtesy of virtual hearings, which were taking longer to resolve and also blamed the retirement of many sitting VCAT members and, of course, the on-going timeframe effects of the COVID-19 pandemic. I accept it continues to remain poorly funded and certainly under resourced, but time will tell whether VCAT will ever get its act together. I will admit though, with the COVID-19 lockdowns and initially working from home, then constantly appearing in court by way of virtual hearings, also did take a toll on me. Once you lose the passion and, most likely, the patience and empathy needed in dealing with crime and family violence matters, in particular, you can't act in the best interests of your clients.

Our rules also provide for any person to make a complaint to the Legal Services Board and Commissioner (LSBC) on the conduct of a legal practitioner. My patience was sorely tested over my 25 years of practice when two complaints were made against me, one which was dismissed by the LSBC. The other complaint involved my acting in a matter where I clearly had a conflict of interest and should not have taken at the time many years later, against a former client on behalf of a trustee in bankruptcy. The fact that this former client tried to run me over in a carpark might have had something to do with it, but I took the penalty on the chin, which was to complete an additional CPDU on conflicts of interest.

The question I keep asking myself is, with the benefit of hindsight, did I enjoy my 25 odd years as a lawyer? It certainly had its ups and downs and I completely understand how some lawyers, after a period of time, suffer from burnout and walk away from the profession. We really have to balance the "scales of justice" and we tread a fine line, having the overall responsibility of the future financial status and, in many cases, the freedom of clients resting on our shoulders.

A recent wellness survey by Meritas Australia and New

Zealand determined that 85 per cent of lawyers experienced anxiety in the workplace with 60 per cent suffering from depression. Such a workplace was best described by the Victorian Law Society President where lawyers were prone to mental illness, solely due to such a high-pressure environment faced by legal practitioners. The issue for all lawyers is, of course, the constant pressure in dealing with clients and their never-ending legal issues and then ensuring the law firm principal is happy with the hours as billed. What budding new lawyers will also find is, effectively, they must be available 24 hours a day, seven days a week, and this combined with the on-going pressure of practising law may lead to mental health issues.

My foray into law since being admitted on April Fool's Day was, to a degree, totally unexpected, particularly given my early lack of education as I preferred to play sport and indulge in other endeavours. The 19-odd years of catching school crooks and giving evidence in court perhaps may have had something to do with it, being cross examined by various learned counsel and thinking I could do a better job. It begs the question though, whether if had my time again, would I have entered the legal profession. The jury is also still out on that one.

21
TIME TO CALL STUMPS

In June 2015, at the ripe old age of 68 and after nearly 20 years as a legal practitioner, I did decide enough was enough and entered retirement phase one, only to return to the profession in 2017 as special counsel. The initial retirement plan was to train and become fit enough to walk the Kokoda Trail and, in the interim, continue playing cricket in the over 60s veterans' competition, in addition to umpiring.

During my two-year hiatus, I was fortunate enough to both umpire and play veterans cricket in Sri Lanka, England, Mexico, Hawaii, New York and even at Sabina Park in Kingston, Jamaica. Playing and umpiring at Sabina Park, being a well-known West Indies Test Cricket Ground, gave me bragging rights over a few fellow cricketer mates. Not that I made many runs.

I then umpired quite well in the second game and honestly thought West Indian great, Brian Lara, came out to bat at the fall of the first wicket. Unfortunately, it wasn't him as he batted right-handed but still smashed the Australian attack to all parts of the ground. We also played a limited overs match against the Jamaican Melbourne Cricket Club and former West Indian fast bowler, Courtney Walsh, thankfully, displayed his talents but only bowling leg spin, bar for one frightening ball from his normal run up.

Unfortunately, I couldn't add Cuba to my umpiring and playing list as, on our arrival in Havana, the capital and the largest city, the Communist Party of Cuba, led by Raul Castro, brother of Fidel, determined that we needed to make a further ex-gratia payment to their coffers in order to play against their expat team of cricketers. We politely declined and spent a short few days touring its cobbled streets with never-ending performing musicians, historic forts and famous restaurants. Indeed, one of my favourite tourist destinations.

The World Veterans' Cricket Championship final in Philadelphia, USA was another crowning moment in my umpiring career, being given the honour to umpire the final between India and Pakistan with my good friend, Martin Betts. Unfortunately, heavy overnight rain determined that the final could not proceed with the pitch and most of the oval under water. However, the match officials, while trying to keep the large crowd happy, advised us we must play at least a ten over match.

Who would have guessed? At the toss it was readily apparent that both sides didn't like each other and only one side wanted to play, but the other team, quite rightly, refused given the state of the ground. Martin and I discussed this impasse with the match officials and, after some lengthy deliberation, they instructed us to walk back out to the middle, shake our heads vigorously as we returned back to the safety of the pavilion.

It was then announced over loudspeakers that the umpires determined, against the wishes of match officials, that the game could not proceed. This was, of course, met by sustained booing being directed at us. I have been booed a few times in my cricket umpiring days, but I look back on this experience with a smile on my face. I also officiated in an International Over 60s "Test" at Geelong between England and Australia, giving the English captain out plum leg before first ball and again booed by their supporters. My veterans' cricket umpiring also took me to Samoa and to assist in the training of their local cricket umpires, but unfortunately, I reported an Australian player, who I knew quite well, for dissent.

My attempt to walk the Kokoda Trail did not eventuate as my knees gave out requiring titanium replacements and I think my many years of wicket keeping may have had something to do with it. I returned to umpiring after my first knee replacement but only lasted one match, which was a veterans' game between Tasmania and Victoria. My knee didn't stand up to well over 80 overs. I also reported two Tasmanian players for their abuse.

I took the view that if I am reporting players in veterans' games, then do I really want to keep umpiring and maybe I should call stumps. My knees would not now last a full day in any event. I already had a reputation in the local cricket association for not taking any rubbish from players and, one certain gentleman, for want of a better word, copped a three-year suspension. He called me a cheating "cee U next Tuesday" during a semi-final match for turning down a leg before wicket, leading to a total of nine charges all up, followed by abusing the tribunal members as he was leaving the hearing, resulting in an additional one-year suspension.

I was still actively involved in Australian Rules, particularly when both my sons played junior football for a number of years. I also did four years as a not-so-successful junior coach, followed by president of the junior club, then I was with the senior club as head trainer and later as president. My role as head trainer commenced in 2005 with the senior team, coached by Alan Quaife. I always wanted to be a medic in the army, so this was probably the next best thing. I often wondered why I had to attend a number of training courses to qualify with a refresher each year to maintain accreditation, particularly in CPR.

Defibrillators were not compulsory at club level back then and my CPR lectures certainly came to the fore after one game in my second season as a trainer. An elderly gentlemen collapsed at the end of one game with no pulse when I reached him, but I was able to continue with resuscitation until the medics arrived some 10 minutes later. I was quite proud of myself at the time as he survived after a stay in hospital. That all disappeared though, when I unfortunately went against our training and tried to put a dislocated finger back in place only to cause a fracture. Rather embarrassing, given that our training always was to leave dislocations to the professionals. Lesson well learnt.

I decided to call stumps on my role as president after three years, as we needed a new and much younger board of management to lead the club and certainly one with more energy and passion. I had also crossed swords with the local shire for many years over their lack of understanding and effort in managing community sporting facilities, so hopefully a new board with a fresh approach and ideas might lead to a change of attitude. Funnily enough, in my last year with the senior club, the players gave me the nickname of "President Joe Biden", but

I don't think I was in the same league as him. Then again, he did only replace Donald Trump.

My involvement in community sport continued for 22 years, including as chairman of a junior football league tribunal, but maybe it is time to also call stumps in that regard. The old age syndrome again reared its ugly head when a president of a junior club threatened to not appear as an advocate for a reported player before the tribunal as, in his view, which he told all and sundry that would listen, I was "too old" to continue to act as chairman. He did appear though and quickly withdrew his defamatory comment when I challenged him. Then again, truth is a defence to defamation!

Whilst old age is a virtue, it was time to finally call stumps and at midnight on 30 June 2023, I ceased to be an Australian lawyer.

ACKNOWLEDGEMENTS

My reference to a number of other lawyers is also a thank you to them for guiding me through my inexperienced early days and after 10 years, considering me as being reasonably competent. I say that, not just with tongue in cheek, but the fact is, no lawyer can say they are reasonably competent until they have at least 10 years of practice. I also pay credit to my numerous clients, well most of them, and I have particularly referred to such clients under a "nom de plume" to protect their confidentiality.

My heartfelt thanks also to my former practice manager, Nadine Smith, for her wise counsel and client memories. Special mention also to lawyer, Ayla Dodson, for not only her encouragement given to me in writing this book, but her careful eye in going over parts of my interpretation of our legal system. A thank you to Malcolm Howell of Jirsch Sutherland for his input to certain chapters and also for his professionalism as a trustee in bankruptcy and company liquidation.

No doubt, some of my colleagues and other well-meaning legal practitioners, will take issue with some of my client case examples and interpretation of the law, and relevant pieces of legislation. I plead ignorance, or should I say our legal system is rather complex, an ass at times, open to interpretation and my book, by no means, is in any way to be considered as an exhaustive analysis of the law. On the other hand, I was admitted to practice on April Fool's Day. I rest my case.

I must also thank Age journalist, John "Sly of the Underworld" Silvester, for his many informative articles on crime and its infamous identities as well as his *Naked City* podcasts. Anthony Dowsley, Patrick Dowling and Andrew Rule of the Herald Sun also need to be acknowledged for their enlightening writing and podcasts on criminals, long forgotten and those crims of today and, of course, Lawyer X.

My family have always been a source of support and inspiration. Thank you to my amazing sister, Susan, for her input about our early days and my two beautiful daughters, Karen and Alison, who have given me five wonderful grandchildren to love. My two sons, Hayden and Patrick, have grown into fine young men and their never-ending love, encouragement and loyalty is and always will be, held by me in high regard.

Thank you to our much loved dogs, firstly Edo, who certainly got me out of several dangerous situations, our beautiful Golden Retriever, Tully, our first family dog who showed us so much loyalty and love and helped heal our hearts during many difficult and sad times with the loss of many friends and family members, and finally our amazing rescue Doberman, Pickle, who taught us all about resilience and never ending love over the four years she was in our lives. They are now in heaven, no doubt eating "schmackos", telling tales about how much we loved them and they loved us in return and looking down on us, making sure we look after our rescue greyhound, Sandy.

To my loving and supportive wife, Michelle, I owe her so much. She not only experienced the ongoing stressful drama of my many callouts in the middle of the night to confront and catch school crooks, but my frustrations as a lawyer and dealing with my shortcomings in the early days. There were also my dealings with certain clients and should I say it, but again with no disrespect, my least favourite tribunal and, of course, certain well-meaning and experienced magistrates.

Michelle's contribution to this book deserves a big "thank you". Mind you, she had plenty of experience in perusing and correcting my comprehension in essays and papers during law school, in particular, my Honour's thesis and then my master's thesis, but this book would not have been possible without her guidance, with a number of suggested amendments, of course, so thank you and love you to the moon and back. Special thanks again to Alana Lambert of Book Burrow for her publishing skills and to Samantha Elley for her editing expertise, particularly for picking up some embarrassing errors.

Finally, this book is certainly not to be taken in any way as providing legal advice to my readers and the legalisation and regulations applicable at the time. Every legal matter has its own set of peculiar facts, applicable to each and every particular situation, so please ensure you obtain relevant legal advice, if and when needed.

June 2025.

GLOSSARY

NOTE: Words may include in some cases both legal and ordinary meaning.

A

Account Stated Statement between a creditor and debtor setting out a series of prior transactions and the total amount owed as per the nominated date.

Acquit An accused is discharged after being deemed not guilty, for example, following a jury trial.

Act of Bankruptcy Action taken by a debtor as a result of an inability to pay debts as owed and due payable to a creditor.

Actus Reus A guilty act. In criminal law, one of the elements required to prove a crime has been carried out by voluntary actions or omissions. Can also be either a positive or failure to act. Also requires mens rea as the other essential element.

Adjourn Court matter is suspended to another specified date, postponed or stood down. Also known as *sine die*.

Administrative Law The legal framework for public administration to be carried out in the decision-making powers and procedures of public servants.

Adversary System The legal system of justice in common law countries where the opposing parties present and argue their case or position before an impartial third party, such as an arbitrator, judge, magistrate, or jury to make a decision.

Affidavit A written document setting out evidence or statement of facts voluntarily made by a person known as the deponent and sworn on oath or by way of an affirmation before a person authorised as a witness, such as a lawyer.

Affirmation A formal declaration by a person who declines to take swear on oath for such reasons, for example, based on religious grounds.

Age of Criminal Responsibility The minimum age a juvenile can be arrested, charged or jailed. The Victorian Government plans to raise such minimum age from 10 to 12 in late 2024, then to 14 by 2027. Also see Doli Incapax.

Aggravated Burglary A criminal offence that involves the use of a weapon to commit another crime when illegally entering occupied premises in order to steal or cause damage.

Aggravated Damages Compensatory damage for distress awarded to a successful party in a civil proceeding. Also see compensatory and exemplary damages.

Alleged A fact that has been stated but has not yet proven to be true.

Amicus-Curiae A friend of the court. Someone who is not a party to the matter but assists the court on questions of law or fact.

Appeal To review a decision from a lower court or tribunal before a higher court.

Appellant A person who appeals a decision from a lower court or tribunal to a higher court.

Apprehended Domestic Violence Order A court order introduced in New South Wales made to protect a person in a domestic relationship by restricting and prohibiting certain types of conduct by the other person.

Arbitration A formal procedure regarding a dispute for a binding decision by a neutral third party known as an arbitrator which cannot be appealed. Often referred to as alternative dispute resolution.

Arrest Taken into custody and usually in order to bring the person under arrest before a court.

Articled Clerk A trainee solicitor under supervision by a qualified legal practitioner.

At Large An animal that was not securely confined to the owner's property. A person may also be deemed to be at large if they have committed a criminal offence or escaped from custody and have not been arrested.

B

Bail A person accused of a crime may be granted bail with certain conditions which may include payment of money or on their own undertaking, to return to court on the adjourned date to answer the charge(s) as laid.

Bail Justice Is a person with designated authority to hear bail applications, usually after hours at a police station with the power to either refuse or grant bail to the accused.

Balance of Probabilities More probable than not the evidence presented in a civil proceeding is true. Compare this to a criminal trial in which the standard of proof is beyond reasonable doubt.

Bankruptcy A legal process where an individual or entity is declared unable to pay their debts to creditors and has entered into bankruptcy. Also see Voluntary Bankruptcy.

Barrister A legal professional called to the Bar specialising in courtroom advocacy and client representation. Usually takes instructions from solicitors.

Basic Income Threshold Amount The actual income threshold amount applying to a bankrupt taking into account the number of dependants that they have. After tax it is currently $68,768.70.

Beneficiary Is a person who derives an advantage, such as money, left from a will, trust, or life insurance policy.

Beyond Reasonable Doubt The highest standard of proof in a criminal trial the prosecution must meet in order to prove the guilt of an accused before a judge or jury. In the event of any doubt, they must be deemed to be not guilty. Compare to the civil proceeding standard of proof of a balance of probabilities.

Blood Alcohol Content Amount of alcohol in a person's bloodstream for which police may test, for example, by way of a roadside random breath test.

Breach of Contract A breach may occur when a party fails to satisfactorily perform services or action agreed to under a contract.

Burden of Proof The requirement in a criminal case for the prosecution to successfully prove, beyond reasonable doubt, the guilt of the accused. The defence is not required to prove anything and can simply maintain innocence unless a particular defence is raised meaning the burden then reverses.

C

Cab Rank Rule Requires any barrister to accept any matter in their field of expertise, meaning a party has a right to be represented by a barrister of their choice. The rule has exceptions such as conflict of interest or unavailability.

Case Law Also known as common law or judicial precedent, refers to decisions of judges in previous cases. Can be a binding or persuasive precedent from a higher court.

Caveat Formal warning or notice that someone has a legal interest (caveatable interest), for example, in land or property.

Character Reference A written statement that sets out an accused's good character, behaviour and reputation. Such a reference should be addressed appropriately, for example, 'The

Presiding Magistrates' or 'Your Honour' and be typed, dated and signed and no longer than one A4 page.

Character Witness A person who provides character testimony in court, in person, on behalf of the accused.

Charge Formal criminal accusation made against a person. Can also be a judge's direction to a jury, a fee for service or a financial burden such as a lien or encumbrance.

Civil Action Legal proceedings between private parties which may also include an action by a plaintiff against the state seeking a legal or equitable remedy.

Civil Law Means non–criminal law relating to civil matters.

Civil Pecuniary Penalty Fines imposed that breach certain laws and regulations, also known as monetary or pecuniary penalty.

Civil Wrong Refers to a cause of action under civil law for a wrongful act. Also see Tort and Breach of Contract.

Coercive Control A pattern to establish and maintain control over another person, particularly in domestic relationships.

Committal Proceedings Hearing held in a Magistrates Court to determine whether there is sufficient evidence to commit an accused to trial in the jurisdiction of a higher court. Sometimes also called a preliminary hearing.

Common Law The component of English Law traditionally derived from common custom and judicial unwritten law.

Community Corrections Order (CCO) A flexible sentencing order with conditions that an offender serves in the community. Most orders will require unpaid work in the community under supervision.

Compensation Order Requires a person convicted of a criminal offence to pay a monetary amount to the victim of that offence as determined by the court. Will not apply if the accused does not have sufficient financial means or ability to pay the compensation.

Compensatory Damages Money paid by way of damages to a successful party in a civil proceeding to compensate them for any incurred loss. Also see aggravated and exemplary damages.

Conciliation An alternative dispute resolution process where the parties to a dispute use a conciliator who meets with the parties in order to try and resolve the dispute by way of a mutual agreement to avoid further costly and time-consuming litigation.

Confidentiality Protection against disclosure, kept private. For example, in a professional relationship, such as doctor-patient, there is an ethical duty of confidentiality. Business relationships often see the parties enter into a non- disclosure agreement (NDA).

Constructive Dismissal A forced resignation when the employee believes that, given the adverse relationship with their employer they are left with no choice but to resign. Can also occur in situations where an employer advises an employee, 'If you don't resign, you will be terminated.'

Contest Mention Hearing Allows the magistrates court in criminal proceedings to efficiently manage the matter in the first instance and provides for any issues in dispute to be resolved between the parties. Applies to summary offences and indictable offences triable summarily in the lower court.

Control Test An analytical examination of the employment relationship to determine who is or, who is not, an employee. In simple terms, under common law an employer has the right to tell an employee what to do, how, when, and why in determining where there was in fact an employment relationship.

Conviction A determination by a court of law that a defendant is guilty of a criminal offence. Despite a guilty finding a court may exercise its discretion not to record a conviction.

Costs The legal fees and disbursements incurred by each party in a proceeding including and not limited to lawyer fees based on work done, filing fees, photocopying and travel. The losing party in most litigious matters will be ordered to pay the other party's costs and can be on a standard court scale basis. Also see damages and costs on an indemnity basis and party-party costs.

Costs Indemnity Basis Awarded by a court against a losing party to fully indemnify the successful party for all their legal costs and disbursements reasonably incurred and, as such, are normally significantly higher. For example, what has been reasonably charged by the law practice is recoverable.

Counterclaim A separate claim made by a defendant against a plaintiff in a civil action. Such a claim might have previously been brought in a separate matter but now the defendant claims by way of counterclaim in addition to filing a defence to the action.

Coward's Punch A strike to the head of an unsuspecting individual that is unprovoked and delivered without warning and often from behind.

Creditor A person or entity who is owed a debt.

Creditor's Statutory Demand A formal letter of demand under the Corporations Act served by a creditor on a debtor company in an attempt to recover the debt as owed to the creditor.

Criminal Culpability In criminal law an accused is held responsible for a criminal act or negligence when found to be at fault and liable for their conduct. Also see Actus Reus and Mens Rea.

Cross-Vesting The transfer of cases between state or territory Supreme Courts or Commonwealth courts. It allows proceedings to be transferred from one court to another within Australia.

Culpable Driving In Victoria the crime of culpable driving causing death can occur when a person driving a vehicle causes another person's death due to driving recklessly or negligently under the influence or affected by alcohol or drugs to a degree they could not control their vehicle.

Custodial sentence Term of imprisonment imposed by a court to prison or some other secure facility.

Custody Legal detention over a person when arrested or sentenced. Also denotes legal right or a duty of care of someone such as a child following parent separation. Also see Remanded in Custody.

D

Damages At common law is a remedy ordered by a court by way of a sum of money to be paid as compensation for loss or injury such as a civil wrong or breach of contract. Also see Compensatory Damages; General Damages; Nominal Damages; Special Damages and Unliquidated Damages.

Debt A sum of money that is owed or due by one party to another.

Debt Agreement A legally binding agreement between a debtor and a creditor to deal with unpaid debts without the need for the debtor to enter into bankruptcy.

Debtor A legal entity such as a person or company that owes a debt to another entity.

Debtor's Petition A formal personal application made by a debtor to the Official Receiver in Bankruptcy. Also known as voluntary bankruptcy.

Deed A legal written document or instrument that is executed between parties, for example, in respect to ownership of property or legal rights.

Deed of Company Arrangement (DOCA) A binding

agreement between a company and its creditors governing how the company's affairs will be dealt with in order to repay its debts after entering into voluntary administration.

Defamation The action of damaging the good reputation of a party either in printed or oral form without any proper justification. Also known as slander or libel.

Default Failure to fulfill an obligation. For example, to repay a loan or Aprea in court. Also see Default Summons.

Default Summons A court document that is issued alleging the debtor or defendant has failed to pay a debt due and owing.

Defendant A person or entity where the party is accused of committing a crime or named in a civil action where a remedy is sought.

Directions Hearing A preliminary hearing at the commencement of a court or tribunal matter in order for directions to be given to the parties as to what further steps need to be taken and how the matter should proceed. Also used to address questions of law and admissibility of evidence. Also see Contest Mention Hearing.

Director's Penalty Notice A formal notice issued by the Australian Taxation office to a company director to recover the company's tax liability for which the director is now personally liable. Such notice will outline the unpaid amount and remission options available.

Disbursement Monies paid out on behalf of a client in a legal matter and may include, for example, filing and search fees etc.

Discovery A process in legal proceedings where the parties involved, for example, in a civil court matter, provide to the other side all documents they intend to rely on in respect of the matter to be heard. In criminal matters, a duty of disclosure also applies in which the prosecution must serve on the defence all material in their possession they intend to rely on in order to prove guilt (or innocence) in the matter before the court. Also see Police Brief.

Diversion Order A diversion plan is typically run in the Magistrates Court where an order is made to allow the matter to be dealt with out of the court system and allow the defendant to avoid a conviction, providing a plea of guilty is entered. A magistrate must agree that the offender is eligible for a diversion plan which will include certain conditions that must be adhered to.

Doli Incapax The common law principle that a child between the ages of 10 to 14 years is presumed incapable of forming criminal intent unless rebutted by the prosecution that such child knew their conduct was morally wrong. Emanated from the Latin phrase "incapable of evil".

Duty Lawyer A legal professional who provides free advice and assistance to a person attending a court or tribunal hearing who is not represented by another lawyer.

Duty of Care A legal obligation or responsibility to take all reasonable steps to avoid causing harm or detriment to another person or property that is foreseeable and if breached, results in injury or harm giving rise to an action in tort.

E

Emphasis Added A phrase commonly used in legal writing to indicate that certain words have been highlighted or emphasised in order to draw attention to a specific text or meaning.

Employment Law Laws that govern the relationship between an employee and their employer and generally covers under a contract of service the rights and responsibilities of both parties including the terms and conditions of the employment such as salary, duties and working hours.

Entrapment May provide a defence to a criminal charge when it is alleged a law enforcement officer induced the person charged to commit a crime they would otherwise not have committed. Must be demonstrated that the person was persuaded or coerced.

Equity A body of law and a system of legal rules that is concerned with fairness and justice outside the common law jurisdiction. Equity also applies to a financial interest in respect of property and goods.

Evidence The information which is used in a court of law to either support or disprove the truth or existence of a fact. Usually obtained from witness testimony, documentary evidence or exhibits such as weapons and clothing.

Executor A person or entity appointed to carry out the terms of a will. Executrix applies if the person appointed is a female.

Ex-Gratia Payment A voluntary payment made by an individual or entity as a gesture of goodwill for damages or a claim but without acknowledgement of any fault by the party making the payment. Ex Gratia is Latin for "by favour".

Exhibit Refers to a piece of evidence or a document presented during a trial, hearing, or other legal proceedings. Can take many forms, for example, emails, contracts, CCTV footage, photographs etc.

F

Family Violence Intervention Order A court order designed to protect individuals, their children and property from harmful behaviour by another family member, partner or ex-partner. Also see Apprehended Domestic Violence Order and Personal Safety Intervention Order.

Family Violence Safety Notice Taken out by Victoria Police to provide immediate protection for individuals facing family violence.

Funds in Court A division of the Supreme Court of Victoria responsible for managing funds paid into court in civil proceedings. Typically used in situations where the funds paid are compensation to persons living with a legal disability.

G

General Damages Compensation paid as damages that is difficult to quantify and prove, such as pain and suffering, loss of reputation and future earnings. Also see Damages.

Guardian A person appointed to protect and manage the personal and financial affairs of another person. A plenary guardian holds all the normal powers for someone who is unable make decisions in their own right. Also known as plenary guardianship.

H

Hand-Up Brief A brief of evidence tendered by the prosecution in a committal hearing on which they intend to rely, setting out the charges, a summary of the evidence and documents, such as witness statements, and may also include a list of any previous criminal or traffic convictions. Also see Police Brief.

Hearsay Evidence An unverified statement based on what a witness has allegedly heard from another person, for which the witness has no personal knowledge or experience and is being offered in court as the truth. Hearsay evidence is normally inadmissible in a court proceeding unless an exception applies to the hearsay rule.

Hung Jury A jury that cannot agree upon a verdict of guilty or not guilty after an extended deliberation and is unable to reach the required unanimous or majority verdict. Can lead to a retrial.

I

Inadmissible Evidence that cannot be used in court to prove or disprove a fact in a case. For example, what could be irrelevant or obtained illegally.

Incorporated Association A recreational, cultural, or charitable entity established under legislation with its own legal identity and structure separate from its members and generally provides protection to such members in legal transactions.

Indemnity Security, compensation or protection against a loss or other financial burden. Also means to indemnify.

Indictable Offence A more serious criminal offence than a summary offence and generally heard before a judge and jury. Some indictable offences can be triable summarily in a lower court such as before a magistrate.

Industrial Manslaughter An employer, contractor or business owner who negligently breaches a health and safety duty under legislation that is owed to a worker resulting in death of that worker and is duly punishable at law.

Infant Is a person who has not yet reached the age where they are legally considered an adult. Specific age can vary depending on the jurisdiction but is generally under the age of 18 years. Such legal terms can also be known as juvenile and as referred to in criminal law, family law and civil proceedings.

Informant Individual who provides privileged information about a person or organisation to an agency such as a law enforcement body. Also, can be referred to as a confidential human source. In criminal matters, an informant is the person who lays the charge and includes a police officer, council officer or other government official.

Injunction A specified court order that compels or directs a party to do a specific act or thing or refrain from doing so.

An equitable remedy depending on the discretion and fairness of the court. Can be interim or may continue indefinitely. If breached can lead to a criminal or civil sanction and also can be seen as contempt of court.

Insolvency Unable to pay debts in full by a person (bankrupt) or company meaning they are in a state of insolvency.

Instalment Order A court can grant an application by a debtor to pay a judgment debt by regular payments either weekly, fortnightly, or monthly.

Inter Alia A Latin term commonly used in legal matters meaning amongst other things. More than one issue but only referring to one particular issue.

Interim Order A temporary order by a court or tribunal agreeing to or preventing certain action or steps being taken to preserve the status quo until the matter is heard in full when a final order can be made as determined.

Intervention Order A court order that prohibits a person (the Respondent) from behaving in a particular matter such as physical, verbal or emotional abuse towards another person (the protected person). See Apprehended Domestic Violence Order, Family Violence Interim Order, Family Violence Safety Notice and Personal Safety Intervention Order.

In-Vitro Fertilisation Complex treatment for infertility that can lead to pregnancy.

J

Judgment Debt The total amount owed to be paid by a debtor under a court order and can include costs and interest.

Judgment Debtor A person or company that is ordered by a court to pay money owed to another person or company.

Judicial Monitoring A sentencing option available to judges and magistrates that allows the court to actively manage and monitor compliance with sentencing requirements and conditions and can include a number of appearances before the sentencing judicial officer.

Judicial Officer Includes judges, Associate judges, Registrars, Magistrates and Justices of the Peace.

Judicial Registrar Generally involved in directions and interlocutory hearings and the management of criminal, civil and family law matters, issue various procedural and case management orders and also can participate in resolution conferences such as pre-hearing conferences in the Magistrates Court.

Judicial Review Review by a court in respect of an executive, legislative or administrative action taken by a public body. Also see Review on the Merits.

Jurisdiction Legal authority given to a court of law to determine a matter before it. Can also relate to mean the geographical boundary in which a court order can be enforced.

Jurisdictional Objection A claim that the Fair Work Commission does not have the power or is limited in the power to hear and decide a matter before, such as an unfair dismissal claim.

Juror Someone who is a member of a jury. In a criminal trial the number of jurors is typically 12 but can vary based on the jurisdiction and specified legal system. Civil trial jurors can also vary from six to 12 jurors but in most jurisdictions, it is normally six.

Jury A sworn body of people (jurors) from the general public convened to hear evidence in order to reach a verdict in a criminal trial based on the evidence presented and determined beyond reasonable doubt of the guilt or innocence of an accused and in civil cases, if proven on a balance of probabilities, the amount to be awarded in damages.

Justifiable Homicide Absolves a person of any criminal liability who killed another, such as in self-defence. Can also be in situations where a police officer acting, not just in self-defence but in situations to prevent a very serious crime being committed by that person.

Juvenile Police Caution Police may issue an informal caution, meaning that no formal action will be taken and it will not be listed on the young offender's record. If the matter is more serious, a formal caution will apply but under similar criteria but not serious enough to justify a criminal charge to bring the juvenile before the Children's Court.

L

Law Enforcement Assistance Program (LEAP) The online database used by Victoria Police that details their interactions with persons in respect of alleged crimes, incidents of family violence and also missing person reports.

Lawyer Client Costs The fees and disbursements rightly charged by a lawyer for providing legal services to a client.

Lawyers Picnic A somewhat colourful expression used by others and even lawyers to describe situations where lawyers are perceived to benefit excessively or overcharging for a particular legal matter.

Legal Aid Provision of free assistance from public monies for persons unable to afford their own legal representation.

Legal Eagle Not only referred to in jest but can also describe a very skilled lawyer or clever student of the law.

Legal Professional Privilege Protects confidential communications and documents between a lawyer and client and can only be disclosed with client permission. It is a cornerstone of the legal system to ensure clients can obtain legal advice and guidance without fear of compromising their rights.

Legislation Also known as Statutes or Acts of Parliament being the written law created by Parliament or delegated bodies.

Letter of Demand A formal letter stating a legal claim which makes a demand for restitution, such as payment of a debt or performance of some obligation or to desist from doing or saying something. Cease and desist letters are largely used in allegations of defamation.

Liability The state of being legally responsible for something, such as in a civil matter, a breach of contract, or criminally liable for committing a crime.

Liquidation The process of finalising a company's affairs and selling its assets to repay creditors and shareholders. Maybe voluntary or compulsory.

Litigant A person or entity involved in a civil legal dispute.

Litigation The act, process, or procedure to settle a matter by way of court proceedings. A litigant is a person involved in a civil case.

Litigation Guardian A person who is appointed on behalf of a party, usually by a court or tribunal, to act for a party who is unable to conduct their own litigation due to mental or physical disability or under the age of 18 years. The litigation guardian stands in the place of the represented party and makes all applicable decisions on that person's behalf.

Local Laws Laws and regulations enacted and enforced by local councils.

M

Magistrate A judicial officer who administers the law and presides over court matters that deal with normally less serious criminal matters and conducts preliminary hearings such as a committal in more serious indictable criminal charges. Also presides over civil matters including victims of crime applications.

Manifestly Excessive Appeal of the sentence in a criminal matter that is considered too harsh or severe and can occur, by way of example, where a sentence is imposed for a number of different offences at the same time, but overall a lack of consideration has been given of the collective effect of all of the sentences together.

Manifestly Inadequate The prosecution may appeal a sentence in a criminal matter on the basis that it is considered too lenient. A Court of Appeal would then consider the merits of the appeal and whether there has been a substantial injustice in respect of the original sentence.

McKenzie Friend A person who assists a self-represented party in a legal proceeding with leave of the court. Such a friend cannot, however, give legal advice or address the court on behalf of that person.

Means Tested The assessment of a person's income and assets in order to determine their eligibility for financial assistance.

Mediation A structured, interactive process used in dispute resolution where an impartial third party assists the disputing parties with a view to resolving a matter without the need to proceed, for example, to arbitration. Also see Conciliation.

Men's Behaviour Change Program A court ordered approved counselling program to assist and support a male in order to address violent and other problematic behavior arising from a relationship.

Mens Rea The intention or knowledge of wrongdoing required to constitute a criminal act. It is the mental element of the state of mind of the accused which can vary from intent to recklessness or even dishonesty and malice. Most crimes committed require proof of both mens rea and actus reus.

Mention Date In the Magistrates Court it is the first date in which a criminal matter is listed and for the court to provide further directions to progress the matter. A plea of guilty can sometimes proceed on the first mention date.

Mitigation In civil matters, the principle that applies to a party to have taken reasonable action to minimise their loss or damage suffered. In criminal matters it is the facts submitted to the court on behalf of the defendant to reduce the severity of the sentence. For example, a plea in mitigation may include remorse, a plea of guilty at the first opportunity and other relevant factors to assist the court in imposing an appropriate penalty.

N

Negligence A fundamental concept in Tort law when a person fails to meet a duty of care directly resulting in harm, loss or damage to another person. Determined on balance of probabilities.

Non-Disparagement Commonly used in a terms of settlement that prevents the parties from saying anything negative about each other or bringing them into disrepute and damaging their reputation.

Nominal Damages A small amount of money awarded to a successful party that suffered a legal wrong but no real financial loss.

Notice of Appearance Legal practitioners normally use a prescribed court form to file an appearance on behalf of a party they are representing, such as an accused in a criminal matter. Can also be given in person in court. 'I appear, Your Honour, on behalf of…'

Notice of Defence Written particulars that set out a response to a Writ and Statement of Claim addressing each of the allegations which can include a denial and on what basis, admissions, or non-admissions. Also referred to as pleadings.

Notice of Intention To Sue A letter by way of demand that puts the other party on notice that in the event they do not meet certain demands, legal proceedings may be commenced without further notice. Commonly used in debt matters.

O

Oath A sworn declaration of evidence to be given, such as the person will swear to 'tell the truth, the whole truth and nothing but the truth, in a court of law. Can be given with one hand on a religious text such as the Bible or by way of affirmation if person does not want to swear such evidence on a religious text.

Offence Can be either a summary offence (minor) or an indictable offence being a more serious offence in breach of Commonwealth or State Laws. Some serious indictable offences are triable summarily in a lower court such as the Magistrates Court.

Offender A person or entity who commits an illegal act.

Official Receiver in Bankruptcy A civil officer who manages a bankruptcy or is appointed by a court to manage the financial affairs of the debtor in bankruptcy.

Ombudsman A public official appointed to investigate and make a recommendation or a decision, following a complaint by an individual or entity made against a public authority such as a government body, Council or against a particular profession or organisation.

Outlaw Motorcycle Gang (OMCG) Also known as bikies, being a motorcycle club subculture where its members use their status and affiliation with the club as a means to conduct criminal activities.

P

Parole The conditional release of a prisoner before completion of a sentence, subject to conditions under a parole order.

Party-Party Costs Costs ordered against an unsuccessful litigant in order to pay the reasonable legal costs of the successful party. Both parties can attempt to agree on the amount to be paid and, in the absence of any agreement, a costs assessor is appointed. Typically, a successful party's reasonable legal costs are partially covered and usually in the range of 70 to 75 per cent of their total legal costs.

Perpetrator A person suspected of or who has committed a criminal offence. Also referred to as the offender or suspect.

Petition for Bankruptcy Formal process taken by a debtor or creditor in order to file for bankruptcy. The petition will disclose all the debtor's financial information such as assets, income, liabilities and debts. Also see Debtor's Petition.

Plaintiff A person or entity also known as a litigant who commences legal proceedings in a court of law against another in respect of a civil dispute.

Pleadings Written particulars that outline a claim or defence in a legal proceeding.

Personal Safety Intervention Order A court order put in place to protect an individual, their family members and property by another person who is not a family member.

Police Caution Given to a person under arrest in that they have the right to remain silent and seek legal advice and anything they do say may well be used in evidence against them.

Police Brief The brief of evidence in which police prepare and serve on a person charred with a criminal offence which will be relied on in a court of law by the prosecution to prove the guilt of the accused.

Pre-Hearing Conference When a defence is filed and served, for example, in a civil matter, the matter may proceed to an informal but compulsory and confidential conference, usually conducted by a court registrar to clarify any issues in dispute and to try and reach a settlement without the need to proceed to a full hearing.

Precedent Principle, rule or doctrine established in a prior legal case which courts are obliged to follow when hearing and making decisions in similar cases. Established from the reasoning given by judges when making decisions and can be either binding or persuasive.

Preliminary Brief Provides sworn early disclosure of the prosecution case and it may not contain a copy of all the witness statements but will detail the alleged facts and evidence that supports the charges as laid.

Presiding Magistrate The judicial officer who presides over proceedings in a Magistrates Court.

Presumption of Innocence The legal principle that any person accused of a crime is considered to have such a presumption until proven guilty in a court of law.

Prima Facie A Latin expression meaning "at first sight" or based on the face of it such as a first impression.

Prima Facie Case A case that has sufficient evidence to prove the facts of the matter as opposed to only speculative.

Prima Facie Evidence Evidence that exists which, unless disproven is sufficient to prove a certain fact or circumstance and in criminal matters a conviction beyond reasonable doubt.

Primary Victim A person who is injured or dies as a result of a violent crime. Compare to secondary and related victim.

Prisoners Compensation Quarantine Fund Initiated by a procedure that allows prisoners to seek compensation for alleged injuries or loss of property that occurred while serving a term of imprisonment. If awarded, it is held in the fund for initially 12 months. In some cases, their victims can make an application to be compensated for the monies held in respect of damages alleged to have been suffered.

Pro-Bono Specialist services provided by a professional, free-of-charge, to an individual or community. The term usually refers to the provision of legal services free of charge.

Professional Indemnity Insurance Type of insurance that protects a person, such as a lawyer, in respect of alleged claims of negligence arising from the performance of their professional duties.

Prohibited Person A person who must not possess, carry or use a firearm.

Prosecution The party conducting a prosecution and presenting evidence against a person charged with a criminal offence.

Protocol Is an agreement of a less formal nature than a treaty or convention.

Provocation Conduct or speech used deliberately to make a person angry or afraid.

Q

Quantum The total amount of money as compensation to be paid as awarded by way of damages.

Quantum Meruit A legal term that infers a promise to pay a reasonable amount such as for labour and materials supplied.

R

Random Breath Test (RBT) A procedure whereby a member of the police force may breath test a vehicle driver at random to detect and measure any alcohol in the driver's system.

Regulation A law or rule made by a government department or statutory body as enshrined by an applicable act of parliament.

Related Victim A person who, at the time of a violent crimes being committed where a person has died, was a close family member or in a personal relationship with the deceased primary victim. Also see Secondary Victim.

Remanded in Custody A person charged with a criminal offence is held on remand in custody, in prison or other facility until the matter is heard in a court of law.

Respondent A person named in a legal matter in respect of whom a case or appeal is brought against. Can also apply by way of a summons.

Restitution Refers to a payment to be made by a person convicted of a criminal offence or in a civil proceeding to make a payment by way of restitution, for example, in respect of property lost or damaged. You can also make restitution under the terms of a contract.

Restraining Order In family law, an order issued by a court to protect a person applying for the order from acts of domestic violence.

Reverse Onus Test Burden of proof shifts from the prosecution to the accused in criminal matters to show compelling reasons or exceptional circumstances in order to be released on bail.

Review on the Merits A review or re-hearing of a decision or ruling made by the primary decision maker in order to reconsider the facts and the law to determine whether it was a just and right decision in the first instance.

Right of Reinstatement A case or matter that has been struck out may be reopened in certain circumstances. For example, it was struck out but with a right of reinstatement.

Rogues Gallery Often referred to as mug shots or other images of criminal suspects kept by police for purposes of identification. Can also be used in the vernacular as a likable rogue.

Royal Commission It is an independent public inquiry conducted in Australia to investigate and make recommendations in respect of matters of particular public importance with specific terms of reference. Generally, only established in rare and exceptional circumstances by the issuing of Letters Patent by the Governor–General. Commonwealth Royal Commissions can only be conducted in respect of matters that relate to the responsibilities of the Commonwealth of Australia.

S

Safe Harbour Relief Refers to specific rules and regulations that can provide relief to taxpayers in certain circumstances. Allows individuals and companies to reduce or eliminate such regulatory liability.

Secondary Victim A person who suffers a physical and /or psychological injury as a direct result of witnessing an act of violence or being the parent or guardian of a primary victim under the age of 18 years. Also see Related Victim.

Self Defence The defence of one's person or interests, which can include the use of physical force but only at a level or degree of response in respect of the criminal act to remove the threat. By way of example, often used as a defence to a charge of assault or even murder on the basis of acting in self defence.

Self-Incrimination A privilege with certain limitations of not making a statement or to do anything that may lead to a criminal prosecution or used in evidence against that person.

Self-Representation To appear in person in a court of law without legal representation.

Sentencing Order The sentence imposed by a court of law following a defendant being found guilty in a criminal matter.

Sequestration Order Order handed down by a court, usually in bankruptcy for the assets of the person now declared bankrupt, to be managed by a trustee. Can also include an order for property to be seized to satisfy a debt.

Serious Indictable Offence A severe crime, such as murder, manslaughter, arson, sexual assault or robbery and usually punishable by more than five years in prison. Also see Indictable Offence.

Show Cause An accused in this situation must show cause and demonstrate why their continued detention is not justified. The prosecution does not have the onus of showing that the person charged poses an unacceptable risk if granted and released on bail. The onus rests with the defendant to demonstrate why bail is justified.

Special Damages Damages that can be easily and clearly determined and may include out-of-pocket expenses, such as medical costs, loss of earnings and rehabilitation costs. Generally awarded in civil litigation to the successful party for significant financial loss.

Spent Conviction Legislation allows the criminal record of the offender to be amended by the removal of certain offences after a period of time, without re-offending and usually those that are minor. In other words, they will no longer exist and can be spent by way of an application and, if removed, need not be disclosed to any person or entity.

Social Justice Justice in relation to a fair balance in the distribution of wealth, opportunities and privileges in a society where individual rights are recognised and protected.

Solicitor A legally qualified practitioner who can deal in most legal matters and appear on behalf of clients in a court of law and tribunals. Also provides written instructions to barristers by way of a brief.

Standard of Proof The designated level of certainty supported by the evidence to establish proof in a court of law. For criminal matters, it is beyond reasonable doubt and for civil matters based on a balance of probabilities.

Statement of Claim Sets out in paragraph form, with particulars, a description of what a plaintiff is alleging and claiming from a defendant.

Statute Also known as an act, being a law enshrined by parliament, either Commonwealth, State or Territory.

Statutory A law enshrined by a parliament or delegated body and can be in the form of an Act, regulation, or local law. If not adhered to a relevant penalty can be applied.

Statutory Body Also known as a statutory authority being a body set up by law defining its powers, objectives and functions as is also empowered to implement certain legislation.

Statutory Declaration A written statement and account of certain facts attested to and signed by the person who solemnly and sincerely declares it to be true before a person so authorised to take such a declaration.

Strict Liability In criminal law a strict liability offence means a defendant can be held liable for committing an act against public policy without requiring proof of intent or mental state (mens rea).

Subpoena A subpoena or witness summons is a form of Writ issued by a court of law compelling a witness to attend at court on a certain day and time, in order to give evidence or produce documents.

Sue To initiate a legal proceeding against a particular party in a civil matter.

Summary Case Conference A meeting between the prosecution and the accused and usually with their legal representative to discuss the charges as laid, the evidence and issues in dispute with a view to progressing the matter before the designated court appearance. Also seen as pre-trial disclosure.

Summary Dismissal Refers to the termination of an employee without notice and usually in respect of serious misconduct.

Summary Offence A minor offence that can be determined in the Magistrates Court without the need for a trial by judge and jury. Typical sentences can include a fine, good behavior bond or community corrections order.

Summons A legal document issued by a court to a named person requiring their attendance at court on a specific date and time.

Surety A promise by a person as guarantor that financial obligations will be met if a party defaults, normally paid into the court by the person providing the surety and, in the event of default, the money paid will be forfeited. Often seen in bail being granted with surety.

Suspended Sentence A prison sentence on conviction for a criminal offence that will only be served if the convicted person defaults by committing further offences. Can be wholly suspended or a combined custody and treatment order.

Sworn Evidence Given when a person first takes an oath or affirmation before providing such evidence.

T

Terms of Reference Sets out the terms for which an inquiry will be conducted or a decision that will be determined.

Terms of Settlement A detailed document that sets out the agreement by way of terms and conditions reached between the parties to settle a dispute. Also referred to as a Deed of Settlement.

Thesis A document submitted in support of candidature for an academic degree or professional qualification detailing the candidate's research and findings. Also known as a dissertation.

Tort A civil wrong that causes harm or loss to a claimant resulting in legal liability and can be intentionally or otherwise, giving rise to a civil claim whereby the claimant can sue for unliquidated damages or even by way of an injunction.

Trafficking In criminal law to deal or trade in something that is illegal such as drugs or humans.

Treatment Order A court order that provides for compulsory mental health treatment in a psychiatric hospital for a person suffering from a mental disorder, as opposed to a prison, when convicted of a criminal offence.

Trespass Unlawful entry onto someone's land or property without permission.

Triable Summarily Indictable offences that are less serious and can be listed before a Magistrate for hearing.

Trust Items held on trust by one party referred to as the trustee for the benefit of the person known as the beneficiary.

Trust Account A nominated bank account held by a legal representative in order for monies to be deposited on behalf of a client and to be held in trust pursuant to strict accounting rules.

Trustee in Bankruptcy The person appointed by the court who oversees and manages the bankrupt's estate and assets and to ensure strict compliance with bankruptcy laws.

U

Unfair Preference Payment A preference transaction by paying a debt made by an insolvent company that provides an advantage to one creditor as against payment to other creditors. Also see Voidable Transaction.

Unliquidated Damages When damages to be awarded are left to the determination of a judge and jury. Can also refer to a debt that remains to be paid or removed by way of an agreement.

V

Vexatious A legal action or proceeding that is initiated by a party without proper basis in order to annoy or cause inconvenience or issues for the other named party and without any possibility of success.

Vexatious Litigant A court or tribunal can declare a person as such if they persistently commence unwarranted and without proper basis, legal action that has no reasonable prospect of success. Such a declared person is then prohibited from commencing legal proceedings without leave of the court.

Victim Impact Statement A written statement provided to the court by a victim of crime setting out the details of their injury, loss or damage as a consequence of the crime.

Visual Audio Recording Evidence (VARE) A formal statement in a criminal matter made by a juvenile to police, either by way of an audio or video recording where a suitably trained police officer will ask the child relevant questions.

Void Has no legal effect.

Voidable Transaction A transaction from a company's assets to another party that occurs at a time when the company was insolvent or otherwise causes a detriment to the company and is, therefore, void. Also see Unfair Preference Payment.

Voluntary Bankruptcy A debtor chooses to go into bankruptcy as against being forced to do so.

Voluntary Liquidation A company chooses to go into liquidation as against being forced to do so, such self-imposed windup or dissolution being approved by its shareholders.

W

Waive Refrain from or give up a legal right or claim relinquished voluntarily.

Warrant A legal document issued by a court authorising an officer, such as a police member, to take certain action, which can include arresting a person to bring before the court or to search premises.

Wilful Blindness A term to describe a situation where a person seeks to avoid civil or criminal liability in respect of a wrongful act by intentionally and deliberately avoiding those facts that would implicate them. Often seen as "turning a blind eye".

Without Prejudice A term used in a legal letter or other form of communication in order to invoke legal privilege in a genuine attempt to resolve a matter or dispute and such communication cannot be used against the communicating party in any future court proceedings.

Without Prejudice Save as to Costs A term used where any communication, usually by way of a letter, is protected except when and if the question of legal costs is then being determined. Often used in a letter of offer to settle a matter and if not settled the letter may then be produced in court on a question of costs as applicable.

Witness A person who witnessed an event and can provide such evidence or knowledge in respect of any fact or issue arising from it.

Writ A formal written order issued by a higher court such as the Supreme or County Court and has attached a statement of claim as part of the first step in a legal proceeding.

BIBLIOGRAPHY

- Banks, Keith (with Ben Smith), *Drugs Guns & Lies*, Allen & Unwin 2020.
- Bezzina, Charlie, *The Job Fighting Crime from the Front Line*, The Slattery Media Group 2010.
- Fair Work Commission, *General Protections benchbook*, Australian Government 2022.
- Fair Work Commission, *Sexual Harassment benchbook*, Australian Government 2023.
- Fair Work Commission, *Unfair Dismissals benchbook*, Australian Government 2022.
- Fitzroy Legal Service, *The Law Handbooks, Your Practical Guide to the Law In Victoria*, FLS 2017-2022.
- Ford, Justine, *The Good Cop*, Pan Macmillan 2016.
- Hardy, J, *The History of Family Law in Australia*, Society, 2016.
- O'Neill, C, *From Vietnam Nasho to Catching School Crooks*, Book Burrow, Australia, 2024.
- Petraitis, Vikki, *Inside the Law 25 years of true crime writing*, Clan Destine Press 2019.
- Quaedvlieg, Roman, *'Tour de Force'*, Penguin Random House Australia 2020.
- Sharpe, Alan & Encel, Vivienne, *Murder: 25 True Australian Crime Stories*, Kingsclear Books Pty Ltd 1997.
- The Secret Barrister, *Stories of the Law and How its Broken*, Macmillan 2018.

MAGAZINES/JOURNALS/REPORTS/ARTICLES

- Australian Competition & Consumer Commission, *Court declares lawyer engaged in misleading debt collection practices* (19 October 2011).
- Australian Criminal Intelligence Commission: *Illicit Firearms in Australia* (2016).
- Australian Federal Police, *Three People jailed in NSW over $5.8 million NDIS Fraud*, Media Release (31 October 2024).
- Australian Government Attorney General's Department, *Presumption of innocence* (2021).
- Australian Government Attorney General's Department, *Draft Report 2020 – Age of Criminal Responsibility* (31 March 2021).
- Australian Government Attorney General's Department, *National Firearms Registry* (December 2023).
- Australian Government Department of Foreign Affairs and Trade, *Commonwealth Firearms infraction Booklet* (2021).
- Australian Government Department of Social Services, *The National Plan to End Violence against Women and Children 2022-2032* (28 October 2022).
- Australian Government Department of Social Services, *Domestic, Family and Sexual Violence Commission* (28 February 2023).
- Australian Government Department of Social Services, *The 'Getting the NDIS Back on Track' Bill has passed* (11 September 2024).

- Australian Institute of Criminology, *Mass shootings and firearm control: comparing Australia and the United States* (2014).
- Australian Institute of Criminology, *Restorative justice in the Australian criminal justice system* (2014).
- Commonwealth of Australia 2022, *Fair Work Commission, Annual Report - Access to Justice 2021-22* (21 September 2022).
- Communications Law Bulletin, *Review of phone tapping law* (Vol 11, No 3).
- Coroners Court New South Wales; *Domestic Violence Death Review* (December 2022).
- Council of Australian Governments, *National Disability Scheme* (2009).
- Crime Statistics Agency, *latest- Victorian Crime data-year ending 30 September 2022* (December 2022).
- Crime Statistics Agency, *latest- Victorian Crime statistics-year ending 30 September 2022* (December 2022).
- Crime Statistics Agency, *latest- Victorian Crime statistics-year ending 30 September 2023* (December 2023).
- Crime Statistics Agency, *Key figures- Victorian Crime statistics-year ending December 2023* (March 2024).
- Crime Statistics Agency, Media Release, *Key crime measures decrease with criminal incident rates at their lowest since the year ending 2005.* (December 2022).
- Crime Statistics Agency, Media Release: *Key crime measures begin to stabilise after pandemic-related declines* (16 March 2023).
- Government of Western Australia, Media Release, *Firearms Crackdown to Include Mandatory Mental Health Checks* (5 February 2023).
- Independent Broad-based Anti-Corruption Commission, Guidance Material *IBAC's legislated powers* (26 December 2017).

- Judicial College of Victoria, *Victorian Sentencing Manual* (9 September 2023).
- Lawyers Weekly, *Melbourne lawyer guilty on 7 counts of professional misconduct* (3 April 2020).
- Lawyers Weekly, *Nicola Gobbo's conduct 'duplicitous, inexcusable' final report finds* (30 November 2020).
- Lawyers Weekly, *Commonwealth government faces class action over NDIS exclusion* (21 September 2022).
- Lawyers Weekly, *Fake Lawyer cops suspended jail sentence* (9 October 2022).
- Lawyers Weekly, *High Insolvency numbers coming, says Big Law partner* (22 January 2023).
- Lawyers Weekly, *Lessons from the 'mercy killing' of the AAT* (6 April 2023).
- Lawyers Weekly, *More awareness needed to combat 'avalanche' of mental health issues in the profession* (26 May 2023).
- Lawyers Weekly, *Victorian lawyer sunk client's money into 'bizarre' scam* (29 May 2023).
- Lawyers Weekly, *Victorian Lawyer jailed for 'abhorrent' $420k theft from clients* (20 June 2023).
- *Lawyers Weekly, Lawyer in $105 mm Plutus Payroll scandal sentenced* (4 July 2023).
- Law Council of Australia, *Council of Attorneys-General–Age of Criminal Responsibility Working Group Review* (2021).
- Law Society Journal, *Gun control: what makes Australian an US laws so different* (26 July 2022).
- Law Society of NSW Journal, *What is a Calderbank offer? Settlement offers and indemnity costs* (4 October 2022).
- Masters Builders Victoria, *The first industrial manslaughter conviction in Australia* (17 June 2020).
- Mc Culloch, *Behind the Headlines* (3 June 1987).

- McNab, Duncan, *Digging up the past: The gruesome bid to cover up the murder of Melbourne solicitor Roger Wilson* (15 December 2019).
- *Minister for the Department of Social Services, Major increases to penalties and criminal offences planned for NDIS providers* (28 October 2024).
- Monash University, *Legal responses to one-punch homicide in Victoria; Understanding the Impact of Law Reform* (December 2018).
- Murderpedia, *Christopher Dale Flannery*.
- National Archives of Australia, *Royal Commission into Aboriginal Deaths in Custody*, (December 1988).
- NDIS, *National Disability Insurance Agency Annual Report 2021-22*).
- NDIS Quality and Safeguards Commission, *Unauthorised uses of restrictive practices in the National Disability Insurance Scheme* (January 2022).
- New South Wales Police, *Operation Amarok leads to the arrest of NSW's most dangerous DV offenders* (31 January 2023).
- New South Wales Police, *NSW's most dangerous DV offenders targeted during Operation Amarok 111*(16 July 2023).
- News and Resources, *Drug Driving- The Lick Test* (10 March 2010).
- Northern Territory Government, *Raising the minimum age of criminal responsibility* (6 December 2022).
- Office of Public Prosecutions, *Best Practice Communication with Victims, A study for the OPP* (RMIT 2017-18).
- Pat Cronin Foundation, *What is the Coward Punch and how do we put an end to One Punch attacks?* (December 2022).
- Platypus Journal- Australian Federal Police, *A Collaborative Approach Towards Combating Fraud* (Article 2000).

- Premier of Victoria Media Release, *Clear laws for Victoria Police's use of Informants* (15 August 2022).
- Premier of Victoria Media Release, *Landmark Reforms To Support Victims of Crime* (6 April 2022).
- Respect Victoria, *Five years On; Respect Victoria Reflects on the Royal Commission into Family Violence* (26 March 2021).
- Right Now Human Rights Australia, *When Justice Fails-Wrongful Convictions in Australia* (2 October 2020).
- Royal Commission *Into the Management of Police Informants; final report* (30 November 2020).
- Sentencing Advisory Council, *Phasing Out of Suspended Sentences Complete from Today* (September 2014).
- Sentencing Advisory Council, *Restitution and Compensation Orders* (June 2017).
- Sentencing Advisory Council, *Firearms Offences: Current Sentencing Practices* (May 2019).
- Sentencing Advisory Council, *Serious offending by People Serving a Community Correction Order*: (2020-2021).
- Sentencing Advisory Council, *Guilty Pleas and Sentencing* (November 2022).
- State Trustees, *(Response to) Victorian Ombudsman Report* (June 2019).
- The Australian Professional Liability Blog, *Sole practitioner gets 3.5 years jail for $1M trust deficiency* (22 November 2006).
- The Australian Professional Liability Blog, *Michael Bakhaazi jailed for 3 years stealing a quarter million dollars* (10 June 2007).
- The Australian Professional Liability Blog, *Law Institute seeks 50-year ban for 62-year-old solicitor* (11 July 2008)
- The California Sunday Magazine, *Nicola Gobbo defended Melbourne's most notorious criminals at the height of the gangland war They didn't know she had a secret* (16 January 2020).

- University of Wollongong Australia, *The operation of Australian 'one punch' laws 2008-2018* (December 2019).
- Victims of Crime Assistance Tribunal -*Relevant Review Cases* (June 2020).
- Victims of Crime Commissioner, *Annual Report 2018-2019*
- Victims of Crime Commissioner, *Annual Report 2020-2021*.
- Victims of Crime Commissioner, *Silenced and Sidelined Report*, (March 2024).
- Victims of Crime, *Victorian Victims Register- offender information* (May 2023).
- Victorian Aboriginal Legal Service VALS Policy Brief, *Fixing Victoria's Broken Bail Law (undated)*.
- Victorian Civil and Administrative Tribunal, *Annual Report 2021-22*.
- Victorian Law Foundation- *Jurors Handbook* 2012.
- Victorian Law Reform Commission, *Improving the Justice System Response to Sexual Offences* (Report September 2021).
- Victorian Law Reform Commission, *The Role of Victims of Crime in the Criminal Trial Process: Consultation Paper* (November 2022).
- Victorian Legal Services Board and Commissioner, *Annual Reports 2013-2022*.
- Victorian Legal Services Board and Commissioner, *Supreme Court bans fake lawyer from undertaking legal work* (15 October 2018).
- Victorian Ombudsman, *Investigation into child sex offender Robert Whitehead's involvement with Puffing Billy and other railway bodies* (25 June 2018).
- Victorian Ombudsman, *Investigation into State Trustees* (27 June 2019).

- Victorian State Government, *Victorian Workplace manslaughter laws now in effect* (media release 1 July 2020).
- West Australian State Government, *Important steps to bolster family and domestic violence response* (medial release 12 September 2023)
- WorkSafe QLD, *First individual convicted for industrial manslaughter* (31 March 2022).
- WorkSafe Vic, *Companies charged with workplace manslaughter* (8 February 2023).
- WorkSafe Western Australia, *Overview of Western Australia's Work Health and Safety Act* 2020.

PRINCIPAL REFERENCE WEBSITES

- www.abc.net.au
- www.afsa.gov.au
- www.asic.gov.au
- www.ato.gov.au
- www.austlii.edu.au
- www.childrenscourt.vic.gov.au
- www.countycourt.vic.gov.au
- www.fairwork.gov.au
- www.fwc.gov.au
- www.fitzroy-legal.org.au
- www.fwc.gov.au
- www.legalaid.vic.gov.au
- www.magistratescourt.vic.gov.au
- www.supremecourt.vic.gov.au
- www.vcat.gov.au
- www.vocat.vic.gov.au
- www.1800respect.org.au
- www.wikipedia.org
- www.trove.nla.gov.au

LIST OF CASES

Proudman v Dayman [1941] HCA 28-67 CLR 536-defence under reasonable mistaken belief	14
R v Lanteri [2006] VSC 225 for an explanation of the sentencing process by Gillard J	14
R v Tania Lee–Anne Herman [2005] VSC 234-Criminal law- sentence	19
DPP v Trent Potts, Phillip O'Donnell, Jake Houldcroft and Jake Mitchell [2022] VCC 1825-Criminal law-sentence	26
R v Mills [1998] VSC 241-Sentencing principles	28
Azzopardi v The Queen [2011] VSCA 372)-Sentencing principles	28
RP v The Queen [2016] HCA 53 *doli incapax* presumption	29
DPP v PM [2023] VSC 560)-doli incapax presumption	30
R v ALH (2003) 6VR 276[2003] VSCA 129-Crown to prove juvenile knew conduct was seriously wrong: criminal liability	31
R v Kirby: Ex parte Boilermakers Society of Australia (1956) 94 CLR 254 -Major case dealing with separation of powers in Australian law	51
Hollis v Vabu Pty Ltd [2001] HCA 44- Principle – question of employee or independent contractor	53
Ogilvy & Mather (NZ) Ltd v Turner [1996] 1 NZLR 64-reasonable notice on termination at common law	58
Quinn v Jack Chia (Australia Ltd [1992] 1 VR 567-reasonable notice on termination at common law	58
Mohazab v Dick Smith Electronics [1995] IRCA 625-leading authority on constructive dismissal	60
Chen v Monash University [2015] FCA 130-whether employee subjected to discrimination or harassment in the workplace–whether court has jurisdiction to hear claim for victimisation	62

Swan v Monash Law Book Cooperative [2013] VSC 326-Tort-Negligence-Duty of Care–Workplace bullying	74
Ms SB [2014] FWC 2014-Workplace bullying-Application of section 789FD of the Fair Work Act	74
Rankin v Marine International Pty Ltd [2001] VSC 150-Employer- employee–claim for wrongful dismissal-allegations of misconduct	75
ACCC v Sampson [2011] FCA 165-Cost on letters of demand for debt	80
Milson & Official Receiver in Bankruptcy [2004] AATA 275-Bankrupt– hardship grounds–income contribution	89
Swaby v Lift Capital Partners Pty Ltd [2009] FCA 749-factors for leave to proceed against company in liquidation	98
Calderbank v Calderbank [1975] ALL ER 333-costs consequences of not accepting offer to settle	104
Hazeldene's Chicken Farm Pty Ltd v Victorian Workcover Authority (No 2)[2005] VSCA 298 13 VR 43 –unsuccessful appeal against discretionary Judgment regarding appointment of damages	105
Steven John Reynolds v Criscon Pty Ltd [2019] QDC 252-Appeal – Criminal law	114
Aaron Guilfoyle and Ardent Leisure Ltd [2020] QMC 13-sentence–breach of Work Health and Safety Act	114
R v Brisbane Auto Recycling Pty Ltd & Ors [2020] QDC 113–sentence- Industrial manslaughter	115
R v Jeffrey Owen [2022] QDSR 168–sentence-Industrial manslaughter	116
Director of Public Prosecutions v Keilor-Melton Quarries Pty Ltd [2018] VCC 2139- sentence–breach of OHS Act	118
Chiro v The Queen [2017] HCA 37-criminal law–sentence	119
Di Aldo DiTonto & Anor v The Queen [2018] VSCA 318 appeal-sentence	119
Keilor- Melton Quarries Pty Ltd v The Queen [2020] VSCA 169-leave to appeal sentence	119

DPP v Phongthaihong [2020] VCC 294–Culpable driving causing death-sentence	130
Phongthaihong v the Queen [2021] VSCA 317–Appeal–Culpable driving causing death- Appeal allowed	130
The Queen v Glascott [2008] VSC 236–sentenced for murder	144
Glascott v The Queen [2011] VSCA 109–resentenced on appeal	144
R v Keogh (unreported, Supreme Court of Victoria, Hampel J 15 February 1989-criminal law–sentence	146
R v Ramage [2004] VSC 508-criminal law-sentence manslaughter	147
R v Sharpe [2005] VSC 276-criminal law-sentence murder	148
Batty, Luke COR 2014 0855[2015] Vic Cor C 23285– finding into death	149
The King v Basham, Adrian James (sentencing) [2023] VSC 79-criminal law - sentence murder	173
DPP v Brown, Adam [2023] VSC 311-criminal law-sentence murder	173
DPP v Benjamin Coman [2023] VSC 159 criminal law-sentence murder	176
DPP v Tan, Joon Seong (Ruling No 1) [2023] VSC 296-Evidence-Hearsay	176
DPP v Tan, Joon Seong [2023] VSC 416-criminal law-sentence murder	177
DPP v McDonough, Paul Philip [2023] VSC 352- criminal law–sentence manslaughter	177,266
R v Loveridge [2013] NSWSC 1638	183
R v Loveridge [2014] NSW CCA 120-criminal law–sentence	183
R v Mc Neil [2015] NSWSC 1198-criminal law–sentence	184
R v Garth (No 2) [2017] NSWDC 471-criminal law–sentence	185
The State of Western Australia v Dimer [2022] WASCA 148-Criminal law- State appeal against sentence	186

The Queen v Martyn [2011] NTCCA 13-criminal law–sentence	186
R v Polutele [2011] VSC 381-criminal law sentence	187
DPP v Closter [2014] VSC 484-criminal law–sentence	187
DPP v Tyrone Steven Russell [2014] VSC 292-criminal law–sentence	187
DPP v Tyrone Steven Russell [2014] VSCA 308-leave to appeal-sentence	188
The Queen v Andrew William Lee [2017] VSC 678-criminal law–sentence	190
Lee v The Queen [2018] VSCA 63-leave to appeal-sentence	190
R v Vincec [2017] VSC 602-criminal law–sentence	191
Vincec v The Queen [2018] VSCA 18-leave to appeal-sentence	191
DPP v Esmaili [2019] VSC 218-criminal law–sentence	192
DPP v Armstrong, Tyson [2023] VSC 374-criminal law–sentence	193
National Disability Insurance Agency v WRMF [2020] FCAFC 79-Human Rights–NDIS	208
R v Knight [1989] VR705-criminal law-sentence murder	214
Knight v Victoria [2017] HCA 29) Constitutional law (Cth)-parole period	214
Minogue v Victoria [2019] HCA 31-Constitutional law (Cth)-parole period	214
The Queen v Martin Bryant–22 November 199 -comments on passing sentence for multiple murders	215
Pickford v Chief Commissioner of Police [2002] VSC 435-prohibited person -application to be deemed not a prohibited person	225
R v Hudson [2008] VSC 389–criminal law–plea–murder	228
Websdale v Chief Commissioner of Police (Review and Regulations [2019] VCAT 666-Firearms Prohibition Order-public interest-Order seat aside	233
Chief Commissioner of Police v Cameron Patterson [2023] VSC 172	233

The Queen v Tibar Omar [2021] VSC 515-criminal law–sentence	235
DPP v Gargaslous (2019) VSC 87-criminal law-sentence murder-reckless conduct endangering life	240
R v Paterson [2006] VSC 268 A Crim R122–Bail-show case- Burden on applicant to show cause-Burden on Crown to show unacceptable risk	243
Re Asmar [2005] VSC 487 Bail-show case-Burden on applicant to show cause-Burden on Crown to show unacceptable risk	243
Hildebrandt v DPP [2008] VSC 198-right to bail-lengthy delay	243
Mokbel v DPP (No 3) [2002] VSC 393;133 a Crim R 141Bail-exceptional Circumstances-indefinite delay in committal and trial	243
Nelson, Veronica COR 2020 0021(2023) Vic Cor C 28312-Finding into death	251
Arnold v CCT (unreported VSC–10 December 1992- special circumstances Assistance for victims of crime	262
DPP v Corfe [2023] VCC 253- criminal law–sentence-Plea-historic child sexual offending	272
DPP v Anthony John Hutchins [2023] VCC 738 criminal law–sentence	274
DPP v Whitehead [2015] VCC–CR-15-00645-criminal law–sentence	274
R v Denyer [1995] 1VR 186–Criminal Law-murder-Sentence-whether non–parole period should have been fixed	281
R v Forde [2007] VCC 1610 -criminal law–sentence	284
DPP v Forde [2023] VCC 1763	285
Anthony John Carolan v The Queen [2015] VSCA 167-Appeal-indefinite sentence	285
Allen v Sir Alfred Mc Alpine & Sons Ltd [1968] 2 QB 229–concept of Amicus curiae	314
McKenzie v McKenzie [1970] 3 All Er 1034-concept of McKenzie friend	315

Collier v Hicks (1831) 109 ER 1290-concept of McKenzie friend	315
Li v So [2021] VSCA32- McKenzie friend and oral submissions	315
Nepal v Minister for Immigration and Border Protection [2015] FCA 366- McKenzie friend and oral submissions	315
Smith v R (1985) 159 CLR 532-Court discretion-McKenzie friend	315
R v Burke [1993] 1 Qd R 166-McKenzie friend-refuse legal aid	315
Livingspring Pty Ltd v Kilger Partners [2008] VSCA 930-Security for costs -Threshold jurisdictional question- Whether reason to believe company will be unable to pay costs	316
Spiel v. Commodity Brokers Australia Pty Ltd (In Liq) (1983) 35 SASR 294) -Security for costs-in granting of order for security may result in an injustice to plaintiff	316
O'Reilly v. SA Waste Management Pty Ltd [2011] FWA 4229) Employer sought security for costs-employee failed to comply with directions- security for costs order granted	316
Victorian Legal Services Board and David Jensen & Ors [2018] VSC 740 -injunction	323
Victorian Legal Services Board and David Jensen & Ors [2022] VSC 603) -Contempt of Court	323
DPP v Domenic Mak [2020] VCC 1233–criminal law-sentence	325
DPP v Cavkic, Athanasi, Clarke [2004] VSC 158-criminal law-sentence murder	325
Briginshaw v. Briginshaw (1938) HCA 34 60 CLR336- How the requisite standard of proof should operate in civil proceedings	325
DPP v Athena Razos [2024] VCC 1077	326
LSB v Francis McGrath (No 2) [2010] VSC 332)-removal of name from roll of practitioners	327
R v Kesik [2006] VSC 493-Sentence-Solicitor-Deficiencies in trust account and thefts	328

LSBC v Kevin Roache VCAT J50/2021-professional misconduct	328
DPP v Kevin Roache [2023] VCC 1034-criminal law–sentence	328
R v Dupas [2006] VSC 481 - Criminal law	330
R v Bakhazzi [2006] VSC 496)-Criminal law-Failing to account for trust money-obtaining property by deception-Procuring the execution of a valuable security	330
R v Gabriel W [2006] VSC 397-Criminal law-Theft, Obtaining financial advantage by deception, trust account deficiency	330
Law Institute of Victoria v DSS [2008] VCAT 1179-Misconduct prosecution	331
LSC v Nguyen [2013] VSC 443)-removal of name from roll of practitioners	331
DPP v David Chapman [2013] VCC 2139-Criminal law-sentence	331
DPP v Kim Charles Blackberry [2019] VSC 279-Criminal law-sentence- multiple charges of obtaining property by deception and using a false document–legal practitioner	331
DPP v Kotsifas [2020] VSC 347-Criminal law sentence-causing Trust account deficiencies and theft	332
Kotsifas v The Queen [2021] VSCA 368)-Appeal against sentence	332
R v Sidaoui [2018] SCR 0220 -Criminal law-sentence-Trust account deficiencies and theft	332
R v Dev Menon [2023] NSWSC 768-Criminal law-sentence	333
R v Johnson [2011] VSC 633)- Criminal law-sentence	337
AB & EF v CD [2017] VSC 350 and EF v CD [2017] VSC 351-Application to prevent release of criminal convictions-dismissed	339
AB v CD & EF [2017] VSCA 338-Appeal rejected	339
AB (a pseudonym) v. CD (a pseudonym); EF (a pseudonym) v CD (a pseudonym) [2018] HCA 58-Criminal law–Prosecution's duty of disclosure -Public Interest immunity	340

Chief Commissioner of Police v Crupi [2024] HCA 34-Special leave to Appeal	344
Madafferi v The Queen [No 2] [2021] VSCA 332-Criminal law-Appeal Bail –refused	344
DPP v Arico (Unreported, County Court of Victoria, Judge Chettle, 10 November 2016, Criminal law-sentence	344
Rocco Arico v The Queen [2018] VSCA 135; 272 A Crim R 450 -Criminal law–appeal-sentence	344
R v Faruk Orman [2009] VSC 538-Criminal law–sentence	345
Faruk Orman v The Queen [2019] VSCA 163-Criminal law–appeal – sentence squashed	345
Zlate Cvetanovski v The Queen [2020] VSCA 272 Criminal law–appeal –sentence squashed	346
Salvatore Agresta v The Queen [2020] VSCA 334 Criminal law–appeal -Bail pending appeal	346
Rob Karam v The Queen [No 2] [2022] VSCA 163-Criminal law –Conviction-Application for leave to appeal against conviction	347
Saverio Zirilli v The Queen [2021] VSCA 2:287 A Crim R 407-Criminal law–Conviction-Application for leave to appeal against conviction-Orders made under section 317 of the Criminal Procedure Act 2009	347
John (Jan) Visser v The Queen [2020] VSCA 327-Appeal dismissed	347
R v Goussis [2006] VSC 168-Criminal law– sentence	348
R v Goussis [2009] VSC 16-Criminal law–sentence	348
Evangelous Goussis v the King [2022] VSCA 255-Application for leave to appeal	348
Antonios Mokbel v The King [2023] VSCA 40-Summary of Judgment	349
Cassidy, Tyler COR 2008 5542[2011] Vic Cor C 12-Finding into death	357
Dale v DPP [2009] VSCA 212-bail–exceptional circumstances	359
R v Miechel [2006] Supreme Court of Victoria, King J, 26 May 2006 (conviction) 18 August 2006 (sentence).	359

David Anthony Miechel v the Queen [2010] VSCA 225-Appeal-sentence	360
Gobbo v State of Victoria (redacted) [2025] VSC 334 Negligence - personal injury	364
Victorian Legal Services Board v Gobbo [2020] VSC 692)- removal of name from roll of practitioners	364
XYZ v State Trustees Ltd [2006] 25 VAR 402-Administrative law- Guardianship and Administration-Appointment of administrator	377

LIST OF LEGISLATION

Commonwealth

A New Tax System (Goods and Services) Tax Act 1999	83
Age Discrimination Act 2004	53
Australian Human Rights Commission Act	54
Bankruptcy Act 1966	77-79, 87-92
Bankruptcy Regulations 2021	79
Classification (Publications, Films and Computer Games) (Enforcement) Act 1995	326-327
Commonwealth Powers Act 1996	51
Corporations Act 2001	90, 93-95, 98-101, 105-107, 110-113
Corporations Regulations 2001	99
Corporations Amendment (Statutory Minimum) Regulations 2021	97
Crimes Act 1914	29
Criminal Code Act 1995	13, 165, 210
Disability Discrimination Act 2004	53, 198, 211
Disability Services Act 1986	198
Defence Services Homes Act 1918	89
Evidence Act 1995	13
Fair Entitlements Guarantee Act 2021	99

Fair Work Act 2009	48, 52-54, 57, 59-61, 65-69, 71-72, 74, 315-316
Fair Work Amendment (Paid Family and Domestic Violence Leave) Act 2022	180
Fair Work Commission Rules 2013	316
Fair Work Regulations 2009	59, 75
Family Law Act 1975	142-143
Family Law Reform Act 1995	142
Industrial Relations Act 1988	52
Industrial Relations Reform Act 1993	52
Insolvency Law Reform Act 2016	101
Invalid and Old Age Pensions Act 1908	197
Judiciary Act 1903	239
Matrimonial Causes Act 1959	142
National Disability Insurance Scheme Act 2013	198-200
National Disability Insurance Scheme Amendment (Participant Service Guarantee and Other Measures) Act 2022	200
National Disability Insurance Scheme (Becoming a Participant) Rules 2016	199
National Disability Insurances Scheme (Restrictive Practices and Behaviour Support) Rules 2018	206
National Disability Insurance Scheme Amendment (Getting the NDIS Back on Track No 1) Act 2024	211
National Handgun Buyback Act 2003	217
Proceeds of Crime Act 2002	195
Public Governance, Performance and Accountability Act 2013	208
Public Service Act 1999	171
Racial Discrimination Act 1975	53
Sex Discrimination Act 1985	53

Superannuation Guarantee (Administration) Act 1992	112
Workplace Relations Act 1996	52
Work Health and Safety Act 2011	115

Australian Capital Territory

Crimes Act 1900	115
Human Rights Act 2004	350
Work Health and Safety Act 2011	115

New South Wales

Crimes Act 1900	184, 222
Crimes and Other Legislation Amendment (Assault and Intoxication) Act 2014	184
Crimes Legislation Amendment (Coercive Control) Act 2022	150, 175
Crimes (Sentencing Procedure) Act 1999	183
Crime (Serious Crime Prevention Orders) Act 2016	178
Coroners Act 2009	172
Firearms and Dangerous Weapons Act 1973	214
Summary Offences Act 1986	222
Young Offenders Act 1997	28

Northern Territory

Control of Weapons Act 2001	221
Criminal Code Act 1983	34, 117, 186
Criminal Code Amendment Act 2024	34
Victims of Crime Assistance Act 2006	34
Work Health and Safety (National Uniform Legislation) Act 2011	117

Queensland

Bail Act 1980	185

Criminal Code Act 1899	185
Domestic and Family Violence Protection Act 2012	174
Domestic and Family Violence Protection (Combating Coercive Control) and Other Legislation Amendment Act 2023.	150-151
Penalties and Sentencing Act 1992	185
Police Powers and Responsibilities Act 2000	221
Safe Night Out Legislation Amendment Act 2014	185
Work Health and Safety Act 2011	115-117

South Australia

Criminal Law Consolidation Act 1935	195

Tasmania

Family Violence Act 2004	151, 175

Victoria

Accident Compensation Act 1985	46
Ambulance Services Act 1986	25
Bail Act 1977	238-243, 245, 247, 249-250, 252-255, 343
Bail Amendment (Stage One) Act 2017(Vic)	240
Bail Amendment (Stage Two) Act 2018(Vic)	240
Charter of Human Rights and Responsibilities Act 2006	13, 233, 239
Children, Youth and Families Act 2005	14, 282, 290
Civil Procedure Act 2010	322
Commonwealth Powers (Industrial Relations) Act	51
Control of Weapons Act 1990	219, 245
Control of Weapons Regulations 2021	220

Coroners Act 2008	205-206
Corrections Act 1986	25, 214, 267, 282
Corrections Amendment (Parole)Act 2014	214
Country Fire Authority Act 1958	16
County Court Act 1958	83, 313
County Court Civil Procedure Rules 2018	316
Crimes Act 1958	25-26, 39-41, 130, 165, 220, 234, 247, 256, 307, 326, 352
Crimes (Mental Impairment and Unfitness to be Tried) Act 1997	47
Criminal Injuries Compensation Act 1972	257
Criminal Organisations Control Act 2012	222
Criminal Procedure Act 2009	15, 122, 158, 272, 289, 294, 313, 332, 345
Disability Act 2006	198
Domestic Animals Act 1994	36
Drugs, Poisons and Controlled Substances Act 1981	291, 359
Education and Training Reform Act 2006	48
Emergency Management Act 1986	25
Employee Relations Act 1992	51
Equal Opportunity Act 2010	53, 73, 75
Evidence Act 2008	13, 161, 325
Evidence (Miscellaneous Provisions) Act 1958	239
Family Violence Protection Act 2008	149-150, 222

Firearms Act 1996	218-219, 222-227, 232
Firearms Regulations 2018	218
Fire Rescue Victoria Act 1958	25
Fisheries (Abalone) Regulations 2004	16
Gender Equality Act 2020	53
Guardianship and Administration Act 1986	377-378
Honorary Justices Act 2014	239
Human Source Management Act 2023	368
Independent Broad-based Anti-corruption Commission Act 2011	355
Judicial Commission of Victoria Act 2016	278
Judgment Debt Recovery Act 1984	111
Juries Act 2000	37-38
Jury Directions Act 2015	38
Justice Legislation Miscellaneous Amendment Act 2018	25
Legal Profession Act 2004	320
Legal Profession Uniform Admission Rules 2015	320
Legal Profession Uniform Continuing Professional Development (Solicitors) Rules 2015	335
Legal Profession Uniform Law Application Act 2014	320
Legal Profession Uniform Conduct (Barristers) Rules 2015	374
Legal Profession Uniform Law Australian Solicitors Conduct Rules 2015	321, 338, 374
Legal Profession Uniform Legal Practice (Solicitors) Rules 2015	321
Legislation Amendment (Parole Reform and Other Matters) Act 2016	214
Long Service Leave Act 1992 (repealed 2018)	53-55
Magistrates Court Act 1989	54, 290, 313

Magistrates Court General Civil Procedures Rules 2010	105
Magistrates Court (Judicial Registrars) Rules 2015	286
Major Crime (Investigation Powers) Act 2004	159
Major Crime Legislation (Office of Police Integrity) Act 2004	360
Motor Car Act 1909	126
Motor Car (Breath Testing Stations) Act 1976	127
Occupational Health and Safety Act 2004	53, 72, 114, 117-121, 124
Occupational Health and Safety Regulations 2017	114, 121
Ombudsman Act 1973	274
Outworkers (Improved Protection) Act 2003	54
Personal Safety Intervention Orders Act 2010	150, 152, 165, 222-223
Police Assistance Compensation Act 1958	262
Prostitution Control Act 1994	17
Public Holidays Act 1993	54
Public Interest Monitor Act 2011	343
Racial and Religious Tolerance Act 2001	53
Road Safety Act 1986	127-129, 131-132, 134, 137-139, 141, 307
Road Safety Amendment Act 2014	129
Road Safety Amendment (Drinking while Driving) Act 2011	132
Road Safety Drivers Regulations 2009	127
Safe Patient Care (Nurse to Patient and Midwife to Patient Ratios) Act 2015	54

Sentencing Act 1991	14, 23, 25, 28, 123, 130, 188-189, 191, 193, 235, 249, 265, 271, 283, 306, 309-310
Sentencing Amendment Act 2010	272
Sentencing Amendment Act 1993	284
Sentencing Amendment (Abolition of Suspended Sentences & Other Matters) Act 2013	272
Sentencing Amendment (Community Correction Reform) Act 2011	272
Sentencing Amendment (Coward's Punch Manslaughter and Other Matters) Act 2014	188
Serious Sexual Offender (Detention and Supervision) Act 2009	285
Sex Work Act 1994	17
Spent Convictions Act 2021	281
Special Investigator Act 2021	350-351, 353, 358
State Liability (Police Informants) Act 2024	364
Summary Offences Act 1966	16, 26, 297, 307
Supreme Court Act 1986	144, 313
Supreme Court (General Civil Procedure) Rules 2015	316, 323
Surveillance Devices Act 1999	163
Transport Accident Act 1985	140, 261
Transport Legislation Amendment (Road Safety and Other Matters) Act 2017	128
Vexatious Proceedings Act 2014	144
Victims Charter Act 2006	267
Victims of Crime Assistance Act 1996	258-267, 286

Victims of Crime Assistance (Amendment) Act 2000	258
Victims of Crime Assistance (Amendment) Act 2007	259
Victims of Crime (Financial Assistance Scheme) Act 2022	288
Victims of Crime Assistance (Special Financial Assistance) Regulations 2021	270
Victims of Crime Commissioner Act 2015	268
Victoria Police Act 2013	25
Victorian Civil and Administrative Act 1998	314, 376
Victorian University Act 2010	46
Victorian University of Technology Act 1990	46

Western Australia

Criminal Code Compilation Act 1913	185
Firearms Act 1973	229
Occupational Safety and Health Act 1984	116
Occupational Safety and Health Regulations 1996	116
Work Health and Safety Act 2020	116

INTERNATIONAL COVENANTS AND DECLARATIONS

International Covenant on Civil and Political Rights 1966	13
Right to Organise and Collective Bargaining Convention 1949(No 98)	50-51
Equal Remuneration Convention, 1951(No 100)	51
Discrimination (Employment and Occupation) Convention 1958(No 11)	51
Declaration on Fundamental Principles and Rights at Work (1998).	51
Convention on the Rights of Persons with Disabilities 2008	198
Declaration of the Basic Principles of Justice for Victims of Crime and Abuse of Power 1985	257
International Covenant on Civil and Political Rights 1976	349

NEWSPAPER AND OTHER MEDIA REFERENCES

AAP

- *Daniel Christie one-punch killing: Shaun McNeil jailed for at least seven and a half years* (27 August 2015).

ABC News

- *Dead policeman's family want king-hit campaign* (17 June 2011).
- *Police killer's sentence increased on appeal* (16 November 2011).
- *One Punch Killers to spend 10 years in jail under new Victorian laws* (17 August 2014).
- *David Cassai death; Man involved in fatal New Year's Eve attack has sentence doubled* (2 December 2014).
- *Richard Vincec fatally punched Jaiden Walker outside Melbourne Bar after kissing his ex, court told* (2 October 2017).
- *One-punch killer Hugh Garth jailed for 10 years over death of Ray Manalad at Rooty Hill party* (8 December 2017).
- *Reward in Shannon Mc Cormack one-punch death investigation raised to $1 million* (1 June 2022).'
- *Teenager sentenced to 10 years in prison over fatal stabbing of Jack Beasley on Gold Coast* (5 August 2022).

- *'Coward punch' campaigner Caterina Politi calls for urgent changes to close legal loopholes'* (17 August 2022).
- *Domestic abuser Paul Philip Mc Donough jailed for manslaughter of Bekkie- Rae Curran- Trinca* (23 June 2023).
- *Corrupt lawyer Dev Menon jailed for 14 years over Plutus Payroll tax fraud* (4 July 2023).
- *Should character references still be used in Australian courts?* (13 September 2023).
- *ACT raises the age of criminal responsibility to 14 with nation first legislation* (1 November 2023).
- *Youths charged with serious crimes to wear monitoring bracelets under Victorian trial* (20 March 2024).
- *24 hours, seven mass shootings- as an election looms, what does a day of gun violence look like for the United States* (7 April 2024).
- *Federal Government commits $160 million for creation of National Firearms Register* (27 April 2024).
- *NSW government proposes higher bail threshold, electronic monitoring for serious domestic violence offenders* (14 May 2024).
- *Victorian Government promises tougher youth bail restrictions, won't raise criminal age to 14* (13 August 2024).
- *Nicola Gobbo in 'very poor health' as Victorian government moves to block her lawsuit against police* (13 August 2024).
- *Gangland murder trail delayed as Victoria Police wins bid to keep source's identity secret* (11 September 2024)
- *Victorian Lawyer X bill passes upper house in last minute deal limiting civil compensation to $1 million* (12 September 2024).
- *Bill Shorten responds to concerns around NDIS changes and defends handling of support list* (3 October 2024).
- *NT's CLP government passes legislation to lower the age of criminal responsibility from 12 to 10, in first week of parliament* (18 October 2024).

- *Tougher bail laws pass both houses after marathon sitting of Victorian Parliament* (21 March 2025)
- *Charges dropped against man accused of murdering gangland lawyer Joseph Acquaro* (2 May 2025)

BBC

- *Dreamworld tragedy sparks industrial manslaughter laws* (23 August 2017).
- *Dreamworld accident; Australian theme park fined over four deaths* (28 September 2020).

The Age

- *Tough Gun laws introduced throughout Australia* (11 May 1996).
- *Long prison terms for lawyer's killers* (11 May 2004).
- *Former top lawyer loses drug appeal* (28 August 2004).
- *Fatal shootings by Victoria Police* (14 October 2004).
- *Provocation defence to be removed* (21 January 2005).
- *Man admits killing wife, daughter* (2 February 2005).
- *Magistrate Criticises Herald Sun Editor* (18 February 2005).
- *Herman to testify against Korp* (29 June 2005)
- *Retrial for three on solicitor's murder* (2 August 2005).
- *Relieving the Walsh Street Murders* (1 October 2005).
- *Rapist jailed indefinitely after 'depraved' attack* (14 December 2006).
- *One dead, gunman at large after city shooting* (19 June 2007).
- *Barrister Pockets $630,000 for Libel* (23 March 2010).
- *Body Cameras for Police; Will It Make Them More Accountable* (18 April 2010).

- *Child porn lawyer struck off roll* (6 August 2010).
- *Court told of 'jailhouse confession'* (28 October 2010).
- *The Real Animal Kingdom* (12 February 2011).
- *It is never too late for justice* (3 June 2011).
- *Loophole That Helped Evil Bully* (9 July 2011).
- *King-hit killer jailed for 10 years* (16 August 2011).
- *Lawyer arrested on drug, gun charges after being 'on the run'* (24 August 2011).
- *Serial Killers Parole Bid Refused* (13 December 2012).
- *Offenders Risk Losing their Licence* (21 March 2013).
- *Former lawyer grabs cash reward for tip off* (15 July 2013).
- *People Love Gangsters* (3 October 2013).
- *Gatto solicitor David Chapman walks free on suspended sentence for drug trafficking* (14 October 2013).
- *Jail term increased for martial arts fighter Tyrone Russell over 'one punch death of David Cassai* (2 December 2014).
- *Mass murderer Julian Knight loses legal bids for compensation and cell privileges* (27 December 2014).
- *IBAC inquiry: Justice Murray Kellam's recommendations into protected witnesses to remain secret* (10 February 2015).
- *'Entrenched' paedophile wins fight against indefinite sentence* (27 June 2015).
- *The Monash University shooting, Huan Yun Xiang, and what came after* (21 October 2015).
- *Magistrate Rodney Crisp Found By Supreme Court Judge to be Wrong in Law* (11 November 2014).
- *Law Students Fight for the Freedom of Man Accused of Murdering Melbourne Lawyer* (12 November 2015).
- *New evidence could spark fresh probe into notorious police slaying of Graeme Jensen* (17 December 2015).

- *Bombers, Contract Killers and the stress of Policing- A Top Cop Tells* (30 March 2016).
- *Underbelly: The Secret Backroom Deals that Cracked Melbourne's Gangland War* (5 May 2016).
- *Catching Tony Mokbel; the big win that proves we lose* (17 March 2017).
- *Is Road Rage a Crime? It Depends on the Case Says Victoria Police* (17 July 2017).
- *At last: Gun laws that will have crooks looking down the barrel* (28 September 2017).
- *Andrew Lee could walk free in five years after one-punch assault that killed Patrick Cronin* (10 November 2017).
- *The Duke's last stand: Prolific hitman Rodney Collins dies, taking murder secrets to his grave* (11 May 2018).
- *Underworld boss Rocco Arico gets two years knocked off sentence* (24 May 2018).
- *Tony Mokbel among underworld figures who could appeal conviction* (4 December 2018).
- *Lawyer X Appeal in tomato tins case fails* (18 December 2018).
- *The harder they fall: Nicola Gobbo, from gangland lawyer to family outcast* (1 March 2019).
- *'No other case like it': The unique case of Lawyer X* (11 April 2019).
- *Appeal court tells cops to make Mokbel document hunt a 'top priority'* (2 May 2019).
- *Victims want acknowledgment during legal proceedings, report finds* (13 May 2019).
- *Police replace QC over stance on public disclosure in Gobbo probe* (23 June 2019).

- *Ombudsman finds State Trustees failed Victoria's most vulnerable* (27 June 2019).
- *Five million dollars paid to victims of dodgy lawyers* (6 November 2019).
- *Gangland lawyer seen assaulting the man later charged with his murder* (11 November 2019).
- *Proposals for a better NDIS need to be heeded* (20 January 2020).
- *Six years' jail for solicitor who robbed clients to fund renovation* (11 June 2020).
- *Jailed Gobbo client wants to know if other lawyer was also an informer* (10 September 2020).
- *Wrongly convicted, jailed for a decade and now finally free to tell his story* (30 October 2020).
- *From Lawyer X to ex-lawyer: Gobbo finally struck off bar roll* (4 November 2020).
- *'Disgraceful' Gobbo condemned but may be out of reach of justice* (30 November 2020).
- *The Nicola Gobbo, Lawyer X scandal explained* (30 November 2020).
- *The lie from which the Gobbo scandal grew* (30 November 2020).
- *Man bailed over tomato tins ecstasy bust Lawyer X appeal* (14 December 2020).
- *One gun crime is too many: New Police unit cracks down on illegal firearms* (11 January 2021).
- *Underworld lawyer Joe Acquaro provided information but was not a registered police informer* (19 January 2021).
- *Former Gobbo clients wait on key documents ahead of appeal hearings* (18 February 2021).

- *Victoria's bail laws are broken and need to be fixed* (7 March 2021).
- *'Exceptional circumstance': Gelato shop murder accused granted bail* (18 March 2021).
- *You Still Battle: Rosie Batty on Five Years of Family Violence* (28 March 2021).
- *The Seven Shots That Took a Life and Changed Another* (9 April 2021).
- *How a murder taskforce solved and thwarted murders, seized millions and stopped the underworld war* (16 April 2021).
- *New prisons or looser bail laws? Labor's unpalatable choice* (15 May 2021).
- *Keep tough bail laws, says police union, as Greens try to wind them back* (17 May 2021).
- *Better Monitoring Needed of Police Body Camera Compliance – Auditor General* (8 June 2021).
- *Phil Cleary Giving Men a Sporting Chance to End Violence Against Women* (16 June 2021).
- *Nothing about us without us: The government should include the disabled when reforming the NDIS* (13 July 2021).
- *Care provider rorted NDIS out of thousands for services never provided* (21 July 2021).
- *Mafia figure Frank Madafferi to be deported after two decades of trying by immigration* (23 July 2021).
- *Plea deals and sitting next to the killer's family: Victims say courts must change* (9 September 2021).
- *Ugly turf war as service providers tussle over NDIS clients with disabilities* (20 September 2021).
- Drug trafficker *Francesco Madafferi denied bail on appeal case* (2 December 2021).
- *Disabled deserve fix for troubled NDIS* (24 April 2022).

- *Commercial vultures must be booted from the NDIS, aged care and home care* (1 May 2022).
- *'Son of Satan'; Man jailed for 25 years for depraved attacks on women* (26 May 2022).
- *NDIS alarm bells must no go unanswered* (15 August 2022).
- *Shifty as a rat: Legal clerk who stole millions was a conwoman with 14 aliases* (27 November 2022).
- *People waiting years to have cases heard at state's 'timely and efficient legal tribunal* (27 December 2022).
- *'Must be stopped': Fraud taskforce nabs NDIS firms charging for services not delivered* (22 January 2023).
- *Andrews government must act now on bail reform (*22 January 2023).
- *'Dangerous, discriminatory': Legal advocates call for urgent bail reform* (24 January 2023).
- *Government to consider bail law reform, but details remain under wraps* (25 January 2023).
- *Victorian bail laws 'incompatible' with human rights charter: Coroner* (30 January 2023).
- *Coroner in tears as he damns bail law findings* (31 January 2023).
- *Magistrate who once told alleged rape victim she had 'buyer's remorse' stood down over fresh complaint* (6 February 2023).
- *Cold-blooded killer': Distraught parents turn and face pregnant daughter's murderer in court* (6 February 2023).
- *New informant legislation risks rerun of Lawyer X scandal, experts and opposition say* (8 February 2023).
- *Andrews government sat on bail reform report for 11 months* (9 February 2023).
- *'Justice for Sam': Life sentence for Phillip Island ex-wife killer Adrian Basham* (27 February 2023).

- *Bail law reforms unveiled as attorney-general concedes state 'cast the net too wide'* (5 March 2023).
- *Cover-ups and justice failures in Veronica Nelson's death* (5 March 2023).
- *Youth crime surges as offences by children aged 10 to 14 increase by more than a third* (16 March 2023).
- *How to fix a justice system that punishes disadvantage* (22 March 2023).
- *Gobbo seeks immunity deal to dob on police* (22 March 2023).
- *Controversial Lawyer X bill stalls at the last minute* (23 March 2023).
- *Government puts faltering Lawyer X bill on ice* (23 March 2023).
- *Ex-magistrate (Richard Pithouse) who once told alleged rape victim she had 'buyer's remorse' accused of sexual harassment* (30 March 2023).
- *'Suffer, you dog': The moment a man who killed the mother of his children was sentenced to 25 years* (31 March 2023).
- *Man's gun prohibition order tossed out despite string of allegations of gun misuse and animal cruelty* (13 April 2023).
- *What makes an informer inform?* (15 April 2023).
- *Juror who researched case to be referred to prosecutors as murder trial aborted* (3 May 2023).
- *Crackdown on prices and junk therapies to slow NDIS spending: Shorten* (4 May 2023).
- *Victoria's deadliest weapon is at the centre of a youth 'madness' wave* (4 May 2023).
- *Going behind the lines to tackle rise in youth crime* (6 May 2023).
- *Police minister says firearms 'too easily accessed' in WA after shots fired at Perth school* (25 May 2023).

- *Pain lingers for victims of Puffing Billy child abuser* (26 May 2023).
- *'You had an opportunity to stop'. Deakin lecturer jailed for savage attack on wife* (30 May 2023).
- *Five-year parole ban to be slapped on serial killers* (20 June 2023).
- *Lawyer X investigator threatens to quit because prosecutors wont charge police* (21 June 2023).
- *Nicola Gobbo was prepared to plead guilty, testify against police* (21 June 2023).
- *'Careful and realistic': Public prosecutor defends lack of Lawyer X charges* (22 June 2023).
- *Lawyer X saga fizzles out with no police officers charged* (27 June 2023).
- *Gobbo's secret lawsuit against police* (1 July 2023).
- *I've reported on gun violence in the US for more than a year and I just can't get used to it* (7 July 2023).
- *Crooks hiding weapons caches to hand over in exchange for sentencing cuts* (10 July 2023).
- *Viper taskforce strikes: One serious criminal nabbed every day in gang blitz* (12 July 2023).
- *How a dogged detective overcame great odds to find a victim- and catch her killer* (22 July 2023).
- *Bail reforms at fixing 'disaster' law face one year wait* (31 July 2023).
- *Taking down a monster; How a dedicated detective brought 'son of Satan to justice* (29 October 2023).
- *Backwards and archaic; Victoria ditches planes to give children presumption of bail* (24 March 2024).
- *Victorian government will track young criminals with ankle bracelets* (21 April 2024).

- *Underworld figures spared witness box as Lawyer X case settles* (25 April 2025)

The Australian Jewish News

- *Assist Victims* (25 July 1980).

Brisbane Times

- *Tell Him He's Dreaming-Lawyer Loses $250k Dennis Denuto Defamation Case* (21 November 2015).
- *Company fine over Eagle Farm deaths was 'disproportionate', judge rules* (17 December 2019).

Canberra Times

- *Payment Plans for Victims* (26 August 1964).
- *Victims of crime get rights in sentencing* (5 October 1995).
- *Carl Williams' killer fighting conviction* (15 December 2021).
- *Australia's first family violence commissioner announced as Micaela Cronin* (27 October 2022).

Courier Mail

- *Meet Bernie 'the Attorney' Balmer and his mate Mick Gatto* (31 May 2013).

Daily Mail Australia

- *Paralegal, 28, who stole $2 million from his property clients and blew it the stock market is jailed for four years* (14 August 2020).

- *Carl Williams' killer Mathew 'The General' Johnson is seen for the first time in years as he makes bombshell move from behind bars where he brutally bashed the underworld figure to death. 'He's had a gutful'* (13 August 2022).
- *One nation, under gun violence: Nashville school shooting is America's 129th mass shooting in 2023 as nation is on course for the MOST mass shootings ever* (28 March 2023).
- *Biden jokes about only being known for 'chocolate chip ice cream and Ray- Bans before calling on Congress to pass assault weapon ban after Nashville shooting* (28 March 2023).
- *Kenneth Ball left with horrific lifelong injuries after coward-punched by Thomas Short in Aldinga Beach, South Australia* (30 July 2023).
- *Mum's heartbreaking plea as one-punch killer Kieran Loveridge walks free from jail 12 years after deadly attack which helped trigger Sydney's nightlife lockout laws.* (4 April 2024).

Financial Review

- *'Dysfunctional' Administrative Appeals Tribunal abolished* (16 December 2022).

Geelong Advertiser

- *Fugitive lawyer on 143 charges* (26 October 2018).

Herald Sun

- *Strike Three for magistrate Richard Pithouse* (4 July 2010).
- *One punch now equals 10 years* (16 August 2014).

- *Con artists: Sara Grasso fooled family and friends with her tales of her fantastic legal career* (14 January 2015).
- *World's biggest ecstasy bust; Bikie John Higgs fails appeal bid* (26 August 2015).
- *Frankston Magistrate Rejects Move for Diversion Program, Says Alleged Victims have a right to be Heard* (10 February 2017).
- *'Carnapping' lawyer banned after running panel beating racket despite repeat warning* (20 March 2017).
- *Why Mokbel's still a big wig inside Victoria's toughest jail* (3 Feb 2019).
- *Duped client uncovers crooked conveyancer's $250k con* (4 June 2019).
- *Time to admit our national shame* (29 August 2020).
- *Knife Victims Soar* (14 December 2022).
- *Ambush horror rocks a nation* (14 December 2022).
- *No ID, no worries for machete buyers* (23 December 2022).
- *Lawyer fought the good fight* (28 December 2022).
- *Lawyer X probe funds dry up* (2 January 2023).
- *X probe needs funds and teeth* (3 January 2023).
- *Muzzle on Registry* (3 January 2023).
- *NDIS rorts rob those in need* (4 January 2023).
- *Sex therapy, tai chi -Wasteful claims on NDIS revealed* (9 January 2023).
- *Fast- track court process effective- Calls to scrap committal test* (11 January 2023).
- *Cops agitate for gun-owner log* (16 January 2023).
- *High Country case gets first big test* (16 January 2023).
- *'X' Factor Hits Court* (23 January 2023).
- Bail change on table (24 January 2023).
- *Libs support (bail) reform* (25 January 2023).
- *Safety first on softer bail laws* (25 January 2023).

- *Harsh bail laws a factor in tragedy* (31 January 2023).
- *Firearm registry at last* (4 February 2023).
- *Awkward Questions for Lawyer who knows 'everything'* (5 February 2023).
- *Disorder in the court- Magistrate benched (Richard Pithouse)* (7 February 2023).
- *Bill to protect informants* (8 February 2023).
- *You have the right to know…This Legislation stinks* (Lawyer X) (12 February 2023).
- *Junior Crims let off* (17 February 2023).
- *Ex-top cop's criminal age fears* (19 February 2023).
- *Tackling a cycle of youth crime* (22 February 2023).
- *Source law 'terrible' – Judge slams 'sloppy legislation'* (24 February 2023).
- *'Abominable' killer will serve at least 30 years – Justice for Sam* (28 February 2023).
- *'Rack off all you NDIS rorters'* (4 March 2023).
- *Mokbel jail time slashed-Sentence cut after Lawyer X Scandal* (8 March 2023).
- *Joffa Court Out* (8 March 2023).
- *Joffa's character flaws* (9 March 2023).
- *Joffa victim's outrage–Painful quest for justice was 'all for nothing'* (15 March 2023).
- *Junior criminals are raising hell* (17 March 2023).
- *Jails failing to make us safer* (22 March 2023).
- *Drug-drive reform push* (26 March 2023).
- *Face up to it: Jailing is failing in Victoria* (22 March 2023).
- *Gobbo shock admission* (22 March 2023).
- *Doubts Lawyer X law fix can protect clients* (23 March 2023).
- *Flawed law risks Lawyer X repeat* (23 March 2023).
- *Ruling in Lawyer X drug case* (26 March 2023).

- *Controversial magistrate quits (Richard Pithouse)* (27 March 2023).
- *More trials were coming – Ex magistrate (Richard Pithouse) faced sex harassment beef (31 March 2023).*
- *NDIS bill's not clear as crystal* (1 April 2023).
- *'Very just' term for murder* (1 April 2023).
- *Cash in, to best of our ability – Greedy NDIS 'middlemen 'gouge government agency, clients say* (16 April 2023).
- *Wrong Arm of Law Court Out- Stealing booze, rudeness and bullying complaints* (19 April 2023).
- *Justice needs a quick fix* (20 April 2023).
- *Crims' welcome mat interstate offenders allowed in* (15 May 2023).
- *Dan gives evil killer hope- Andrews rejects plea to lock up Denyer forever* (18 May 2023).
- *Government 'unsure' how to reverse NDIS blowout* (27 May 2023).
- *Hannah's Law Snub* (29 May 2023).
- *Russian Roulette – Law change plea on domestic violence* (29 May 2023).
- *The legal change that could help Victoria Police save lives* (30 May 2023).
- *Hannah's law could save lives* (30 May 2023).
- *Thieving lawyer 'trashed' his name* (30 May 2023).
- *Killer's Insta Post of love* (31 May 2023).
- *Jail time Weight and see* (2 June 2023).
- *Heartbreaking history- Letters of grief that changed Australia* (16 June 2023).
- *No release for Denyer* (19 June 2023).
- *Victory for serial killer – Betrayed* (22 June 2023).
- *Lawyer X probe judge vows to quit over feud* (22 June 2023).

- *Justice denied without charges* (22 June 2023).
- *Lawyer X marks the spat* (23 June 2023).
- *Victim's father tells Dan he is sick of 'BS'* (23 June 2023).
- *Dan's unfettered powers make sufferers of us all* (23 June 2023).
- *Let investigator lay the charges- Opposition bid to see heads roll in Lawyer X scandal* (24 June 2023).
- *Evil crim in bid for freedom- brutal rapist to appeal* (26 June 2023).
- *Another test on law and safety* (26 June 2023).
- *Just charge Lawyer X and take your chances* (27 June 2023).
- *OSI closure bombshell ruins hope of charges* (28 June 2023).
- *Dan denies Lawyer X Royal Commission a waste of money* (28 June 2023).
- *NDIS cops make $11m sting- Shorten says alleged fraud 'organised crime'* (1 July 2023).
- *Police face payout as Lawyer X sues* (1 July 2023).
- *It's 'Gun Dependence' Day* (5 July 2023).
- *Student reprieve after cop assault – Officer now 'fears' the job* (5 July 2023).
- *Lawyer X 'She should have kept an open mind – judicial delay on the cards for Mokbel* (11 July 2023).
- *Crime-busting taskforce marks first year* (12 July 2023).
- *Patton warns new arrest laws will put children and victims at risk* (15 July 2023).
- *Special investigators wanted DPP to charge Victoria's former police chief 'Let off the Hook'* (17 July 2023).
- *Killer's confession panned: Judge: it was self-serving, not sign of remorse* (22 July 2023).
- *Drug-driving challenges* (24 July 2023).
- *Overland ties to close for Judd* (27 July 2023).
- Crims win in 'secret deals' (4 August 2023).

- *Victim: This is torture Rapist in bid to walk free* (8 August 2023).
- *Game up for the 'worst of worst'* (9 August 2023).
- *Eliminate the scourge of DV* (9 August 2023).
- *Bail win for crims – Vic laws to be relaxed* (15 August 2023).
- *If only she knew he was out of jail* (22 August 2023).
- *Victims register needs reform* (22 August 2023).
- *Family fury as 13yo boy cleared of teen murder* (21 September 2023).
- *'Joffa' case is a blight on our state's justice system* (22 September 2023).
- *'Crooks' ripping off NDIS-Syndicates in $400m scam, bam thank you* (25 September 2023).
- *Bail back flip points to flaws* (6 October 2023).
- *Bail Laws to be relaxed* (18 October 2023).
- Cops nab 900 DV dodgers (23 October 2023).
- *Jail for rip-off rorters-NDIS bosses vow to get tough on gougers* (28 October 2023).
- *Victoria to throw away Denyer key- Allan's chance to reset state* (1 November 2023).
- *'Nowhere to hide', violent abusers told* (27 April 2024).
- *System is failing brave women who fought for their lives* (27 April 2024).
- *Get tough on DV breaches* (29 May 2024).
- *State will strengthen bail test on violence* (13 August 2024).
- *Youth Crime Crisis- Outrage forced Allan's U-Turn-Police Support youth justice backdown* (14 August 2024).
- *Dodgy NDIS claims* (3 October 2024).
- *A better deal for victims of crime* (17 October 2024).
- *He's not yet free, but he's close* (5 April 2025).
- *Keeping track of teen crims* (11 May 2025).

- *As Premier urged to completely outlaw machetes – Thugs rush to beat sales ban* (27 May 2025).
- *Lawyer X payout fails – Judge: Informer risk 'inherent'* (14 June 2025).

The Guardian

- *Australia's baby-faced killer Carl Williams dies in jail* (20 April 2010).
- *Sydney siege; magistrate unaware Man Haron Monis on bail at time of alleged sex assaults* (17 August 2015).
- *Inquest into Sydney siege to examine why Man Haron Monis was on bail* (16 August 2015).
- *Government called in private law firms to fight a third of NDIS cases, figures show* (11 November 2020).
- *Bourke Street attack coroner laments 'agonising' failures that led to massacre* (19 November 2020).
- *Melbourne gangland lawyer Joe Acquaro gave police information on former client* (19 January 2021).
- *Victorian Magistrate who suggested alleged rape victim had 'buyer's remorse is counselled* (Magistrate Richard Pithouse) (9 March 2021).
- *Inquest hears of Hannah Clarke's attempts to save her children from her estranged husband* (21 March 2022).
- *Government to crack down on NDIS provider fraud amid warning scheme will soon costs $50bn annually* (25 October 2022).
- *Terry Irving spent 1,671 days in jail for a crime he didn't commit– and 25 more years seeking justice* (19 January 2023).
- *Over 17,000 weapons surrendered in first year of Australian Firearms amnesty* (21 January 2023).

- *Greens threaten Andrews government with possible defeat in parliament over bail laws* (7 February 2023).
- *'We have to fight': the over 65's challenging NDIS age exclusions* (20 February 2023).
- *Andrews takes cautious approach to overdue bail reforms* (10 March 2023).
- *Lawyer X royal commission concerned about new informant bill* (20 March 2023).
- *Victoria's major parties and opposition are backing Legalise Cannabis effort to change 'unfair' road safety laws* (8 March 2023).
- *Informant's plea deal behind decision not to lay charges over Lawyer X scandal, says Victorian DPP* (22 June 2023).
- *Biden names Harris to lead first federal gun violence prevention office* (22 September 2023).
- *New Disability Rights Act needed to end abuse and exploitation, royal commission finds* (29 September 2023).

The Sydney Morning Herald

- *Former judge says Victoria Police are corrupt* (11 January 2007).
- *Police shot first to hit Tyeler's legs* (16 December 2008).
- *Kieran Loveridge fails in High Court Appeal bid over 10-year sentence for killing Thomas Kelly* (12 December 2014).
- *Dreamworld deaths coronial findings* (24 February 2020).
- *Barrister with a Heart of Gold* (11 February 2021).
- *NSW Police eye Supreme Court orders to prevent domestic violence homicides* (31 January 2023).
- *'No licence to kill people': Dodson says his gut must act on 'national disgrace'* (5 March 2023).
- *NDIS now 'exact opposite of what was intended', says scheme's godfather* (30 June 2023).

The West Australian

- *Jaylen Denny Dimer: WA's top prosecutor says sentence for one-punch death of Guiseppe Raco 'inadequate'* (3 February 2022).
- *First workplace manslaughter charge in Vic* (25 October 2022).

ABOUT THE AUTHOR

Colin served in Vietnam as a National conscript during 1968-69. On his discharge from the Army, he resumed working for the Victoria Police Department as an unsworn member. In 1974, Colin was appointed Head of School Security for the Victorian Education Department in the prevention and detection of school crime.

He then entered the legal profession, being admitted to practice in 1996 as a Barrister and Solicitor mainly practicing in the areas of crime, family violence and industrial relations. He retired in 2022 and lives on the Mornington Peninsula in Victoria with his wife, Michelle.

www.ingramcontent.com/pod-product-compliance
Lightning Source LLC
Chambersburg PA
CBHW011128070526
44583CB00023B/2947